Dan Jones is an acclaimed historian and award-winning journalist. *The Plantagenets: The Kings Who Made England* was a *Sunday Times* and *New York Times* bestseller. He is a columnist for the *Evening Standard*, and also writes for *The Sunday Times*, *Wall Street Journal*, *Mail on Sunday*, *Daily Telegraph* and *Spectator*. He has presented documentaries for the BBC and Channel 5. He lives in London with his wife and two daughters.

Further praise for *The Hollow Crown*:

'Jones is a born storyteller, peopling the terrifying uncertainties of each moment with a superbly drawn cast of characters and powerfully evoking the brutal realities of civil war. With gripping urgency he shows this calamitous conflict unfold.' Helen Castor, *Evening Standard*

'If you're a fan of *Game of Thrones* or *The Tudors*, then Dan Jones's swashbucklingly entertaining slice of late medieval history will be right up your alley. Exploring the world of the War of the Roses with a near-novelistic degree of pace and intrigue, while always remaining scholarly and insightful, *The Hollow Crown* is every bit as entertaining and readable as Jones's previous history blockbuster, *The Plantagenets*.' Alex Larman, *Daily Express*

'Jones, though a young man, is a traditional narrative historian in the mould of Starkey, Taylor and Trevelyan. In other words, he tells a good story.' Gerard DeGroot, *The Times*

'*The Hollow Crown* is exhilarating, epic, blood-and-roses history . . . Jones's material is thrilling . . . There is fine scholarly intuition on display here and a mastery of the grand narrative; it is a supremely skilful piece of storytelling.' Jessie Childs, *Sunday Telegraph*

'Jones navigates the violence and treacheries that follow in such vivid prose that everything, even a non-battle, seems incredibly dramatic and exciting . . . Fast-moving, witty and humane, *The Hollow Crown* is narrative history at its best.' Leanda de Lisle, *Literary Review*

'Dan Jones's fine new history . . . locates the conflict not in the tedious familiarity of modern power plays, but in the fascinating strangeness of the attitudes and belief systems of that distant age: a world in which piety and politics converged, and where the outcome of war was nothing less than the manifestation of divine judgement.' John Adamson, *Mail on Sunday*

'[Jones's] greatest skill as a historical writer is to somehow render sprawling, messy epochs such as this one into manageable, easily digestible matter; he is keenly attuned to what should be served up and what should be omitted. It makes for an engrossing read and a thoroughly enjoyable introduction to the Lancastrian–Yorkist struggle.' Sean McGlynn, *Spectator*

'Written with the pace and flair of a novel, Jones's book catapults readers back to the 15th century, when England was "battered on every side by catastrophe and hobbled by weak leadership." His melodramatic narrative, all battles, coups and murders, and teeming with memorably cold-blooded characters, sometimes reads like a real-life *Game of Thrones*. But this is not just an impressive example of old-fashioned narrative history, it is an epic soap opera based on serious scholarship.' *Sunday Times* Books of the Year

'You could build your own castle out of all the books that have been published on the Wars of the Roses, but few can match Dan Jones for blood-and-guts drama. As well as being a terrific story-teller, he's got a particular knack for making his characters spring off the page.' *Mail on Sunday* Books of the Year

The Hollow Crown

*The Wars of the Roses and
the Rise of the Tudors*

DAN JONES

ff

FABER & FABER

First published in 2014
by Faber & Faber Limited
Bloomsbury House
74–77 Great Russell Street
London WC1B 3DA

This paperback edition published in 2015
Typeset by Faber & Faber Limited
Printed in the UK by CPI Group (UK) Ltd, Croydon, CRO 4YY

A CIP record for this book
is available from the British Library

ISBN 978–0–571–28808–3

4 6 8 10 9 7 5 3

For Jo

Summer of Blood: The Peasants' Revolt of 1381
The Plantagenets: The Kings Who Made England

Contents

CONTENTS

List of Illustrations

Henry V. Oil on panel portrait by an unknown artist, fifteenth century. (*National Portrait Gallery, London, UK/Bridgeman Images*)

Catherine de Valois funeral effigy. Painted wood, 1437. (© *Dean and Chapter of Westminster*)

Henry VI. Oil on panel portrait by an unknown English artist, sixteenth century. (*Society of Antiquaries of London, UK/Bridgeman Images*)

Margaret of Anjou. Illumination (detail) from the 'Shrewsbury Book', *c.*1445, British Library MS Royal 15 E.VI f. 2v. (© *The British Library Board*)

Richard duke of York. Stained-glass, Trinity College, Cambridge, *c.*1425. (*Master and Fellows of Trinity College, Cambridge*)

Edward IV. Oil on panel by an unknown English artist, *c.*1540. (*Ann Ronan Pictures/Print Collector/Getty Images*)

Elizabeth Woodville. Oil on panel portrait by an unknown artist, *c.*1480. (*Print Collector/Getty Images*)

Edward V. Painted panel by an unknown artist, St George's Chapel, Windsor, sixteenth century. (*A. F. Kersting/akg-images*)

Edward IV. Tempera on vellum, illumination from *Chronicle of the History of the World from Creation to Woden, with a Genealogy of Edward IV*, Philadephia Free Library, MS Lewis E201 f. 1.
(*Free Library of Philadelphia/Bridgeman Images*)

Genealogy of Henry VI. Illumination from the 'Shrewsbury Book', *c.*1445, British Library MS Royal 15 E.VI f. 3.
(*British Library/Robana via Getty Images*)

Genealogy with Tudor symbols. Illumination from *Motets*, Flanders, *c.*1516, British Library MS Royal 11 E.XI f. 2.
(*British Library/Robana via Getty Images*)

Title page of *The Union of the Two Noble and Illustre Famelies of Lancastre & Yorke . . .* by Edward Hall, 1550. (*The William Andrews Clark Memorial Library, University of California, Los Angeles*)

Every effort has been made to trace or contact all copyright holders. The publishers would be pleased to rectify at the earliest opportunity any omissions or errors brought to their notice.

Maps

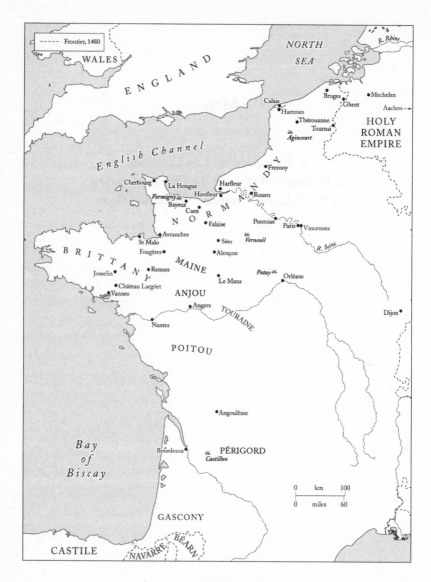

1. France and the Low Countries

2. England and Wales in the Fifteenth Century

3. Noble Landholdings in England and Wales

Genealogical Tables

The House of Lancaster
The House of York
The House of Tudor

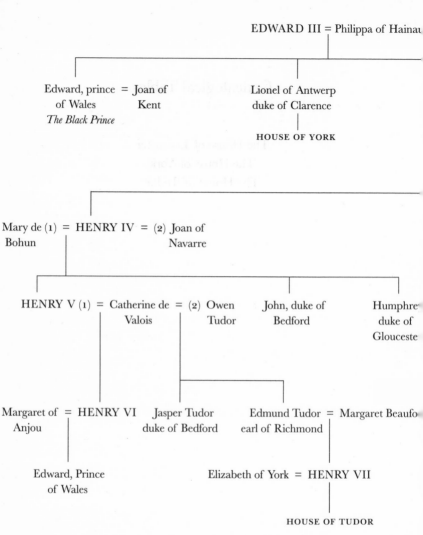

EDWARD III = Philippa of Hainau

Edward, prince = Joan of
of Wales   Kent
The Black Prince

Lionel of Antwerp
duke of Clarence

HOUSE OF YORK

Mary de (1) = HENRY IV = (2) Joan of
Bohun   Navarre

HENRY V (1) = Catherine de = (2) Owen
              Valois   Tudor

John, duke of
Bedford

Humphre
duke of
Glouceste

Margaret of = HENRY VI
Anjou

Jasper Tudor
duke of Bedford

Edmund Tudor = Margaret Beaufo
earl of Richmond

Edward, Prince
of Wales

Elizabeth of York = HENRY VII

HOUSE OF TUDOR

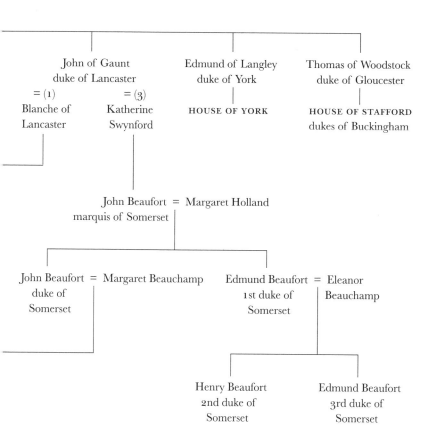

John of Gaunt
duke of Lancaster
= (1)
Blanche of
Lancaster

= (3)
Katherine
Swynford

Edmund of Langley
duke of York

HOUSE OF YORK

Thomas of Woodstock
duke of Gloucester

HOUSE OF STAFFORD
dukes of Buckingham

John Beaufort = Margaret Holland
marquis of Somerset

John Beaufort = Margaret Beauchamp
duke of
Somerset

Edmund Beaufort = Eleanor
1st duke of   Beauchamp
Somerset

Henry Beaufort
2nd duke of
Somerset

Edmund Beaufort
3rd duke of
Somerset

THE HOUSE OF LANCASTER

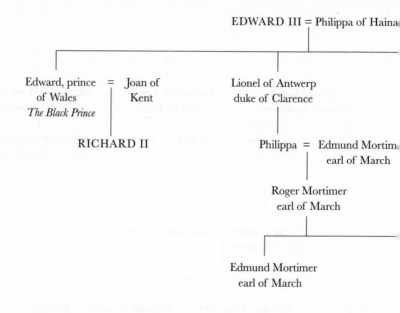

EDWARD III = Philippa of Haina

Edward, prince = Joan of
of Wales   Kent
The Black Prince

RICHARD II

Lionel of Antwerp
duke of Clarence

Philippa = Edmund Mortim
           earl of March

Roger Mortimer
earl of March

Edmund Mortimer
earl of March

THE HOUSE OF YORK

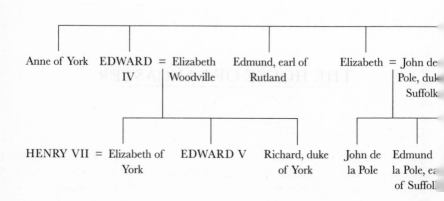

Anne of York EDWARD = Elizabeth   Edmund, earl of   Elizabeth = John de
              IV   Woodville   Rutland   Pole, duk
                                                                      Suffolk

HENRY VII = Elizabeth of   EDWARD V   Richard, duke   John de   Edmund
            York   of York   la Pole   la Pole, ea
                                                                    of Suffol

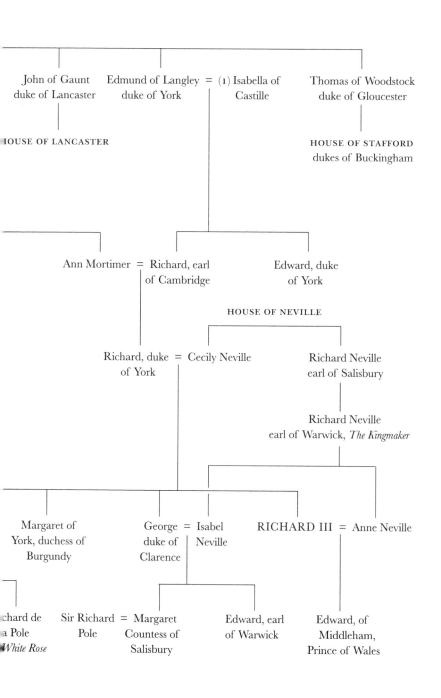

John of Gaunt
duke of Lancaster

Edmund of Langley = (1) Isabella of
duke of York   Castille

Thomas of Woodstock
duke of Gloucester

HOUSE OF LANCASTER

HOUSE OF STAFFORD
dukes of Buckingham

Ann Mortimer = Richard, earl
of Cambridge

Edward, duke
of York

HOUSE OF NEVILLE

Richard, duke = Cecily Neville
of York

Richard Neville
earl of Salisbury

Richard Neville
earl of Warwick, *The Kingmaker*

Margaret of
York, duchess of
Burgundy

George = Isabel
duke of   Neville
Clarence

RICHARD III = Anne Neville

Richard de
la Pole
White Rose

Sir Richard = Margaret
Pole   Countess of
                   Salisbury

Edward, earl
of Warwick

Edward, of
Middleham,
Prince of Wales

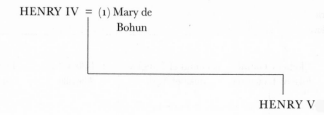

HENRY IV = (1) Mary de
Bohun

HENRY V

THE HOUSE OF TUDOR

HENRY VI

see **HOUSE OF LANCASTER**

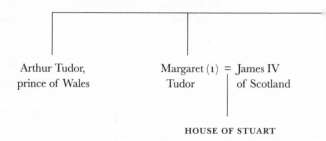

Arthur Tudor,
prince of Wales

Margaret (1) = James IV
Tudor   of Scotland

HOUSE OF STUART

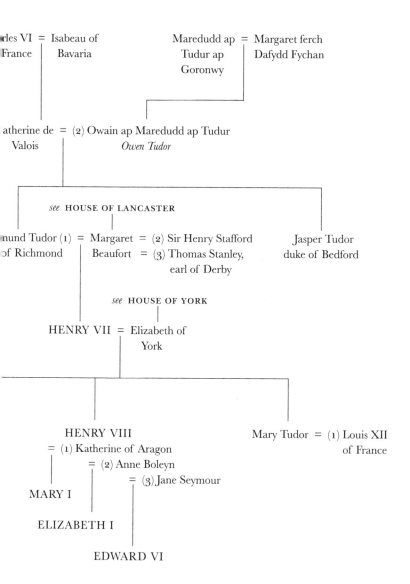

Charles VI = Isabeau of
of France   Bavaria

Maredudd ap = Margaret ferch
Tudur ap   Dafydd Fychan
Goronwy

Catherine de = (2) Owain ap Maredudd ap Tudur
Valois   *Owen Tudor*

see **HOUSE OF LANCASTER**

Edmund Tudor (1) = Margaret = (2) Sir Henry Stafford
earl of Richmond   Beaufort = (3) Thomas Stanley,
earl of Derby

Jasper Tudor
duke of Bedford

see **HOUSE OF YORK**

HENRY VII = Elizabeth of
York

HENRY VIII
= (1) Katherine of Aragon
= (2) Anne Boleyn
= (3) Jane Seymour

MARY I

ELIZABETH I

EDWARD VI

Mary Tudor = (1) Louis XII
of France

Note on Names, Money and Distances

The names of principal characters in this book have generally been modernised for the sake of familiarity and consistency. Thus Nevill becomes Neville, Wydeville becomes Woodville, Tudur becomes Tudor, and so on. Latin, French and archaic English sources have been translated or rendered into modern English except in a very few cases where original spellings have been maintained to illustrate a historical point.

Where particularly pertinent, sums of money have been translated into modern currencies with the assistance of the conversion tool at http://www.nationalarchives.gov.uk/currency/, which gives modern values for ancient, and also has a 'purchasing power' function. Readers should be aware, however, that the conversion of monetary values across the centuries is a perilously inexact science, and that the figures given are for rough guidance only. As an approximation, £100 in 1450 would be worth £55,000 (or $90,000) today. The same sum would represent ten years' salary for an ordinary English labourer in the mid-fifteenth century.

Where a distance between two places is given, it has usually been calculated using Google Maps Walking Directions, and thus tends to be calculated according to the fastest route via modern roads.

The family trees presented at the start of this book are designed to clarify the complex dynastic links described later in the text. For reasons of space and sense, these have been simplified. In some places, siblings have been placed out of order of age.

Who wot nowe that ys here
Where he schall be anoder yere?

ANON. (1445)

For God's sake, let us sit upon the ground
And tell sad stories of the death of kings;
How some have been deposed; some slain in war,
Some haunted by the ghosts they have deposed;
Some poison'd by their wives: some sleeping kill'd;
All murder'd: for within the hollow crown
That rounds the mortal temples of a king
Keeps Death his court . . .

WILLIAM SHAKESPEARE, *Richard II* (*c.*1595)

Introduction: The Wars of the Roses?

At seven o'clock in the morning on Friday 27 May 1541, within the precincts of the Tower of London, an old woman walked out into the light of a spring day. Her name was Margaret Pole. By birth, blood and lineage she was one of the noblest women in England. Her father, George duke of Clarence, had been the brother to a king and her mother, Isabel Neville, had in her time been co-heir to one of the greatest earldoms in the land. Both parents were now long gone, memories from another age and another century.

Margaret's life had been long and exciting. For twenty-five years she had been the countess of Salisbury, one of only two women of her time to hold a peerage in her own right. She had until recently been one of the five wealthiest aristocrats of her generation, with lands in seventeen counties. Now, at sixty-seven – ancient by Tudor standards – she appeared so advanced in age that intelligent observers took her to be eighty or ninety.[1]

Like many inhabitants of the Tower of London, Margaret Pole was a prisoner. Two years previously she had been stripped of her lands and titles by an act of parliament which accused her of having 'committed and perpetrated diverse and sundry other detestable and abominable treasons' against her cousin, King Henry VIII. What these treasons were was never fully evinced, because in truth Margaret's offences against the crown were more general than particular. Her two principal crimes were her close relation to the king and her suspicion of his adoption of the new forms and doctrines of Christian belief that had swept through Europe during the past two decades. For these two facts, the one of birthright and the second of conscience, she had lived within London's stout, supposedly impervious riverside fortress, which bristled with cannon from its whitewashed central tower, for the past eighteen months.

Margaret had lived well in jail. Prison for a sixteenth-century aristocrat was supposed to be a life of restricted movement tempered by decent, even luxurious conditions, and she had been keen to ensure that her confinement met the highest standard. She expected to serve a comfortable sentence, and when she found the standards wanting, she complained.[2] Before she was moved to London she had spent a year locked in Cowdray House in West Sussex, under the watch of the unenthusiastic William Fitzwilliam, earl of Southampton. The earl and his wife had found her spirited and indignant approach to incarceration rather tiresome and had been glad when she was moved on.

In the Tower, Margaret was able to write letters to her relatives and was provided with servants and good, expensive food. Her nobility was not demeaned. Earlier in the year Queen Catherine's tailor had been appointed to make her a set of new clothes, and just a few weeks previously more garments had turned up, ordered and paid for directly by the king. Henry had also sent his cousin a nightgown lined with fur and another with Cypriot satin, petticoats, bonnets and hose, four pairs of shoes and a new pair of slippers. More than £15 – roughly the equivalent of two years' wages for a common labourer at the time – had been spent on her clothing in just six months. As she walked out into the cool morning air, Margaret Pole could therefore have reflected that, although she was due to be beheaded that morning, she would at least die wearing new shoes.

Her execution had been arranged in a hurry. She had been informed only hours previously that the king had ordered her death: a shockingly short time for an old lady to prepare her spirit and body for the end. According to a report that reached Eustace

Chapuys, the exceptionally well-infor... to England, the countess 'found the thing... had no idea 'of what crime she was accused,... been sentenced'. Few, in truth, would ever quite und... threat this feeble old lady could have posed to a king as... and self-important as Henry VIII.

A thin crowd had gathered to bear witness. They stood by a pathetically small chopping block, erected so hastily that it was simply set on the ground and not, as was customary, raised up on a scaffold. According to Chapuys, when Margaret arrived before the block she commended her soul to her creator and asked those present to pray for King Henry and Queen Catherine, the king's two-year-old son, Prince Edward, and the twenty-five-year-old Princess Mary, her god-daughter. But as the old woman stood talking to the sparse crowd (Chapuys put the number at 150; the French ambassador, Charles de Marillac, suggested it was fewer), a feeling of restlessness went around. She was told to hurry up and place her neck on the little piece of wood.

The Tower's regular executioner was not on duty that morning. He was in the north, alongside King Henry, who had visited the farthest reach of his kingdom to dampen the threat of rebellion against his rule. The Tower's axe had therefore been entrusted to a deputy: a man of tender years and little experience in the difficult art of decapitation. (Chapuys described him as a 'wretched and blundering youth'.) He was faced with a task wildly inappropriate to his ability. Only one other noblewoman had been executed in England since the Norman Conquest: the king's second wife, Anne Boleyn. She had been beheaded in a single stroke with a sword by a specially imported French executioner. *This* was not *that*, and the hapless executioner knew it. When the signal was given to strike, he brought the weapon down towards the block. But he botched the job. Rather than cutting cleanly through Margaret's neck in one stroke, he slammed the axe's blade into

She did not die. He brought

n. It took several more blows

t in which the inept axeman

pper body to pieces. It was a

d shock everyone who heard of

ardon her soul,' wrote Chapuys,

uous and honourable lady.'³

ned Imperial ambassador

ery strange', since she

nor how she had

erstand what

powerful

*

el just another casualty of the reli-
gious wa...   he sixteenth century, in which followers of the old faith – ... n Catholicism – and various splinter
groups of the new faith – Protestantism – sought to smite one
another into submission. These wars took different forms. Occasionally they were fought between kingdoms allied to opposing
faiths, but far more often, the religious wars were civil and dynastic conflicts that ripped individual kingdoms asunder. This was
certainly the case in England during the 1540s, and Margaret's
execution in that sense represented a reforming king's deliberate
strike against a powerful family who clung to the old faith.

Yet her death could also be seen as the undignified final act
in a long spell of non-religious aristocratic violence that had
begun nearly a century earlier. These were wars of politics and
personality that had sprung from a struggle for hegemony following the slow but catastrophic collapse of royal authority from
the late 1440s onwards. This conflict, usually assumed to have
been closed on the accession of Henry Tudor as Henry VII in
1485 and his defence of the crown at the battle of Stoke in
1487, in fact continued to haunt sixteenth-century politics long
afterwards. Certainly it played a role in Margaret Pole's death,
for this old woman was one of the last surviving members of the
Plantagenet dynasty and a living relic of what we now call the
wars of the roses.

Dozens of Margaret's immediate and extended family had fallen victim to these wars. Her father, George duke of Clarence, was twenty-eight when his brother King Edward IV had him executed for treason – drowned in a butt of the sweet Greek wine known as malmsey, in memory of which Margaret was said always to wear a tiny wine keg on her bracelet.[4] Two of her paternal uncles had been slaughtered in pitched battles during the 1470s and 1480s. Both of her grandfathers had also died on the battlefield; one ending his days with his head impaled on the city gates of York, a paper crown nailed to his skull. Margaret's brother Edward, styled but not officially recognised as earl of Warwick, had spent most of his twenty-four years of life imprisoned in the Tower of London. Henry VII had ordered his execution by beheading in November of 1499, when rumours spread of a plot to break him out of jail. Margaret's eldest son Henry Pole, Lord Montague, was executed in January 1539; her eldest grandson, Montague's heir, also called Henry, would die while incarcerated in the Tower some time after 1542. The whole history of the Pole family between the 1470s and 1540s was one of brutal destruction undertaken by three different kings. And in this the Poles were far from exceptional. They were simply the last of the great aristocratic families to be persecuted to extinction in the wars of the roses.

That England was used to killing its most illustrious men and women did not detract from the profound shock that Margaret Pole's callous execution caused around Europe. By 13 June the news had reached Antwerp, and a week later it had spread to the Imperial Court.[5] In early August the countess's second son, Reginald Pole, a renegade Catholic churchman who had risen to the rank of cardinal, wrote bitterly to Juan Alvarez de Toledo, cardinal archbishop of Burgos, that his mother had 'perished, not by the law of nature, but by a violent death, inflicted on her by one from whom it was the last due, as he was her cousin'. Reginald's only consolation in his mother's savage murder was that she had suffered a martyr's death. 'To suffer as Christ, his Apostles, and so many martyrs and virgins suffered, is not ignominious,' he wrote, but Pole nevertheless went on to compare Henry VIII unfavourably to the ancient tyrants Herod, Nero and Caligula. 'Their cruelty is far surpassed by the iniquity of this man, who, with much less semblance of justice, put to death a most innocent woman, who was of his own kin, of advanced age, and who had grown old with a reputation for virtue.'[6]

To paint Henry VIII as a brute killer in a long line of otherwise virtuous kings was somewhat disingenuous. Henry was certainly capable of violence and cruelty towards members of his own family, but such were the times. Indeed, if anything could be said for Margaret's death it was that it marked the end of the bloodbath that had been continuing on and off since the 1450s. When her poor, mangled body finally dropped to the ground, there remained barely a single drop of Plantagenet royal blood in England, other than the little which flowed in the veins of Henry VIII and his three children. Nearly a century of butchery was coming to an end not by choice but by default: almost all the potential victims were now dead.

*

One of the earliest recorded uses of the phrase 'the wars of the roses' came from the pen of the nineteenth-century British writer and royal tutor Lady Maria Callcott. Her children's book *Little Arthur's History of England* was first published in 1835. In describing the violent upheaval that convulsed England in the fifteenth century, Callcott wrote, 'For more than thirty years afterwards, the civil wars in England were called the wars of the Roses.'[7] She was right and she was wrong. The precise phrase is not recorded before the first quarter of the nineteenth century, but the idea of a country torn in half by the rival houses of Lancaster and York, represented respectively by the emblems of red and white roses, went back in some form to the fifteenth century.

Roses were a popular symbol throughout Europe during the middle ages, and their colours, whether deployed in politics, literature or art, were judged to have important and often opposing meanings. The fourteenth-century Italian writer Giovanni Boccaccio used red and white roses in his *Decameron* to symbolise the entwined themes of love and death.[8] Roses were doodled in the margins and illuminated letters in books of prayer, calendars and scientific texts.[9] Aristocratic families in England had included roses in their heraldic badges since at least the reign of Henry III in the thirteenth century.[10] But in the later fifteenth century in England, red and white roses began to be associated closely with the fortunes of rival claimants to the crown.

The first royal rose was the white rose, representing the house of York – the descendants of Richard duke of York, who asserted his right to the crown in 1460. When Richard's son Edward became King Edward IV in 1461, the white rose was one of a number of symbols he used to advertise his kingship. Indeed, as a young man Edward was known as 'the rose of Rouen', and on his military victories his supporters sang 'blessed be that flower!'[11] In later decades, the white rose was adopted by many of those who chose to align themselves with Edward's memory, particularly if they wished to stake their claim to royal pre-eminence by virtue of their relationship to him.

The red rose was far less common until it was adopted and promoted vigorously by Henry Tudor (Henry VII) in the 1480s. The earliest quasi-royal use of the red rose was by Henry Bolingbroke (later Henry IV), who had his pavilions decorated with the flowers during his famous trial by combat against Thomas Mowbray in 1398.[12] There is some (slight) evidence that red roses were also associated with Henry IV's grandson, Henry VI. But it was only after the battle of Bosworth in 1485 that red roses flourished as a royal badge, representing Henry VII's claim to the crown through his connection to the old dukes of Lancaster. The red rose was then used as a counterpoint to the white, puffing up the weak Tudor claims to royal legitimacy. ('To avenge the White, the Red Rose bloomed,' wrote one chronicler, studiously follow-ing the party line after Bosworth.[13]) As king, Henry VII had his scribes, painters and librarians plaster documents with red roses – even going so far as to modify books owned by earlier kings so that their lavish illuminations included roses of his own favoured hue.[14]

The red rose was more often invoked retrospectively, as its principal purpose after 1485 was to pave the way for a third rose: the so-called 'Tudor rose', which was a combination of white and red, either superimposed, quartered or simply wound together. The Tudor rose was invented to symbolise the unity that had sup-posedly been brought about when Henry VII married Edward IV's daughter Elizabeth of York in 1486, entwining the two warring branches, the houses of Lancaster and York, together. The story this rose told was of politics as romance: it explained a half-century of turmoil and bloodshed as the product of two divided families, who were brought to peace by a marriage that promised to commingle the feuding rivals. When Henry VII's son Henry VIII came to the throne in 1509, the court poet John Skelton, who grew up during the worst of the violence, wrote that 'the Rose both White and Red / In one Rose now doth grow'. The idea of 'wars of the roses' – and, most importantly, of their resolution with the arrival of the Tudors – was thus by the early sixteenth century a commonplace. The concept took hold because it offered up a simple, powerful narrative: a tale that made the world, if not black and white, then red and white. It implicitly justified the Tudors' claim to the crown. And to writers over the centuries – including the Tudor historians Edward Hall and Raphael Holinshed, Elizabethan dramatists such as William

Shakespeare, eighteenth-century thinkers such as Daniel Defoe and David Hume, and nineteenth-century novelists like Walter Scott, all of whom invoked the roses in their depictions of the wars – the idea was irresistible. But was it really true?

The answer, alas, is no. Modern historians have come to understand that the wars of the roses were far more complex and unpredictable than is suggested by their alluring title. The middle-to-late decades of the fifteenth century experienced sporadic periods of extreme violence, disorder, warfare and bloodshed, an unprecedented number of usurpations of the throne, the collapse of royal authority, an upheaval in the power politics of the English nobility, murders, betrayals, plots and coups, the savage elimination of the direct descendants of the last Plantagenet patriarch, King Edward III, and the arrival of a new royal dynasty, the Tudors, whose claim to the throne by right of blood was somewhere between highly tenuous and non-existent. It was a dangerous and uncertain period in which England's treacherous political life was driven by a cast of quite extraordinary characters, men and women alike, who sometimes resorted to unfathomable brutality and cruelty. The scale of the violence, the size and frequency of the battles that were fought, the rapidly shifting allegiances and motivations of the rivals, and the peculiar nature of the problems that were faced were baffling to many contemporaries and have remained so to many historians. This is one very good reason why a simple narrative of warring families split and reunited took root in the sixteenth century and has endured so long afterwards. But it is also true that this version of history was deliberately encouraged in the sixteenth century for political ends. The Tudors, particularly Henry VII, promoted the red rose/white rose myth vigorously, drawing on methods of dynastic propaganda that had been employed reaching far back to promote the dual monarchy of England and France during the Hundred Years War. Their success is self-evident. Even today, with several generations of modern historians having put forward sophisticated explanations for the 'wars of the roses', drawing on research into late medieval law, economics, culture and political thought, the simple Lancaster/York narrative is still the one that prevails when the fifteenth century becomes the subject of screen drama, popular fiction and discussion in the press. Victory to the Tudors, then: the very notion of 'the wars of the roses' continues to reflect that dynasty's innate genius for self-mythologising. They were masters of the art.

This book tells several overlapping stories. In the first place it seeks to draw an authentic picture of this harsh and troubled period, looking where possible past the distorting lens of the six-teenth century and of Tudor historiography and viewing the fif-teenth century on its own terms. What we will find is the disastrous result of a near-total collapse in royal authority under the kingship of Henry VI, who began his rule as a wailing baby and ended it as a shambling simpleton, managing in between to trigger a crisis unique in its nature and unlike any of the previous constitutional moments of the late middle ages in England. This is a story not of vain aristocrats attempting to overthrow the throne for their own personal gain – of 'bastard feudalism' gone awry and 'overmighty nobles' scheming to wreck the realm (both have, at times, been explanations put forward for the wars) – but of a polity battered on every side by catastrophe and hobbled by inept leadership. It is the story of a realm that descended into civil war despite the efforts of its most powerful subjects to avert disaster.

For nearly thirty years, Henry VI's hopeless rule was held together by the endeavours of fine men and women. But they could only strain so hard. The second phase of our story exam-ines the consequences of one man's decision that the best solution for this benighted realm was no longer to induce a weak king to govern his realm more competently, but to cast him aside and claim the crown for himself. The means by which Richard duke of

York did this were not unprecedented, but they proved extremely destructive. To a crisis of authority was added a crisis of legitimacy as the 'Yorkists' began to argue that the right to rule was not only a matter of competence but was carried in their blood. The second part of our story charts this stage of the conflict, and its eventual settlement under the able and energetic king Edward IV, who re-established the authority and prestige of the crown and, by the time of his death, appeared to have brought England back to some semblance of normalcy and good governance.

The third part of our story asks a simple question: how on earth, from this point, did the Tudors end up kings and queens of England? The family spawned by the unlikely secret coupling of a widowed French princess and her Welsh servant during the late 1420s ought never to have found themselves anywhere near a crown. Yet when Edward IV died in 1483 and his brother Richard III usurped the crown and killed Edward's sons, the Tudors suddenly became extremely important. The third strand to our story tracks their struggle to establish their own royal dynasty – one that would become the most majestic and imperious dynasty that England had ever known. Only from the slaughter and chaos of the fifteenth century could such a family have emerged triumphant, and only by continuing the slaughter could they secure their position. So as well as examining the wars of the roses as a whole, this book drills down into the early history of the Tudors, presenting them not according to their own myth, but as the fifteenth century really found them.

Finally, this book examines the Tudors' struggles to keep the crown after 1485 and the process by which their history of the wars of the roses was established: how they created a popular vision of the fifteenth century so potent and memorable that it not only dominated the historical discourse of the sixteenth century, but has endured up to our own times.

That, then, is the aim. My last book, *The Plantagenets*, told the story of the establishment of England's great medieval dynasty. This book tells the story of its destruction. The two books do not quite follow chronologically from one another, but they can, I hope, be read as a pair of complementary works. Here, as before, I aim to tell the tale of an extraordinary royal family in a way that is scholarly, informative and entertaining.

As ever I must thank my literary agent, Georgina Capel, for her brilliance, patience and good cheer. I also owe a great debt of thanks to my visionary editor at Faber in the UK, Walter Donohue, and to the equally wonderful Joy de Menil at Viking in the US. They and their teams have made this book a pleasure to write. I am grateful also to the staffs at the libraries, archives, castles and battlefields I have visited during the writing of this book – and most particularly to the staff at the London Library, British Library and National Archives, where I have spent a great deal of my time over the last few years. The book is dedicated to my wife, Jo Jones, who, with my daughters Violet and Ivy, has once again suffered my scribbling with love and humour.

And so to our story. In order fully to comprehend the process by which Plantagenet rule was destroyed and the Tudor dynasty established, we open not in the 1450s, when politics began to fracture into violence and warfare, nor in the 1440s, when the first signs of deep political turmoil emerged, nor even in the 1430s, when the first 'English' ancestors of the Tudor monarchs were born. Rather, our story starts in 1420, when England was the most powerful nation in western Europe, its king the flower of the world, and its future apparently brighter than at any time before: a time when the idea that within a generation England would be the most troubled realm in Europe would have been little short of preposterous. As with so many tragedies, our story opens with a moment of triumph. Let us begin.

DAN JONES

Battersea, London, February 2014

I

BEGINNINGS

1420–1437

'We were in perfect health.'

KING HENRY VI (aged seventeen months)

Chapter 1

BEGINNINGS
1420–1437

'We were in perfect health.'
KING HENRY VI (aged seventeen months)

1 : King of All the World

She was married in a soldier's wedding. Shortly before midday on
Trinity Sunday in June of 1420, a large band of musicians struck
up a triumphant tune as the elegant parish church of St Jean-au-
Marché in Troyes filled with splendidly dressed lords, knights and
noble ladies, gathered to observe the union of two great families
who had long been set against one another. The archbishop of
Sens conducted the solemn proceedings in the traditional French
fashion as Catherine de Valois, youngest daughter of the mad
king of France, Charles VI, and his long-suffering wife, Isabeau
of Bavaria, was wedded to Henry V, king of England.

Catherine was eighteen years old. She had delicate features, a
small, prim mouth and round eyes above high cheekbones. Her
slender neck bent very slightly to one side, but this was a lone
blemish upon the fine figure of a princess in the flush of youth.
The man she was about to marry was a battle-hardened warrior.
He had pursed lips and a long nose, characteristic of the line
of Plantagenet kings from whom he was descended. His dark,
slightly protruding eyes bore a close resemblance to those of his
father, Henry IV. His hair was cropped fashionably short and his
face was drawn and clean-shaven, showing scars including one
deep mark dating back to a battle fought when he was just sixteen, when an arrowhead had lodged deep in his cheek, just to
the right of his nose, and had to be cut out by a battlefield sur-
geon. At thirty-three, Henry V was the finest warrior among the
European rulers of his day. His appearance on his wedding day
was appropriately grand. 'Great pomp and magnificence were
displayed by him and his princes, as if he were at that moment

[3]

king of all the world,' wrote the high-born and well-connected French chronicler Enguerrand de Monstrelet.[1]

The war-torn countryside around Troyes, the ancient capital of the French county of Champagne, nearly one hundred miles south-east of Paris, had been bristling for a fortnight with English soldiers. Henry had arrived in town on 20 May, accompanied by two of his three brothers, Thomas duke of Clarence and John duke of Bedford, a large number of his aristocratic war captains and some sixteen hundred other men, mostly archers. There was no room for them within the town walls, so most of Henry's regular men had been quartered in nearby villages. The king himself was staying in the western half of town at a smart hotel in the marketplace called La Couronne ('The Crown'). From this base he conducted himself in high majesty during negotiations for a final peace between the warring realms of England and France.

In the seven years that had passed since his father's death in 1413, Henry V had settled an anxious realm. His father's reign had been beset by crises, many of them stemming from the fact that in 1399 he had deposed the ruling king, Richard II, and subsequently had him murdered following an attempt to rescue him from jail. This was the violent beginning to an unstable reign.

Richard had not been a popular king, but Henry IV's usurpation had triggered a crisis of legitimacy. He had suffered long-running financial problems, a massive insurgency in Wales under Owain Glyndwr and a series of northern rebellions, during one of which the archbishop of York was beheaded for treason. He had been very ill for long stretches of his reign, which had led to clashes with his sons – particularly the young Henry – as they strove to exercise royal authority on his behalf. For all that Henry IV had tried to govern as a mighty and authoritative king, he had found himself reliant on the men who had helped him acquire the throne in the first place: principally his retainers from the duchy of Lancaster, which had been his private landholding before he was crowned. This caused a long-running split in English politics, which only his death could remedy. It came, after his final illness, in the Jerusalem Chamber of the abbot's house in Westminster on 20 March 1413.

The accession of Henry V – king by right, rather than conquest – reunited England under an undisputed leader. Henry was a vigorous, charismatic, confident king: an accomplished general and an intelligent politician. His reign was notable for success in almost every area of government and warfare. Early on he made significant gestures of reconciliation, offering forgiveness to rebels of his father's reign, and exhuming Richard II from his burial place in King's Langley, Hertfordshire, and transferring his remains to the tomb Richard had commissioned, alongside his first wife, Anne of Bohemia, in Westminster Abbey. The central mission of his reign was to harness his close relations with his leading nobles to lead a war against France. In this he had been wildly successful: in less than two years of fighting Henry had pushed English power further into the continent than at any time since the rule of Richard the Lionheart more than two centuries before.

Catherine's marriage to this energetic young warrior-king represented the culmination of this audacious foreign policy. Kings of England had been fighting their French cousins for centuries, but only rarely with real success. Since 1337 the two kingdoms had been engaged in a period of particularly bitter hostility, which we now call the Hundred Years War. Many territorial claims, counter-claims and squabbles were folded into this complex and long-running dispute. Underpinning them all was a claim first made by Henry's great-grandfather, Edward III, to be the rightful king of both realms. Not even Edward, a superb campaigner and wily politician, had managed to realise this aim, but in marrying Catherine, Henry was about to come tantalisingly close. With the treaty of Troyes, sealed in the city's cathedral on 21 May, Henry had not only secured for himself a French bride. He also became, as he announced in a letter he dictated, '*Henry* by the Grace of God, *King of England, Heir and Regent of the Realm of France*, and *Lord of Ireland*'.[2] The treaty of Troyes redirected the French succession, disinheriting Catherine's seventeen-year-old brother Charles, the last surviving son of Charles VI and Queen Isabeau, in favour of Henry and his future children. The French crown would pass for the first time into English hands.

*

The treaty of Troyes and the royal marriage that followed were made possible by the woeful condition of the French crown. For nearly thirty years Charles VI had been suffering from a combination of paranoia, delusion, schizophrenia and severe depression, which came in bouts lasting for months at a time. He suffered his first attack while leading an army through the countryside near Le Mans on a hot day in August 1392. Dehydrated, highly stressed by a recent assassination attempt on one of his close friends, and frightened by a local madman who had shouted out that he faced treachery on the road ahead, he had been overcome by a violent fit and had attacked his companions with his sword, killing five of them in an hour-long rampage.[3] It took him nearly six weeks to recover, and from this point his life was dogged by psychotic episodes.

Physicians at the time blamed Charles's mental abnormality on an excess of black bile, the 'wet' or melancholic humour which was thought to make men susceptible to stress and illness. It was also speculated that his weak constitution was inherited: Charles's mother, Jeanne de Bourbon, had suffered a complete nervous breakdown following the birth of her seventh child, Isabelle.[4] Whatever the diagnosis, the political effects of the king's condition were catastrophic. Incapacitating bouts of madness returned every year or so, crippling him physically and mentally.

He would forget his own name and the fact that he was a king with a wife and children. He treated the queen with suspicion and hostility and tried to destroy plates and windows bearing her arms. At times he trembled and screamed that he felt as though a thousand sharp iron spikes were piercing his flesh. He would run wildly about the royal residence in Paris, known as the Hôtel St Pol, until he collapsed from exhaustion, worrying his servants so much that they walled up most of the palace doors to stop him from escaping and embarrassing himself in the street. He refused to bathe, change his clothes or sleep at regular inter-vals for months on end; on at least one occasion when servants broke into his chambers to attempt to wash and change him they found him mangy with the pox and covered in his own faeces. A regency council was established to rule France during his increas-ingly frequent periods of indisposition. Yet even when Charles was deemed sane enough to rule, his authority was debilitated by the fact that he might at any moment relapse into lunacy.

The madness of King Charles had caused a power vacuum in France. All medieval crowns relied on a sane and stable head beneath them, and Charles VI's derangement was responsible for – or at the very least severely exacerbated – a period of violent unrest and civil war which erupted in 1407 between two power-ful and ruthless groups of French noblemen and their supporters. The initial protagonists were Philip the Bold, duke of Burgundy, and Louis de Valois, duke of Orléans, who was the king's brother. They quarrelled over land, personal differences and – above all – their relative influence over the regency council. When Louis of Orléans was stabbed to death in the streets of Paris on 23 November 1407 by fifteen masked men loyal to Philip the Bold's son and heir John the Fearless, murder and treachery became the defining characteristics of French politics. Louis's eldest son, Charles, built an alliance with his father-in-law, Bernard count of Armagnac, and France swiftly divided into two rival power blocs as the leading men of the realm split their allegiance between the warring parties. The stand-off between the Burgundians and the Armagnacs had begun.

Henry V had played the two sides of the French civil war against one another with startling success. In 1412 he signed a treaty with the Armagnacs, offering them his support in return for a recognition of English lordship over several important territories in south-west France: Poitou, Angoulême and Périgord, all of which had ancient connections to the English crown. The treaty did not last long. By 1415 Henry had increased his demands to include English sovereignty over Normandy, Anjou, Maine, Touraine and Brittany. This was no arbitrary clutch of estates: he was claiming the lands once controlled by his twelfth-century Plantagenet ancestors, Henry II and Richard the Lionheart. When the Armagnacs refused, Henry invaded Normandy and besieged and conquered Harfleur, the port town at the mouth of the Seine. He then raided his way across the French countryside before finally engaging an enormous French army at Agincourt on St Crispin's Day, Friday 25 October 1415.

The two armies met on a ploughed field, the mud beneath their feet thickened by heavy rain. Despite the size of the French army, which was perhaps six times as large as Henry's, superior tactics and outstanding generalship gave the English the advantage. Henry relied heavily on the use of longbows, which were capable of causing havoc on a crowded battlefield. The king protected his archers from cavalry attacks by driving sharpened stakes into the ground around them. And the bowmen repaid him: firing volley after volley through the air towards the French and their horses, and the men-at-arms who attempted to cross the battlefield on foot. Numerical advantage meant nothing when the sky rained arrows, and a terrific slaughter ensued. In the words of one eyewitness, 'the living fell on the dead, and others falling on the living were killed in turn.' The deaths were disastrously one-sided:

more than 10,000 Frenchmen were killed for the loss of perhaps as few as 150 English.[5]

To prevent any threat of the enemy regrouping, Henry ordered thousands of prisoners and casualties to be killed when the battle was over, with only the highest-ranking spared for ransom. Yet despite this unchivalrous and ruthless command, he had won an astonishing victory, and was hailed as a hero. When the news of Agincourt reached England, wild parties broke out, and when Henry returned to London following the battle he was greeted like a new Alexander. Girls and boys dressed as angels with golden face-paint sang 'Hail flower of England, knight of Christendom', and huge mock-castles were erected in the streets. 'It is not recorded', wrote one admiring chronicler, 'that any king of England ever accomplished so much in so short a time and returned to his own realm with so great and glorious a triumph.'[6]

In the years that followed Agincourt, Henry returned to France to make even more spectacular gains. In July 1417 he launched a systematic conquest of Normandy, landing in the mouth of the river Touques, before besieging and brutally sacking Caen, followed by the important military towns of Exmes, Sées, Argentan, Alençon, Falaise, Avranches and Cherbourg, along with every significant town and castle in between.[7] Rouen, the capital of the duchy, was besieged and starved inhumanly into submission between July 1418 and January 1419: refugees cast out of the city were refused passage through the English lines and simply left to die of hunger in no-man's land. By the late summer Henry had become the first English king effectively in command of Normandy since his ancestor King John had been chased out by Philip II of France in 1204. Paris lay within his sights.

With the English menacing their way down the Seine towards the French capital, all of France descended into terrified chaos. Had the Burgundians and Armagnacs been able to resolve their differences and oppose Henry as one, the realm might have been saved. They could not. At a crisis meeting held between the factions on a bridge in the town of Montereau on 10 September 1419, John the Fearless, duke of Burgundy – who had claimed control of the king, queen and court – was murdered by an Armagnac loyalist who smashed his face and head with an axe. (Many years later the duke's skull was kept as a curiosity by the Carthusian monks at Dijon; the prior of the monastery, showing the skull to the visiting King François I, explained that it was through the hole in his cranium that the English had entered France.) Queen Isabeau and the Burgundians now viewed any other end to the war as preferable to making peace with the detested and treacherous Armagnacs. They sued for peace with Henry, offering him the greatest gift in their possession: the French crown.[8] Charles VI was so far gone that he was quite unfit to take part in the negotiations pertaining to the future of his own crown. The peace was sealed in the cathedral of Troyes on 21 May 1420. Its very first clause provided for the marriage of the princess Catherine and Henry V, king of England and now '*Heir and Regent of the Realm of France*'.

Catherine's marriage was therefore momentous for both royal houses. French princesses had married Plantagenet kings before: indeed, it was the union between Edward II of England and Isabella of France in 1308 that had mingled rival royal blood sufficiently to provoke the Hundred Years War in the first place. Never before, however, had an English and a French dynasty come together with the specific aim of settling their two crowns on a single king, as would now be the case whenever the merciful death of the poor, demented, fifty-one-year-old Charles finally came.

The ceremony had its moments of splendour. One later chronicler recorded that on their betrothal Henry had given Catherine a beautiful and priceless ring as a token of his esteem.[9] He certainly gave a generous cash gift of two hundred nobles to the church in which they were married. French protocol was followed, so a procession would have made its way on the night of the wedding to the couple's chamber, where the archbishop blessed the royal bed and gave them soup and wine for their supper.[10]

When Henry's English guests wrote newsletters home, they referred to the celebrations in only the most cursory fashion. There were more important matters at hand. Immediately after the couple were married, the king told the knights in his company that they would be leaving Troyes directly the next day to lay siege to Sens, a day's march to the west, where Catherine's brother Charles, now a pretender to the throne, was ensconced with his Armagnac supporters. There would be no ceremonial jousting held to mark the royal wedding. According to a Parisian diarist of the times, Henry told his men that fighting for real at Sens was of infinitely greater value than the mock-battle of the tournament field: 'We may all tilt and joust and prove our daring and worth, for there is no finer act of courage in the world than to punish evildoers so that poor people can live.'[11]

As Henry and his followers marched off to pursue their long and bloody war, Catherine was allowed to travel with her mother and father. She spent the winter watching her husband's men move from town to town, laying sieges and either starving or slaughtering their enemies into submission. On 1 December 1420 she watched as her father accompanied Henry on his first formal entry into Paris, where the treaty of Troyes was formalised and the official process of disinheriting her brother – referred to in official English documents as '*Charles*, bearing himself for the *Dauphin*' – was completed.[12] Two months later Catherine set sail from Calais for Dover, leaving behind the country of her birth to begin a new life across the sea. She landed on 1 February 1421 and immediately prepared for her coronation.

*

The England in which Catherine arrived early in 1421 was a strong, stable realm, more politically united under Henry's leadership than perhaps at any time in its history.[13] During the long centuries of Plantagenet rule, English kings had steadily increased the scope of their power, governing in (usually) fruitful consultation with their great magnates, barons, the commons in parliament and the Church. England was unmistakeably a war state, taxed hard to pay for adventure overseas, but in the aftermath of Agincourt and the steady succession of victories that followed, the realm endured its financial burdens buoyed by a strong sense of triumph. Although Thomas Walsingham, a monastic chronicler based in St Albans, Hertfordshire, wrote that the year preceding Catherine's arrival had been one 'in which there had been a desperate shortage and want of money . . . even among the ordinary people scarcely enough pennies remained for them to be able to lay up sufficient supplies of corn', he noted that it was also 'a year of fertile crops and a rich harvest of fruit'.[14]

The most common medieval analogy for a state was the literal body politic, with the king as the head. 'When the head is infirm, the body is infirm. Where a virtuous king does not rule, the people are unsound and lack good morals,' wrote the contemporary poet and moralist John Gower.[15] In this respect, England and France could not have been more different. Henry was without doubt a virtuous – perhaps even a virtuoso – king and his realm had accordingly flourished. He had enjoyed a thorough political education in adolescence that in adulthood manifested itself in strong and capable kingship based confidently on his birthright. He was personally charismatic, liked and trusted by his leading nobles, and successful enough in war to create a tight-knit military fraternity. He had three loyal and able brothers: Thomas duke of Clarence, John duke of Bedford and Humphrey duke of Gloucester, all of whom were of great value both in governing the realm and in pursuing the war abroad. Henry met with the approval of the English Church for his vigour in hunting out Lollards, a heretical sect who followed the teachings of the scholar John Wycliffe and held unorthodox views about the dogma of the Catholic Church and the validity of her teachings. He taxed his realm relentlessly, but his personal household expenses were markedly frugal, his exchequer competently run and his war debts relatively controlled. He pleased the people in the shires of England with a tough but impartial drive to re-establish the rule of royal law and stamp out the disorder that had bedevilled his father's reign. Criminals were often drafted into military service, where their violent instincts could be safely satisfied pillaging and burning among the villages of France.[16]

> May gracious God now save our king,
> His people and his well-willing;
> Give him good live and good ending,
> That we with mirth may safely sing,
> *Deo gracias!* [Thanks be to God!][17]

So went a popular song of the time – and with good reason, for the prosperous kingdom of England reflected all the virtue of its mighty ruler.

Catherine's place in her new realm was established immediately on her arrival. The French chronicler Monstrelet heard that she was 'received as if she had been an angel of God'.[18] The nineteen-year-old queen was provided with a personal staff of her husband's choosing. The information that reached Walsingham from court was that the queen's household consisted almost entirely of noble Englishwomen. 'Nor did any Frenchman remain in her service except for three women of good birth and two maidservants.'[19] On 24 February she was crowned at the church of St Peter in Westminster, and celebrated with a feast attended by most of the English nobility and James I, king of Scotland, a long-term captive at the English court. (James had been seized by pirates off the English coast in 1406 when he was twelve and had inherited the crown during his captivity, over the course of which he also received a full education and was generally treated as an honoured guest.) The feast was a show-case for English cuisine. Since it was Lent, no meat was served, but the tables groaned with eels, trout, salmon, lampreys, hali-but, shrimps and prawns, great crabs and lobsters, whelks, jellies decorated with fleurs-de-lis, sweet porridges and creams. The 'subtleties' – non-edible but visually extraordinary dishes that announced each course of the meal – featured pelicans, pan-thers, and a man riding on the back of a tiger. In each subtlety the new queen was represented as St Catherine with her wheel, defending the honour of the Church.[20]

After the coronation, Catherine left Westminster and joined the king on a tour of the midlands. She travelled through Hert-ford, Bedford and Northampton on her way to Leicester, where she celebrated Easter with Henry. She found England a profitable and hospitable country. 'From the cities thus visited the king and queen received precious gifts of gold and silver from the citizens and prelates of each town,' wrote the chronicler John Strecche.[21] But Henry did not tarry long in England. Shortly after Easter he received news that his eldest brother, the duke of Clarence, his deputy and lieutenant in France, had died fighting in Normandy. The war would not wait, and in June 1421 the king and queen crossed the channel again for Calais. Catherine was three months pregnant.

*

The queen's condition meant that she did not stay long in France. She left Henry campaigning against her brother and returned to England to give birth to a rival heir to the French crown. For good fortune on the perilous journey through childbirth Catherine brought with her a treasured relic: the foreskin of the Holy Infant, which was known to be a valuable aid to women in labour.[22] With its help she delivered a healthy baby boy in the royal palace at Windsor on 6 December, the feast day of St Nicholas. Every bell in London was rung at once to celebrate the news, and Te Deums were sung in the city's churches.[23] Inevitably, the child was named after his father. But the two Henries were never to meet.

Henry V's heroic victories on the battlefield had enabled him to manufacture a situation in which he could claim to be the rightful king of two realms. The task of turning this into a political reality, however, strained every fibre of his formidable being. His intervention in French politics had deepened the rift between the Burgundians and Armagnacs, since to the latter the war now appeared to be nothing less than a struggle for existence. Forces loyal to the dauphin dug in, garrisoning castles wherever they could, determined to resist Henry at any cost. Conquest, it was clear, would be a slow and increasingly draining endeavour.

From October all through the winter of 1421–2, Henry led an operation to besiege Meaux, a small town a few miles north-east of Paris. Meaux was heavily fortified and its defenders put up a fierce resistance. The siege began late in the year, lasted for more than six months, and was a miserable experience for both sides: the garrison was slowly starved while the besiegers outside suffered the horrible privations of winter warfare. It was a long and ugly way to fight a war, but if Henry was to force the whole of France to observe his rights under the treaty of Troyes, he would have to break the most entrenched of the resistance to his rule.

Towards the end of May, Catherine returned to France to visit her husband, leaving her baby son at home in England, under the care of his nurses. She spent a few weeks at his side, along with her parents. But it was clear as summer arrived that not all was well with the king. At some point, probably in the squalor of the siege of Meaux, Henry V had contracted dysentery. The 'bloody flux', which brought the agonies of intestinal damage and severe dehydration to the sufferer, was very often fatal, and Henry knew it. He was an experienced soldier and would have seen many of his men suffering the same fate. Henry was cogent and pragmatic enough as the illness worsened to make a detailed will, outlining his wishes for the political settlements in England and France after his death. He died in the royal castle at Vincennes between two and three o'clock in the morning on 31 August, a little more than two weeks short of his thirty-sixth birthday. With the same bewildering swiftness that had characterised his life's every action, England's extraordinary warrior-king was gone. At home a baby not quite nine months old was set to inherit the crown, the youngest person ever to become king of England.

If the new king were to live beyond infancy – and of this there was no guarantee – England would now face the longest royal minority in its history. Precedent was not promising. Three English kings since the Norman Conquest had inherited the crown as children, and all had endured very difficult times. Henry III was nine years old when he became king in 1216, and in his early years he was dominated by overbearing ministers who used royal power to enrich themselves and their followers. Edward III had been thrust upon the throne at fourteen in 1327 after the forced abdication of his father, Edward II, and for the next three years power had been greedily and murderously wielded by his mother, Isabella of France, and her feckless lover, Roger Mortimer, until they were deposed in a bloody palace coup. Richard II was the most recent king to have inherited the crown as a child, in 1377, when he was ten years old. An attempt had then been made to govern as if the boy-king was a competent adult. It was a dismal failure. Within four years of his accession England's government had almost been brought down by the Peasants' Revolt – the great popular rebellion of 1381 – and Richard's subsequent path to adulthood was beset by political faction and upheaval. He bore the psychological scars to his death.[24] The book of Ecclesiastes expressed perfectly England's experience of immature monarchs: 'Woe unto thee, O land, when thy king is a child . . . !'[25]

Matters grew even more complicated when, on 21 October 1422, Charles VI died. He was fifty-three and probably died from causes connected to his longstanding illness. The infant Henry of Windsor was now not merely the new king of England. He was also, under the terms of the treaty of Troyes, the heir to the English kingdom of France, a political entity that was still the subject of a furious war. The French king's body was laid to rest in the mausoleum at the abbey church in St Denis. His queen Isabeau would continue to live in the Hôtel St Pol in what was now effectively occupied Paris. Once a powerful, if controversial, force in guiding the realm during her husband's bouts of lunacy, her political days were now over. The English spread scurrilous (and most likely false) stories of her outrageous promiscuity and claimed, all too conveniently, that the dauphin was not really the son of Charles VI. As far as the conquerors from across the sea were concerned, the death of the mad king left them in charge of France. At Charles VI's funeral, Henry V's eldest surviving brother, John duke of Bedford, had the sword of state carried before him, a gesture intended to demonstrate that he was now, as his nephew's representative, the effective power in the realm.

Yet for all the grandstanding and triumphalism, there was no getting away from the truth, which was that the first king of the dual kingdom was a tiny, helpless baby. An unprecedented and extremely delicate military situation would have to be managed for nearly two decades without a competent hand to guide the way. Only disaster, surely, could await.

2 : We Were in Perfect Health

Boy-kings were not unknown in the fifteenth century, but they presented a realm with many difficult questions. A king who was a baby, a toddler, even a young man was perfectly able to *reign*, but he was not in any practical sense able to *rule*. At nine months old, Henry VI had been accepted unquestioningly as rightful and legitimate king. Yet until he came of age, or began to show enough discretion to start taking part in government, it would be necessary to make all the decisions of his public and private life on his behalf. As a child, the king was incapable of choosing his officials and servants or giving direction in war and justice, and insufficiently competent to make critical decisions about succession, on which the security of England rested. Yet these matters could not be ignored for eighteen years until the boy became a man.

This problem had been anticipated, in part at least, by his father. As Henry V lay dying in August of 1422, he had gathered his companions around him and given them instructions for the care of his son and his kingdom after his death. Codicils to his will established that responsibility for the young Henry VI's person would fall to his great-uncle, Thomas Beaufort, duke of Exeter. The duke was to have overall governance of the royal person, with responsibility for choosing his servants. In this, he was to be assisted by two men who had been conspicuously loyal to the old king: Sir Walter Hungerford, a long-serving steward to the royal household, and Henry, Lord FitzHugh, a trusted chamberlain. One or other was to attend the king at all times. (They were later succeeded in their positions by two more soldiers who had been loyal to the old regime: John, Lord Tiptoft and Louis de Robesart.) But when it came to the practicalities of raising a tiny child, a mother knew best. Catherine de Valois – herself only recently out of childhood – played an equally important role in her son's early life and upbringing.

Catherine's household was institutionally separate from her son's, but in practice they overlapped a great deal. The dowager queen's household finances supplemented those of her son and Catherine was influential in his choice of servants. As a baby, Henry VI was attended chiefly by women: he had a head nurse called Joan Asteley, a day nurse, Matilda Fosbroke, a chamberwoman, Agnes Jakeman, and a laundress, Margaret Brotherman; little is known about any of the women, but it is impossible to imagine that Catherine had no say in their selection, for they would spend far more time with the boy than she did. When Henry was two years old, Catherine's former servant Dame Alice Boutiller was appointed as royal governess, with an official licence from the king's council to chastise Henry from time to time, without fear of reprisals if and when he took offence at his necessary discipline. Even when the king grew older and more men were added to his company, Catherine's hand was still visible. In 1428, Richard Beauchamp, earl of Warwick, took over responsibility for Henry's education, with a mandate to imbue him with the qualities of chivalrous, knightly kingship. But Henry's confessor, George Arthurton, and the head knight of his chamber, Sir Walter Beauchamp, had both been former servants in the queen's household.[1]

The young dowager queen held extensive lands and properties throughout England and Wales – including the vast Welsh castles of Flint, Rhuddlan and Beaumaris, the imposing fortress of Knaresborough in Yorkshire and, further south, Hertford Castle, Leeds Castle and Pleshey in Kent, and Wallingford, an ancient royal castle that had been extensively repaired and fitted out for her comfort and benefit. She divided her time between her favourite residences, but for the most part, she stayed near her son in the magnificent royal palaces of the Thames valley, and particularly at Windsor, Westminster and Eltham.

Eltham, in Kent, a favourite royal residence for more than a century, affords a glimpse of the young king's early life. It offered space, grandeur, luxury and comfort for Queen Catherine and plenty of intriguing corners for a toddler to explore. It was surrounded with acres of parklands, and landscaped gardens planted with vines. Stone bridges arched elegantly across its moats and led to a network of outbuildings: the young king could stumble upon the cooks at work in the kitchen and buttery, the comforting scents of the morning's bread drifting up from the bakery and the more exotic foreign flavours of the spicery. The palace had come into royal hands in 1305 and had been significantly redeveloped three times since the 1350s. In the early years of Henry's reign, yet more money was spent ensuring that it offered all the clean and modern facilities needed to raise a young king.[2] Smart wooden apartments with stone chimneys were joined by cloisters to a grand private chapel. Catherine could entertain her guests at night in the hall and a specially constructed dancing chamber, while the king's household kept to his rooms, centring on a private chamber warmed by two roaring fires and lit by stained-glass windows, decorated with birds and grotesques and the personal symbols of Henry's paternal grandfather, Henry IV. Royal badges and crowns surrounded the old king's motto: *soueignex vous de moy*; remember me.[3] In this chamber, and others like it around the palaces of England, young Henry began his path to manhood and kingship: playing with toys and jewels given to him as gifts at New Year, taking his academic lessons from his tutor, the Oxbridge scholar and medical doctor John Somerset, learning devotions by rote from his prayer book, laughing on feast days at court entertainers like Jakke Travaille or the performing troupe called the Jews of Abingdon, learning to play the two musical organs he possessed, and receiving early instruction in the martial arts, while wearing his specially built 'little coat armours' and wielding a long sword. In private, Henry lived the life not of a king, but of a young prince – raised and taught and loved and entertained and (occasionally) punished much like other royal boys before him. Yet in the public sphere of kingship, things were far more complicated.

England was a realm whose government spun like a wheel around the hub of the king's person. Institutionally, it was sophisticated, mature and complex. The king was obliged by his coronation oath to consult his senior noblemen on matters of state, either through a formally composed council or the more informal means of taking counsel, or considered advice, from the great men of the land as he saw fit. When taxes were required, he had to work in partnership with the realm via the gatherings of lords and commons that met when he called a parliament. Justice was dispensed by increasingly professional public servants answerable ultimately to the court of chancery, and public finance was managed through another ancient and very bureaucratic institution, the exchequer.

But although it was big and complicated, English royal government was not a machine that could operate of its own accord. Indeed, the machine's smooth operation, and by extension, the fortunes of the realm at large, still depended fundamentally on the personal competence of the king. The magic ingredient that made royal government work was the absolute freedom of the royal will, and it was by exercising his royal will that the king could settle disputes between the great men of the realm, correct abuses and corruption in the system, and generally give a sense of leadership and direction to the country. Thus, a confident, decisive, persuasive and soldierly king like Henry V was able to govern a united and peaceful realm. By contrast, a wavering, untrustworthy king without luck or skill on the battlefield and bereft of good judgement, such as Richard II had been, could swiftly see his rule unravel and disorder tear apart the realm.[4]

Self-evidently, it was impossible for a child to fulfil this part of kingship, which marked the essential difference between *reigning* and *ruling*. Yet from the very day that England learned of Henry V's death, there was an astonishingly sophisticated and united effort by virtually the entire English political community to operate the young king's power responsibly and carefully on his behalf.

On his deathbed, Henry had given instructions that led to his eldest surviving brother, John duke of Bedford, taking responsibility for French affairs.[5] This was uncontroversial: Bedford was the heir presumptive to the French crown, a sober, pious, hard-working man, a canny politician and an effortlessly impressive lord, who projected princely magnificence in everything he did. More controversial were the measures Henry had proposed for government at home in England. One of the codicils to Henry's will suggested that his youngest brother, Humphrey duke of Gloucester, would be appointed as *tutela* during Henry VI's minority. It may well have been that this term implied simply that Gloucester should have personal responsibility for the education and upbringing of the new king. However, it was also possible to interpret the term to suggest that Gloucester would wield full regency powers in England, accountable only to the king himself.

Many in England would have approved of this interpretation, for in the country at large Gloucester was held in high esteem. He was a literate and cultured man, with knowledge and interests in every direction, from English, French and Italian poetry and the humanist learning of Italy to alchemy, which was then popular in educated circles. He employed foreign scholars as his secretaries, spent large sums on patronising and promoting artists and writers, collected books and fostered a learned, courtly atmosphere in his household. Moreover, he was a veteran of the battle of Agincourt, and the beautiful Jacqueline of Hainault, whom he married in 1423, was a princess generally beloved by the people of England. He held implacably aggressive views on foreign policy and, although these were not shared by many of his fellow noblemen, Gloucester was seen in London as the champion of mercantile interests and someone who would stand up for native traders.

Yet for all these qualities and his undeniable popularity among the English, Gloucester did not command the devotion of everyone around the new king. Although he was a deep drinker of high culture, he could also be pompous and self-regarding. In his military career he had pursued an image of chivalry, but he was decidedly less impressive than his three elder brothers: for while Henry V had been a peerless commander and a magnetic character, Thomas of Clarence a suicidally brave soldier and John of Bedford a sober strategist, Gloucester tended to place mindless belligerence above all other tactical considerations. His desire for popular worship alienated others who had a claim to power as well, and made him a curiously shallow leader. Meanwhile, his pretensions to chivalry would founder in 1428 when he callously cast aside Jacqueline of Hainault, having their marriage annulled in order to take up with one of her ladies-in-waiting, a smart and seductive baron's daughter by the name of Eleanor Cobham. Like his older brother Bedford, Humphrey duke of Gloucester cultivated a reputation for stateliness and grandeur. His simply rang hollower.

It was perhaps no surprise, then, that when the conditions of Henry V's will became known, a concerted effort was made to prevent Gloucester from taking up the personally dominant position in government that he craved. This resistance was led by Bedford, in alliance with other lords of the royal council. In December 1422, during the first parliament of the new reign, Gloucester was summoned to be told he had been awarded the title of 'Protector and Defender of the kingdom of England and the English church and principal councillor of the lord King'. Even if it sounded grand, this title was designed to be strictly limited, and it would lapse whenever the more senior Bedford visited England. Neither Gloucester nor anyone else was going to be a lieutenant, tutor, governor or regent. The duke was simply the pre-eminent man in what would prove to be a very carefully constructed conciliar protectorate – the first such experiment in English history, and one which acted under a very singular fiction. Government was carried out on Henry's behalf, but it also continued as if the child-king was in fact a fully functioning public figure.

Gloucester was bitterly disappointed. Not even the large salary he received in his new role could mask the fact that he had been passed over in a manner that suggested not even his own brother, with whom he maintained generally good relations, considered him fit to govern England independently. Yet to his credit, Gloucester did not withdraw from politics or begin to think of rebellion. Despite the sting of personal rejection, he appears to have recognised the same facts that had struck everyone else close to the English crown: that Henry V's death left England in a very dangerous position and that without a collective attempt to create a stable form of minority government that could last for a decade or more, the realm could very easily end up in the same disastrous condition as that which had afflicted their French neighbours across the sea. Seen in this light, the decision to pass over Gloucester in favour of a form of conciliar rule serving the conceit that the baby king was a genuine ruler was both a piece of wholly artificial constitutional backbending and a stroke of brilliance.

*

King Henry VI presided over parliament for the first time at Westminster in the autumn of 1423, when he was not yet two years old. A medieval parliament had no power of its own to speak of, save that derived from the sovereign, whether he was a baby, a grown man or a dribbling geriatric. On Friday 12 November, therefore, Queen Catherine prepared to bring her son from his nursery at Windsor down through the affluent towns and villages that stood on the north bank of the Thames, to Westminster, where he would meet representatives of his subjects in the time-honoured fashion. Windsor was grander than Eltham, a fairytale castle imbued with all the pious chivalric trappings of English kingship: a moated and walled forest of towers and turrets, with glorious painted chambers and sumptuous living quarters, as well as the magnificent chapel of St George, home to the Order of the Garter. It was from this tranquil place that in the second week of November, the twenty-three-month-old king – a toddler now, with the beginnings of his own will – was about to be removed.

Henry was not impressed by the prospect of the trip. Although the start of the journey was smooth, and the infant king was well attended by his nurses and nannies, the travelling did not much agree with him. After the first day on the road the royal party spent the night at Staines. Then, on the morning of Sunday 13 November, as Henry was carried towards his mother, seated in her coach and ready to travel onwards to Westminster via Kingston, he threw a royal tantrum. 'He cried and shremed [i.e. shrieked and thrashed about and wept] and would not be carried further,' wrote one London chronicler, 'wherefore he was borne again into his inn, and there bode the Sunday all day.'[6] Only twenty-four hours later, after a day of mollification in his lodgings, would the toddler consent to be taken on towards parliament. Finally, on 18 November he arrived, was presented to the realm on his mother's lap and listened, presumably with no interest whatsoever, to the Speaker, the lawyer and MP John Russell, expressing the thanks of all concerned for their great 'comfort and gladness to see your high and royal person to sit and occupy your own rightful see and place in your parliament'.[7]

If all this seemed rather a strained and strange political dance, it nevertheless had profound importance to the men who performed it. Kingship was a sacred and essential office, and in the 1420s every effort was made to draw the young Henry into its symbolic rituals. Day-to-day government was carried out by a council with clear rules and a fixed membership. Seventeen councillors were initially appointed, articles of conduct for their meetings were agreed and a quorum of four was deemed necessary to make decisions binding. The council kept detailed minutes, including the names of those who had made decisions, and it limited itself to carrying out only the essential functions of kingship. It sold offices and titles only for the financial benefit of the Crown, rather than for private political patronage. It held absolute and secret control over the royal finances. It was as close to a disinterested political body as could be conceived.

Yet the king was still brought into play whenever it was possible. In the first month of Henry's reign, a solemn ceremony had been held at Windsor to mark the transfer of the great seal of England – the essential tool in royal government – out of the hands of the old king's chancellor, Thomas Langley, bishop of Durham. The baby was surrounded in his chamber by the greatest nobles and bishops of the land, who watched carefully as the 'chancellor delivered to King Henry the late king's great seal of gold in a purse of white leather sealed with the said chancellor's seal, and the king delivered the same by [the duke of Gloucester]'s hands to the keeping of [the keeper of the chancery rolls], who took it with him to London . . .'[8] The next day the seal was taken to parliament and solemnly handed over to a clerk of the royal treasury for safekeeping.

It was pure theatre, but the fabric of English government was materially sustained when the king's soft and tiny fingers passed over the fine white leather of the seal's purse. The same ceremony was repeated nearly two years later at Hertford Castle, when the king was again called upon to hand the seal over to his great-uncle Henry Beaufort, bishop of Winchester, who had been appointed chancellor in his turn.[9] When the king was five years old, the lords of his council recorded in their minutes an astonishingly clear summary of their position: 'How be it that the king as now be of tender age nevertheless the same authority resteth and is at this day in his person that shall be in him at any time hereafter.'[10]

This attempt to affect personal kingship was, at times, comical in its confection. Official letters survive, written in the very first years of Henry VI's reign, which were framed not as instructions from older men ruling on the behalf of a baby, but with the pretence that the baby himself was a fully functioning adult dictating his royal despatches in person. One such, written to the duke of Bedford in France, on 15 May 1423, when the king was still a couple of weeks short of eighteen months old, began, 'Right trusty and most beloved uncle we greet you well with all our heart and signify unto you as for your consolation that at the time of the writing of this thanked by God we were in perfect health of person trusting to our Lord it as we desire in semblable wise ye so be . . .'[11] Five years later, the king was described in parliament as showing signs of readiness to rule: 'The king, blessed be our lord, is . . . far gone and grown in person, in wit and understanding, and like with the grace of God to occupy his own royal power within [a] few years.'[12] He was six years old.

In fact, conciliar government continued throughout the 1420s. In areas where an adult king would traditionally have intervened in person, such as arbitrating disputes between the great nobles in the shires, a system of mutual oath-taking served to keep the peace. It was not always straightforward, but order was generally maintained. Only in 1425 did a personal feud threaten to destabilise the administration completely, when a dispute flared up between two of the most powerful and potentially dangerous men in England: the frustrated protector, Humphrey duke of Gloucester, and the king's rich and influential great-uncle, Henry Beaufort, bishop of Winchester.

*

On 29 October 1425, the city of London boiled with excitement. A new mayor, John Coventry, had been elected and was taking office, but as he sat down to his official feast, he received an urgent message summoning him with all the most important men in the city to a meeting with the duke of Gloucester. When he arrived in the duke's presence, he was instructed to secure London as swiftly as possible for the night ahead. He was told that a large armed force was gathering under the leadership of Beaufort on the south side of London Bridge, in the suburb of Southwark. Archers, men-at-arms and a whole array of other men loyal to the bishop were said to be preparing to invade London the next day, determined to do harm to anyone loyal to Gloucester, and to cause mayhem in the city. A long, sleepless night lay ahead. The citizens were told to keep watch, and to ready themselves for a fight.

The background to the quarrel was complex. Gloucester and Beaufort were both capable and experienced men, with vital roles in the minority government. In the absence of the duke of Bedford, they bore, between them, a large responsibility for keeping the peace, but their views on foreign policy and domestic issues frequently clashed, producing mutual suspicion and hostility.

Gloucester's outsized personality was well known, but Beaufort was also an imposing figure. The second son of Henry VI's great-grandfather, John of Gaunt, and his third wife, Katherine Swynford, he had been made a cardinal and legate by Pope Martin V in 1417. The cardinal's personal power and wealth came from his diocese of Winchester, the richest in England, and his public standing came from a long life of service. At fifty, he had held high office in England for more than twenty years, often helping to prop up Crown finances by means of vast and generous loans. In 1425 he was the chancellor of England and probably the leading advocate of the conciliar system of government. It was likely that Beaufort, naturally conservative, had helped co-ordinate opposition among the lords of the council to Gloucester's regency. All this meant that the two men were, as one chronicler laconically put it, 'not good friends'.[13]

By 1425 their animosity and mutual suspicion was intense. The principal fault lay with Gloucester who, the previous summer, had led a popular but extremely unwise military expedition to the Low Countries, in pursuit of his wife's claim to the county of Hainault. Unfortunately, the man who now held Gloucester's wife's possessions was her first husband, John of Brabant, who was supported by the duke of Burgundy, a key ally of the English in their war with Armagnac France, and a man whom Beaufort had spent a great deal of time and effort courting. That Burgundy was greatly upset and antagonised by Gloucester's heedless aggression was bad enough. To make things worse, the campaign was a total failure. It also stirred up violent anti-Flemish feeling in London, which bubbled over into xenophobic riots and disturbances in the streets. Beaufort, as chancellor, was left to try and calm the capital. He appointed a new keeper of the Tower of London, one Richard Woodville, as a precautionary peacekeeping measure, but this was interpreted as an attempt to intimidate the citizens by putting the fortress that loomed over the city in the hands of a government stooge, and had the effect of arousing still more popular ire. By 1425, Cardinal Beaufort had become the chief public enemy in the capital, perceived to be a friend of foreigners and enemy of native Londoners.

Thus it was that on the evening of 29 October, tensions exploded. Beaufort had come to believe that it was his cousin's intention to travel from London to Eltham to take personal command of the young king, a symbolic appropriation of the source of power that would have amounted to a full *coup d'état*. It is unlikely that Gloucester really meant to kidnap the king, but Beaufort was not prepared to gamble on the duke's trustworthiness. He had thus garrisoned Southwark, and, when day broke over a wakeful city, the citizens rushed to the riverbank to see that that the south side of London Bridge had been barricaded, with huge chains drawn across it and heavily armed men standing guard at windows, 'as it had been in the land of war, as though they would have fought against the king's people and breaking of the peace'. On the north side of the bridge, Gloucester and London's new mayor had closed the city gates. It was a stand-off whose most likely conclusion appeared to be a deadly confrontation on the bridge itself. There was panic throughout the city. 'All the shops in London were shut in one hour,' wrote one breathless chronicler.[14]

Yet battle was never joined. There was enough passion on both sides of the Thames to have foamed the eddies beneath London Bridge's narrow arches with blood, but England luckily had cooler heads than those of the two disgruntled uncles of the king. Chief among them were Henry Chichele, archbishop of Canterbury, and Pedro, prince of Portugal and duke of Coimbra, a much-travelled cousin of King Henry, who was then staying in England as an honoured guest of the court.[15] They led frantic negotiations throughout the day on 30 October, their messengers riding eight times between the opposing camps until eventually a truce was brokered.

Bad blood lingered on both sides. The next day, Beaufort wrote an indignant letter to his nephew, John duke of Bedford, begging him to return from France and take command of the troubled regime. 'As ye desire the welfare of the king our sovereign lord and of his Realms of England and of France, and your owne wele [i.e. well-being] and ours also, hasten you hither,' he wrote, 'for by my troth [if] ye tarry, we shall put this land in adventure with a field [i.e. a battle]. Such a brother ye have here. God make him a good man.'[16] Bedford returned in January and spent a year restoring calm.

This was a significant act: in a sense his return to mediate between his sparring kinsmen had the duke playing surrogate king. But it worked. Cardinal Beaufort resigned as chancellor, his attentions soon diverted by instructions from the pope to lead a military crusade against the Hussites, a reforming sect of heretics in Bohemia. Yet Beaufort's climbdown did not mean that Gloucester was allowed to feel he had emerged victorious: under Bedford's instruction the regulations that had established the careful conciliar government of 1422–4 were re-enacted, and in January 1427 two separate meetings were held in the Star Chamber at Westminster and Gloucester's inn in London, where Bedford and Gloucester both swore to the assembled lords of the council on the Holy Gospels that they would support a conciliar form of government. Both agreed they would be 'advised, demesned [i.e. dealt with] and ruled by the lordes of the council and obey unto the King and to them as for the King'. Gloucester evidently gave his oath in bad faith, for less than one year later he would again demand an expansion of his powers over domestic government, huffily threatening to boycott all future parliaments unless he was granted what he desired. Yet once again, he would be unequivocally slapped down, told in parliament to satisfy himself with the powers that the realm had deemed sufficient for him and asked forcefully to confirm 'that you desire no greater power'. In the face of every serious crisis of authority, a general commitment to preserving and defending royal government triumphed.

Nevertheless, no matter how diligently the principles of conciliar rule were observed, royal government without the king could only ever be temporary, and each challenge to the existing order inevitably tested the ability of all around the council table to preserve their constitutional pact. The crisis of 1425–7 illustrated

precisely why there was such eagerness to see in the child-king
the ability 'to occupy his own royal power within [a] few years'.
Recalling Bedford from France had been a desperate measure
that would not prove practical or desirable to repeat. In short,
as the 1420s progressed it became very clear that Henry would
have to grow up – or be forced to grow up – as rapidly as could
be managed. Yet it would not be domestic affairs that prompted
Henry's most significant advancement. Rather, it was events
across the Channel that impelled England's surrogate rulers to
thrust the first real vestiges of kingship upon a seven-year-old boy.

3 : Born to Be King

On 17 August 1424, eight thousand men stood ranked together
on the plain outside the fortified town of Verneuil, in eastern
Normandy, and braced themselves for the charge. Opposite them
bristled a massive army, loyal to the dauphin – or, as he would
have it, Charles VII of France. Charles himself was not present,
but his distant cousin Jean, count of Aumale, a twenty-eight-year-
old prince of the French blood who had been fighting the English
since his teenage years, commanded between fourteen and sixteen thousand troops, all heavily armed and prepared to fight
to the death. Above Aumale's army blew flags and pennons representing men of various origins: Frenchmen stood shoulder to
shoulder with six and a half thousand Scottish men-at-arms and
archers and a contingent of Spaniards, all of whom were flanked,
most menacingly, by two divisions of cavalry from Lombardy, a
region of northern Italy famous for producing the finest armour
and the most terrifying and stoutly protected mounted warriors
in Europe. The juddering approach of these powerful and heavily shielded horses, together with the bright glint of the lances
and breastplates of their riders, was enough to strike mortal fear
into the hearts of any man who saw them. There may have been
as many as two thousand of these galloping agents of death in the
French army. The wide, unprotected plains of Verneuil were the
perfect territory for them. It was a fearsome sight.[1]

The eight thousand men who prepared to confront these fearsome horsemen and the thousands of infantry they accompanied
were an army of Englishmen and Normans under the command
of John duke of Bedford. The regent of France led his army

wearing a surcoat decorated with both the white cross of France and the red of England – a potent sign of the dual monarchy he represented. Over the top he wore the blue velvet robes of the Order of the Garter. Beside him in the field stood Thomas Montacute, earl of Salisbury, a grizzled veteran who, at thirty-six, was one of the most famous soldiers in Europe. They formed an impressive pair of leaders, but for all their personal honour and experience, they could not ignore the facts of the battlefield, which seemed overwhelmingly to favour the enemy.

Bedford and Salisbury's men were arrayed to anticipate the danger that the cavalry, in particular, would pose. An armoured horse and rider charging at full speed could just as well knock a soldier to the ground and crush him as gore him with the thrust of a lance. The force of hundreds of cavalry arriving at the same time could scatter an army into terrified chaos before the hand-to-hand fighting even began. So just as at the battle of Agincourt, the English archers protected their lines by hammering sharp wooden stakes into the ground, as vicious obstacles to check the cavalry charge. The large body of English and Norman men-at-arms – dismounted knights who fought in armour with swords, axes and daggers – were grouped together in one huge division. Horses and baggage wagons were tied together behind them to create further defensive barricades. The rest was entrusted to God.

The battle began, as expected, with a charge of the Lombard cavalry, who hurtled towards Bedford and Salisbury's centre. They collided with such force that they drove straight through the middle of the English line, splitting the entire army in two, emerging at the rear and proceeding to attack a lightly armoured reserve force who had been kept back to guard the baggage train. The reservists leapt on their horses and fled from the battlefield in fear. The Lombards gave murderous pursuit. Behind them, the French and Scottish men-at-arms waded towards the now broken line of English foot-soldiers and the chaotic one-to-one crowded fighting known as the mêlée began.

'The battle was a bloody one; no one could tell who was winning,' wrote a Parisian diarist, who was not an eyewitness at Verneuil, but managed to capture in one phrase the reality of so many medieval battles.[2] As soon as the cavalry charge had passed, the duke of Bedford is said to have exhorted his troops to fight not for 'winning or keeping worldly goods, but only to win worship in the right of England'.[3] Thereafter he showed them the way, fighting manfully with a poleaxe, while Salisbury displayed the martial skill and bravery that had made him a hero of the French wars. It was a desperate fight, waged with violent intensity on both sides. At one point the English standard – the flag that marked the central position of the army – fell to the ground. Traditionally this was a sign that an army was defeated, but a Norman knight threw himself into the French lines and managed single-handedly to retrieve it.

The day was eventually won by this sort of courage: Bedford's men simply ground their way to victory in hand-to-hand combat rather than by following any orders of tactical military brilliance. Noble-blooded men-at-arms fought alongside peasant-born archers, all devoted to the same cause. They managed to slaughter enough of the French and Scots to ensure that when the Lombards returned to the field following their rout of the English reserve, they found the battle already over, and English horsemen now thundering about a broken enemy, despatching anyone within reach as they tried to flee.

It had been a most extraordinary victory. Accounts of the battle credit Bedford with generalship at its purest and most inspirational. More than seven thousand French and Scots were massacred in the fields of Normandy that day. Some of the dauphin's finest commanders were killed, including Aumale and the two Scottish leaders, the earls of Buchan and Douglas. Several others were taken prisoner. When Bedford returned to Paris to give thanks for his victory at Notre-Dame, the people of the city turned out dressed all in red and cheered him in the streets. He was received, said one writer, 'as if he had been God'.[4]

The battle of Verneuil was the military high point of John duke of Bedford's regency in France, and of English fortunes on the continent as a whole. For the duke's reputation it was a triumph: he had won against the odds, seemingly through the sheer application of honour, bravery and personal skill. It was a fitting triumph for a man who would always strive above all other things to preserve the memory of his eldest brother, Henry V. Verneuil also fitted well with another of Bedford's great devotions, to the cult of St George. (The portrait of the duke in the Bedford Hours, a sumptuously illustrated devotional text that he commissioned in 1423, shows him kneeling in fine embroidered robes before the solemn figure of his favourite saint, who wears full armour and the robes of the Order of the Garter.[5]) The victory seemed to give the Almighty's own approval to the cause of the dual kingdom: a sign that all the lives and all the money that had been spent by the English pursuing the dreams of Henry V and his Plantagenet forebears had been justified.

If Verneuil was the apex of England's military fortunes and of Bedford's personal command, the years that followed comprised a slow and painful descent from glory, victory and supremacy. The occupiers sought with increasing futility to convince first the enemy, and then themselves, that the English kingdom of France was something that could be realistically maintained.

*

It is not hard to understand why Henry V, on his deathbed, had recommended his brother for the regency of France. Tall, strong-limbed and physically imposing, with a large, beak-like nose, the duke was level-headed and conspicuously faithful. He was deeply pious and, although capable of severity and even cruelty to those who offended him, genuinely committed to fair governance and the provision of justice. He had a good understanding of the realities of occupation, and in Normandy in particular he strove to govern through the native institutions, employing Normans in positions of power and making sure that large numbers fought in the armies that defended their territory from Charles VII's forces. Although Bedford lacked a major military victory until Verneuil, he was trusted and aided by experienced and tough English war captains such as Salisbury, Sir John Fastolf, Thomas, Lord Scales, Sir William Oldhall and John Talbot. Bedford was also personally invested in the wider politics of the French wars: he was married to Anne of Burgundy, the sister of England's most important foreign ally, Duke Philip, and together the couple established a stunning court. It gathered in Bedford's numerous houses in Paris, Rouen and elsewhere, all of which fairly groaned with the vast collections of art, books, treasure, tapestries and religious vestments to which Bedford had long devoted himself. As a later fifteenth-century chronicler would write, the duke physically 'represented the person of the King of France and England', and he made sure that he lived up to the image his position demanded.[6]

The position, however, was not a simple one. The English kingdom of France was on the face of it the fullest occupation of its sort in Europe for nearly four hundred years, since William the Conqueror had invaded and conquered Anglo-Saxon England in 1066. The Anglo-Burgundian alliance controlled nearly half the landmass of the realm, from the county of Flanders in the north to the duchy of Gascony in the south, and from the borders of Brittany in the west to the banks of the river Meuse in the east. A heavy garrison policy in Normandy had entrenched English rule across the duchy. In addition to the men who could be summoned from these garrisons to fight on the front line, a regular stream of hired soldiers contracted for six months or a year at a time swelled the English forces during campaigning season.

The twenty-one-year-old dauphin was exiled from the sacred heart of his own realm as the English flag flew over Rouen, the capital of Normandy, and the three holiest sites of French kingship: Reims, where French kings were consecrated; Paris, where they ruled; and St Denis, where they were laid to rest. Newly minted French coins bore the arms both of France and England, an angel resting a hand on each. Meanwhile, laws had been passed in Normandy forbidding any reference to the enemy as Frenchmen: those who opposed the English occupiers were only to be known by their factional name of Armagnacs, while Charles VII was to be described merely as 'he who calls himself the dauphin'. Punishments for flouting the new rule, whether in speech or in writing, were severe: a fine of ten *livres tournois* (£583) would be levied for a first offence by a nobleman and a hundred *sous* (£292) for a commoner, with the tariff increased tenfold for a second offence, rising to confiscation of all goods for a third.[7] These were vast sums, equal to many years' income; if offenders could not pay they were to have their tongues pierced or their foreheads branded.

Yet English authority, dominant as it was, could not be described as universal. For as long as the dauphin was at large, there was an alternative centre of political power in France. Without a full military victory, Bedford could not claim full legitimacy for English rule – a state of affairs further undermined by the fact that Pope Martin V adamantly refused to endorse the treaty of Troyes, denying the full moral weight of the Church to Henry VI's claim to the crown. There was a lean, dangerous Norman resistance movement: gangs of brigands roamed free, kidnapping, robbing, extorting, looting, burning property and taking – and sometimes torturing – hostages. These insurgents combined a basic self-help ethic and criminal instinct with the timeless righteous resentment of a conquered people. One band of thieves and robbers in Normandy, led by the brigand captain Jean de Hallé, did not baulk at kidnapping monks, or torturing women by forcing them to drink vast amounts of water until their stomachs and intestines ruptured. Hallé's crew robbed for personal gain, but also wore uniforms and swore a general oath to 'do everything in [their] power to damage and injure the English'.[8]

So as Bedford waged war to defend English authority, to pacify the population in the conquered lands and to attempt to push the Armagnacs further south below the banks of the river Loire, he also embarked upon a propaganda campaign designed to appeal to all Frenchmen living under the nominal rule of the young king across the water, who in French regnal terms was to be known as Henri II. Little did Bedford know that the means by which he carried out this campaign would be much imitated in England, many decades after his death.

*

In 1425 a canon from Reims was forced to seek a pardon from the English regime for visiting the cathedral of Notre-Dame in Paris and vandalising a large bill-poster that had been hung on the wall by Bedford's orders.[9] The image he had damaged was a family tree illustrating King Henry VI's descent from the ancient kings of both England and France. It had been placed there on the orders of the duke of Bedford, and it was one of many such posters which had been mass-produced and distributed about France in order to convince the common people that in Henry and his representative, Bedford, they had a ruler who was king not merely by right of conquest, but also by blood. Throughout the occupied territories, English genealogies were distributed as handbills or hung in churches and cathedrals to capture the eye and, it was hoped, the imagination of the common people.

We know what the Notre-Dame family tree probably looked like from a later copy, made on the order of John Talbot, earl of Shrewsbury, during the 1440s.[10] (See plate section.) It was both

complicated and alluringly simple. At the top was a roundel showing Louis IX of France – St Louis as he had been known since
his canonisation in 1297 – the pious and magnificent Capetian
king who had reigned in the thirteenth century. Behind the roundel was a large teardrop-shaped background decorated with tiny
fleurs-de-lis. Beneath Louis came his descendants, Philip III and
Philip IV, followed by Philip IV's four children, Louis X, Philip
V, Charles IV and Isabella: the last generations in the house of
Capet. Meanwhile, running down either side of the poster were
two subsidiary lines of descent. On the left was the house of Valois,
on the right the English royal house of Plantagenet, beginning
with Edward I. On the English side, the table showed Philip IV's
daughter Isabella marrying Edward II of England in 1308. Following that union came an apparently direct line of descent from
Isabella to Henry V. In neat symmetry on the French side, the title
of the house of Valois was shown to descend from Philip VI to
Catherine de Valois. Catherine meets Henry V at the bottom of
the poster – their marriage under the treaty of Troyes depicted in
neat, diagrammatic form – and from those two apparent scions
of the royal houses, out popped the last image in the table: Henry
VI himself, sitting regally upon a throne, with angels swooping
down to place two crowns upon his head.

The message was clear: Henry VI was king of France because
of who he was, not what his father's armies had done. A claim
staked out in blood was more permanent and sacred, and Henry's
emergence at the end of a lineage begun with the holy figure of
St Louis implied that his very being was a source of unity rather
than division. He was the true heir of France's holiest ruler; his
destiny to be the restorer of a divided house. And all of this was
done not by conquest, but by rightful inheritance. The tidiness
and symmetry of the genealogy and the historical story it told
gave the poster an intrinsic, satisfying beauty.[11]

Posters like this were usually accompanied by a poem composed by one of Bedford's clerks, Lawrence Calot, which outlined the claim in more detail.[12] In England the poem was translated by the court poet John Lydgate, its content very little changed. To quote Lydgate's version, the poem praised 'Henry the sext, of age ny five yere renne, / Borne to be king of worthie reamys two'. It then made direct reference to the genealogy it accompanied, and proclaimed at great length Henry VI to be:

> An heir of peace by just succession,
> This figure maketh clear demonstration
> [. . .]
> That this Harry in the eighth degree
> Is to saint Louis son and very heir
> [. . .]
> That this Harry standing in the line,
> Through God's hand and purveyance divine,
> Is justly born, to void all variance,
> For to be king of England and of France.

Like the dynastic diagram it commented upon, the poem – both Calot's version and Lydgate's translation – was rather elegant. It was also a total deception: fudging numerous genealogical facts and pointedly ignoring the French principle of Salic law, which dictated that the crown could never pass through a female. In a limited sense this did not matter: as punishment for his act of vandalism the clerk from Reims was forced to pay for two new copies of Henry's doctored family tree. But in the broader scheme of politics, it mattered very much. It was not bloodstock that would decide who triumphed in France, but blood spilled on the battlefield.

*

Although the duke of Bedford was forced to split his attention between England and France in order to keep order between his brother and his cousin, in the aftermath of Verneuil the war effort continued broadly successfully, so that by September 1428 the dauphin's forces had been pushed back almost wholly beyond the river Loire. That month, English forces began a siege of the town of Orléans. It ought to have been a straightforward matter, but it proved to be the point from which the whole English position started to deflate, thanks to the improbable intervention of a young woman called Jehanne d'Arc (usually anglicised to Joan of Arc), nicknamed the Pucelle, or the Maid. The political confidence and propaganda value she offered the dauphin and his allies would prove to be worth more to the French cause than any number of dynastic handbills.

The army that besieged Orléans was commanded directly by Salisbury, with an authority that stood largely independent of Bedford's. This arrangement had been made in England by the duke of Gloucester, who envisioned a much more aggressive foreign policy than most of the rest of the council, particularly Bedford and Beaufort. Bedford's conservative strategy was to attack the relatively lightly defended town of Angers, but this advice was ignored as Salisbury and his large, well-equipped and handsomely paid-for army instead marched 150 miles further up the Loire to attack the far more difficult and prestigious target of Orléans.

Orléans was a large city, stoutly defended both by the geography of the Loire and a series of massive walls, gates and towers. Salisbury stormed the nearby countryside, cutting off Orléans from the neighbouring settlements of Jargeau, Meung and Beaugency. Then he besieged the town, firing on its walls with cannon and instructing his miners to dig below its fortifications. All seemed promising until, as a long siege through the winter months beckoned, disaster struck. Salisbury was surveying the town's defences on 27 October when he was hit by debris thrown up by a stone cannonball fired across the river from the turrets of

Orléans. Shards of flying masonry tore off half the flesh from his face: a mortal injury from which he took a full agonising week to die.

Salisbury's death was a disaster. '[He] was a noble lord and a worthy warrior among all Christian men,' wrote the author of the Brut Chronicle.[13] The English were from this point committed to a lengthy siege, but had lost the only commander in their ranks who was capable of winning it. Salisbury was replaced by William de la Pole, the thirty-two-year-old earl of Suffolk – a valiant and experienced soldier, but not of the same stature as the man he replaced. The English attempted to rally under Suffolk, battering the walls of Orléans with guns and fortifying the countryside where they could to make it as inhospitable and dangerous as possible to any who might think of coming to the aid of the citizens. But there remained a basic shortage of men. The English could not storm the heavily defended city; indeed, they remained unable even to surround its entire circumference. Inside Orléans the townsmen settled in for a long winter siege. The English beyond the walls did what they could to prevent anyone passing in or out. The winter months ground by in a long, tedious and uncomfortable stalemate.

Then, at the end of February, Joan of Arc appeared. The seventeen-year-old, illiterate peasant girl had travelled from Domrémy in south-east France to the dauphin's court at Chinon, disguised beneath drab, grey male clothes and a pudding-bowl haircut. She had been driven, she later said, by divine voices that had been guiding her actions since the age of thirteen.[14] She believed it was her mission to raise an army, relieve the siege of Orléans and escort the dauphin to Reims in order to have him crowned king of France. At Chinon and Poitiers she was repeatedly interrogated by Charles's clerics, who were puzzled by this curious, intrepid and determined countryside maid. In the end, they decided that there was little to be lost by testing her out. Joan was granted her wish. In late April she dressed in male armour and rode to Orléans aboard a white horse. Behind her was an army several thousand strong, with a group of priests by her side and armed with an ancient sword, later rumoured to be that of Charles Martel, the legendary eighth-century king of the Franks. They reached the city on 29 April and found the besieging forces' lines weak and undersupplied.

When the English first heard about Joan they scoffed and screwed up their faces in disgust. A woman riding in male armour, with her hair cropped short, was nothing short of abominable: cross-dressing was forbidden by biblical law, and Joan's appearance seemed to be yet another sign of the decadence and godlessness of the French. Joan had dictated letters to the English from the dauphin's court some weeks before her arrival at Orléans, in which she warned Suffolk and his men to clear out of the occupied lands or lose their heads by her hand. At the time this had been treated as an absurdity, and Joan was dismissed as nothing more than an Armagnac whore. Yet now, here she was: armed to the teeth, bursting with godly zeal and backed by a substantial body of troops with which she aimed to drive the English away from the walls of Orléans and relieve the long and miserable siege.

On her arrival, Joan wasted little time. Her men attacked the English where their thinly spread lines were feeblest: to the east of the city, where a single small fortification was easily overwhelmed by a concerted French assault. With almost astonishing ease a hole was punched in the siege lines, and it remained open long enough for the radiant Joan to gallop into an overjoyed city, waving a white flag and resembling – to the citizens at least – a vision sent from heaven. She was given a townhouse for her lodgings and then, remarkably, began to direct relief operations from behind Orléans's long-battered walls.

With Joan inside the town, and her army outside led by Jean

count of Dunois – a man better known by his sobriquet 'the bastard of Orléans' – operations to relieve the town began in earnest. On 4 May the French army began to raid and burn English siege fortifications, starting at the weakest point in the east, the same spot where Joan had been spirited in behind the walls. In one day's fighting, the bastard of Orléans's men did enough damage to open a permanent route in and out of the town. This was a serious blow to Suffolk's siege effort: six months of numbing boredom, during which the English had tried to starve their opponents into submission, was ended in twenty-four hours. The next day, Joan sent another message to the enemy to warn them that this was only the beginning. 'You men of England, who have no right in this kingdom of France, the King of Heaven orders and commands you through me, Joan the Pucelle, to abandon your strongholds and go back to your own country,' announced a note fired into the English camp by an archer on 5 May. 'If not, I will make a war cry that will be remembered forever.' Once again, the English laughed. But this time their laughter was decidedly less assured.

At dawn on 6 May, another Armagnac assault began, driven by a new zeal, which seemed almost visibly to radiate from the person of the Pucelle. As the English siege positions came under fierce attack, she rode around in the centre of the fighting, her white standard fluttering as blood sprayed up around her. At one point the blood was her own: an arrow fired from an English-held tower sliced through the flesh of one of her shoulders. God, however, was smiling upon his appointed agent, and Joan staggered on, almost oblivious to her wound, spurring the Frenchmen forward. Relieving troops and liberated citizens alike swarmed over the English positions, capturing them one by one, slaughtering enemies and sending waves of sheer panic through the living. At night, bells of celebration clanged and jangled from the churches of Orléans, rung with glee by men and women who knew that they were winning their freedom. Within three days the French had fully relieved Orléans, and the English were retreating up the Loire at such speed they were forced to abandon their cannon and heavy weaponry as they went.

The loss of Orléans began a serious collapse in the English position. Reinforcements were sent, but more strongholds began to fall along the Loire. On 18 June 1429 the confused English army was drawn into a battle at Patay, just north of Orléans, for which they were totally unprepared. They were annihilated by the French vanguard: more than two thousand men were killed and every captain save Fastolf was captured. In a matter of months, fortunes in occupied France had been dramatically reversed. The dauphin's forces marched through Anglo-Burgundian territory, towns falling before them without a fight. On 16 July the dauphin entered Reims, and the following day he was anointed with holy oil and crowned King Charles VII, with Joan of Arc standing proudly by the altar. All the genealogical propaganda in the world could not obscure the fact that France now had a ceremonially anointed king – and that he was not called Henry.

*

The dreadful news from France was described in the minutes of the English privy council as 'diverse great and grievous adversities'. It demanded an urgent response.[15] There was one obvious course of action. In the first week of November 1429, after a period of very hasty preparation, London and Westminster welcomed the young king, still only seven years old, to his English coronation.

The ceremony by which kings were crowned was one of the most important spectacles in English political life, and it had become increasingly elaborate over the centuries since the Norman Conquest. In 1423 a book outlining the order of service for crowning French kings had come into the duke of Bedford's hands, and the English ceremonial had been upgraded once again to give it Frankish pomp. Events took place over several days. The first stage was Henry's formal entry to the capital. 'The Friday, the third of November, the King with his lords . . . rode from Kingston over London Bridge,' wrote the author of the Brut Chronicle. 'And the Mayor and the Aldermen, all in scarlet hoods, rode to meet the King.' The citizens accompanied him to the Tower of London where, the next evening, Henry sat in splendour to receive thirty-two young noblemen, who were ritually washed and dubbed knights of the Order of the Bath. On Sunday he proceeded out of the Tower to parade before his subjects, and to make his way to Westminster Abbey for the coronation proper. He rode bareheaded through the cramped streets of the city accompanied by his great lords, who were dressed for the most part in gold. Inside Westminster Abbey a great scaffold had been erected, to allow a good view to the congregation. Henry's mother Catherine and her ladies sat in pride of place near the altar, near the king's cousin Pedro, prince of Portugal, who had returned in haste to the country he had visited earlier in the decade, in order to attend the ceremony.[16]

The earl of Warwick carried Henry into the church, then led him up the scaffold to his seat in the centre, from where he surveyed the crowds around him, according to Gregory's chronicle, 'sadly and wisely'. Henry Chichele, archbishop of Canterbury, addressed the assembled realm, telling them Henry had come before God and the Holy Church, 'asking the crown of this realm by right and descent of heritage'. The congregation gave a roar, throwing their hands in the air and crying 'ye, ye', while young Henry walked before the great altar and prostrated himself for a long time before it.

What followed took hours. Throughout the ceremony bishops gave readings and sang anthems over the king's body, while he was made to lie down, stand up, lie down and stand up again, as well as being undressed, redressed and paraded around in the most elaborate costumes: first girded with the spurs and swords of a warrior, then in a bishop's robes and sandals, before finally being arrayed in gleaming cloth of gold, with Richard II's crown placed on his head since the traditional crown of Edward the Confessor was deemed too weighty for a seven-year-old. At the heart of the ceremony was the anointing: the most mysterious and permanent part of kingship, a rite that could never be undone. Henry stood in his undershirt while his little body was touched systematically with a miraculous oil said once to have been given by the Virgin Mary to St Thomas Becket. Holy oil was poured from a golden eagle-shaped ampulla onto Henry's breast 'and the midst of his back, and his head, all across his two shoulders, his two elbows [and] his palms of his hands'.[17] These were then dabbed with a soft white cotton cloth, while a white silken coif was placed on his head. It was to be worn for eight days, at the end of which a group of bishops would ceremonially clean Henry's head with lukewarm white wine. (This was one of the least comfortable aspects of the coronation: Henry's grandfather, Henry IV, had developed head lice after he was crowned in 1399.) After many hours of such solemn proceedings, capped by the celebration of the mass, the newly crowned king processed from the abbey to Westminster Hall for a feast in which every dish carried messages about the splendour of Henry's dual kingship. The first course featured (edible) fritters decorated with fleurs-de-lis and a decorative 'subtlety' showing Henry being carried by St Edward the Confessor of England and St Louis of France – his two holiest royal ancestors. The second course saw more tarts dusted with fleurs-de-lis. The subtlety brought out with the third course featured Henry presented to the Virgin and Child by St George and St Denis. A poem accompanied its presentation, praising the young king, 'Born by descent and title of right / Justly to reign in England and in France'. Then, as soon as the festivities at Westminster were over, preparations began to take the young king to his much-advertised second kingdom.

On St George's Day, 23 April 1430, a massive expedition left the ports of Sandwich and Dover, bound for Calais. This was essentially a mobile court, complete with hundreds of servants, cooks, clergymen, clerks, soldiers, doctors, the king's teachers, eight dukes and earls, and the king himself. After a short stay in Calais, the court moved slowly to Rouen, and bided their time until the route up the Seine to Paris was thought safe enough for the king to travel.

They would wait more than a year. After heavy fighting, aided by large numbers of soldiers sent from England at vast cost, a route was finally cleared. The process was helped immensely by the capture by Burgundian forces of Joan of Arc on 23 May 1430 during a skirmish outside the besieged town of Compiègne. Although she attempted several times to escape from prison, she was always recaptured. She was finally sold to the English and tried as a heretic, in deeply partisan proceedings underpinned by the occupiers' desire for revenge on a woman who had humiliated them for many years. Just over a year after her capture Joan was burned to death in the market square at Rouen on 31 May 1431. Her ashes were scooped up and thrown in the Seine.

In early December Henry made his way north-east to Paris. It remained impossible to crown him in Reims, but the ceremony could just as well be held at the cathedral of Notre-Dame, where all Anglo-Burgundian France could gather with sufficient magnificence. The king entered the city beneath a giant azure canopy decorated with fleurs-de-lis, and rode along dirty streets sanitised by being draped with linen. One was turned into a river of wine, thronging with mermaids, while seasonal Christmas plays were performed on an outdoor stage by citizens in elaborate disguise. A giant lily spouted milk and wine for the crowds to drink. In a presentation to the king at the Châtelet (a seat of government on the right bank of the Seine), a pageant was displayed on a stage decked with gold, tapestries and the dual arms of England and France: a lookalike Henry VI sat centre stage in state, wearing a scarlet hood, while actors playing the dukes of Bedford and Burgundy held up to him more English and French arms, along with various documents advertising the king's 'rightwiseness'.[18] All of this pageantry was highly amusing and agreeable even to the most sceptical observers. Yet there was heartbreak amid the festivities: Isabeau of Bavaria, widow of the mad king Charles VI, grandmother of the young king and mother of the dauphin, was present in the city, staying in the Hôtel St Pol. An eyewitness wrote: 'When she saw the young king Henry, her daughter's son, near her, he at once took off his hood and greeted her, and she immediately bowed very humbly towards him and then turned away in tears.'[19]

On a freezing Sunday 16 December 1431, Henry's second coronation finally took place. Despite all the grandstanding, it did not strike observers as anything like as impressive an occasion as that which had taken place in Westminster. It was carried out in a hurry, and the Parisians felt peeved that Cardinal Beaufort performed the coronation, rather than a native bishop. Due to the crush of people, pickpocketing was rife. The hall prepared for the banquet was too small, and the food, wrote an eyewitness, was 'shocking'. It had been cooked too far in advance and was not even considered suitable to be sent as leftovers to the city's paupers.[20]

The court enjoyed Christmas in Paris, but Henry was whisked back to Rouen by the first week of the new year, and left Calais for Dover on 29 January 1432. It was noted that he left Paris without carrying out any of the usual bequests of a new king: releasing prisoners, cutting taxes and offering a few legal reforms. Henry was the first king ever to be anointed as ruler of the two realms. But it was very clear which one he preferred.

He returned to London on a bright, windy Thursday in March and was greeted with a now familiar scene. 'He came to London, and there was worshipfully received of the citizens in white gowns and red hoods,' wrote one chronicler.[21] The sheer volume of public display and spectacle announcing the child's all-conquering status was visually dazzling, technically impressive and very expensive. It also spoke to the seriousness with which Henry's polity on both sides of the Channel took his claim to the dual monarchy, and how fervently they were willing to protect his father's legacy. Yet at the same time, it demonstrated the hollowness of the two crowns. The louder the English shouted about Henry's hereditary right to rule over France, the more obvious was their basic insecurity. As long as the dauphin lived, an anointed rival with a separate centre of political gravity and claim to rightful kingship, English propaganda was just that: parchments and pageantry inflicted on an increasingly uneasy populace.

4 : Oweyn Tidr

The Welshman was fleeing through Warwickshire, heading in
the direction of north Wales, when messengers sent from the
royal council caught up with him. He had left the capital in a
hurry, acutely aware that his liberty depended on getting out of
England as quickly as possible. He was travelling light, because
he had packed in haste, and also because he had had very little
to pack in the first place. The valuables in the baggage train that
accompanied his small party were a hotchpotch of treasure and
trinkets: a dozen expensive gold cups and a few silver salt cellars,
vases, a pair of candlesticks, spice-plates, chapel ornaments and
– rather strikingly – two basins decorated with roses and heraldic
arms in the bottom and smaller gilt roses around the rims. This
haul was later valued at £137 10s 4d – a decent sum, but hardly
a fortune for a man who had until recently been living in regal
comfort.[1] The messengers told him he was to travel swiftly back
to London, and he would be protected on his journey by a grant
of safe-conduct. This was a promise which the man looked upon
with great scepticism, telling the messenger 'that the said grant
so made sufficed him not for his surety'.[2] He had seen enough
of English politics to know that a Welshman's safety was never
entirely guaranteed when he ventured east of the borderlands.
But the messengers insisted. So the man turned back, heavy-
hearted, towards London.

His name, to English tongues at least, was Owen Tudor. His
ancestors were famous in their homelands, the ancient principality of Gwynedd in north Wales, which included the rugged,
chilly mountains of Snowdonia and the fertile isle of Anglesey.

They were known as a line of administrators, priests and soldiers who had given loyal service both to the native princes and to the English kings who had conquered Gwynedd in the late thirteenth century. Tudur was a popular name for the men of the family: Owen's great-great-grandfather was called Tudur Hen; his grandfather was known as Tudur ap Goronwy, and his father was Maredudd ap Tudur ('ap', in Welsh, means 'son of'). In Wales Owen had therefore been known as Owain ap Maredudd ap Tudur – until confused English attempts to normalise the barbaric and strange Celtic language came up with 'Owen Fitz Meredith', 'Owen Meredith', 'Oweyn Tidr' and, eventually, 'Owen Tudor'.

The generations of distinguished Welshmen from whom Owen Tudor sprang had established a dynasty with land and plenty of local prestige. But Owen's father and uncles had fallen into disgrace after allying with their cousin Owain Glyndwr against King Henry IV during the great Welsh revolt that broke out in 1400 and raged until 1415. Owen was born around the beginning of the revolt, so he grew up in a family embroiled in more than a decade's plotting and violence, and who suffered accordingly when the rebels' fortunes began to fail. Glyndwr was commanding guerrilla-style raids between 1409 and 1412 but by September 1415 he had disappeared into hiding and retirement. He probably died the following year, and although his son and successor was pardoned by Henry V in 1417, many others who had fought in the revolt on the Welsh side were dealt with severely: stripped of their lands, banned from officeholding and replaced by loyalists. Maredudd ap Tudur had his estates confiscated for bearing arms against the crown, and Maredudd's brother Rhys was executed for treason in Chester in 1412.[3] The stain of rebellion and treachery had lain upon Owen almost since birth. It was in his blood.

Despite all this ignominy, however, Owen Tudor had done something extraordinary in the thirty-seven years or so that he had been alive. He had not merely raised himself up to the status of gentleman and Plantagenet associate that had been enjoyed by his predecessors, but had gone well beyond – embedding himself in the very heart of English royalty. For the last decade, he had been the lover, husband and secret companion of Catherine de Valois, queen dowager of England.

*

Catherine's life in England had not been quite what she expected when she married Henry V in Troyes. A twenty-year-old widow within two years of her arrival in the foreign realm, for much of the next decade Catherine was defined principally by her motherhood. Her life was arranged around the needs and occasional public appearances of the infant king. She travelled everywhere with him, and her income – drawn from the generous dower settled upon her by parliament – contributed handsomely to the running costs of the king's household, at the rate of £7 a day. She was a prominent figure on religious feast days and at great occasions of state – which included sitting in pride of place next to the altar at Henry's English coronation in 1429. When the king was taken to France she accompanied him as far as Rouen, although she returned to England long before his Paris coronation, which spared her the uncomfortable sight of seeing her son crowned in direct rivalry to her brother, Charles VII. But when the king came home, Catherine's role diminished. From 1430 the queen ceased to live with her son. Their households became formally and financially separate, never to be reunited. She continued to describe herself in letters as 'Catherine, queen of England, daughter of King Charles of France, mother of the king of England, and lady of Ireland', but she travelled on her own itinerary and joined the royal court only on ceremonial occasions.[4] Otherwise, her life was her own.

Freed from the daily responsibilities of motherhood, Queen

Catherine's position was thus now a curious one. England's other dowager queen – Henry IV's widow, Joan of Navarre – was over sixty, coming to the end of a life that had petered out on the fringes of aristocratic importance, her reputation tainted by false and outrageous accusations of witchcraft cooked up against her in 1419 by her own confessor. Catherine, by contrast, was young, wealthy and endowed with estates spread far and wide across England and Wales. In a world bonded by landed power, she was an attractive woman, and according to the tittle-tattle of one English chronicler, she was 'unable fully to curb her carnal passions'.[5] This phrase rings with the same sort of snide misogyny that had been hurled at Catherine's mother, Isabeau of Bavaria, but all the same, it reflected the fact that Catherine had – by virtue of her sex and sexuality – the potential to influence English politics if she should remarry. And indeed, after young Henry's coronations, the queen mother's sexual conduct became a matter of high intrigue.

Queens dowager did not, as a rule, marry Englishmen. If they wedded at all, they did so out of the country, to make a clean break from the politics of the crown.[6] A queen mother who married into the English nobility could give her husband an invaluable position of proximity and access to the king. For a strong, self-possessed, adult king this would not necessarily be a concern, but these were not the conditions of the minority. Those who had read enough royal history to recall the dark days of the 1320s knew that upon the accession of fourteen-year-old Edward III the queen dowager, Isabella of France, had ruled for three years in her son's name, and that her rule had been perverted by her lover, Sir Roger Mortimer, who used his easy access to power for tyrannical ends. Mortimer had taken advantage of his position to order the murder of the king's father and to stage the judicial murder of the king's uncle. He convinced the king to agree to a shamefully one-sided treaty with the Scots, then rewarded himself with the grand new title of earl of March, sustained by a massive land-grab on the estates of disaffected English noblemen, many of whom were forced into exile for fear of their lives. Mortimer had only been removed when the teenage king ordered a violent coup to reclaim control of his own crown. One hundred years on, the English council could ill afford a repeat performance.

In the mid-1420s, however, it was rumoured that Catherine had formed an attachment to Edmund Beaufort, count of Mortain, the young nephew of Cardinal Beaufort. He was five years younger than her and an ambitious soldier whose elder brothers had seen service in France and spent long spells in French imprisonment. He was also of Plantagenet birth – a grandson of John of Gaunt with a keen sense of his own high blood and chivalric status. In spite, or perhaps because, of this the rumours of his familiarity with the queen provoked sharp alarm among the royal council, and particularly in Humphrey duke of Gloucester. There could be no more worrying situation to Gloucester than for the king's mother to marry into the circle of his Beaufort rivals, a scenario that the protector felt was not only to the detriment of national stability, but also a personal threat.

It seemed that Gloucester's fears of a union between Catherine and Edmund Beaufort were well founded when, at the Leicester parliament of 1426, a petition was introduced asking the chancellor 'to grant to king's widows permission for them to marry at their will'.[7] There was no direct reference to Catherine, but it could hardly have referred to anyone else. The petition was deferred by the chancellor for 'further consideration', but at the next parliament, which opened in Westminster in the autumn of 1427, an unambiguous response was given. A statute was made that expressly forbade queens from remarrying without the 'special licence' of an adult king. It claimed to seek 'the preservation of the honour of the most noble estate of queens of England'; in effect, its purpose was to prevent Catherine from being wedded to an Englishman for at least a decade. The wording of the legislation made it clear that the cost of marrying the queen dowager was nothing short of financial ruin. 'He who acts to the contrary and is duly convicted will forfeit for his whole life all his lands and tenements.'

And so Edmund Beaufort's dalliance with Catherine came to an abrupt, legalistic end. We do not know if Edmund and Catherine continued to have a physical relationship, or if indeed they ever had one. If so, then Beaufort in particular would have been taking a massive personal risk, of the sort that he would in later life show every inclination to avoid. In any case, by 1431 the queen had defied parliament's ruling by another means – not by marrying a Beaufort, but by falling in love with a charming Welsh squire by the name of Owen Tudor.

Quite how Tudor came to meet Queen Catherine remains a mystery, the truth buried beneath a number of romantic and comic stories spread in the centuries that followed – some designed to laud Owen's memory, and others to deride it. Certainly Catherine had links with Owen's homeland: the lands assigned to her after Henry V's death comprised great swathes of north Wales including Beaumaris, Flint, Montgomery, Builth and Hawarden. It is also possible that Owen had links with the queen's home country. In his late teens or early twenties he may have gone to war in France: a man listed as 'Owen Meredith' served alongside Henry V's steward Sir Walter Hungerford in 1421, and since Hungerford was later the steward of young Henry VI's household, we can reasonably suggest that this may be how Owen found his way into Catherine's domestic sphere. More than that is hard to say. Mischievous stories dating from the late fifteenth and sixteenth centuries variously claim that he was the son of a tavern-keeper or a murderer, that he fought at Agincourt, that he became the queen's servant or her tailor, that he and Catherine fell in love because she caught sight of his naked body while he swam in a river, or that they were smitten after he got drunk at a dance and fell insensible into her lap. Whatever the case, they met around 1430 and Catherine decided that this lowly Welshman, born of a family of rebels, was the man she would take as her second husband.

Her second marriage could scarcely have been more different from her first. A later writer suggested that the queen did not realise she was marrying so far below her station: 'Queen Catherine being a French woman born, knew no difference between the English and Welsh nation . . .'[8] But it would have been an astonishingly unobservant woman who lived in English royal circles for a decade without realising the pariah status of the Welsh – even those who, like Tudor, could boast impressive ancestry. Penal laws passed in 1402 forbade Welshmen from owning property, holding royal office, convening public meetings or wearing armour on the highways. Welsh law was suppressed and Welsh castles were to be garrisoned only by pure-blooded Englishmen, who could not be convicted of a crime on the testimony of a man of Wales.[9] These penal laws applied equally to Welshmen and Englishmen who married Welsh women: it had long been clear that the mingling of blood was unacceptable, and Catherine would have been not simply a foreigner but a fool not to have noticed.

The most likely explanation is that Catherine, chafing against the council and parliament's ban on her remarrying, decided to take a husband who was a political nonentity: one who already possessed so few rights to property and rank that the threat of legal ruin meant very little. Nevertheless, their marriage was contracted in secret, probably while most of the English court were abroad for the king's French coronation in Paris. Shortly afterwards their first son was born, at the manor of Much Hadham in Hertfordshire, the great timber-framed country palace belonging to the bishops of London. The boy was named Edmund. It has been suggested that this was because the real father was Catherine's old flame Edmund Beaufort – implying that the queen married Owen Tudor as an expedient to prevent the law's cruel ruin falling upon her real lover. This seems very unlikely.[10]

Catherine's marriage was kept discreet during her lifetime. It was a matter of privileged court gossip, rather than public knowledge. But those who saw the queen – particularly Cardinal Beaufort and his followers, with whom she remained close – could be under no illusion. More children were born in quick succession: a second son, Jasper was born at Bishop's Hatfield in Hertfordshire; there was probably a third son, Owen, who was entrusted to the monks of Westminster and lived a long, quiet life as a monk, and a daughter, called either Margaret or Tacine, who may have died young, for nothing certain is known of her.[11] All came before 1436 – and as many as four full pregnancies in little more than five years could not possibly have been concealed. Had the father been a man with any independent political status or ambition, the birth of children who were half-siblings to the king would have caused a crisis. But as it was, Catherine and her new young family managed to live quietly and uneventfully and Owen was accommodated formally into the realm. Letters of denizenship were granted to him in the parliament of 1432, conferring on 'Owen Fitz Meredith' the status of a faithful Englishman for the rest of his life.[12] Two years later he was granted interests in the queen's lands in Flintshire, reflecting his family's ancient position in north Wales. Yet although Owen Tudor enjoyed a degree of protection from the law, his security was completely dependent on his wife.

By 1436 the queen had fallen ill, with a lingering disease that progressively weakened her body and mind. By the end of the year she had moved into Bermondsey Abbey, a Benedictine monastery which regularly tended the sick and wounded, on the south bank of the river Thames, directly opposite the Tower of London.[13] She lay there through a bitter winter, when a 'great, hard,

biting frost . . . grieved the people wonder[fully] sore', froze the
chalk in the walls to dust and killed the herbs in the ground.[14] The
discomfort was too much. On New Year's Day 1437, Catherine
made her will, in which she complained of a 'grievous malady,
in the which I have been long, and yet am, troubled and vexed',
and named the king as her sole executor. Two days later she died,
aged thirty-five.

Catherine de Valois was buried in the Lady Chapel at Westminster Abbey on 8 February, her coffin carried below a black
velvet canopy hung all around with bells, and topped with a delicate wooden effigy painted as if it were alive (see plate section),
which can still be seen today. But Owen Tudor did not have much
time to grieve. He realised that the death of the queen dowager
amounted to more than the sad loss of his wife. It placed him in
immediate personal danger. He had broken a statute made in
parliament, fathered a number of children who were half-blood
relations to the king, and could now expect to be pursued. His
enemies were not long in showing themselves. As soon as Catherine was laid to rest, the council, driven by the tireless Humphrey duke of Gloucester, went after Owen. Thus it was that the
messengers sent from London had caught up with him in Warwickshire as he travelled towards Wales, and sent him down to
Westminster, wearily, to face the music.

*

On arrival at Westminster, however, Owen Tudor chose not
to present himself to the council. Instead he threw himself on
the mercy of the abbey, where he claimed the right of sanctuary, 'and there held him many days, eschewing to come out
thereof'.[15] After a while, the ministrations of friends persuaded
Owen that by staying behind the walls of Westminster Abbey, he
was only making his case worse. It was said that the young king
had been stirred to anger, although the records of Owen's arrest

and interrogation before the council give the strong impression that any real royal wrath was stage-managed by the duke of Gloucester, and that Henry VI had not interested himself very deeply, if at all, in the details of his stepfather's flight.[16] Nevertheless, after a fashion, Owen emerged from Westminster and was brought before the king. He 'affirmed and declared his innocence and his troth, affirming that he had no thing done that should give the King occasion or matter of offense . . . against him'. It was a performance good enough to earn him release and passage back to Wales. But as soon as he arrived in his homelands, he was promptly rearrested for breaking the terms of his royal safe-conduct. This was rather a dubious charge, since he had not accepted safe-conduct in the first place. But it did not matter. Now Owen's valuables were seized, taken into the treasury and given away to royal creditors, and Owen himself was shut up in the grim surroundings of the notorious Newgate prison in London, with only a chaplain and servant for company.

Although Newgate had been completely renovated in the 1420s and early 1430s, and had a code of rules supposedly to protect prisoners from the worst horrors of confinement, it was not a pleasant place to stay. Its inmates – both male and female – were held there for offences ranging from debt and heresy to thieving, fighting, treachery and murder. Many were waiting to be brought before a judge, and plenty of those were certain to swing on the hangman's rope – or worse.[17] Some prisoners there were clapped in irons, others were tortured, and extortion was commonplace by jailers who could make a handsome private profit by charging their prisoners for privileges and even basic comforts such as food, bedding and candles. There were a few decent rooms with lavatories and chimneys, and even access to a chapel and a flat roof above the main gate, where exercise could be taken, but other parts of the prison – dungeons known as the 'less convenient chambers' – were dark, cramped and diseased.

Fortunately, Newgate prison was corrupt enough to make escape a realistic possibility, and Owen Tudor determined to do precisely that. In January 1438 his chaplain helped him organise a bid for freedom. It was briefly successful: Owen fought his way out of the prison compound in a dash so violent that his jailer was 'hurt foule'. But his flight was short-lived. He and his accomplices made it out of the prison, but were rearrested within days and promptly sent back. It was not until July that Owen's friends, represented by none other than his late wife's one-time sweetheart, Edmund Beaufort, secured his transfer to the more salubrious surroundings of Windsor Castle, where he was put under the watch of Walter Hungerford, the captain under whom he may have served in France nearly two decades previously. Eventually, in July 1439, Owen was deemed to have suffered enough for his temerity in disobeying parliament. He was given his freedom and pardoned. It had been a painful two years.

The Welsh bard Robin Ddu, writing some years later, composed a poem that lamented the fate of this adventurous but unlucky Tudor. 'Neither a thief nor a robber, neither debtor nor traitor, he is the victim of unrighteous wrath,' he wrote. 'His only fault was to have won the affection of a princess of France.'[18]

Owen Tudor's journey, however, was not quite over, for his marriage to Queen Catherine had produced more than just tall stories and trouble. As the Welshman emerged from his imprisonment, his two eldest sons, Edmund and Jasper, were taking the first steps of their own lives – which would, in time, prove just as remarkable as that of their enterprising father.

*

Katherine de la Pole, abbess of Barking, had every reason to be pleased with the religious house over which she ruled. The elegant, richly furnished buildings of the abbey, set around the large double-fronted church of St Mary and St Ethelburga, enclosed one of the wealthiest and most prestigious nunneries in England, home to around thirty ladies in holy orders, served by a large staff of male servants and priests.[19] Wealthy daughters and widows from the titled aristocracy and upper gentry came to Barking to retire from the world as inmates, where they followed the Benedictine Rule in a life of prayer, charity, high-born company and scholarship. Good connections had, over the years, brought Barking money, property, honour and fame: Katherine – who as abbess held the same privileged rank as a male baron – controlled thirteen manors and lands in several different counties, besides the hundreds of acres that surrounded Barking itself. A glance out of one of the western windows of the nuns' dormitory (known as the dorter) revealed the scale of the abbey's endowment: swathes of the flat, green woodland and countryside of the Thames estuary which stretched towards the broad horizon. In the distance, not more than a day's ride away, was London, the hub of England's wealth and power.

In the spring of 1437, Katherine welcomed two young visitors from the capital: two boys referred to in records by the tortuously quasi-Welsh names of 'Edmond ap Meredith ap Tydier and Jasper ap Meredith ap Tydier'. They were the sons of the late queen and her shortly-to-be-imprisoned Welsh widower, Owen Tudor.[20] Edmund was aged about seven, Jasper a year or so younger, and by any standards the little boys had endured a shocking and turbulent year. Katherine's task was to offer them respite and shelter from the sudden chaos, a place to grow up away from the dangerous and unpredictable throng of London and the court. When Edmund and Jasper rode through the arch of the gatehouse and into Barking's precincts, and first saw the soaring spires of the abbey church, the quiet gardens that lay within the cloisters and the little outbuildings that surrounded the abbey proper, they should have been reassured that they were coming to a place of peace and stability. It would be their home for the next five years.

Barking was used to taking in children. The abbesses often stood as godparents for Essex's well-to-do families, whose privileged offspring had been placed in the abbey for the early stages of their education since the time of the Venerable Bede in the eighth century. But half-brothers of a king brought with them special requirements. Katherine was not expected to spare any expense in raising Edmund and Jasper. It cost the abbey the enormous sum of £13s 4d a week merely to feed the boys and their servants, quite apart from the further expense of their lodging, education, clothing and entertainment. Over the years that followed, the abbess would have to write on many occasions to the royal exchequer asking for large sums to recompense her for Edmund and Jasper's upkeep.[21] Although on occasion the exchequer was slow to pay her bills, there was no question of shirking the abbey's responsibilities.

Rich, refined and intellectually advanced, Barking Abbey was a wonderful place to grow and learn. Latin and French as well as English were used by the nuns in an age where the vernacular was becoming the standard language of communication and discourse. The library contained volumes by Aristotle, Aesop, Virgil and Cicero, collections of saints' lives, books of sermons, meditations on the life of Christ and even an English translation of the Bible, which the nuns were specially licensed to own. One Mary Chaucer had been a nun at Barking in the fourteenth century, and the abbey owned a copy of her relative Geoffrey Chaucer's *Canterbury Tales*. The abbey church held the bones of its first abbess, St Ethelburga, as well as a particularly fine ornamental cross in the oratory, which drew large crowds of penitents and pilgrims on feast days. One famous ritual was the Easter play: a recreation of Christ's harrowing of hell, in which nuns and their priests paraded through the church holding candles and singing antiphons, before symbolically releasing from damnation all the souls of the prophets and patriarchs.

There was, however, another reason for Edmund and Jasper to be domiciled there at such expense. This was Katherine herself. She was a tenacious, astute woman who was sufficiently impressive to have been elected to her post at only twenty-two or twenty-three. She was also the sister of William de la Pole, fourth earl of Suffolk, a member of the royal council, steward of the royal household, and an increasingly close companion of the young king. It is very probable that William recommended Barking to the king as the Tudor boys' new home, for his advice counted heavily at court and in the council. Certainly, at the moment that Edmund and Jasper arrived in his sister's care, Suffolk was beginning to establish his position as a central figure in the young Henry VI's government. He was the man around whom almost every important political decision of the following decade was to turn.

And so, thanks to these generous connections, Owen Tudor's sons remained peacefully at Barking for the next five years, even while their father fought to stay out of prison. It would be more than a decade before their closeness in blood to the king was formally recognised and they were elevated to positions of importance at court. In the meantime, it was their half-brother, Henry VI, whose emerging personality became the focus of English politics – with results more disastrous than anyone could ever have foreseen.

II

What Is a King?

1437–1455

Thus began sorrow upon sorrow, and death for death . . .

THE BRUT CHRONICLE[1]

5 : My Lord of Suffolk's Good Lordship

King Henry VI grew up beneath an almost crushing burden of expectation. Through no fault of his own, he was the first Plantagenet king finally to achieve what many had attempted: to be crowned king both of England and of France.[1] His father had been one of the most famous men in the Christian world, a conquering hero smiled upon by God, whom English propagandists considered 'able to stand among the Worthy Nine' (i.e. the Nine Worthies of ancient history) and who even his enemies had been forced to admit was a paragon of wisdom, manliness and courage.[2] The length of Henry's minority had caused the old king's reputation to soar to even greater heights. In 1436, the Venetian poet and scholar Tito Livio Frulovisi was commissioned to write Henry V's posthumous biography, the *Vita Henrici Quinti*. Frulovisi's patron was Humphrey duke of Gloucester, and one of Gloucester's chief purposes in commissioning the Italian was to produce a work that would encourage the sixteen-year-old Henry VI to honour his father's warrior spirit. 'Imitate that divine king your father in all things,' wrote Frulovisi, 'seeking peace and quiet for your realm by using the same methods and martial valour as he used to subdue your common enemies.'[3] This was a lot to ask of a teenager who had grown up without ever actually seeing his father – or indeed anyone else – rule England as a king.

Henry was an innocent-looking young man. In adulthood he stood five foot nine or ten. His face would remain round and boyish well into his mature life. A high brow and curved eyebrows sat above large, wide-spaced eyes, a long nose and a small, delicate mouth much like his mother's. His most famous portrait, produced in the sixteenth century but probably copied from a lost life-likeness, depicts him with smooth, plump cheeks and a weak chin, wearing a look of faint surprise.[4]

Henry seems to have been a solemn and sober youth. Certainly he was well educated, and could read and write in English and French with equal fluency. At his English coronation he was seen to gaze 'sadly and wisely' at the congregation before him, as if he were older than his years. Foreign observers found him to be a good-looking young man possessed of kingly dignity.[5] By the late autumn of 1432, as he approached his eleventh birthday, he had come to terms with some aspects of his status as an anointed king: on 29 November, Richard Beauchamp, earl of Warwick, Henry's personal tutor, who took responsibility for overseeing his upbringing and education, sat in a session of the royal council and informed them – as the minutes of the meeting attest – that the king was 'grown in years, in stature and also in conceit and knowledge of his high and royal authority and estate, the which naturally causes him . . . more and more to grouch with chastisement and to loath it'.[6] Warwick requested more powers to insure himself against the king using his royal prerogative to defy or punish his teacher whenever he felt disgruntled or indignant about his lessons.

Yet this was not Warwick's only concern. In the same meeting, he asked the council to grant him powers to keep 'ungoodly or unvirtuous men' away from the royal presence, and similarly to banish anyone whom he deemed 'suspect of misgovernance and not behoveful nor expedient to be about the king'. The council agreed, recognising an eleven-year-old boy who might easily be swayed by the wrong people unless a careful eye were kept on him. Here was the first inkling of a problem that would be magnified as his life went on: Henry would remain a highly impressionable and suggestible king, permanently childlike in his preference for allowing others to make decisions for him. He could be extremely enthusiastic about certain matters – he was an avid reader of chronicles and histories, and given to religious pet projects, such as his attempt in 1442 to secure sainthood for the great Saxon king Alfred. Yet he remained blandly impassive about serious matters of public and national policy, lacking any real ability to drive government or take charge of the unavoidable business of foreign warfare. These were not the qualities of a mighty king.

The most vivid pen-portrait we have of Henry VI was written by his personal confessor, John Blacman, towards the end of Henry's life.[7] Understandably, given its author's vocation, Blacman's memoir makes great play of Henry's simplicity, his religious fervour, and the general godliness of his life. In places the account is obviously distorted to play up the king's saintliness, ignoring Henry's taste for fine clothes, jewels and the trappings of royal pageantry and display, which began to develop from his teenage years. 'It is well known that from his youth up he always wore round-toed shoes and boots like a farmer's,' wrote Blacman. 'He also customarily wore a long gown with a rolled hood like a townsman, and a full coat reaching below his knees, with shoes, boots and foot-gear wholly black, rejecting expressly all curious fashion of clothing.' This description seems to chime more with a desire on Blacman's part to exaggerate the king's piety – plenty of other accounts recall Henry dressed in rich and vivid splendour on state occasions.

All the same, much of the rest of Blacman's account agrees with other descriptions and criticisms of Henry as he emerged from the shadow of childhood in the 1430s, from passing references in official records to scornful tracts condemning English foreign policy. The older he grew, the more his unusually limp and often downright vacant personality became apparent. He seems to have been gripped with a crippling sense of inertia in the face of his royal duties. He appeared absent and distracted when engaged in conversation. He spoke simply and in short sentences, and seemed to prefer studying holy scripture to attending to government business. When he wore his crown on grand state occasions, he also wore a hair shirt. According to Blacman, the foulest curse that would pass his lips was 'forsothe and forsothe', and he told off those around him who used bad language, for 'a swearer was his abomination'.[8] He was at heart a gentle and malleable soul, timid and reluctant in the extreme to take any significant decisions, squeamish about human flesh, agonised by conflict and war, and virtually incapable of leading men, least of all into battle. He may have been chaste, generous, pious and kind, but these were not very useful qualities in a king who was expected to direct government, keep the peace between his greatest subjects and sail across the ocean at regular intervals to slaughter the French. By these crude measures of kingship, Henry VI would grow up to be a tragic failure.

*

During the mid-1430s, however, Henry's adult personality was still a work in progress, and the men of his council could maintain reasonable hope that he would soon begin to feel for the levers of power. History, after all, was encouraging: Edward III had been seventeen in 1330 when he led an armed coup against his mother's government; Richard II was fourteen when he faced down the Peasants' Revolt in 1381; Henry's own father had been sixteen when, as prince of Wales, he had led troops at the battle of Shrewsbury. But the vague hope became an urgent necessity in 1435, when Henry was fourteen, and England suffered two severe blows to her policy in France.

The first concerned the realm's longstanding alliance with Burgundy. This was the diplomatic bedrock on which all the success of the past two decades had rested. It was the quarrel between the Burgundians and Armagnacs that had destabilised

France sufficiently for England to conquer her, and it was the Burgundian alliance that had allowed Henry V to broker the treaty of Troyes and claim the French crown. Burgundian soldiers had captured Joan of Arc and eventually handed her over to the English to be tried, and it was only through good relations with Burgundy that England could hope to continue as a credible occupying force in Normandy and other parts of France. Yet in 1435, at a peace council held in the buzzing Flemish merchant town of Arras, a place famous across Europe for its beautiful woven tapestries, the Anglo-Burgundian alliance dramatically unravelled.

The congress of Arras, held between July and September 1435, was supposed to be a chance to secure a truce between England and France, and to broker a marriage between Henry VI and a French princess. But Henry VI's embassy, led by Cardinal Beaufort, was comprehensively outmanoeuvred by brilliant French diplomacy, designed to collapse the talks with maximum blame attached to the English. Various proposals were offered by Charles VII's ambassadors, all of which appeared generous, but effectively demanded that Henry give up his claim to be the rightful king of both realms, return everything won since Agincourt, and hold Normandy only in feudal deference to the French crown. Beaufort did everything he could to negotiate more acceptable terms, but he was refused in such a way that the English were made to look unbending and arrogant. Eventually, on 6 September 1435 Beaufort stormed out of the talks, leaving Burgundy and France to negotiate directly with one another. His retainers were caught in a rainstorm on the way out of Arras and their vermilion cloaks, the word 'honour' sewn into their sleeves as a protest against the deceitful tactics to which they had been subjected, were drenched.[9]

But worse was to follow. On 14 September, a week and a day after the English delegation left the talks, John duke of Bedford, whose health had been failing for some time, died in Rouen, broken by the strain of many years spent overseeing his nephew's second kingdom. He was forty-six. Bedford left behind him a vast and magnificent household with a large collection of books, plate, tapestries and treasure.[10] But no amount of riches could mitigate the loss of his personal influence. For nearly fifteen years he had been a living link between the spirit of Henry V's conquests and the demands of the present. 'Much moan [was made] amongst Englishmen that were [at] that time in Normandy; for as long as he lived, he was doutet [i.e. feared] and dread among the Frenchmen,' wrote the author of the Brut Chronicle.[11] In France Bedford had been a majestic regent and an inspiring general. When he had been summoned home to England, he had exercised his unique standing as an invaluable mediator, a great nobleman who stood above faction, commanding the obedience of all. He was the only figure able to hold the peace between his uncle Cardinal Beaufort and his brother Humphrey of Gloucester. His death robbed England of its most important figure of consensus, authority and stability – the nearest thing it had to a surrogate king.

Seven days later Philip the Good, duke of Burgundy, arrived at the abbey of St Vaast to sign a treaty by which the two warring factions in France's civil war agreed to be reconciled. Burgundy would recognise Charles VII as the rightful king of France; in return Charles promised to take action against the men who had killed Philip's father in 1419. In a matter of weeks England's whole diplomatic position, carefully constructed over more than twenty years, had been swept away. Their greatest ally had switched sides. It was a blow from which English ambition could never recover.

In the eighteen months that followed Arras, the English position in France began to collapse. In the spring Paris was liberated by forces loyal to Charles VII and his new ally, the duke of Burgundy. After the departure of the last Englishmen from the capital on 17 April 1436, the French began to address their attacks towards the duchy of Normandy, forcing the English into a war of defence and retrenchment. At home, meanwhile, there was a deliberate and desperate attempt to foist adult rule upon the fourteen-year-old Henry VI.

He was brought into his first council meeting on 1 October 1435, and orders began straight away to be made under his authority rather than by the command of the lords of the council alone. This fact was widely publicised: in letters sent to foreign councils and courts it was remarked quite deliberately that the king had begun to attend to his own affairs. In May 1436 the earl of Warwick was dismissed as the royal tutor, and no replacement appointed: a sign that Henry's period of education was over and his induction to the full scope of kingly duties had begun. Two months later Henry started to sign petitions with his own hand, writing 'R.H.' and '*nous avouns graunte*' below requests that he formally approved.[12] The message to the outside world was clear: the minority had come to an end.

Or had it? Superficially Henry had begun to rule. Yet there was much about his kingship that was unsatisfactory. Council minutes began to include notes suggesting that the king was signing off requests which were not just ill-advised but actively damaging to the crown. 'Remember to speak unto the King to beware how that he granteth pardons or else how that he doeth them to be amended for he doeth to himself therein great disavail,' read one, from 11 February 1438, when Henry had granted a petition impoverishing himself to the tune of two thousand marks.[13] The very next day another, near-identical note proposed that it should be explained to the king that his injudicious granting away of the constableship and stewardship of the castle of Chirk in north Wales had cost him another thousand marks. Tellingly, no attempt was made to take Henry back to Normandy to command his own armies, or even to serve as a figurehead despite the peril resulting from Bedford's death and Burgundy's betrayal. Clearly, the boy was not made in his father's mould.

*

The combination of Bedford's death and the young king's inability to step up to the task of vigorous rule left England with a kind of governmental vacuum. And into this vacuum, over the course of the 1430s, stepped William de la Pole, fourth earl of Suffolk.

Suffolk's life until this point had been spent in a broadly conventional career of aristocratic soldiering. His father Michael had died of dysentery at the siege of Harfleur; his elder brother, also called Michael, had suffered a rare and unlucky death – for an Englishman – in being killed at the battle of Agincourt. William had therefore unexpectedly become the fourth earl of Suffolk at the age of nineteen. He spent the next decade and a half building up his military experience and establishing a record of total loyalty to the crown. He was a capable soldier, who fought with sufficient distinction in Brittany and Normandy to be named as a knight of the Garter in 1421; later he was awarded several important offices and grants of land in captured territory and served as an ambassador to the Low Countries in 1425.

His final experience of fighting in France, however, had not been a happy one. He was in a position of high command when Orléans fell to Joan of Arc and her army in 1429. In the aftermath he had attempted to lead the retreat of a few hundred Englishmen along the banks of the river Loire. Five or six thousand Frenchmen, led by the duke of Alençon and Joan of Arc, were in fierce pursuit, and it had been all that Suffolk could do to direct his troops to shelter in the town of Jargeau, a small but reasonably well-defended settlement about eleven miles upstream from Orléans, with a town wall and fortifications around a bridge across the river. Once they reached the town, Suffolk commanded his men and the inhabitants of Jargeau to barricade the walled part of the town for the inevitable siege. And sure enough, no sooner had the English settled in than the French 'immediately surrounded them on all sides, and commenced to attack them very sharply and to assault them in many places'.[14]

Suffolk had twice attempted to negotiate a short truce and twice the French had rejected his overtures – first because he was deemed to have breached chivalric protocol by negotiating with a captain of low status, rather than with the duke of Alençon, and subsequently because Alençon claimed that the noise of the French assaults was such that he simply did not hear the messages being brought from the town. Given the size of the cannon that the French had deployed to smash down the walls of the bridge and town – including one absolutely massive gun called 'Shepherdess', after Joan of Arc – it is just possible that Alençon was telling the truth. In any case, the bombardment was brutal and effective. Although one enterprising Englishman had managed to hit Joan on the head with a rock thrown from the town walls, cracking her helmet in two and knocking her briefly to the ground, her galvanising presence had been enough to spur the French to victory. Jargeau fell in less than a day, Suffolk and his brother Sir John de la Pole were both captured, and another brother, Alexander de la Pole, was killed, along with more than one hundred other defenders. It was a dismal defeat, alleviated only slightly for Suffolk by the fact that he had managed to knight his captor – a lowly soldier rather than a nobleman – before formally surrendering, thereby avoiding the utter chivalric humiliation of having to give his lordly person up to a man of mean status.[15]

After Jargeau, Suffolk had been taken to Orléans and imprisoned for a number of months. He was finally released in 1430 – for a ransom he would later claim was an eye-watering £20,000, or about seven times his annual income during the wealthiest period of his life. Back in England he began building an extensive and deep-rooted base of power that straddled court, countryside and council and eventually put him in control of the mainspring of royal authority.

Suffolk built up his influence through a combination of boldness, good fortune, excellent connections and old-fashioned stealth. His starting point was the lands associated with his earldom, which gave him a substantial power bloc in East Anglia: he was the dominant nobleman in Suffolk and Norfolk.[16] A marriage to the distinguished, stunningly beautiful and extremely rich widow Alice Chaucer, dowager countess of Salisbury, brought more lands in Oxfordshire and Berkshire, close to the centre of royal government; it also introduced Suffolk into the spheres of national politics, since the Chaucers were close associates of Cardinal Beaufort and Catherine de Valois. These connections may well have lain behind Suffolk's appointment to the royal council in 1431 – but here he was also undoubtedly helped by his easy relations with the other leading voice in the minority government, Humphrey duke of Gloucester. Rare was the man who could straddle the Beaufort–Gloucester split, but Suffolk showed from very early in his political career that he was a pragmatist who preferred working across factional divides to taking sides. He was not an exceptionally charismatic or commanding individual, but what he lacked in personality he amply made up for in diligence and the ability to render himself agreeable to mutually hostile colleagues.

Between 1431 and 1436 Suffolk gradually built up a reputation for assiduous royal service. He was one of the keenest attenders on the royal council, served alongside Cardinal Beaufort in the disastrous embassy at the congress of Arras, and even returned, briefly, to military service following Bedford's death, attempting to pacify areas of Normandy. In this he joined up with the young and ambitious Richard duke of York, who led an army during the campaigning season of late summer and autumn

1436. Just as importantly, however, from 1433 Suffolk served as steward of the royal household. The steward enforced discipline and supervised all the day-to-day running of a domestic operation involving several hundred officers, servants and assistants. Out of necessity, he had regular, informal and largely unchecked personal contact with the king at all hours of the day. Therefore at the royal court it was an important position, one that Suffolk valued so much that he made sure to have it guaranteed by the council before he left to fight in France. By the second half of the 1430s he had thus established himself as both a stalwart of the administration and the central figure in the king's household. Other personages, particularly Beaufort and Gloucester, still outranked him and had their own access to Henry; but gradually, through his diligent attendance at council meetings and his pre-eminence at court, Suffolk became, in effect, the main channel for official and unofficial approaches to the king. Throughout the 1430s, as Henry's councillors attempted to nudge the young king into ruling in his own right, there was a to-and-fro of power between the household and the council chamber. Wherever the power went, Suffolk was there too.

This was not, it should be said, a purely self-interested power-grab on Suffolk's behalf. Undoubtedly he was ambitious, and he would later brazenly accrue offices and lands for his own personal gain. But Suffolk was allowed to take on the role of royal puppeteer thanks to a general consensus among both his aristocratic colleagues and other important figures at court, driven by the realisation that someone would have to co-ordinate government behind the scenes until such time as the king summoned enough character and maturity to do it for himself. Nevertheless, Suffolk's omnipresence allowed him to wield influence in a variety of ways and throughout every aspect of government policy and royal activity – which is why we can detect his hand beneath the decision in 1437 to send Edmund and Jasper Tudor to live with his sister Katherine de la Pole at Barking Abbey. And as the years passed it would make him one of the most powerful men in England: Margaret Paston, doyenne of the famous letter-writing East Anglian dynasty, wrote that without Suffolk's blessing, no one in England could defend their property or enjoy their life. Unless, as she put it, 'ye have my Lord of Suffolk's good lordship, while the world is as it is, ye can never live in peace'.[17]

However, as Suffolk amassed and exercised his considerable wealth and power, ruling quietly in the name of a wavering and inert king, he was inadvertently creating a dangerous political situation. For to operate kingship by stealth – even with the noblest intentions – was to play with fire. As the years passed, the dangers of manipulating the natural means of royal rule steadily increased. Soon enough, the problems of Suffolk's 'good lordship' would be brutally exposed.

6 : A Dear Marriage

A nervous crowd stood waiting on Blackheath. It was Friday 28 May 1445 and the large grassy area of common land on the south bank of the Thames, just downriver from Southwark, swarmed with London's most notable citizens: the mayor, the aldermen of London's governing council, representatives of all the wealthy liveried companies of the city, all former London sheriffs and a group of minstrels. The city had been preparing for this day for the better part of a year and everyone of note was dressed identically, in custom-stitched gowns the colour of the bluest summer sky, trimmed with red hoods and embroidered with the crest of the wearer's profession. The design of these fine robes had been a matter of intense civic debate, causing arguments that had raged for several weeks in the council chamber the previous August. It had taken considerable political energy to defeat the idea that the aldermen ought to be wearing saffron rather than blue. These were no petty squabbles. It was vital that the leading citizens of London represent the city at its most dazzling, for they had gathered to celebrate the arrival of a highly esteemed visitor.[1]

She was Margaret of Anjou, fifteen-year-old daughter of Duke René of Anjou, a famous but impoverished nobleman from central France. René held a number of splendid-sounding titles – he was, in theory, king of both Sicily and Jerusalem – but he was also a penniless and serially unlucky soldier, who had spent most of his daughter's youth locked in his enemies' jails or being beaten in wars on the Italian peninsula (a fact that had allowed the women of his family to wield a relatively large degree of political power and autonomy on his behalf). Nevertheless, René was the brother of the queen of France, which made Margaret the king's niece. Her father may have been a relative pauper but the young girl was born of high blood, and her family was well connected, which was why Margaret had come to England to fulfil a political role of her own. She was the new bride and queen consort of King Henry VI.

Margaret's marriage to Henry was Suffolk's brainchild. The girl's father was so poor that she came with a pitiful dowry – a measly twenty thousand francs and the hollow promise that one day the English king would inherit René's claim to the crown of Majorca. But marrying Henry to the French king's niece seemed to serve two greater purposes: it would bring England a diplomatic and military truce in the French wars and it would enable Henry and Margaret to rebuild the dwindling stock of the English royal family.

Since Bedford's death in 1435, England's French policy had been a mess. A famine caused by crop failures in England and Normandy between 1437 and 1440 had impoverished the realm on both sides of the Channel and the Crown was heavily indebted and in arrears with its payments to captains and troops. Parliaments now grumbled loudly when asked to approve new taxes for the never-ending war. At no point since his French coronation had any really serious effort been made to take Henry back to France at the head of an army. (Neither would the king ever be taken to Scotland or Ireland.) It was true that his rival Charles VII had also avoided taking command in the field, but Charles was at least a vigorous director of strategy. The same could not be said of his nephew. During the early 1440s Henry VI had thrown a great deal of his energy into supporting the foundation of Eton College, a grammar school dedicated to the Virgin Mary whose architectural plans he pored over and annotated with his own hand. At the same time he had sponsored the establishment of King's College, Cambridge, a large, rich place of higher education explicitly founded for 'poor and indigent scholar clerks'. Few Plantagenet kings ever took as keen an interest in popular education as Henry VI. But few ever took less interest in warfare. Thus in England a series of confused, conflicting and counterproductive policies had been pursued under the leadership of various loud voices in government.

In 1440 Cardinal Beaufort had gambled away one of England's most valuable diplomatic chips by permitting the release of the duke of Orléans, a prisoner taken at the battle of Agincourt in 1415, who had spent the ensuing twenty-five years writing romances in English castles, including the first recorded Valentine's poem. ('*Je suis déjà d'amour tanné / Ma très douce Valentinée . . .*' – 'I am already sick of love / My very sweet Valentine . . .') Orléans's release had enraged Humphrey duke of Gloucester, whose chief desire never wavered from all-out attack on France. Gloucester saw it as a disgrace to Henry V's memory and made his feelings widely known, though he would soon be compelled to direct his attentions closer to home.

In 1441 a scandal blew up involving the duke's second wife, Eleanor Cobham, the spirited young lady-in-waiting for whom he had abandoned his first wife, Jacqueline of Hainault, in 1428, when their childless marriage was annulled by the pope. The circumstances of the marriage were somewhat controversial, given Eleanor's relatively lowly social status. But she proved to be a stately and intelligent woman who revelled at the head of the sumptuous Renaissance court that she and her husband held at their manor of Greenwich, where they hosted poets, musicians and playwrights.

The death of Bedford meant that Gloucester was heir presumptive; by extension Eleanor found herself potentially the next queen. The thought clearly thrilled and intrigued her, and she began consulting astrologers and necromancers to predict the date of the king's death and thus, by extension, 'King' Humphrey's accession. But in this matter she had grievously overreached. The astrologers whom she consulted were men of considerable academic standing – for this was an age when the realms of science and superstition largely overlapped. But if her diviners were well schooled, they were also politically naïve. They predicted that, in the summer of 1441, Henry VI would sicken and die. Eleanor, or those around her, found it impossible to keep this a secret, and rumours of the king's death began to swirl around the capital and the country.

The high standing of her husband was not enough to protect Eleanor. In July she was arrested, tried and, as one chronicler put it, 'damned for a witch and an heretic, and put in perpetual prison'. Her associates were put to death, but Eleanor managed to escape the flames. She was sentenced to a very public and humiliating penance: ordered to walk barefoot, carrying a candle, about the streets of London on three occasions in November. She was forcibly divorced from the duke and sentenced to an indefinite jail term, which she served at ever more remote castles in Kent, Cheshire, the Isle of Man and finally, from 1449, Beaumaris on Anglesey.[2] Gloucester was personally shaken by the loss of his wife and his public standing never recovered from the scandal: his credibility and the scope of his political influence were at a stroke smashed.

With Gloucester's fall, Cardinal Beaufort's influence grew. He had long been the largest financial creditor of the Crown and a consistently cautious voice on the royal council. But in 1442 the cardinal abandoned his own long-favoured policy of containment and reconciliation and turned heedless aggressor. He convinced the council and parliament to permit a military expedition to France led by his nephew John Beaufort, duke of Somerset. Its purpose was ostensibly to join up the two main blocs of English power in Normandy and Gascony by conquering further territory in the region around Maine. Somerset's expedition, undertaken in the late summer of 1443, was an aimless fiasco, which looked like a shallow attempt by the Beaufort family to endow themselves with booty seized and lands conquered in central France. It annoyed Richard duke of York, who succeeded Bedford as lieutenant of France only to find his authority undercut by Beaufort's independent commission. And it wasted a vast amount of money. Somerset died shortly after his return, humiliated by his failure and very possibly driven to suicide. Cardinal Beaufort now joined his rival Gloucester in effective political retirement.

All this left England with an acute need for peace. Suffolk, now the chief force in English politics, was determined to meet the challenge. He departed for France early in 1444 with the aim of taking decisive action to bring a temporary halt to warfare. He came back with Margaret's hand in marriage as the seal on an agreement with her uncle Charles VII for a two-year truce, a window in which to negotiate for a longer and more lasting peace.

Following the usual diplomatic protocol, Suffolk had personally stood in for Henry and married the fourteen-year-old Margaret by proxy. In the presence of the French king and queen and a vast array of French nobles, he had taken the girl's hand and slipped on the marriage band in the cathedral at Tours on 24 May 1444. The first response of all who heard about the match was apparently one of joyous relief. At the French banquets that followed Margaret's proxy marriage it was said that the common people 'made joy and mirth, and song (all with high voyce) Nowell! Nowell! Nowell! and peace, peace, peace be to us! Amen!'[3]

The great English war captain John Talbot, earl of Shrewsbury, commissioned for the new queen the most magnificent book of hours, which still survives complete with a copy of the royal genealogy with which the duke of Bedford had bombarded Normandy during the 1420s, showing Henry VI as the rightful lineal heir to the crown of France.[4] (See plate section.) On his return to England, Suffolk was promoted from earl to the rank of marquess. (In 1448 he would be raised yet again, to become a duke.) The following year he crossed the Channel to collect the king's bride and bring her back in triumph to her new kingdom. Among his companions on the trip was one Owen Meredith – most likely Owen Tudor, who was now around forty-five years old.

So it was that Margaret landed at Southampton on 9 April 1445, frail from a longstanding illness made worse by seasickness following a very stormy crossing of the Channel aboard the *Cock John*. While recovering her health she slowly made her way from the south coast towards the capital. Her journey took her through rural Hampshire, where her first appointment was at Titchfield Abbey, a modest house of Premonstratensian canons more famous for the austere and scholarly lives of its brethren than for the abundance of its hospitality. In this quiet, monkish setting Margaret finally married Henry in person. The king gave her a fine gold ring set with a ruby, remoulded from the sacred ring he had worn during his coronation as king of France.[5] Then they made their way together towards London. And so it was that on 28 May 1445, when England's new queen rode up to London she was not just greeted by the ranked welcome party of London's azure-clad worthies; behind them the whole city had been decked out to celebrate her arrival.

London excelled at pageantry. Though the city was not looking quite its best – the wooden steeple of St Paul's had been set alight during the winter by a direct lightning strike, and the city gates were in need of repair – it still had the power to dazzle and enthral. Streets had been tidied and houses secured to celebrate Margaret's arrival. Gutters were cleared, roofs strengthened to support clambering spectators, and tavern signs made safe to prevent them from falling on partygoers' heads. Thousands of pounds raised by a council grant and public subscription had been spent on a series of eight lavish pageants with spoken

English captions, each showing and hailing Margaret in a similar light: as the bringer of peace, the saviour of Henry's two realms and a gift sent from heaven. The young queen travelled in a litter through the streets thronged with merrymakers, seeing tableaux that likened her variously to the dove that brought Noah his olive branch and to the virgin St Margaret, who tamed 'the might of spirits malign'.[6] She was lodged in the Tower of London until, two days after her formal entry into the city, she emerged dressed all in virginal white with a crown of gold and pearls, to be drawn in a carriage to Westminster and crowned. England greeted its new queen with three days of feasts and jousting. Soon, it was hoped, Margaret would use her connections to help bring a long-awaited and lasting peace.

*

At the time of Henry and Margaret's marriage the future of the English royal line was a matter of uncertainty. True, there was little chance that Henry VI would emulate his father by dying anywhere near a foreign battlefield. But as the poet John Lydgate wrote, 'experience showeth the world is variable'.[7] Life was short and death could be sudden and unpredictable. The last formal provisions for the royal succession had been made in parliament by Henry IV in 1406, when it was agreed that the crown should fall first to Henry V and the heirs of his body, and subsequently to Henry V's three brothers and their heirs: Thomas duke of Clarence, John duke of Bedford and Humphrey duke of Gloucester. By 1445 Clarence and Bedford had both died without issue and Gloucester, despite marrying twice, had only fathered two bastards, whose names, Antigone and Arthur, reflected his interests in classical literature and British mythology. He was fifty-five years old, his marriages had failed without providing him with a single legitimate heir, and his disgrace following the fall of Eleanor Cobham had severely compromised his status as heir apparent.

Henry VI was thus the only surviving grandchild of Henry IV, and he was near-certain to remain so. Who might follow him if he were unexpectedly to die was not wholly clear. This did not, in itself, put Henry's hold on the crown in danger. But it promised plenty of uncertainty for the next generation. For outside Henry's immediate family there was a tremendous profusion of men with some degree of royal blood in their veins. At least four families could claim descent from Henry VI's great-great-grandfather, Edward III.

The first was represented by Richard duke of York. Born in 1411, York inherited royal blood from both his parents: by his mother he was descended from Edward III's second son, Lionel; from his father he was the heir of Edward III's fourth son, Edmund. (See House of York genealogical table.) His other ancestors included members of many of the greatest noble families in England's recent history: Mortimer, Clare, Despenser, de Burgh and Holland.[8] Throughout the early part of the fifteenth century, his father's side of the family had been involved in rebellions in which they were trumpeted as the rightful kings of England. One great-uncle, Sir Edmund Mortimer, had joined Owain Glyndwr's revolt against Henry IV, proclaiming another uncle – Edmund earl of March – to be the true heir to the crown. York's father shared the belief and was found guilty in 1413 of plotting to depose Henry V and put March on the throne, a crime for which he was beheaded as a traitor.

But if rebellion and ambition ran in the blood, it was a mark of England's relative stability during Henry's long minority that Richard had not been tainted by his relatives' earlier crimes. Over a period of several years leading up to 1434 he had been allowed to inherit all his family's extensive estates: he held the duchy of York and the earldoms of March, Cambridge and Ulster, all of which were traditionally associated with the Mortimer family from whom he was descended. His lands lay right across England,

Wales and Ireland, and his properties included mighty castles on the coasts and in the Welsh marches (the collective name given to the large swathes of land on the borders of England and Wales, which stretched in some places as far west as the coast.) In truly princely fashion, York also owned stunning, palatial fortresses like Fotheringhay on the banks of the river Nene in Northampton-shire, and farms and forests from Yorkshire to Somerset.[9] His personal connections reached even further: in 1429 he had married Cecily Neville, a daughter of one of the greatest noble families of the north. He was knighted at the age of fifteen, brought to court at eighteen and admitted to the Order of the Garter when he was twenty-one. In 1436, after Bedford's death, the twenty-five-year-old York was appointed to the lieutenancy of France, a post he was given not just because he was considered a talented young soldier, but because he was, as his commission papers put it, a '*grant prince de nostre sang et lignage*' and '*nostre beaucousin*' ('a great prince of our blood and line' and 'our dear cousin').[10] Huge grants of land in Normandy were given to him in 1444, which at a stroke made him the most important English landowner in the duchy.[11] In short, Richard duke of York was the richest layman and mightiest landlord in England after the king.

He was not, however, anything more than that. In the early 1440s, while he was serving in France, there were no suggestions whatever that he harboured designs on the crown. He was ambitious, to be sure, and conscious of his status. His wife, Cecily, produced a great brood of children: their first daughter, Anne, was born in 1439, a short-lived son named Henry arrived in 1441, and eleven more children followed over the course of the next ten years. The eldest of the surviving sons, Edward and Edmund, were shown exceptional royal favour. By 1445 Edward – then no more than three years old – had been created earl of March and Edmund, a year younger still, had been made earl of Rutland. The main purpose of elevating York's infant sons to the peerage seems to have been to marry one of them to a French princess. But if these were extraordinary honours, there was little sign that the young duke dreamed of creating a rival royal dynasty. His family's own history amply demonstrated that the exercise of naked ambition was a certain way to lose one's head. At the time of the king's marriage to Margaret of Anjou, York was generally committed, like his peers, to maintaining the form of rule by which England muddled along, with Suffolk leading government quietly from the household, with the tacit backing of those magnates who wanted to keep an underwhelming king from losing control of his twin realms.[12]

All the same, so long as the king remained childless, some thought had to be given to the status of those like York, who were near to him in blood. During the 1440s three other families profited from their descent from Edward III, and around the time of the king's marriage all of them were elevated in status, giving the sense, albeit rather a confused one, of an extended royal family.

The Beauforts, kinsmen of Cardinal Beaufort, were the most prominent members of this greater royal family. Their descent, like the king's, came through John of Gaunt and the house of Lancaster. Gaunt's third wife, Katherine Swynford, had borne him three sons. They were considered illegitimate – not unreasonably, since they had been born while Gaunt was married to someone else – and although in later years Gaunt and Katherine had been married, and the children's taint of bastardy removed by an act of parliament, it had been made very clear – again by parliamentary law – that they were debarred from ever inheriting the crown.

In the 1440s, Cardinal Beaufort was the only surviving son of Gaunt and Katherine Swynford, but the family continued through the cardinal's nephews. In 1443, John earl of Somerset was raised to the rank of duke, and given specific precedence over the duke of Norfolk, the head of one of the oldest and most prominent families in England. As we have seen, this grand elevation did John Beaufort very little good, for he died in unhappy circumstances following his woeful 1443 expedition to France. The family's involvement in politics passed to John's younger brother Edmund Beaufort, who took over the Somerset title in 1448 and fathered a clutch of children of his own. Finally, there was Joan Beaufort, who had been married to James I of Scotland and enjoyed an exciting career in the north, where she served for a brief time as regent, while her son, James II of Scotland, was a minor.

The Beauforts were thus closely connected to the crown, even if technically they were barred from any future succession. So were others. The Holland family traced their own royal ancestry through Henry IV's sister Elizabeth. In January 1444 the most senior Holland, John earl of Huntingdon, was promoted to duke of Exeter, with precedence over all other dukes except for York – another elevation specifically credited to his closeness in blood to the king. John Holland died in August 1447, and his son Henry Holland eventually succeeded to his duchy.

Then there were the Staffords, another family with direct links to the Plantagenet dynasty. The Staffords were descended from Thomas of Woodstock: Edward III's youngest son and the bitterest enemy of the deposed King Richard II. In 1444 Humphrey Stafford, the most senior member of the family, was made duke of Buckingham, and three years later he was, like York, Somerset and Exeter, given a special precedence: specifically, he was to rank above all other dukes who would be created in the future, unless they were of the king's blood.[13]

Thus, around the time of the king's marriage, a loose sort of succession plan had been made – or at the very least there was a hierarchy of aristocracy, in which York, Somerset, Exeter and Buckingham all knew their rank. With a new queen there was now the promise of further expansion of the dynasty. Was a new generation finally stepping forward to take command of England's destiny?

*

The personal relationship between Henry VI and Queen Margaret seems to have been close and even tender. The king's confessor, John Blacman, wrote in his memoir that 'when he espoused the most noble lady, Lady Margaret . . . he kept his marriage vow wholly and sincerely . . . never dealing unchastely with any woman'. (This chastity was in large part temperamental, since Blacman also records that the king was mortified by the sight of nudity and 'was wont utterly to avoid the unguarded sight of naked persons'. When one Christmas 'a certain great lord brought before him a dance or show of young ladies with bared bosoms . . . the king . . . very angrily averted his eyes, turned his back on them and went out to his chamber'. He was also apparently shocked by the sight of naked men when he visited a warm spa in Bath.)[14]

There was chivalry and even real romance. When Margaret arrived in England, Henry kept up his family's tradition of greeting his new wife incognito, dressed as a squire, and only later revealing his identity. After their marriage the couple spent much of their time together in the royal palaces dotted near the banks of the Thames: Windsor, Sheen, Eltham and Greenwich. Henry bought his wife jewellery and numerous horses in which she particularly delighted. He allowed her to found Queen's College in Cambridge in 1448 to mirror his own foundation of King's seven years earlier.[15] In a warrant for payment to one London jeweller, Henry describes Margaret as 'our most dear and most entirely beloved wife the queen'.[16] A touching vignette is preserved describing the royal couple during the New Year festivities not long into their marriage, receiving gifts as they lay in bed together, staying there all morning and apparently enjoying one another's company. Yet if they shared a happy bed, it was not a fruitful one. Eight years would pass between their marriage and the birth of their first child.

This was a problem in its own right. More serious, however, was the complete failure of Margaret's arrival in England to bring about the glorious peace that the marriage had seemed to promise. In July 1445 a magnificent diplomatic delegation – including Margaret's father, René of Anjou – arrived from France to meet with the English in London. It was the greatest peace council of its sort to have taken place in thirty years. There were high hopes – not least from the king, who seems genuinely to have had a desire for peace with the French and whose appearance before the ambassadors at the beginning of the talks was marked by warmth and friendliness. Henry greeted the French diplomats personally, and although royally dressed in red cloth of gold, he raised his hat to them, patted them on the back and appeared to be quite overcome with brotherly love and rejoicing.

Henry's ministers, led by Suffolk, hoped that improved relations with France would lead to a settlement in which they could keep the conquered lands in complete sovereignty. But the French had no intention of agreeing to such terms. They stipulated that for a final peace to be made, the English would be allowed to hold on to their historical lands in and around Gascony, along with Calais and Guînes, but everything else should be surrendered, and English claims to the French crown dropped. Henry and his advisers could not countenance such terms. After a promising beginning an impasse was reached and a mere seven-month extension to the truce was agreed. Plans were made for Henry and Margaret to travel to France in 1446 to continue talks face-to-face with Margaret's uncle, Charles VII.

They never went. Instead, in the autumn of 1445 another French delegation arrived in London, followed by a flurry of letters between Charles, Henry and Margaret. In October the French proposed new conditions: there would be no final peace, but in return for a twenty-year truce the English were asked to surrender possession of the county of Maine to Margaret's father, René. It is possible that this had been the French plan ever since the first negotiations for Margaret's marriage, and it may have been suggested to or even verbally agreed by Suffolk at Tours in 1444 or Henry in July 1445. But it was just before Christmas 1445 that the deal was actually done. On 22 December Henry wrote to Charles VII, saying that since 'it appeared to you that [ceding Maine] was one of the best and aptest means to arrive at the blessing of a peace between us and you . . . favouring also our most dear and well-beloved companion the queen, who has requested us to do this many times . . . we signify and promise in good faith and on our kingly word to give and deliver . . . Maine by the last day of April next coming . . .' This may have been a necessary move towards peace, but the consequences for England, and for the young queen's reputation, would be disastrous.[17]

By agreeing to surrender Maine and its capital Le Mans, Henry had placed his government in a difficult position. The terms were basically humiliating – the surrender of hard-won territory for mere promises and talk from the French. The deal was bound to upset both the duke of York, whose authority in France was once more undermined, and Edmund Beaufort, the future duke of Somerset, who stood to lose a great deal of land and his title of count of Maine. Worst of all, surrendering Maine gave the French a fresh military route to attack the English both in Normandy and in Gascony. And it confirmed the general sentiment that the English war effort was one of retreat and slow humiliation.

Attempts were made to keep the deal secret. Henry's proposed personal embassy to France now appeared to be a dangerous liability at which any number of further calamitous concessions might be made, and Suffolk stalled desperately through 1446 and 1447 to delay sending the king for a follow-up mission and giving back the promised land. But it was pointless. Charles VII was a shrewd negotiator and an accomplished king. The English, who were attempting through Suffolk to govern around the king, were diplomatically outflanked.

There was huge disaffection, bordering on mutiny, among the English soldiers who garrisoned Maine and Le Mans. They dragged their heels at every order to co-operate. As a result, Maine and Le Mans were not physically surrendered until the spring of 1448, but returned they were: the start of the final collapse of England's position in the Hundred Years War, whose preservation had been Henry V's most important legacy, had begun. Chroniclers with the benefit of hindsight would much later write that Henry's wedding 'was a dear marriage for the realm of England'.[18]

Marginalised since his wife's disgrace in 1441, Humphrey duke of Gloucester had become a meek bystander, openly mocked by Suffolk in front of the French ambassadors. As a mark of his dwindling relevance he was not included in the peace negotiations of 1445. And yet, as news began to filter out that the cession of Maine was the price to be paid for a long-term truce, Gloucester's insistent hostility to the French seemed finally vindicated. It did not require much imagination on the part of those who had made the deal to see that when the news became fully public, Gloucester might be thrust back into the heart of politics. It was possible that a new faction, opposed to Suffolk's concessions, might be drawn together around the ageing Humphrey. If the king (and therefore Suffolk and probably the queen) really were to leave England to negotiate further terms with Charles VII, then Gloucester would have a very good claim on exercising the powers of regency in his absence. Late in 1446 a decision was taken by Suffolk and his closest allies to silence the duke before he had a chance to embarrass them.

In February 1447 a parliament was summoned to meet in the unusual location of Bury St Edmunds, a 'safe' venue in the heart of Suffolk's territory. According to the records of the parliament, the weather was 'fervent cold . . . and biting'.[19] Gloucester had been summoned to appear before the parliament. Clearly he was suspicious, for he came to Bury ten days after it had opened, with a huge retinue of armed Welshmen. It is possible that he came in the hope of bargaining for the release of his former wife Eleanor from her jail cell on the Isle of Man. But it was obvious that he was in considerable danger. Rumours had been put about of a plot to kill the king, rumours which were quite probably fabricated in order to place Gloucester under suspicion and facilitate an attempt to destroy him on charges of treason. Contemporary chroniclers were in very little doubt: the parliament, said one, 'was made only for to slay the noble duke of Gloucester', and the prime mover in the conspiracy was Suffolk.[20]

When Gloucester arrived at Bury shortly before 11 a.m. on Saturday 18 February his fears were confirmed. He was prevented from going to meet his nephew the king and was advised 'that he should take the next way to his lodging' at St Saviour's Hospital, the abbey infirmary, just outside the north gate of the city.[21] The journey took him through the town's horse market and down a small street known as the Dead Lane. It was a prophetic path to tread. After Gloucester had eaten dinner a delegation of peers arrived to arrest him on the authority of the royal council. His head servants were also arrested, and the more menial ones were ordered to disperse. The most senior judges in England – the chief justices of the courts of King's Bench and Common Pleas – had been instructed to suspend their business and come to parliament. It seemed that a trial, one likely to be concluded with the duke's final disgrace, was inevitable.

But fate intervened. On Thursday 23 February at around 3 p.m., some five days after he was arrested, Gloucester was dead.

'How he died or in what manner the certainty is unknown, but only to God,' wrote one chronicler. 'Some said he died for sorrow, some said he was murdered between two feather-beds; and some said he was thrust into the bowel with an hot burning spit.'[22] In fact, he had probably suffered a stroke, for he lay three days in a coma before finally expiring.

Gloucester was buried in St Albans. Before he was laid in his tomb, his body was displayed openly in an effort to dispel any talk of foul play. In the weeks that followed the end of the Bury parliament, several members of the duke's household were tried and found guilty of plotting to kill the king and rescue Eleanor Cobham from prison. They were pardoned on the gallows – suggesting that the charges against them were either invented or had been exaggerated for effect, and that the whole campaign against Gloucester was one designed to discredit him and silence any criticisms of Suffolk's peace with France. These grotesque and unsubtle tactics would backfire. Over the years, as the situation in France deteriorated, a legend of Humphrey the 'good duke' arose. This was quite a distortion: in life Gloucester had been quarrelsome, factious, somewhat conceited, impossibly aggressive and at times the single greatest danger to the stability of the realm. His most lasting achievements were in the realm of scholarship, where his patronage of Italian Renaissance artists and scholars was at the forefront of English secular learning, and his library numbered among the finest in the country. But his reputation would swiftly outstrip reality. The 'good duke' would be contrasted ever more fiercely and contemptuously with hostile portrayals of Suffolk and King Henry himself. This hostility would soon erupt in the most fearsome demonstration of popular anger seen in England for nearly seventy years.

7 : Away, Traitors, Away!

On Wednesday 5 August 1444, in the town of Reading a horse set out slowly through the crowded streets, pulling behind it a cart containing a prisoner. In procession behind came the sheriff of Berkshire and others, following closely as the prison cart bumped and trundled slowly towards Reading's western outskirts, before turning around and traversing the town slowly in the opposite direction. The prisoner was one Thomas Kerver, a moderately wealthy local gentleman, until recently the bailiff of the abbot of Reading. He was being paraded around the town in which he had lived his life in a ritual of social humiliation. This would be his very last tour of Reading, for he was shortly scheduled to meet his death at the county gallows near Maidenhead.[1]

Kerver's cart left town by the London road, heading east towards open country. A few miles down the road it stopped. Kerver was brought down from the cart and attached to a far less comfortable device – either a wooden hurdle or a rope tied to a horse's tail. Then for several miles he was dragged painfully along the ground, each stone, rut and pothole in the road scraping against his body and head. In this bloodying fashion he was hauled around another public circuit, this time through Maidenhead and the riverside village of Bray, until eventually his journey reached its end, alongside the gallows where the court of King's Bench had decreed that he was to die. Hauled up from behind the horse, Kerver had a noose placed around his neck and was then strung up to dangle. He did not die – hanging was an experience designed to torture a criminal by choking him, rather than killing him outright by snapping his spine. Everyone who

[98]

looked on would have known what to expect next: the hangman's knife cutting through Kerver's stomach to pull out his entrails; the same knife hacking off his genitals which would then be burned in front of him. The body finally being cut down, beheaded and chopped into rough lumps. This was the ritual of hanging, drawing and quartering, the most fearsome punishment in English law.

Yet at the critical moment, Kerver's punishment was interrupted. He was not slaughtered with a blade, but simply cut down from the gallows, then handed over by the sheriff to another party who had been watching the execution. The men who received him then disappeared at speed, taking with them the prisoner, who was presumably bloodied, bruised, half-conscious and very, very frightened.

Thomas Kerver's near-death experience had come about because the court of King's Bench – one of the highest in the land – had found him guilty of treason: of having 'falsely and traitorously . . . schemed, imagined, encompassed, wished and desired the death and destruction of the king and his realm of England and with all his power traitorously proposed to kill the king'. On the Monday and Tuesday after Easter in April 1444 he was said to have tried to recruit others to join in a plot against the royal life, asking them whether the country was ruled by a king or a boy, and scornfully suggesting that the king was not as great a man as the dauphin. He repeatedly condemned the financial embarrassment of the English Crown, stating that 'it would have been worth more than a hundred thousand pounds to England if the king had died twenty years ago'. It had taken only a few months for Kerver to be arrested, imprisoned in the Tower of London, and found guilty by a jury.

Kerver's rescue on the gallows had come as the result of a secret last-minute order from the royal council, who had decided to show clemency on behalf of the pious young king. This fact was not widely known – it was thought that Kerver's reprieve at

Maidenhead had only taken place so that, as one chronicler imagined, he could be 'thence drawn to Tyborn gallow, and hanged . . . and then his head smitten off, and set on London Bridge'.[2] In fact, Kerver was jailed at Wallingford Castle for a few years and then quietly released. The point, however, had been made. Treasonous words spoken against the king would not be tolerated.

Kerver's case was exceptional for two reasons. His release had shown that Henry VI's personal piety could be a tempering factor in criminal cases. But far more striking was the fact that the full weight of the law had been used against a fairly innocuous malefactor whose ostensible plans to kill the king as detailed in the legal records smack of nothing more than hot air. What was notable about the case was the intensity of the judicial response to words which in reality posed little or no threat.

Yet it is also possible for us to understand the feelings of the government that lay behind the prosecution. For during the 1440s, England was full of muttering and grumbling about the mounting problems faced by the realm both at home and abroad. An insecure regime could sense itself tottering. Occasionally it needed to lash out.

*

There is nothing new about grumbling against authority. Even the greatest kings in history have known that somewhere in their kingdom a drunkard is probably railing against them. But England in the 1440s was especially rich in public disaffection, as it was beset by increasingly serious political problems. In 1448, a man from Canterbury was recorded complaining that Queen Margaret 'was none able to be Queen of England'. The complainant boasted that if he were a peer of the realm he would strike the queen down 'for because that she beareth no child, and because that we have no prince in this land'.[3] In 1450 two farmers from Sussex, John and William Merfeld, were indicted before a court for saying that the king was a simpleton who would hold a staff with a bird on the end, playing with it like a clown, and that some other king ought to be found.[4] Songs lamented the poverty and incompetence of the Crown and the royal government. The parliamentary commons, theoretically representing the people, complained in February 1449 that 'murders, manslaughters, robberies and other thefts, within this . . . realm [are] dayly increasing and multiplying'.[5] These were formulaic complaints, of the sort made by plenty of parliaments over the years, but in the early spring of 1449 there was some truth to the argument that law and order were beginning to falter.

There were two basic functions to kingship in the middle ages. The first was to uphold justice. The second was to fight wars. There was no sense in the 1440s that Henry VI was capable of doing either.[6] Disorder had been increasing steadily in England for several years. Disputes between magnates went unresolved. One especially nasty feud had boiled up in the west country, where a private war had broken out between the Bonville and Courtenay families. The feud had been directly caused by Henry VI, who in 1437 had granted a prestigious and lucrative office – that of the stewardship of the duchy of Cornwall – to two men simultaneously. Latent rivalry between two of the most important families in the region spilled into roadside brawls and physical violence, which the king and his officers seemed worryingly unable to stem. Over the course of the 1440s, the dispute would escalate, resulting in murder, home invasion, the raising of private armies and sieges on property. And this was far from the only area in which such problems were brewing. Disorder was growing markedly across England, not least in the north, where rival magnates held and jealously guarded near-autonomous regional power, and in East Anglia, where the duke of Suffolk was finding his role as private lord and covert executor of royal government increasingly difficult to balance.

Problems were even more pronounced in France, where the English position following the cession of Maine had gone from uneasy to positively perilous. Richard duke of York's commission as lieutenant had expired in 1445, and in 1447 he had been removed from the French wars and appointed to serve with broad and sweeping powers as lieutenant of Ireland, an area traditionally associated with the Mortimer side of his family. He took up his post in June 1449, and in the meantime he was replaced in France by Queen Catherine de Valois's old courtier Edmund Beaufort, now the head of his family and honoured with the title of duke of Somerset.

This turned out to be a very unwise reorganisation of personnel. Despite receiving his commission in 1446, Somerset delayed crossing the Channel to take up his command until the spring of 1448, arriving just in time to see the truce collapse. Blatant breaches of the peace had been taking place on both sides for months, but none sufficient to provoke a return to all-out war. However, on 24 March 1449 English forces under the trusted Spanish mercenary François de Surienne attacked and captured the Breton town of Fougères, robbing its wealthy merchant citizens and sacking the townsfolk's houses. The attack was presented as a spontaneous piece of violence by a renegade captain, but in reality it was planned and ordered in London, by none other than the duke of Suffolk. But the plan, intended as a cunning means by which to curry favour with a potentially dissident ally of Charles VII, backfired spectacularly when the duke of Brittany, whose authority had been offended by the raid on his territory, appealed to Charles VII for assistance.[7] This was just the opportunity the French king had been waiting for, and in July he announced that he was no longer bound to keep the peace with England. He declared war on 31 July, launching a full and swift military invasion of Normandy. French forces swept through the duchy, dragging with them huge siege engines and a number of cannon. In many cases these were enough to convince English fortresses to surrender without a fight. Morale throughout the duchy quickly collapsed, a process hastened by the lack of swift support or reinforcement from England.

The Norman capital of Rouen fell on 29 October 1449. Somerset shamefully and unchivalrously saved his own skin by fleeing the city under a safe-conduct from Charles VII, for which he agreed to a monstrous ransom of fifty thousand ecus, to be paid within the year. Desperate to hold on to whatever they could of Normandy, the council scrambled two thousand additional troops to the duchy, funded by the treasurer, Lord Saye, who pawned the crown jewels to pay the bills. But it was too little, too late. Rouen's fall was swiftly followed by the losses of Harfleur, Honfleur, Fresnoy and Caen. By the spring the English had been driven back almost to the sea. They had no choice but to stand and fight. On 14 April 1450 they met a joint French–Breton force in battle at Formigny, near Bayeux. Amid the boom of cannon fire, the English army was slaughtered and many of their best captains taken prisoner. Their control of Normandy was at an end. It was nothing short of a catastrophe.

Although accomplished quickly, the collapse of the English kingdom of France was still a human disaster. As town after town fell to besiegers, streams of inhabitants were forced to flee. Women trudged out into the countryside with as many of their belongings as they could carry, their children strapped to their bodies with scraps of linen. Garrisons were cleared of their male inhabitants: soldiers and landowners who had made their whole careers in the defence of Normandy were now abruptly forced out into hostile terrain. Some would stay on and find employment in the newly French territory or even serve in Charles's armies; but many hundreds, probably thousands of others would join a flood of refugees making their way in pitiful fashion to England. Cheapside – the main thoroughfare through London – was daily occupied by miserable families wheeling their life's possessions on carts in the street. It was, said one chronicler, 'piteous to see'.[8]

Losing the war in Normandy was not just militarily humiliating: it triggered severe financial problems for the Crown. At the parliament of November 1449 it was said that the Crown was indebted to the dizzying tune of £372,000, against an annual income of just £5,000.[9] Not all of this was due to the war. The running costs of the royal household alone were estimated at £24,000, meaning that, as it was somewhat tortuously expressed in parliament, 'your expenses necessary to your houshold, without all other ordinary charges . . . exceedeth every year in expenses necessary over your livelihood'.[10] Even with the income taxes granted by parliaments for war finance, individual loans, customs revenues, the special tax on wool and the practice of purveyance (by which the travelling royal household requisitioned supplies and goods without payment), the Crown still could not keep up with its obligations. During his relatively short time as lieutenant in France, Richard duke of York had accrued personal costs of £20,000 – five times the yearly return of all his extensive estates in England and Wales – for which he had great trouble in extracting repayment.[11] A similar sum was owed in unpaid wages to the Calais garrison.

This seemed all the more perplexing given that, in theory, Henry VI ought to have had greater private resources than any of his ancestors in living memory, since he had the fewest living relatives to endow. All three of his uncles (Bedford, Clarence and Gloucester) were dead. So was his mother, and Henry IV's widow, Joan of Navarre. Queen Margaret's household had inflated the running costs, but she was far from the most profligate queen consort England had ever had (Edward III's wife Philippa of Hainault had been the *grande dame* of reckless extravagance). Other than the queen there was no one left alive who absolutely required their own landed endowment from the Crown. The royal couple had produced no children, so the king still held the principality of Wales and the duchy of Cornwall in his own right. His duchy of Lancaster was by far the largest private estate in England. And yet Henry was broke.

It was not wildly unusual for the king to be insolvent or even technically bankrupt – throughout the middle ages the Crown was almost always in debt – although it must be said that Henry's financial problems were unusually severe.[12] The greater problem was one of perception: debt was generally tolerated in times of military success, domestic order and convincing royal leadership; at times of distress and disorder, it became a serious political problem. The common idea, which in many ways reflected reality, was that lands which should have supplied a stable income to the Crown, even if only to cover the costs of the royal household, were carved up for personal gain by the men who governed in the king's name. 'So poor a king was never seen,' went the subversive popular song.[13] Technically this was not entirely accurate, but the impression was what mattered.

The first utterances of public disaffection were probably in the taverns and townhouses, from the mouths of men like the unfortunate Thomas Kerver. But in November 1449, when a parliament met to address the dire distress of Normandy, the anger of England's political classes was made absolutely plain. Parliament opened in Westminster, before moving to Blackfriars in London for a few weeks, on account of the 'infected air'. Whatever plague hung in the air, it was not nearly so deadly as the wrath of England's commons.

Parliament had ostensibly been called by the king to deal with 'certain difficult and urgent business concerning the governance and [defence] of his realm of England'. But very swiftly the search began for someone to blame. The news of Rouen's loss was fresh and raw. Every day brought new defeats, and there was a fear that once Normandy fell, Calais would be next. Since it was impossible for parliament to turn on the king himself – direct criticism of the king was politically dangerous and implied serious constitutional crisis – his leading ministers would have to suffer for their evil counsel.

The first to face retribution was Adam Moleyns, the bishop of Chichester, keeper of the privy seal and a man whose hand touched virtually every aspect of royal business. For fifteen years Moleyns had served as a high-ranking ambassador and clerk (and subsequently a full member) of the privy council. Closely allied to Suffolk, he had been a key figure in the negotiations for the royal marriage, and a member of the diplomatic party that had formalised the cession of Maine. He had fallen out with Richard duke of York, publicly accusing him of corruption and incompetence during his French lieutenancy. Moleyns was a thoughtful and talented humanist scholar, but his career as a politician had ultimately been a failure and he was associated with almost every disastrous decision that had been made with regard to France. Having attended the first session of the parliament, he was granted royal leave to stand down from his secular duties and leave the country on a pilgrimage. He never made it out of England. He was in Portsmouth on 9 January 1450 when he was attacked and murdered by one Cuthbert Colville, a military captain who was waiting to embark to fight in France.

It was widely said that as he died, Moleyns cursed Suffolk as the author of all England's misfortune. Whether this is true we will never know, but the rumour spread far and wide throughout England. The king's chief minister would clearly be the next to face the anger of the realm.

Parliament broke for Christmas. As soon as it reconvened on 22 January, Suffolk tried to pre-empt the attack he knew to be coming. In the Painted Chamber at Westminster, richly decorated on every side with ancient murals of scenes from the Old Testament, he stood before the king and parliament and denounced 'the odious and horrible language that runneth through your land, almost in every commons' mouth, owning to my highest charge and most heaviest disclaundre [i.e. slander]'. The de la Pole family, he argued, had been conspicuously loyal, sacrificing almost everything in the name of the Crown: Suffolk's father had died at Harfleur, 'mine eldest brother after . . . at the battle of Agincourt'. Three more brothers had died in foreign service and he himself had paid £20,000 in ransom money after being captured at Jargeau in 1429. He had borne arms for thirty-four winters. He had been a knight of the Garter for thirty years. Since returning from war, he pleaded, he had 'continually served about your most noble person [fifteen] year[s], in the which I have found as great grace and goodness, as ever liegeman found in his sovereign lord'.[14] The impassioned appeal to Henry's pity would save Suffolk's life, but not for long.

How had it come to this? Since the 1430s, Suffolk had played a vital role in English government, managing relations between the royal household, the council and the nobility, and in general he had done so with the approval of those who understood just how disastrously ineffective and inert the king was. Yet in the winter of 1450, Suffolk was on his own. The nobility who might have been expected to rally to the defence of Normandy had conspicuously failed to do so. In fact, gradually since 1447, many of them had stopped attending council meetings and stayed away from court. Effectively, they had abandoned the government, leaving Suffolk and his diminishing group of allies looking increasingly like a domestic clique around the king, subverting his power for their own gain and ruining the country in the process.[15] When he was deserted by his fellow peers, Suffolk's method of rule – directing government minutely but disguising his hand – was brutally exposed. Since he, even more than Moleyns, had been at the heart of royal government for the years of greatest calamity, he would have to take the blame.

Suffolk's plea of loyalty had no effect whatever on the commons. The lower house of parliament tended to be far less sympathetic to failures of noble government than the lords. Four days after the duke's speech, they petitioned the king for Suffolk to be jailed on 'a generalty' – a non-specific charge by which he could be held until a detailed impeachment case could be put against him. There was something close to hysteria whipping around parliament. 'From every party of England there is come among them a great rumour and fame, how that this realm of England should be sold to the king's adversary of France,' stated the petition, by way of justifying its demands: a ludicrous notion, but one that spoke of the extreme political tension in the air.

On 7 February 1450 Suffolk was formally impeached of 'high, great, heinous and horrible treasons'. He was accused of inviting the French to invade England, stirring the king to release Charles duke of Orléans, giving away Maine and Le Mans, passing diplomatic and military secrets to the French, embezzling money through grants of office, tricking the king into granting him lands and titles, including the earldom of Pembroke, which he had held since 1443, giving money to the queen of France, and generally aiding and abetting Charles VII against the English Crown. Scurrilous gossip was written up into formal accusation, including the somewhat implausible suggestion that the night before the duke's capture at the battle of Jargeau, 'he lay in bed with a nun whom he took out of her holy orders and defiled'.[16] A month later, on 9 March, the duke, having been given time to prepare his defence, knelt before the king and parliament and denied the charges one by one, 'and said, saving the king's high presence, they were false and untrue'.[17]

On 17 March, Henry VI summoned all the lords of parliament, including Suffolk, to his private chamber, 'with a gable window over a cloister, within his palace of Westminster'.[18] Kneeling before the assembled lords and king, Suffolk once more protested his innocence, pointing out that it would have been quite impossible for him alone to have committed the long list of crimes of which he was accused. He waived his right to trial by his peers, and threw himself on the king's judgement. Then Henry, through the chancellor, told the lords that he did not find Suffolk guilty of any counts of treason. Rather, he said, there were several lesser charges (known as misprisions) for which the duke could be held responsible. Rather than condemning Suffolk to a traitor's death, he banished him from the kingdom for five years. The sentence was to begin on 1 May.

Despite the lack of a formal trial by peers, it is likely that this was a judgement that had been taken with the lords, whose desire to prevent one of their number from being humiliated by the commons outweighed their desire to see all blame for the realm's ills conveniently fall on Suffolk's shoulders. No record exists of this news being transmitted to the commons, but it is safe to speculate that it was met with something between astonishment and rage.

On 19 March, in the dead of night, the duke was removed from London and taken to his manor of East Thorp, in the county of Suffolk. The journey was supposed to be secret, but around two thousand angry Londoners nevertheless chased the party, jostling and abusing Suffolk's servants all the way. By removing the target of popular disgruntlement, the lords had only served to increase the thirst for blood among their countrymen. A riot broke out in London two days later, in which the leader, a vintner's servant called John Frammesley, was heard to shout, 'By this town, by this town, for this array the king shall lose his crown.'[19] Parliament was prorogued for Easter on 30 March. By now it was clear that the situation in and around London would be too dangerous for it to continue sitting after the break.

The final session on 29 April thus opened in Leicester, one hundred miles to the north of the capital. On the first day of the new session the king was presented with yet another petition: this time calling upon him to issue an act of resumption, by which all lands originally belonging to the Crown or to the king's private estate, the duchy of Lancaster, 'in England, Wales, and in the marches therof, Ireland, Guînes, Calais, and in the marches thereof, the which ye have granted by your letters patent or otherwise, since the first day of your reign' would be taken back, in an attempt to bolster the royal income. In other words, everything that had been given away by royal favour would now be taken back. It is quite likely that this had been demanded for some time, but demands were now all the louder and more persistent. The king had chosen to save his favourite. The government would therefore have to satisfy the calls for reform in some other radical way.

As the Leicester session of parliament debated the proposed act of resumption, Suffolk was on the east coast of England, in Ipswich, preparing to leave for his sentence of banishment. He and his servants set sail on 30 April in a small fleet of two ships and 'a little spinner' – a lighter craft, which we would now call a pinnace – heading for Calais, from where he could make his way to the duke of Burgundy's lands. Before leaving, Suffolk swore on the sacrament that he was innocent of the charges put before him. Others, however, were not so sure.

The ships reached the straits of Dover the following day and the pinnace had gone ahead to make contact with the Calais garrison when, as one correspondent put it, they 'met a ship called Nicholas of the Tower, with other ships waiting on them, and [from those in the pinnace] the master of the Nicholas had knowledge of the duke's coming'. Suffolk's ships were intercepted and the duke was persuaded or commanded to board the *Nicholas*, 'and when he came, the master bade him, "Welcome Traitor"'. According to the same correspondent, Suffolk was held aboard for twenty-four hours, with the agreement of all its crew. The writer heard a rumour that the crew had set up their own tribunal to re-try the duke on the charges he had faced in parliament.

What is more certain is that after a period of time aboard the *Nicholas* Suffolk was removed to a smaller boat with a chaplain to shrive him, 'and there was an axe and a stoke [i.e. a chopping block], and one of the lewdest of the ship' – later named in court as a sailor from Bosham called Richard Lenard – 'bade him lay down his head . . . and took a rusty sword, and smote off his head within half a dozen strokes'. Suffolk's servants were put ashore, robbed but unharmed, to tell their tale. Two days later the duke's body was found dumped on Dover beach, with his head standing next to it on a pole.[20]

*

The news of Suffolk's death reached parliament in Leicester on 6 May. It was the final shock that forced the royal government to accept the act of resumption (albeit with an extensive list of exemptions, which somewhat blunted its practical effect). A sense of general crisis had by this time escaped the confines of parliament. Towards the end of May 1450 men began to gather in bands across south-west Kent. The county had been in a state of some alarm for around six weeks: the military collapse in Normandy had awakened fears that once Charles VII's soldiers reached the coast, they would cross the Channel and attack or even invade England, in which case Kent would be one of the first places to suffer. Coastal raids were bloody and terrifying experiences. On 14 April the royal government had issued a commission of array: a command to raise the county militia in every Kentish hundred (the local unit of county administration), assessing each community for its readiness to protect the realm. Men were selected to serve in a potential defence force and provided with clothing, some equipment, money and armour. A night watch of the coast would have been organised. Perhaps most importantly, constables were appointed to take command of each hundred's militia.[21]

This was a perfectly reasonable notion, given the gravity of the perceived threat from across the Channel. However, at the same time as the county was being put into a state of military readiness, Suffolk's murder triggered a panicked rumour that the king intended to hold Kent communally responsible for the death of his favourite. It was said variously that a visiting court would carry out exemplary hangings of ordinary Kentish folk and that the whole county was going to be razed and turned into royal forest. The people of Kent were therefore armed, organised, angry, frightened and ready to go to war to defend the realm from its enemies.

Unfortunately, they did not see enemies only in the spectre of plundering Frenchmen aboard landing craft. Like the parliamentary commons, they began to see the true threat to the king's realm as the clique around him: ministers and household men like the treasurer Lord Saye, the prominent councillor and royal confessor William Aiscough, bishop of Salisbury, the diplomat John, Lord Dudley and several others. On 6 June word reached these men, and the rest of parliament assembled at Leicester, that Kent had risen in rebellion, and armed bands were assembling around Ashford, in the south-east. It was said that they had elected as their leader and the 'captain of Kent' a man called Jack Cade, who was going by the suggestively aristocratic name of John Mortimer – a name he may have adopted to imply an affiliation to the duke of York's family, who in past generations had been the instigators of rebellion and dynastic plot. (See above, p. 88.) This was nothing more than fantasy, however: Cade had no contact or connection with York, who was then still in Ireland providing loyal service to the Crown.

Cade was to prove a highly effective captain and leader capable of articulating a sophisticated programme of reform that appealed to men of considerable status: his lieutenants included the Sussex gentleman Robert Poynings, the son of a peer who agreed to serve as Cade's sword-bearer. One song that survives makes the rebels' high intentions – a purge of government – quite clear:

> God be our guide,
> And then shall we speed.
> Whosoever say nay,
> False for their money ruleth!
> Truth for his tales spoileth!
> God send us a fair day!
> Away, traitors, away![22]

Henry VI was sent back to London, and two separate commissions of lords were sent to Kent to try and squash the rising: one headed by the king's cousin Humphrey Stafford, duke of Buckingham, and the other a party of decorated war veterans led by Viscount Beaumont, the constable of England.

By the time they had ridden south, the rebels had moved west: by 11 June they were encamped on Blackheath, just downriver of London. This was the camping-ground of the men who had risen in the so-called Peasants' Revolt, during the summer of 1381. By 13 June the king was lodged in St John's Priory in Clerkenwell, most of the important lords and bishops were in London, and Jack Cade's men had been established just a few miles from the capital for several days.

After an uneasy stand-off, on 16 June negotiators from the government met with the rebels at Blackheath to try and establish their terms for dispersal. The king would not come in person, and after two days of fruitless discussions, on the night of 17 June the rebels retreated from Blackheath back into Kent. But this was no wilting. Sir Humphrey Stafford and William Stafford, kinsmen of the duke of Buckingham, led a force of about four hundred men into Kent to chastise the rebels. Yet when they went into battle near Tonbridge, they were ambushed and slaughtered. Both Staffords were killed.

A half-hearted attempt was made to subdue Kent, but it had little effect. Large numbers of the forces supposedly loyal to the king and his magnates lost their nerve and threatened to defect to the rebel side. Calls went up from the Crown's own troops for the trial of so-called traitors: Saye, Dudley, Aiscough and others. On 19 June, London dissolved again into rioting, and in response to the mayhem Henry gave his permission for Lord Saye's arrest as a traitor and imprisonment in the Tower of London. The following day word was given that further offenders would be arrested.

On 25 June Henry and his council abandoned London, leaving the defence of the city to the mayor. There was deep discomfort in the king's household. Henry and his retinue rode north to Kenilworth in Warwickshire, where they took shelter in the splendid palace-fortress, hiding behind the moat and thick stone walls and sending urgent word to nearby counties asking for the recruitment of soldiers to guard Henry's life.

As soon as he heard of the king's flight, Cade immediately marched his men back to Blackheath. They arrived between Wednesday 1 July and Thursday 2 July, then moved upriver to Southwark, where they took over the local inns and taverns, effectively occupying the suburb at the foot of London Bridge. At the same time a rising in Essex saw men marching out of the countryside on the north bank of the Thames, fanning out before the city walls around the Aldgate. Just as it had been in 1381, London was besieged.

Unlike in 1381, when the demands of the rebels had been somewhat vague and jumbled, Cade's men had a very clear idea of their political demands. The sixteenth-century antiquarian John Stow collected and transcribed a number of original documents relating to the revolt, one of which is Cade's manifesto.[23]

In the first place, the 'commons of Kent' repeated the rumour that 'it is openly noised that Kent should be destroyed with a royal power, and made a wild forest, for the death of the Duke of Suffolk, of which the commons of Kent were never guilty'. The manifesto went on to condemn various detestable practices in government, complaining that the king was being stirred by his minions to 'live only on his commons, and other men to have revenues of the crown, the which hath caused poverty in his excellency and great payments of the people'. It was claimed that 'the Lords of his royal blood have been put from his daily presence, and other mean persons of lower nature exalted and made chief of his privy council'; that purveyance – the odious practice of forcibly requisitioning goods from ordinary people to support the royal household – was 'undoing' the 'poor commons of this Realm'; that the legal process for protecting land and goods and obtaining justice in the royal courts was being subverted by 'the King's menial servants'; that an inquiry was needed to investigate the loss of royal lands in France; that MPs in Kent were not being freely elected; that the offices of tax collectors were being distributed by bribery; and miscellaneous other local laments and grievances.

At every point in his rebellion Cade attempted to prove that he was more than simply a freewheeling lout, but rather that he spoke to and for the 'poor commons' both in Kent and the realm at large. This was no easy task since, like all principled popular risings, Cade's rebellion had attracted large numbers of unscrupulous criminals who used the general mood of chaos as an excuse to burn, loot, pillage and murder. This was not just the case in London: as word of the disorder spread throughout England, violent attacks were made on all manner of hated local officials and dignitaries, including most shockingly Bishop Aiscough of Salisbury, who was robbed and murdered by a mob in Wiltshire on 29 June. All the same, in London, at the heart of the rebellion, Cade did his best to lead his men with a semblance of military order, which included beheading one of his captains on Blackheath for indiscipline.

Even this sort of exemplary justice could not keep all the rebels in check. Henry, hiding terrified in Kenilworth, played directly into Cade's hands. When the rebel leader arrived at Southwark he received word from the king's household that he was to be allowed to set up a 'royal' court to try traitors. The Crown had sunk so far into torpor and fear that its authority could now be exercised by anyone who rose up to take it. On 3 July Cade and his men advanced from Southwark to London. They were resisted by the London militia, but managed to fight their way across London Bridge, cutting the ropes of the drawbridge to ensure that it would remain open after they entered the city. Cade made proclamations around the city that order was to be kept and that robbers would be executed, then moved on to the Guildhall to set up his court for traitors.

Around twenty prisoners were brought before the court, where the mayor and aldermen were forced to sit in judgement. The unfortunate victims were led by the royal treasurer Lord Saye, who was dragged out of the Tower of London to face his fate. Saye begged for a trial before his peers, but Cade refused. The mob wanted blood. He was permitted only to see a priest before being dragged to Cheapside, where he was beheaded on a block in the centre of the street. Later his son-in-law, William Crowmer, the sheriff of Kent, was pulled out of the Fleet prison and taken outside the city gates to Mile End, where he too was hacked to death. Saye's body was roped to Cade's horse and paraded around the city. The treasurer's head was stuck on a spear, and displayed at various places in the city, where it was made to 'kiss' Crowmer's similarly impaled head, in a grotesque and morbid puppet show.

A number of other men were similarly slaughtered under Cade's temporary rule. Predictably, the longer the captain kept his men in the city, the more futile his attempts to keep order became. By the evening of 5 July, the mayor and aldermen had

managed to array a military force under Lord Scales and Mat-
thew Gough, two veterans of the French wars, and were prepared to lead a counter-attack against the occupying rebels. A
battle began on London Bridge at around 10 p.m. and raged
through the night, concluding long after sunrise the next morning. Hundreds of men crowded onto the tight causeway across
the Thames, fighting hand to hand by torchlight. Cade, in an
act of desperation, had broken open the Marshalsea prison in
Southwark, flooding his ranks with freed prisoners. But he could
not break past Scales and Gough's defensive lines. In a final act of
reckless rage, the rebels set fire to the wooden drawbridge, choking the battle site with smoke and sending men at the heart of the
fight tumbling from the bridge to drown in the cold water below.
Finally, in the mayhem, the gates on the London side of the
bridge were bolted shut. Hundreds of bloody and burned bodies
were left outside, including that of Gough and the alderman John
Sutton. The rebels had been driven back to Southwark.

The following day, 7 July, on the advice of the queen, who
had – remarkably and bravely – remained during the rebellion
at her manor of Greenwich, the Kentishmen were offered a
chance to take charters of pardon and disperse. Many welcomed
the opportunity, but Cade refused, preferring to withdraw once
again to Kent, taking with him goods and treasure that had been
plundered (quite at variance with his own commands) and vow-
ing to continue the fight. But his luck had run out. On 10 July
Cade was officially denounced as a traitor and a bounty of one
thousand marks was put on his head. After several days' flight
he was captured 'in a garden' at Heathfield in Sussex by Alexander Iden, who had replaced the unlucky Crowmer as sheriff
of Kent.[24] Cade fought to the last, and although he was taken
alive, he died of his injuries on the road. Justice thereafter could
only be symbolic: Cade's corpse was beheaded at Newgate on
16 July, taken around the city as far as Southwark for public

viewing, then returned to Newgate to be chopped into quarters. His head, rather appropriately, was put on a pole above London Bridge, lifeless eyes staring down over the scorched remains of an extraordinary urban battle site.

Cade's revolt was over but tension smouldered throughout the summer. The king, his household and the nobles who had joined him at Kenilworth crept back towards London at the end of the month: on 28 July a service of thanksgiving was held at St Paul's Cathedral, and a month later a high-ranking judicial commission of oyer and terminer, including Humphrey duke of Buckingham, the archbishops of Canterbury and York, and the bishop of Winchester, was sent into the country to investigate the abuses that had been decried in the rebel manifesto.

Many towns and villages in the south-east of England remained dangerously volatile: several other individuals tried to raise Kent, Essex and Sussex into rebellion during the autumn, gangs of robbers roamed the countryside looting and killing, and London simmered constantly. Soldiers returning from Normandy swelled the urban population and veterans committed several offences against the heraldic arms of Lord Saye, including vandalising the stone that marked his burial place at the Greyfriars. In August the Tower was broken into and the armoury there was robbed of many of its weapons. The autumn saw disturbances in reaction to the routine election of a new mayor, while bill-posters railing against the government appeared all over the city and at one stage a disgruntled keeper of Newgate prison started a riot by setting all the inmates free.

At every level, 1450 had been a year of strife, violence, chaos and terror, the product of a gradually building crisis in government that stemmed ultimately from the vacuity of the twenty-eight-year-old king. For years Henry's semi-absent kingship had been managed by a succession of patches and muddles: first by a minority council that balanced the differing views of his uncles against the corporate will of the lords, then by the rule of Suffolk, whose command of government was constructed through his own connections in the council, the royal household and the countryside. Neither of these had proven to be a satisfactory solution and Suffolk's rule had collapsed into murderous chaos and rebellion, of which Suffolk himself had been the first victim. Yet if they had succeeded in destroying a supposed governing clique, the protestors had done precisely nothing to address the root of all the country's ills. Following Suffolk's death and Cade's rebellion, Henry's personal incompetence remained as pressing a problem as ever. Another man would soon thrust himself actively into the centre of political life in an attempt to address it. In September, Richard duke of York returned from Ireland to make his own bid to rescue England from its dizzying decline.

8 : Then Bring In the Duke of York

A small fleet of ships sailed towards Beaumaris, a port town on the south-eastern tip of Anglesey that jostled in the shadow of a vast, turreted stone fortress. The castle, with its deep outer moat, defensive walls soaring more than thirty feet in the air, and twenty-two stout and round towers slitted all over with arrow-holes, had been the most expensive of Edward I's large ring of Welsh fortresses. It was so huge, and its design so ambitious, that parts of the building, begun over 150 years earlier, had never been fully completed. What did stand was an ominous symbol of English royal power on the fringes of the king's territories. Beaumaris was a formidable place to approach.

It was early September 1450 and the ships had been expected for some days. They carried Richard duke of York, the king's cousin and lieutenant in Ireland, and his men. York had left Dublin on 28 August, and the news of his coming had shaken Henry VI and his advisers. Instructions had been issued for the town to be on its guard. The captain of Beaumaris, Thomas Norris, was waiting along with several other local officers of the Crown. They had been told very firmly to delay York, and they sent a message to the duke at sea informing him (as he would later complain) 'that I should not land there, nor have vitaile [i.e. food], nor refreshing for me and my fellowship . . . for man, horse nor other thing that might turn to my worschip or ease'.[1] York was told that the commands issued directly from William Say, usher of Henry VI's chamber, who was convinced that he came unbidden, as a 'traitor'. He was refused permission to disembark; his ships were forced to stay at sea in search of another, friendlier, landing spot.[2]

York's ships finally landed near the mouth of the river Clwyd, some twenty-five miles along the coast of northern Wales. By 7 September the duke and his retinue had reached his own castle at Denbigh. From there they rode to Ludlow, and from Ludlow they crossed the midlands. As York travelled, he amassed followers: armed men from his extensive lands throughout Wales and England. On 23 September a writer in Stony Stratford, Northamptonshire, saw the duke appear in stately magnificence: 'riding in red velvet, on a black horse and Irish hobby'. He would lodge that night in a tavern outside the town gates, called the Red Lion.[3] He did not stay long: on 27 September he arrived in London, entering the city with three to five thousand men under his banner, marching through the streets and then out of the gates and down the short road from London to Westminster, where he was received in a short meeting by his beleaguered cousin, the king.

The panic that York's unscheduled return from Ireland struck into the heart of the royal administration was easy to understand. Jack Cade, whose rising had brought an entire summer of chaos to the realm, had called himself 'John Mortimer', deliberately implying that he was related to the duke. Cade's articles of grievance warned that, unless there was reform, the commons of England would 'first destroy the king's friends and after himself and then bring in the duke of York to be king'.[4] And plenty of other, pettier rebels had also invoked York's name in opposition to the royal government.

In 1449, when Henry VI had been travelling to Leicester for the session of parliament, he had also ridden through the town of Stony Stratford. A local writer recorded that as the king's entourage passed through the streets one 'John Harris, sometime a shipman dwelling in York' approached the king waving a flail – a wooden agricultural tool, sometimes used as an improvised weapon, consisting of a long handle with a shorter pole attached to the end by a chain. Egged on by others in the town, Harris had beaten the ground in front of Henry with the flail, crying that he meant 'to show that the Duke of York then in Ireland should in like manner fight with traitors at the Leicester parliament and so thrash them down as he had thrashed the clods of earth in that town'.[5] For this impudence Harris was arrested, thrown in the dungeon at Northampton Castle and later hanged, drawn and quartered. But his point had been made: as the people of England rejected the regime around Henry, so they projected their dreams of national recovery onto the duke across the Irish Sea.

There is no reason to believe that York had courted this. He was unquestionably the greatest English lord, a man of royal blood and huge landed power, which gave him much the same status as had once been possessed by John duke of Bedford and Humphrey duke of Gloucester. He was relatively untainted by the political failures of the previous three years: his time as lieutenant of France had preceded the dramatic loss of Normandy that took place on the duke of Somerset's watch, and his time as lieutenant of Ireland had taken him away from the centre of politics at precisely the moment when Suffolk's regime dissolved into blood and blame.

But this is not to say that York was a rebel-in-waiting. He would always claim that his return from Ireland was an act of obedience: a move designed to assure the king of his loyalty against 'diverse language . . . said of me to your most excellent estate which should sound to my dishonour and reproach' – in other words, to demonstrate that whatever claims were being made of his ambition, he was a loyal subject. In bills drawn up and sent to the king, probably in the first weeks of his return from Ireland, he wrote that he had come to England in order to assure the king of his loyalty and to 'declare me your true man and subject as my [duty] is'.[6] Yet touring England and Wales in the company of thousands of armed retainers was a provocative way to demonstrate loyalty. Why, then, did he come?

It is possible, but unlikely, that York left Ireland out of dynastic ambition. His 'true blood' had been noted by the Kentish rebels, but this was hardly a novel observation. The king was certainly childless and the matter of his heir apparent had not been formally addressed, but by the same token none of the noble promotions of the dukes of Somerset, Exeter or Buckingham constituted a direct threat to York's lineage. In the case of Exeter, York's superior blood-status was explicitly recognised in the first duke of Exeter's articles of ennoblement. The first duke died in 1447, but his heir, the young Henry Holland, was even more closely tied to York's family: he was married to York's daughter Anne, and had been in York's custody when he was a minor. As recently as 1448 York and the duke of Somerset had been granted lands in joint trusteeship – a sign that there was no division (yet) perceived between those two men.[7] Humphrey duke of Buckingham showed no signs of anything other than diligent loyalty to the Crown. In short, there was no dynastic crisis calling York home: despite the turbulence of the reign and the wild claims of Cade's men, the king was not ill and showed no signs of imminent death, merely prolonged ineptitude.[8]

In 1451 Thomas Young, MP for Bristol and one of York's legal counsellors, would stand in parliament and suggest that for the security of the realm the king should name his heir apparent. Unsurprisingly Young nominated York and was duly arrested for his impertinence. If anything, such claims actively damaged York's political standing. Whatever the rebels of Kent, the tavern-room gossips or upstart lawyers in the commons thought, York's desire to force his claim to the crown, either immediately or in the near future, was precisely nil.

What he saw for himself, rather, was a role as a sort of saviour of both crown and country. York and his wife Cecily had initially sailed to take up residence in Ireland on 22 June 1449. During the fourteen months that he had spent overseas, England had suffered the worst collapse of government, foreign policy and public order in a lifetime – arguably since the early thirteenth century. Normandy had been lost, parliament had revolted wholesale, the duke of Suffolk had been murdered, a violent and continuing popular rebellion had engulfed the entire south-east of England. And while it was true that York had played his part in the makings of the crisis – he was a prominent member of the nobility that had allowed, or at least acquiesced in, the rule of Suffolk and the royal household over a non-functioning king – he had also, by his fortunate removal from France and posting to Ireland, avoided any serious blame. Quite the opposite, in fact: all the news that reached him in Ireland would have given him the impression that his destiny and duty was now to rescue England from the chaos into which it had sunk. His royal blood gave him the prerogative. The thousands of men whom he could put at his disposal gave him the means. York had served as the king's hand in France and now in Ireland; the logical next step was to offer his services for the same role within England itself.

What the duke had perhaps not fully calculated, however, was the extent to which his desire to respond to calls for his return might be seen by some around the king not as a kindly offer but as a grave threat. First his ships were turned away from Beaumaris. Then, as York had ridden through north Wales, he had learned of rumours that a number of knights connected with the royal household intended to capture him, imprison him in Conwy Castle and 'strike off the head' of a number of his servants, including his chamberlain, the veteran soldier Sir William Oldhall. Finally, he had heard that certain unspecified judicial commissions had been issued to indict him for treason, and thereby to 'undo me, mine issue and corrupt [my] blood'.[9] He returned to England hoping to claim his position as the king's reformer-in-chief but found on his arrival that this cast him in the role of the government's most dangerous opponent.

*

York's armed parade through London on 27 September put the febrile city in an even greater state of excitement than usual. Following his short meeting with Henry at Westminster, the duke lodged for a fortnight at the bishop of Salisbury's house in London. From there he began to stake his claim to the central position in government for which he had come out of Ireland.

Since his arrival in England, York had been exchanging bills and letters with the king. His first bill, sent shortly after landing in Wales, complained that he had been treated as a traitor and a criminal at Beaumaris. This was dealt with matter-of-factly in the reply from Henry, which explained patiently that since for 'a long time the people hath given upon you much strange language . . . saying that you should be fetched home with many thousands' to seize the crown, the coasts had been instructed to guard against such a thing. In other words, Henry suggested, his men had overreacted and 'we declare, repute and admit you as our true faithful subject and as our well beloved cousin'.

York remained affronted. At some point after their meeting in Westminster he sent Henry a second bill, ignoring the king's calming words and pointing out that law and order appeared to be collapsing in England, and that 'I your humble subject and liege man Richard Duke of York . . . offer . . . to execute your commandments'. He offered, in effect, to take over command of English government in its moment of crisis. This bill, unlike the first, seems to have been widely publicised among the people of London. It was somewhere between an open letter and a manifesto.[10] Once again, he was politely rebuffed. Rather than handing over government to York, Henry said he intended to 'establish [a] sad and substantial council . . . in the which we have appointed you to be one'.[11] This was plainly not the answer that York was looking for. He left London on 9 October, heading first for East Anglia, and then touring his estates in the midlands. Behind him, London stewed in a state of barely contained agitation. The streets were overrun with soldiers, who rioted during the mayoral elections on 29 October. There were frequent clashes between those who supported and those who opposed the duke of York: across the city the royal arms were torn down and replaced with those of York, restored and then torn down again. If England's capital reflected the mood in the country at large, then peace lay a long way away.

Among the chief impediments to York's taking a central role in government was the fact that someone else had already taken that post. Edmund Beaufort, duke of Somerset, had come back from his catastrophic tenure in Normandy not to be censured or chastised, but rather to find himself appointed to more or less the position that York envisaged for himself.[12] Within two weeks of his returning from France in August of 1450 he was attending council meetings. On 8 September he had been put in charge of stamping out the embers of revolt in Kent and the south-east and on 11 September he was appointed constable: the highest military post in England.

Like York, Somerset was a kinsman of the king. Unlike York, he had close links to Queen Margaret, just as he had been close to Henry's late mother, Catherine de Valois. As a nephew of Cardinal Beaufort he was a familiar and comforting figure to Henry, whereas York was more of an outsider. Somerset also benefited from having no significant landed estates to manage; he was able to devote his full attention to the business of government, taking on tasks that had previously fallen to Suffolk: those of concealing the vacuity of the king, allying the disparate interests of house-hold, council and nobility, and somehow attempting to cope with the righteous anger of the commons. Assuming this task set Somerset on a direct collision course with York. Tension between the two men would dominate politics over the next five years.

Parliament met at Westminster on 6 November 1450, and immediately the two dukes and their supporters collided. Chains had been erected in the streets of London in an attempt to limit the excesses of what the chancellor, Cardinal John Kemp, archbishop of York, described as 'the people of riotous disposition'.[13] It was hard to avoid the sense that the capital was on the point of eruption, and that the fate of England hinged on the next action taken by the duke of York.

He arrived at Westminster on 23 November, one day before John Mowbray, duke of Norfolk, his chief ally since his return from Ireland. Both men, and indeed all the lords who attended the November parliament, brought with them large armed retinues. The author of one chronicle of the period describes seeing York come 'riding [through] the city his sword born afore him', a mark of great pomp and authority.[14] There was an atmosphere of barely constrained violence. One important element in York's adoption of the mantle of reform was to take a bitterly critical stance towards the 'traitors' who had allowed Normandy to be lost. No one was under any illusion: this meant Somerset. On 30 November a series of rancorous arguments broke out within the parliament chamber at Westminster Hall. Several MPs demanded that justice be done against those who had failed so miserably to protect the king's possessions in France.

During parliament's session Somerset was staying at the Blackfriars, a pleasant Dominican house within the western wall of the city just next to the Ludgate, at the point where the river Fleet spilled down into the Thames. On Tuesday 1 December, while the duke was eating, a large band of soldiers tried to break into the house in an attempt to arrest him. The danger to Somerset's life was so acute that he was smuggled out of the house by the riverside quay and taken downriver on a boat, while the rioters remained at Blackfriars, ransacking and looting. Intriguingly, Somerset's saviours were the mayor of London and another increasingly close Yorkist ally, Thomas Courtenay, earl of Devon, who was said to be acting on York's direct instructions.

Earlier that day, the same group of men had authorised the public execution of a rioter. As London's streets seethed with protest and disaffection, York was attempting to play both reforming firebrand and lawgiver. Like the late Humphrey of Gloucester, whose memory he seemed increasingly to cherish and defend, York wished to use his popularity with the common people as a platform from which to disrupt the political process and state his own claim to pre-eminence. In fact, he was just being a nuisance.

It was not York's actions that eventually put the city into some sort of order, but a parade of all the lords of England united, riding through London on 3 December. As one chronicler put it, '. . . upon the Thursday the next day following the king with all the lords come through the City all in harness [i.e. wearing full armour] and the citizens standing upon every side of the street in harness, which was the gloriest sight that ever man in those days saw.'[15]

London's mood began to cool. York's pandering to the populace had won him no favour whatever with the majority of the lords. He remained close to the duke of Norfolk, but when Christmas came, parliament recessed and the streets ceased to seethe, York found that his support was drifting away. He was appointed to a judicial commission in the new year to carry out justice on the Kent rebels, forcing a natural separation from the men who had cried his name the loudest.

In the new year, Somerset, released from his protective custody in the Tower, resumed control of government, this time with some success. He took the king into the shires to suppress another uprising, this time led by one Stephen Christmas. This was followed by further exemplary punishment of rebels. In an attempt

to bring more landed revenue back under Crown control Somerset allowed a new act of resumption to pass parliament and
began to try to raise money to defend Gascony, the next portion
of English France that Charles VII was determined to conquer.
He even managed to deal, after a fashion, with a long-running
private war between the warring Courtenay and Bonville families, whose murderous feuding continued to cause chaos in the
west country.[16] York, meanwhile, appeared ever more to resemble
a rabble-rouser rather than the agent of order and peace. His
client and counsellor Thomas Young's parliamentary petition of
May 1451 demanding that York be recognised as heir presumptive caused parliament to be more or less instantly dissolved and
for York to be wholly excluded from any role in government. The
duke's great play to rescue the crown by inserting himself at its
right hand had, it seemed, come to nothing. He spent the rest of
the year on his estates, brooding.

*

The collegiate church of St Martin-le-Grand in the north-west
quarter of the city of London, abutting the Greyfriars on one side
and the Goldsmiths' Hall on the other, had a long history of independence. Anyone who entered the college claiming the right of
sanctuary could – if their request was granted – be hidden inside
the precincts, shielded by the charters of privilege which had long
ago been granted to its inhabitants. For this reason, the college
had for years been a favourite hideaway for criminals, ne'er-do-
wells and escaped prisoners to run to for protection from the vengeance of the law.[17]

Among its community in January 1452 was Sir William Oldhall, chamberlain to the duke of York, and a prominent politician
who had served as the Speaker of the November 1450 parliament. Oldhall had taken to St Martin-le-Grand before dawn on
23 November 1451, prompted, as the dean of the college would

later write, 'by fear of heavy imprisonment, and greatly alarmed for his life'.[18] He was accused, most immediately, of having taken part in the looting of Somerset's possessions from the house of the Blackfriars in 1450, but there were also wild allegations circulating that he had been plotting on York's behalf to stage a coup in which the king was to be kidnapped. That such a plan was really afoot seems highly improbable, but Oldhall's fear for his life was very real.

So too was Somerset's desire to punish him. During the night of 18 January Walter de Burgh – the man who had accused Oldhall of looting Somerset's goods – was attacked in the street by three strangers and left for dead. In response, Somerset sent a high-ranking delegation to St Martin's. The earls of Salisbury, Wiltshire and Worcester, along with two barons, one of London's sheriffs and a posse of servants, broke into the college shortly before midnight. They were, in the dean's pious words, 'armed with grievous force, not having the fear of God before their eyes', and they proceeded to smash 'all the doors and chests' they could see, looking for Oldhall's hideout. Eventually they found him, concealed in the nave of the church. Oldhall was dragged out, loaded onto a horse and bundled off to the palace of Westminster to be interrogated.

Breaches of sanctuary were serious matters. They were both illegal and offensive to God. And indeed, Oldhall's removal caused such outrage and protest at St Martin-le-Grand that within forty-eight hours he had been returned and placed back under holy protection, where he would remain for more than three years. It was a miserable period in his life. But more significantly, Oldhall's removal from sanctuary marked an escalation in the feud between the duke of York and the government, represented as it was by Edmund duke of Somerset.

York's position was impossible to sustain. He was too great a lord to be alienated from the government of a king whose inane rule demanded co-operation between the greatest men in the realm. In any event, alienation was one thing; directly attacking York's closest servants was another. It was too much to be ignored. Evidently furious with Somerset for the insult to his honour, York sent letters to most of the towns in southern England demanding that they join an orderly march on London to remove Somerset from power in the name of restoring good government to the realm. York made a great play of the fact that Charles VII's forces had all but overrun English possessions in Gascony and occupied the key city of Bordeaux: he reminded England's townsfolk of the 'derogation, loss of merchandise, lesion of honour, and villany' that had taken place in France already, and insisted that the vital trading port and last foothold of Calais was about to fall too. York insisted that he was 'the King's true liegeman and servant (and ever shall be to my life's end)'. He complained bitterly of the 'envy, malice, and untruth of the said Duke of Somerset', who, he said, 'laboreth continually about the King's highness for my undoing, and to corrupt my blood, and to disinherit me and my heirs, and such persons as be about me'.

York wished to raise his quarrel above the personal: he stressed the importance of the common weal, or the good of the country at large, and placed his personal enmity with Somerset in the context of a battle for the basic survival of England. 'Seeing that the said Duke ever prevaileth and ruleth about the King's person, and that by this means the land is likely to be destroyed, [I] am fully concluded to proceed in all haste against him with the help of my kinsmen and friends; in such wise that it shall prove to promote ease, peace, tranquillity, and safeguard of all this land,' he wrote.[19] Then, as his letters circulated, York ordered the tenants of his broadly scattered estates to take up arms and march once again with him to London.

As York marched south at the end of February, Somerset brought the king and an armed retinue out to meet him. While

York had his personal retainers and two significant allies in the earl of Devon and Lord Cobham, the king was joined by a large number of bishops and at least sixteen other lords, including the three other most senior dukes in the land: Exeter, Buckingham and Norfolk, York's erstwhile ally. It was a show of near-total unity from the lords.

The royal force camped at Blackheath, and York eventually brought his several thousand men to rest about eight miles to the east, at Dartford. They were equipped with cannon in the field, and seven ships loaded down with baggage and materiel in the Thames. Negotiations took place on 1 and 2 March. York presented a long list of grievances, 'for the great welfare and the common avail and interest of your majesty royal and of this your noble realm'. Most were levelled against Somerset, who was blamed for the loss of Normandy, for inciting the breaking of the French truce at Fougères, for failing to defend English garrisons, for plotting to sell Calais to the duke of Burgundy and for embezzling money received at the abandonment of Maine.[20]

York's grievances were insufficient to impress the king, or – more pertinently – the rest of the lords who had gathered around him determined to maintain England's fragile peace. Far from being handed control of government and Somerset's head, York was taken to London, effectively a prisoner. Word quickly circulated that the king had tricked him into submission at Dartford, by pretending that he would agree to his articles of reform and to have Somerset imprisoned on condition that York break up his army, only to go back on his word.[21] If true, this was a remarkable and unworthy piece of humbug on the part of the king and his counsellors.

Trickery or no, a fortnight after the encounter at Dartford, the duke was humiliated in public. At a ceremony in St Paul's Cathedral, he was forced to swear a long oath of allegiance to the crown. He announced himself to be a 'humble subject and liegeman' to Henry VI, and promised to bear him 'faith and truth as to my sovereign lord, and shall do all the days unto my life's end . . . I shall never hereafter take upon me to gather any routs, or make any assembly of your people, without your commandment or licence, or in my lawful defence.' As York spoke he laid his hand first upon the holy gospels, and then on the altar cross; finally he was administered the sacrament to confirm that 'with the grace of our Lord I never shall, anything attempt by way of fear or otherwise against your royal majesty and obeisance that I owe thereto'.[22]

Beyond London, England remained perilously unstable: scattered risings continued to break out in Suffolk, Kent, Warwickshire, Lincolnshire, Norfolk and elsewhere, revealing the fundamental difficulty of ordering political society at the highest level in the absence of a powerful and forthright king. Separate armed disputes continued between the greater families in Derbyshire, Gloucestershire and East Anglia, while the west country continued to convulse thanks to the dispute between the Courtenays and the Bonvilles. In Warwickshire the arrival of a new lord, Richard Neville, earl of Warwick, resulted in several serious disturbances, while in Yorkshire, a very serious clash was brewing between Neville's extended family and the traditionally dominant Percys: a dispute that would descend by the mid-1450s into something akin to a northern civil war. The dissolution of stable relations between the magnates of England gradually undermined their collective ability to stand together as they did at Dartford in March of 1452. In the short term, however, the faith of the political community lay with Edmund duke of Somerset rather than Richard duke of York. For the second time in eighteen months, York's efforts to impose himself on the crown in the name of the common good had come to nothing.

*

York's defeat handed Somerset an unquestionable mandate and he began to exert himself in government. Out of nowhere, Henry VI suddenly seemed to become a vigorous and energetic king. Law and order remained a problem, but in other areas the government began to make progress. The earl of Shrewsbury was sent to Kent to continue attempts to stem the stream of rebellions in the county. Judicial proceedings were launched against those who had supported York in his abortive Dartford rising, including a thorough destruction of Sir William Oldhall, whose life in sanctuary at St Martin-le-Grand was made daily more miserable by legal action that stripped him of most of his property and loaded him with the shameful status of an outlaw. York's position as lieutenant of Ireland was given to James Butler, the young earl of Ormond and Wiltshire, who had been close to York in 1451 but now moved decisively towards Somerset's circle. In a further mark of confidence, the court toured the marches of Wales and the east of England – areas where York held large tracts of land – dispensing justice and bringing the king into the view of his people.

There was even limited success across the Channel. Early in 1452 the government had begun to suggest, apparently in all seriousness, that the king might lead a military campaign to rescue what remained of England's possessions in Gascony. This did not come to fruition, but in October 1452 news arrived that an advance force sent under John Talbot, the formidable earl of Shrewsbury, had won several splendid victories. Bordeaux had been recaptured with ease from the French and much of the area around the city rallied back to the English flag. This was the best news to have arrived from France in many months, and when parliament met at Reading in March 1453 it responded generously, voting a subsidy in the form of a fifteenth and tenth (a fixed tax on property), as well as a tax payable on wool exports which was to be paid every year for the rest of the king's life.

The parliament also received a petition concerning two young men who had grown up in relative quiet amid all the turbulence and danger of the 1450s: Edmund and Jasper Tudor. In November 1452, as a way to bolster the ranks of the immediate royal family, the Tudor boys, now in or approaching their early twenties, had been elevated jointly to the peerage. Edmund was made earl of Richmond, while Jasper was created earl of Pembroke. The parliament of 1453 was successfully moved to declare them legitimate half-brothers of the king. The Latin petition began by praising the 'famous memory' of Queen Catherine de Valois, and then calling on parliament 'to esteem highly and to honour with all zeal, as much as our insignificance allows, all the fruit which her royal womb produced', in this case, 'the illustrious and magnificent princes, the lords Edmund de Hadham and Jasper de Hatfield, natural and legitimate sons of the same most serene lady the queen'.

The praise was uncommonly high: 'By their most noble character they are of a most refined nature,' the petition read; they were also lauded for 'their other natural gifts, endowments, excellent and heroic virtues, and other merits of a laudable life'. Notwithstanding the fact that, being half Welsh and half French, neither had a drop of English blood in their veins, they and their heirs were confirmed in their right to hold property and titles. The Tudor boys, having left almost no mark on the historical record since their education in Barking Abbey during the late 1430s and early 1440s, were suddenly promoted into the front rank of the aristocracy, their noble blood and royal relations trumpeted. In a highly unsubtle dig at York, lands seized from the now ruined Sir William Oldhall were granted out as part of Jasper earl of Pembroke's new landed estate.

At almost exactly the same time came more good news. In the early spring of 1453 Queen Margaret, who had for so long been the object of public derision for her failure to produce an heir, became pregnant. Notwithstanding the difficulties of childbirth and the infant mortality rate of the time, there was a real prospect that a direct heir to the crown would soon provide England with a new focus – and that any questions of noble precedence would finally wither away. The queen was delighted, and on discovering her pregnancy immediately set out for Walsingham in Norfolk to give thanks at the famous shrine to the Virgin Mary. Henry VI rewarded the servant who brought him the news with a jewel known as a 'demy ceynt'. All England stirred in happiness: even York's wife Cecily – whose relations with the queen were more cordial than those between her husband and the king – was moved to write to Margaret, remarking that her unborn child was 'the most precious, most joyful, and most comfortable earthly treasure that might come unto this land and to the people thereof'. Finally, after so much misery, so much strife, it appeared that God was smiling on the reign of King Henry VI.

Then, on 17 July 1453, in a field near Castillon, a town on the banks of the Dordogne just twenty-six miles east of Bordeaux, an English army under Talbot was annihilated by the cannon and cavalry of a French force commanded by Jean Bureau. Talbot, the brilliant veteran of half a century of warfare who was known as the 'English Achilles' and the 'Terror of the French', died alongside thousands of his men, charging headlong into a hail of artillery fire. The English were routed and within three months Bordeaux would once again fall under French control. It would prove to be the final, unequivocal defeat in a war that had been waged since 1337, and was greeted in England as the calamity it was. No one reacted more terribly to the news than Henry VI. In August, as the court was touring the west country, Henry fell into a form of stupor – the crippling, vacant, catatonic insanity of a waking coma under whose grotesque spell he would remain for fifteen months. At a stroke, England was once again kingless. And soon madness would engulf not just the king, but his kingdom, too.

9 : Smitten with a Frenzy

Henry's illness came upon him while he was staying at his hunt-ing lodge in Clarendon, near Salisbury. It struck suddenly and overwhelmingly, and although for several weeks the king's con-dition remained a secret, when he failed to recover it became impossible to conceal the fact that he was profoundly and shock-ingly unwell. The men around him had no specific name for his ailment; they could only describe its symptoms. 'The king . . . suddenly was taken and smitten with a frenzy and his wit and reason withdrawn,' wrote one. To another he was merely 'sick'. He became completely helpless, removed both from his wits and the world around him to the point of total vacuity. He recognised no one. He could not speak or respond in any way to questions. He could neither feed nor clean himself, since he had no control of his arms or legs and could not even keep his head up. He had no sense of time. No physician could stir him. No medicine could stimulate him.[1] His grandfather Charles VI of France had also suffered numerous bouts of insanity, but, whereas Charles's madness had led him to scream in pain, smear himself in his own waste and run deranged through the royal palaces, Henry was simply mute and inert: a kingly nothing.

Even when sane, Henry had been a fairly weak and impotent force in government. Now that he was so obviously indisposed, however, Somerset and the rest of his counsellors were presented with a dire problem. When the king was healthy, they possessed an animated if ineffectual puppet through whom government could legitimately be carried out by a small group working as his chosen ministers. But with the king devoid of reason and will, their mandate to rule in his name disappeared. The king had all the will and capacity of a newborn baby, which meant that a situation similar to Henry's long minority in the 1420s was once again upon the realm. There was a royal person who could be said to reign, but he had no ability whatever to rule. Just as in the 1420s, a communal response was required.

Although the turbulence in England and the dire situation in the meagre rump of English France demanded constant attention, a political reaction to Henry's illness was nevertheless delayed as long as possible, probably with the dual aim of hoping, rather vainly, that he would recover and waiting for the queen's pregnancy to reach its term. The second of these came to pass, on 13 October 1453 – the feast day of Edward the Confessor, one of the holiest and most venerated saints in England, with special importance to the royal family. In a chamber at Westminster, Margaret of Anjou was delivered of her first child, a boy. The child was called Edward, a princely name that not only spoke to the auspicious day of his birth but recalled times of greater glory: the days of the baby's great-great-great-grandfather Edward III. 'Wherefore the bells rang in every church and Te Deum [was . . .] sung,' wrote one observer.[2] The duke of Somerset stood godfather at Prince Edward's baptism.[3]

If the birth was cause for great joy, it was also clear that the torpor of the boy's father could no longer be ignored. It was important to construct a working government, and it was vital that this government should be genuinely inclusive. The king's mental collapse had coincided with, and may indeed have contributed to, a huge escalation of violence, particularly in the north of England. Long-simmering hostility between the Neville and Percy families, who were rivals for power in Yorkshire, Cumbria and Northumberland, had descended into more or less open warfare. On 24 August 1454 Thomas Percy, Lord Egremont and an army of retainers numbering perhaps a thousand ambushed a wedding party celebrating the marriage of Sir Thomas Neville and Maude Stanhope. The immediate cause was a disputed inheritance: the beautiful manor and castle of Wressle, which had once belonged to the Percys, would come into the hands of the Nevilles by way of Sir Thomas's marriage to the Stanhope heir. But this was one small battle in a much bigger struggle: the Percys sensed, with some justification, that the Nevilles were gradually displacing them as the most powerful family of the north. This, in turn, was a pressing problem for central government. The north of England appeared to be on the brink of civil war, as all pleas and instructions to cease hostilities issued by Somerset's government had been ignored. Since the feud involved the two most powerful families in the region, there was no authority save the king's that was able to put a stop to massive and disastrous bloodshed.

As soon as Prince Edward was born, a great council of all the senior lords and churchmen in the realm was summoned to meet as soon as possible. At first, the intention was to exclude York from its membership, but on 24 October a letter was sent, addressed 'By the king' to his 'right trusty and well-beloved cousin', summoning the duke from his estates to attend the gathering in London. It is not clear who drafted the letter, since it is signed in Henry's name. However, the messenger who took the letter was told to advise York to put aside 'the variance betwixt' him and Somerset, and to 'come to the said Counsail peaceably and measurably accompanied', with the aim of securing 'rest and union betwixt the lords of this land'.[4]

York arrived at Westminster on 12 November, but he did not come in a conciliatory mood. His first action was to have his sometime ally the duke of Norfolk launch a vehement attack on Somerset before the council, once again accusing him of treason in losing France. Norfolk demanded Somerset's imprisonment and in the confusion and crisis of the moment, browbeaten by his aggressive demands, a majority of the lords assembled consented. The duke was arrested and sent to the Tower to await trial. A few days later the lords once again gathered in council at the Star Chamber, and were individually 'sworn on a book' that they would keep their 'troth and allegiance . . . to the king'.[5] After several years of failure, York was now finally at the centre of affairs.

He did not occupy his position unchallenged. In January 1454 the queen, having recovered from the birth of Prince Edward, made her own bid for power. Margaret had long been close to Somerset and to the royal household through which so much of government had proceeded, and it seems that her intention was to fight York's dominance by any means she could. The dumbstruck King Henry had shown no signs of recognising his son – when Margaret and Humphrey duke of Buckingham took the baby to see his father at Windsor Castle, 'all their labour was in vain, for they departed thence without any answer or countenance saving only that once he looked on the Prince and cast down his [eyes again] without any more'. Nevertheless it was clear that, in possession of the baby, Margaret had the opportunity to build a different, rival power base to York's. In the new year she published 'a bill of five articles' in which she demanded 'to have the whole rule of this land', as well as the right to appoint all the great officers of state, sheriffs and bishops, and 'sufficient [livelihood] assigned her for the King and the Prince and herself'.[6]

Margaret's efforts were bold, but they were not unprecedented. Although female rule was uncommon in the fifteenth century, it was not completely unknown. England's own history held examples: Queen Isabella had ruled as regent for Edward III between 1327 and 1330, and before her Eleanor of Aquitaine had been granted extensive powers of governance during the reigns of her husband Henry II and her son Richard the Lionheart. Perhaps more pertinently, Margaret had in her early life seen her mother and grandmother taking command of government in Anjou and Naples while Duke René languished in captivity.[7] However, in the crisis of 1453–4, the last desire of the English lords (or, for that matter, the parliamentary commons) was to experiment with a new model of female rule. Margaret's bill was cordially rejected. As a mollifying measure on 15 March 1454, the five-month-old Edward was created prince of Wales and earl of Chester. This was as far as accommodation with the queen went.

A week later Margaret's close ally, Cardinal Kemp, archbishop of Canterbury and chancellor of England, died. In desperation the lords sent another delegation to the king, to see if they could coax from him some indication of whom he wished his new archbishop to be. Once again, they reported to the parliament, which took a keen interest in the king's condition, that they could get 'no answer nor sign'. The lords left 'with sorrowful hearts'.[8] The crisis of authority had worsened. On 27 March the lords in parliament agreed to elect Richard duke of York as protector of the realm and chief councillor. His rise was complete.

There were many who held grave reservations about York's suitability for the role of protector. Their fears were not realised. Although he appointed as the new chancellor Richard Neville, earl of Salisbury – patriarch of the Neville family whose feuding with the Percys was tearing apart the north – York's government attempted in general to be tough, even-handed and non-partisan. He went in person to the north to make a serious attempt to arbitrate between the Nevilles and the Percys. In the course of this he imprisoned his own son-in-law, the violent and feckless Henry Holland, duke of Exeter, in Pontefract Castle, as punishment for involving himself in the northern war and thereby directly disobeying the oath sworn by all the lords to keep and respect 'royal' authority during the king's illness.

York appointed himself captain of Calais and resumed his lieutenancy of Ireland, but these were actions natural and conducive to strong leadership rather than representative of his seizing the spoils of office. Other grants, which were modestly made, were given out on non-partisan lines: the queen, the duke of Buckingham, and Jasper and Edmund Tudor all received lands or offices during York's protectorship, whereas men supposedly closer to him – such as Salisbury's eldest son the earl of Warwick (also called Richard Neville) – received nothing.[9] Yet there was one glaring area in which York's policy of peace and conciliation failed: he could not normalise relations with Edmund Beaufort, duke of Somerset. Throughout 1454, Somerset remained locked away in the Tower. He kept keenly abreast of news from the outside world through a network of undercover agents: 'spies going in every Lord's house of this land: some gone as [friars], some as shipmen . . . and some in other wise; which report unto him all that they can see . . .'[10] To have killed Somerset would have been a destructively divisive act. In prison, therefore, he was able to study the situation and bide his time, hoping, as the popular image had it, that Fortune's wheel would shortly give another turn.

*

On Christmas Day 1454, more than a year after he had been stricken, Henry VI woke up. His senses flooded back as quickly as they had first rushed out of him. Two days after Christmas he was ordering his almoner to deliver gifts of thanks to the shrine at Canterbury, and on Monday 30 December Queen Margaret took the fourteen-month-old prince to see his father. Henry 'asked what the prince's name was, and the Queen told him Edward; and then he held up his hands and thanked God thereof'. He had no memory of anything that had been said or done during his stupor. But he seemed extremely happy to have recovered. When his ministers found that he could once more speak to them 'as well as he ever did', they 'wept for joy'.[11]

The same could not be said for York. Henry's recovery did not simply end the protectorate: it led directly to the reversal of most of the means York had pursued over the course of the last year. By 26 January 1455 Somerset had been released from prison and by 4 March the charges of treason against him were dropped. York was formally stripped of the protectorate on 9 February. In a sign of the absolute repudiation of York's primary case against Somerset – that he was treasonably negligent in his dealings with the French – York was stripped of his captaincy of Calais and it was awarded once more to Somerset. York's ally Richard earl of Salisbury was forced to resign the chancellorship. In mid-March Salisbury's son, the earl of Warwick, was ordered to release Henry Holland, the scheming and belligerent duke of Exeter, from his entirely deserved place in prison at Pontefract.

As Somerset and his allies raced back into their old positions in government and at the side of the king, York and the Nevilles were forced to abandon court. Despite the protector's genuinely purposeful actions in trying to maintain government during the royal madness, he now found himself stripped of his posts, authority and dignity as though he had been a usurper. The only possible conclusion York could draw was that with Somerset beside the king, he would forever be treated as an enemy of the crown: denied his proper place in the realm as if he were nothing but a scoundrel and a rebel. York had been bound by the king and a council of the lords to keep his peace with Somerset until June, on pain of a fine of twenty thousand marks. But peace was no longer an option. With the Nevilles, York now went north to follow the only course of action that was left to him: he began to raise an army.

York and the Nevilles – led by the earls of Salisbury and Warwick, father and son – were now thrown together in a friendship of common cause. Between them, they controlled much of northern England, and since the Nevilles existed in a state of war-readiness owing to their struggles with the house of Percy, it did not prove difficult for the allies to raise their retainers to form a small army during the spring of 1455. They had, by their own later admission, 'great might of men in diverse countries, much harness [i.e. armour] and great habiliments of war'.[12] It is important to note that for York the purpose of raising an armed force was to remove Somerset and the 'traitors' around the king; this to his mind was a very different matter from rebellion – and certainly *dynastic* rebellion – against Henry VI himself. It is questionable, however, how many of the men who served beneath him would have appreciated the subtle difference. All the same, they were raised with efficient haste in April and May, and the news of York and the Nevilles' mobilisation, although perhaps not its scale, soon reached the court and council at Westminster.

Somerset at this point panicked and dithered. Notwithstanding the London populace's general preference for York over him, the obvious course of action ought still have been to raise a royal army, set to defend the capital, and allow a repeat of the Dartford conflict of 1452 to occur. Instead, a decision was taken to move the king's household and the lords attending the king north. A great council – not quite a parliament, although the summonses went out on a broad scale to England's lords, along with a selection of hand-picked knights expected to be favourable to Somerset's regime – was called to meet at Leicester, a town in the heart of the duchy of Lancaster, the king's private landholding.[13] York and his allies were invited, so it seems that at least one aspect of the Dartford episode was in mind: the government hoped to impose a new settlement upon Somerset and York, and most likely one that would embarrass York in public with an oath of loyalty of the type he had been forced to swear at St Paul's.[14] This was not something York was prepared to countenance. He may also have thought of the fate of Humphrey duke of Gloucester, who had been summoned to a parliament in Bury St Edmunds in 1447 and had never returned.

There was the distinct possibility of armed confrontation at Leicester. In mid-May, as the king and his supporters prepared to travel north, requests were sent to lords and townsmen along the route, requiring them to send armed men to the king 'wheresoever we be in all haste possible'.[15] The destination for assembly was the town of St Albans, in Hertfordshire, which lay conveniently along the road between London and Leicester. On the morning of Tuesday 20 May the king and his entourage set out from Westminster along this very route. Ahead of them went messengers with letters to York, Salisbury and Warwick, demanding that they disband their armies immediately and come to the king attended by no more than 160 men each in the Nevilles' case, and two hundred in the case of York.

By the time the letters reached York and the Nevilles, they had reached Royston, a town a few miles south-west of Cambridge, and less than a day's ride from St Albans. They replied to the orders to disband with a letter addressed to the chancellor who had replaced Salisbury: Thomas Bourchier, the forty-four-year-old archbishop of Canterbury. 'We hear that a great rumour and wonder is had of our coming, and of the manner thereof, toward the most noble presence of the king oure most [re]doubted sovereign lord,' they wrote. It was vital for York and his allies that they should establish themselves as the true defenders of the common good in the face of Somerset's treacherous government, so they added that 'we intend not with God's grace to proceed to any matter or thing, other than with God's mercy shall be to his pleasure, the honour, prosperity and weal of our said sovereign lord, his said land and people'. More ominously, the Yorkists also promised the chancellor that for the sake of the kingdom they would do whatever 'accordeth with our duty, to that that may be the surety of [the king's] most noble person, wherein we will neither spare our bodies nor goods'.

By the time the letter reached Chancellor Bourchier, the king's party had left Westminster. The men around Henry hardly consisted of a partisan group: the king was attended by men as diverse in their political outlooks as his faithful half-brother Jasper Tudor, earl of Pembroke, the Percy patriarch Henry Percy, earl of Northumberland, the independent-minded Humphrey duke of Buckingham, the former Yorkist ally Thomas Courtenay, earl of Devon, and the earl of Salisbury's brother William Neville, Lord Fauconberg. Other great nobles included the earl of Wiltshire and Lords Clifford, Ros, Sudeley, Dudley and Berners. Perhaps in anticipation of confrontation, Queen Margaret was left behind, and only one bishop travelled with the king – although several others probably followed at a safe distance. The party passed out of London and by nightfall on Wednesday 21 May they were lodged in Watford, seven miles south of St Albans. At dawn they rose to continue their journey, planning to arrive in the town in good time to settle and enjoy their midday meal at the splendid abbey. But as morning arrived, so did a messenger, bearing the alarming news that York and his army were close by: they had camped the night in Ware, and not only were they ahead of the king's party on their way to St Albans, but they were said to have with them around three thousand men. The king's party numbered closer to two thousand.

The sense that something between an armed showdown and a pitched battle was looming sparked action in the royal party. Conciliatory action was urgently required. Early on the morning of Thursday 22, Somerset was abruptly relieved of his post as constable of England, by which he commanded the king's military forces. He was immediately replaced in the office by Humphrey duke of Buckingham, who as the most senior duke at the king's side had the presence to represent the royal interest, but was far less personally obnoxious to York and the Nevilles. Buckingham seems to have believed that he would be able to negotiate a settlement without bloodshed.

The party rode on to St Albans, arriving at about 9 a.m. The Yorkists had arrived two hours earlier, and were camped in the Key Field, just to the east of the town centre. There were 'diverse knightes and squiers unto ther party', and they were perfectly visible to the king's party as they came to a halt in the middle of St Albans on St Peter's Street, below the massive silhouette of the abbey church.[16] The townsmen, realising that their lives and homes were in some peril, manned the defences, which took the form of barricades around the unwalled settlement. They were reinforced by knights loyal to the king, and between 9 and 10 a.m. messengers passed between the two sides as they tried to negotiate a settlement.

The talks with York were conducted by the dukes of Buckingham and Somerset, who claimed that they were speaking directly for the king. It is unlikely that Henry knew very much about what was happening: he had not seen York's initial petitions and one of the first stages of negotiation involved York's demand that the letters he had sent should actually be placed under the royal nose. Henry may have recovered from his illness, but his role at St Albans remained passive and symbolic.

York's principal demands had not changed but only hardened since Dartford. He wanted Somerset and he was prepared to use any means to obtain him. In response to this, Buckingham could do little but stall for time, and await both the bishops who were following behind the royal party and the military reinforcements that had been requested from around the country. He asked York to remove his men to a nearby town for the night, while negotiations could continue through suitable proxies. And he absolutely refused to hand over the duke of Somerset.

Whether or not York was prepared to continue negotiations into a second day will never be known. At around 10 a.m., while talks were continuing, men under the earl of Warwick grew sick of waiting and began an assault against the barricades on the fringes of the town. Within St Albans, the king's banner was raised over the royal forces. The talking time was over. Fighting had begun.

Defence of the barricades was commanded by Thomas, Lord Clifford, an experienced soldier who had served for some time in the north, battling the Scots in the marches. He was later considered to have manned the barriers to St Albans 'strongly', and probably held the line outside the town for about an hour.[17] York, however, had the superior numbers, and around 11 a.m. the skirmishing was turning in favour of the attacking forces. Warwick took a flanking party to the thoroughfare known as Holywell Street, which led into St Peter's Street, where the royal party were massed. They smashed down palisades and the walls of houses and finally broke open an entry point between two inns, known as the Key and the Chequer, through which their men could pour into the town, blowing trumpets and shouting 'Warwick! Warwick! Warwick!' at the top of their voices. As soon as they clapped eyes on the king's forces, 'they set on them manfully'.[18]

St Albans was soon overrun. Amazingly, it seems that Buckingham and Somerset had failed to prepare for the possibility that the barricades would fall so swiftly, for as the town bell was rung in urgent alarm and fighting spilled from street to street, there was a general scramble for the defenders to pull on their full armour. They were unprepared and overwhelmed, and when one of York's allies, Sir Robert Ogle, brought several hundred men crashing into the marketplace, blades slashing and arrows fizzing through the late morning air, the short conflict was effectively decided in favour of York's men. From the puncturing of the barriers the fighting lasted around half an hour. But it was a shocking experience all the same.

In the middle of the mêlée stood the king himself, terror presumably spreading across his pale, round face, for the son of Henry V had managed to reach the age of thirty-three without ever having stood before a siege or in the chaos of a battle. Like the best of his lords, he was imperfectly armoured, and was lucky to survive when a stray arrow bloodied his neck. ('Forsothe and forsothe,' the king is said to have remarked, employing his favourite and only oath, 'ye do foully to smite a king anointed so.'[19]) For his protection, if not the maintenance of his royal dignity, Henry was hustled into a nearby tanner's cottage to hide while the street fighting played out. As he left, his banner, which in every battle was to be upheld to the death, was easily pulled to the ground, its defenders scattering into the streets.

After only a short stay in his reeking hideaway, Henry was captured and taken away to proper safety in the precincts of the abbey. York's men had absolutely no interest in doing him physical damage, for it was a crucial component of the duke's political campaign to argue that he was fighting for and not against the king. But Henry's companions were not so lucky. York and the Nevilles had come to St Albans to eliminate their enemies, and in the disorder they had created, they were able to achieve their goal. By midday, when hostilities came to a conclusion, the streets groaned with bloodied and injured men. Given the numbers of combatants – probably around five thousand in total – it is slightly surprising that fewer than sixty were killed. But of the dead men there were three of great significance. First was Thomas, Lord Clifford, who had so bravely held the town's defences while the first hour's blows were traded. Second was Henry earl of Northumberland, the most senior male in the Percy family and as a result the chief enemy of the Nevilles. And third was the greatest enemy of them all: Edmund Beaufort, duke of Somerset.

Somerset had fought for the duration of the battle of St Albans. Although he may have been an unlucky commander, he was at least used to seeing military action during his long service in France. Several chronicles of the battle record that after the king had been taken to the abbey, and as fighting was coming to its conclusion on St Peter's Street, Somerset was pushed back into defending a tavern under the sign of the Castle. At his side was his son Henry Beaufort, nineteen years old and already a courageous warrior. Whereas the earl of Wiltshire had timidly, if pragmatically, fled the scene of the battle disguised as a monk, the Beauforts stood their ground and struggled to the very last. Young Henry Beaufort was wounded so severely in the fighting that he left St Albans dragged on a cart and close to death. His father was not so fortunate. It was he over whom the whole conflict had arisen, and he was a marked man from its outset. Eventually overcome by his enemies, Somerset was dragged from the tavern and hacked to death in the street. With the end of his life arrived the end of the battle. Troops aroused by the bloodshed continued to create havoc in the streets, but this was now an armed rout, rather than a purposeful battle. Safe beneath the high vaulted ceilings of the abbey church, York, Salisbury and Warwick respectfully took Henry VI before the shrine of St Alban himself, then requested that they now be received as his faithful subjects and advisers. The king, who had absolutely no choice in the matter, accepted that the lords had 'kept him unhurt and there . . . granted to be ruled by them'.[20] As soon as this was done, York gave the order for all violence outside the abbey to cease. His orders were eventually obeyed. But it was only some time later that anyone dared to gather up the bloodied corpses of Somerset and the rest of the men killed on the streets of St Albans, in a day of violent upheaval that would leave its stain on England for two generations to follow.

*

Henry was escorted back to London by the Yorkists on Friday 23 May and deposited in his apartments in the palace of Westminster, before moving on to the bishop's palace. The following day he was paraded before the city of London 'in great honour

. . . the said duke of York riding on his right side and the earl of Salisbury on the left side and the earl of Warwick [bearing] his sword', and on Sunday 25 May in a ceremony at St Paul's he sat in state and was handed his crown by the duke of York.[21] All this presented a picture of majesty and kingly authority, but it was even more spurious than it had ever been. For even if he could be presented to the public in stately highness as 'a king and not as a prisoner', beside the three lords who had emerged victorious from St Albans, it was quite obvious that now more than at any time before, Henry VI was a royal cipher.[22]

Meanwhile, as York worked to establish for the second time his authority as the chief councillor of the king and the effective governor of England, stories of the battle of St Albans began to spread. They circulated in England and they crossed the Channel: within days the fracas was the talk of diplomats across Europe. On 31 May 1455 the Milanese ambassador, who had left London earlier in the month, wrote a letter from Bruges to the archbishop of Ravenna in which he reported the 'unpleasant' news that in England 'a great part of the nobles have been in conflict'. 'The Duke of York has done this, with his followers,' wrote the ambassador, recounting the deaths and injuries that had befallen Somerset and his allies. Yet if the violence was shocking, there was a seasoned pragmatism in the ambassador's report. York, he wrote, 'will now take up the government again, and some think that the affairs of [the] kingdom will now take a turn for the better. If that be the case, we can put up with this inconvenience.' Three days later the ambassador filed an update confirming his earlier notes. 'Peace reigns,' he wrote. 'The Duke of York has the government, and the people are very pleased at this.'[23]

Even if this was true, it would not last for long.

III

The Hollow Crown
1455–1471

I spoke quietly to his Majesty about English affairs . . .
He remarked with a sigh that it is impossible to
fight against Fortune.

SFORZA DE BETTINI OF FLORENCE,
Milanese ambassador to the court of Louis XI[1]

10 : Princess Most Excellent

In 1456 Coventry was one of the richest and most densely populated cities in England: beyond London, only Bristol and Norwich could claim to be bigger or more prosperous. Coventry's busy cloth market was the beating heart of a proud and bustling community, living both within and beyond the recently renovated city walls, surrounded by a ditch and accessed on three sides by ornate, ancient gates. The river Sherbourne wound its way by the southern wall, and three of England's busiest roads passed within twenty miles of the city. Coventry boasted all the features of a thriving urban centre: elegant churches and a grammar school; inns for revellers and travellers under the signs of the Swan and the Bear; a magnificent guildhall built on the remains of a castle ruined nearly three hundred years earlier; two hospitals and a hermitage; townhouses belonging to local dignitaries and merchants; and four religious houses, one of which was the cloistered college of the vicars choral, whose voices marked the liturgical rhythm of the day. In the south-east of the city proper was a rare expanse of open space: the vineyard which had once belonged to the castle. Densely populated suburbs spread out from the walls, houses dotted between pockets of marshland regularly flooded by the region's several waterways. This was a vibrant centre of trade and power, well connected to the realm beyond.[1] It was a place fit for a king – and more importantly, for a queen.

On 14 September 1456, Margaret of Anjou entered Coventry in high splendour. She came with her young son Prince Edward, who was a month short of his third birthday. Henry VI – husband, father and still in his deeply unremarkable way king of England – had come to the city several days before the rest of his family. He was not an impressive sight. Sickness had left him feebler than ever: still blandly pious and easily swayed by whoever had command of him, he was now also physically weak and quick to tire. Henry was only thirty-four years old, but more than a decade of criticism and disappointment had left him miserably reduced. He had begun planning his tomb in Westminster Abbey, and at times acted as though he were ready to crawl into it. Pope Pius II, watching England from afar, would later describe Henry in this phase of his life as 'a man more timorous than a woman, utterly devoid of wit or spirit, who left everything in his wife's hands'.[2]

It was therefore Margaret's arrival in Coventry, and not Henry's, that was marked with the greatest pageantry and display. The city was famous for its mystery plays, and the citizens put all of their dramatic expertise into celebrating the arrival of a woman who, since the serious decline in her husband's health, was becoming one of the most formidable political actors in England. As she processed into the town she was greeted in verse (albeit somewhat pedestrian in its composition) by figures arrayed as Isaiah and Jeremiah, St Edward, St John and Alexander the Great, and players dressed as the seven cardinal virtues and the Nine Worthies. She was hailed as a 'princess most excellent, born of blood royal' and 'Empress, queen, princess excellent, in one person all three'. (The actor playing Joshua, king of the Israelites, called her 'the highest lady that I can imagine'.) Her son Edward was accorded similarly high praise: St Edward the Confessor called his young namesake 'my ghostly child, whom I love principally', while St John gave thanks that 'the virtuous voice of prince Edward shall daily well increase'. The figure of Alexander the Great, one of the greatest soldier-kings in history, offered Henry the unlikely title of 'noblest prince that is born, whom fortune hath famed . . . sovereign lord Harry, emperor &

king'. This was very much a token gesture among a pageant that celebrated the queen's majesty above all. It drew to an end with the sight of St Margaret taking to the stage to slay a dragon with 'a miracle'.[3] Evidently satisfied with what she had seen, Margaret would remain in Coventry with the king, prince and royal court for much of the next year, and return frequently for the rest of the decade. Although England's bureaucratic machinery remained in Westminster, the realm would henceforth be ruled, effectively, from the midlands.

Since the battle of St Albans, Margaret's power had increased steadily. At twenty-six, she was now a mature and experienced public figure, confident, capable, and connected to a large circle of supporters and allies. Most importantly, she had possession of Edward, the heir to the crown, and it was through her own queenly influence and her importance as keeper of the little prince that she set about establishing herself as an alternative hub of power to Richard duke of York.

Women were not often able to exercise outright political control in the fifteenth century. Contemporary political thought held them to be weak, hysterical and physically incapable of carrying out the fundamental duties of kingship – not least riding into battle, swinging an axe, ready to make war upon their enemies. Female rule was considered unnatural, and attempts by women to seize power unilaterally were rare and usually futile. But that was not how Margaret saw it. Growing up in Anjou, she had witnessed her mother and grandmother taking charge of her father's territories during his long periods of imprisonment, ruling in the name of a man and wielding 'his' authority, but in reality acting on their own. Why should she not do the same in England, either through her husband or her son?

York's policy following his victory at St Albans had been to establish a second protectorate, similar to that which had existed during the king's illness. He secured reappointment as protector on 15 November 1455 and for four months did his best to exercise royal authority in the cause of unity among the lords and good governance. But whereas during York's first protectorate the king had been obviously and totally incapacitated, during the second protectorate he was attempting to exercise royal power without any such urgent mandate.

He was obliged to reward his Neville allies handsomely for their help in ridding the realm of Somerset. Richard earl of Warwick was awarded the captaincy of Calais and a slew of grants in Wales, where Somerset had held land and titles. The Bourchier family was also well rewarded, but few other families benefited, which gave the impression that the second protectorate was a narrow clique rather than the national enterprise York seems genuinely to have imagined he could create. Politics had become far more strained and factious in the aftermath of the violence York had provoked, and although he enjoyed a few successes – restoring order to the south-west by stamping out the worst excesses committed between the Courtenay and Bonville families – this was not enough to convince the realm that Yorkist government in Henry VI's name was the solution to its problems.

York ran into severe difficulty in early 1456, when parliament demanded another full-blooded act of resumption, by which lands granted away from the Crown would be swept back into royal possession in order to bolster the king's finances. Since York had a mandate to try to bring some order and stability to royal government, he stood behind the policy and did his best to convince his fellow lords to do the same. But here again he found that the base of his support was extremely narrow. There was a distinct apathy towards his protectorate – and certainly he did not possess enough enthusiastic support throughout the realm to encourage men who had been personally enriched by grants from the Crown suddenly to give them up with no prospect of recompense. The Act was rejected by a large number of England's lords and York felt he had no choice but to resign the protectorship on 25 February 1456. He tried to remain involved in government throughout the summer, organising military defences when the king of the Scots raided the northern border and trying to deal with pockets of disorder in Wales. But his authority was almost visibly ebbing away. In public he was scorned: a display of five dogs' severed heads was erected on Fleet Street in London in September, with each dead mouth holding a satirical poem against York, 'that man that all men hate'. By the autumn it was clear that his rule was over. His allies and supporters began to be dismissed from their offices, and were replaced by men loyal to Queen Margaret.[4]

From late 1456, then, the queen tried to impose herself on the affairs of state. A correspondent watching events in London during the end of York's second protectorate wrote to the East Anglian knight Sir John Fastolf that 'the Queen is a great and strong-laboured [i.e. much petitioned] woman, for she spareth no pain to sue her things to an intent and conclusion to her power'.[5] A chronicler writing later went further, noting that 'the governance of the Realm stood most by the Queen and her Council'. And a third writer, a partisan of York, reckoned that the queen 'ruled the realm as her liked, gathering riches innumerable'.[6] It was rumoured that she was attempting to persuade her husband to abdicate, resigning the crown to his young son, who would become, by implication, a puppet strung even more tightly to her fingers.

In part Margaret's motivation in opposing York was sheer personal enmity. The queen had been deeply offended by the duke's actions in 1455. Whatever the constitutional niceties of York's argument, Margaret could not ignore the fact that the duke had raised an army, left two peers – one of them her friend Somerset – bleeding to death in the streets of St Albans, and taken the king as an effective captive back to London. York, for his part, resented the queen moving towards the centre of power. A woman, and a

Frenchwoman at that, supplanting the natural role of a duke of the royal blood was completely unacceptable. Added to this was the fact that this particular woman appeared to hate him with every fibre of her being, and was committed to undermining his attempts at government. It was no surprise that relations between the two camps were strained.

During 1457 Margaret built up her territorial power in the midlands, staffed her son's council with loyal household men and, where she could, advanced trusted allies both through offices and other means, such as marriages. Thus in April 1457 Henry's half-brother Jasper Tudor, earl of Pembroke, was appointed as constable of Carmarthen and Aberystwyth, Welsh offices that had recently been in the hands of York himself. Meanwhile, Jasper's elder brother Edmund Tudor, earl of Richmond, was a focus for the queen's interests in south Wales, where he busied himself with a private war against two of the duke of York's retainers, Sir William Herbert and Sir Walter Devereux.

Edmund Tudor had been granted a handsome elevation through his marriage in the autumn of 1455 to Margaret Beaufort, the twelve-year-old niece of the late duke of Somerset and daughter of the disgraced soldier John Beaufort, the duke who had died, possibly by suicide, when Margaret was one year old. Margaret was the richest heiress in England, and her hand brought with it immense wealth and power. By the summer of 1456 Margaret was pregnant. But Edmund Tudor would never see his child. He died of plague on 1 November 1456 following a short imprisonment by York's retainers in Carmarthen Castle. Just under three months later, on 28 January 1457, in Pembroke Castle, the thirteen-year-old Margaret was traumatically delivered of a son, named Henry Tudor. Even in an age where girls became wives and mothers early in life, this was a young age at which to bear a child. Margaret was probably physically and mentally traumatised by the birth: certainly this was the last child she would ever bear.

Queen Margaret, meanwhile, did not only favour those close to the royal camp. York and his allies were excluded from the king's council and kept firmly away from court, but they were not totally isolated following the failure of the second protectorate. The duke's commission as lieutenant of Ireland was renewed for ten years, and he was financially rewarded for the properties and offices he lost to men like the Tudors. In the summer of 1457, when there was a fear that the French were planning an attack on the English coastline, York and his friends were appointed to muster infantry and archers to defend the realm. York's daughter Elizabeth was married to John de la Pole, the fifteen-year-old duke of Suffolk, only son of the murdered William de la Pole. Likewise, the Neville family received cautious royal patronage. The earl of Salisbury was employed as chief steward in some northern parts of the king's duchy of Lancaster, and he was included in defences against Scotland. Salisbury's son Warwick was allowed to continue as captain of Calais with control of the large garrison there – a critical post given the delicate situation in France. So if there was tension as a result of Margaret's displacement of York, there was also a hope for cautious reconciliation – this perhaps emanating from the king, whose only apparent wish in government was a pious but simple-minded desire for rapprochement. This came to a head on 25 March 1458 in London, when the Crown held a curious procession known as a Love Day.

*

The deaths incurred on the royalist side at St Albans were not easily forgotten. Both Edmund Beaufort, duke of Somerset, and Henry Percy, earl of Northumberland, had left sons and heirs who harboured a rancorous determination to avenge their families' losses. Henry Beaufort, the third duke of Somerset, was twenty years old in 1456 and lucky to be alive at all, having been grievously wounded fighting shoulder to shoulder with his father at St Albans. Henry Percy the younger, who became the third earl of Northumberland, was thirty-six, and with his younger brother Thomas, Lord Egremont, bore a fierce resentment against the Neville family. These young men and their friends were widely known to carry a 'grudge and wrath' against the Yorkists – a situation scarcely promising for the future stability of the kingdom.[7] Henry, or those around him, decided that, rather than allow blood feud and personal vendetta to spill into further murderous violence, the two sides should be brought quite literally hand in hand to make peace and foster friendship under the royal blessing.

The court had moved from Coventry back to the south-east in the autumn of 1457, and a great council was summoned to London early in the new year. By the end of January the city's largest lodging houses were packed with lords and their large bands of armed retainers. The duke of York brought four hundred men and stayed in his own city residence, Baynard's Castle. Salisbury came with five hundred, and his son Warwick arrived from Calais with six hundred followers, all dressed in 'red jackets, embroidered with a ragged staff', Warwick's personal emblem.[8] Their rival magnates came arrayed even more forcefully: Henry duke of Somerset came to London in the company of the duke of Exeter and eight hundred men, and he was followed by the Percys – Northumberland, Egremont, Sir Ralph Percy – and John, Lord Clifford, whose father, Thomas, had also been killed fighting on the king's side at St Albans. These northerners brought a massive force of fifteen hundred men. By early March, when the king and queen came up to Westminster to open council proceedings, London resembled a war zone. The city authorities kept an overnight watch, banned the public carrying of weapons and put men-at-arms on patrol in the streets to try to hold the peace, while thousands of royal archers could be seen posted both inside and outside the city, guarding the whole Thames corridor from Southwark down to Hounslow.

The air fairly crackled with violent intent, but mercifully the great council opened in peace, and after long discussions a deal was brokered between the Yorkists and their young opponents. York and Warwick agreed to give substantial sums of money in compensation to the bereaved families, as well as paying for St Albans Abbey to sing masses for the souls of the dead, a process supposed to hasten a spirit's journey through Purgatory. The Neville and the Percy families both agreed to undertake four-thousand-mark bonds to keep the peace for ten years. This having been formally agreed, on 25 March – known generally as Lady Day, the feast of the Annunciation – the reconciled lords went out in public to show off their newfound mutual affection.

They processed along the militarised streets of London in rather astonishing fashion, each aggrieved lord walking arm in arm with the person towards whom he held the sharpest hatred. At the head of the parade went the fresh-faced Somerset, linked at the elbow with old Salisbury. Behind them came Exeter, walking in harmonious and brotherly tandem with the earl of War-wick. And at the back marched the oddest couple of them all: the regal person of Queen Margaret accompanied by her bitterest foe, Richard duke of York. Between them all, holding no one's arm, came the faintly ridiculous figure of King Henry VI, master of the Love Day and supposed reconciler of his fractured realm. The party walked with all pomp towards the giddying spire of St Paul's Cathedral, which was crammed with 'the greatest multitude of people that day that was ever seen', and a service gave thanks to God for the peace that had descended on England. The peace was further celebrated with a series of jousts and tournaments at the Tower of London and in the queen's castle at Greenwich. But if the Love Day was meant to strike observers as two sets of lords now joined together in friendship, a perceptive watcher could have noted that the divisions between the realm's noblemen, written in blood at St Albans, had in fact been sharpened and polarised by a reconciliation in which they were forced to relive events before being lined up and marched before the watching populace as if in opposing teams.

Government in 1458 continued to bump along in financially constrained failure. Queen Margaret took the king and prince back to Coventry following the Love Day, and most of the lords who had filled London with armed men returned to their estates. But the city remained racked with riotous disorder, as did the south-west, Wales and the marches, and northern East Anglia. As the country seethed, the queen and the Yorkists continued to vie for power. In the autumn Margaret began to dismiss adherents of York and the Nevilles from their official posts, and bolstered her command by taking control of the royal revenues and official appointments.

One official position she could do nothing about, however, was that of Richard earl of Warwick as captain of Calais. Throughout the political turmoil of the late 1450s Warwick had held on to the post, which gave him command of the town's garrison, a powerful standing force of royal soldiers. He had significant military resources, whose loyalty to him made him difficult to remove. This became a serious problem as Warwick turned his office to ends that were increasingly embarrassing and awkward for the government on the other side of the Channel. The Calais garrison was perpetually broke and payments to its men forever in arrears. To address this issue, and also to help cultivate his own buccaneering image, Warwick had begun to use Calais as a base for what amounted to piracy. Merchant ships from the Low Countries and Italy were attacked by rogue vessels launched at Calais, as was a fleet of ships carrying salt belonging to the Hanseatic League – the guild of trading cities along the coast of the North and Baltic Seas. Goods were plundered and sailors were bloodily slain. A similar fate befell a fleet of twenty-eight Spanish sails, which was ambushed by ships connected with Warwick in the summer of 1458. The seamen 'bickered', to use one chronicler's understated phrase. Actually, a massive naval battle was fought, in which the sea foamed red as more than two hundred Spaniards and eighty men of Calais lost their lives, with three hundred more wounded 'right sore'.[9]

Warwick was summoned to Westminster in early 1459, to attend a council called to discuss matters that included further rumours of a planned French attack on the south coast of England. He came only reluctantly, aware that there was a strong feeling that he should be removed as soon as possible from his captaincy. His reticence was soon justified. While he was at court, a brawl broke out between his men and several of the king's household, 'insomuch that they would have slain the earl'. Whether or not this was a manufactured quarrel designed to do away with Warwick, it certainly seemed that way to him. When a further rumour reached him that he was to be imprisoned in the Tower, Warwick fled London on his barge and returned to Calais, undismissed but deeply troubled that he had narrowly escaped assassination. Relations between the Yorkists and the court were rapidly deteriorating.

From the late spring of 1459 both sides began to prepare once more for armed conflict. Margaret did so through her son's authority. In May the court decamped again to Coventry, and letters were sent around the nearby counties requesting a military levy to come to the royal side: those who would not comply were threatened with prosecution. All around the midlands and the north-west men were privately recruited to the royal retinue and given little badges of allegiance in the form of Prince Edward's livery: a swan with a crown around its neck. A great council was scheduled for June. Suspecting the worst, York and the Nevilles refused to attend, as did a number of their sympathisers, including Thomas Bourchier, archbishop of Canterbury. For their non-attendance the Yorkists were openly denounced by Queen

Margaret. It seemed highly likely that the next step would be for the Crown to declare them traitors and to have them attainted: their families ruined forever by an act of parliament that stripped them of their lands and titles and reduced them to nothing. In York's case, this would have meant removing his status as a member of the extended royal family and future claimant to the crown. It was the final provocation.

On 20 September Warwick returned from Calais, gathering several hundred men about him as he rode via Warwick Castle for a rendezvous with York and Salisbury at York's base of Ludlow in the Welsh borders. Salisbury had already recruited an army: he had perhaps five thousand men behind him as he set out to ride south from the family seat at Middleham in Yorkshire. The chronicles of the time make it clear that Salisbury had raised his men not for show but for the fight, 'dreading the malices of his enemies and especially of the queen and her company the which hated him deadly'.[10] He was not mistaken. News of his army's movement reached Coventry, and the court despatched James Tuchet, Lord Audley, to attempt an interception and seize the rogue earl.

Audley was an elderly man. At sixty-one, he had not seen action in the field since his last involvement in the French wars some twenty-eight years earlier. All the same, he was a powerful lord in the west midlands, who was able to raise large numbers of men from his lands in Cheshire, Staffordshire and Shropshire, and deploy them along the route on which the earl of Salisbury was marching. In a matter of days he assembled a force numbering somewhere between eight and twelve thousand, at the heart of which was a bristling cavalry: knights aboard powerful horses, both men and beasts heavily protected by clanking plate armour, helmets and breastplates that glinted dangerously when they caught the light. Audley's large cavalry contingent was clearly intended to impress Salisbury and suggest to the Yorkists that facing down the Crown and its loyal servants in a military show of strength would be no idle task.

On the morning of 23 September, Audley marched his men along the road that ran between Newcastle-under-Lyme and Market Drayton in Shropshire. Scouts soon encountered the first signs of Salisbury's army. To block Salisbury's path Audley drew his men up in battle formation at Blore Heath, a large open patch of sloping ground bounded by a light wood and a small stream now known as Hempmill Brook. It was behind this stream that Audley's forces stood, their front perhaps a mile long and partially defended by a thick band of hedgerow.[11] Salisbury's men were ranged opposite them on the slope, their front only around two-thirds as long, but their lines well defended. Behind them was a deep trench, and in the front line Salisbury's archers stood protected by deadly sharpened stakes hammered into the ground, a classic device for thwarting and slaughtering onrushing horsemen, who would impale their animals on the fierce spikes if they decided to charge rather than dismount and fight on foot. On the flanks, Salisbury and his men were sheltered by the wood and a formation of wagons which had been chained together to form a barricade. While his defences were tight, the earl nonetheless realised that the odds were against him: not only was he outnumbered by perhaps two to one, but the queen was waiting less than ten miles away in Eccleshall with a second army, and a third army under the Stanley brothers – Thomas, Lord Stanley and Sir William Stanley – hung back slightly closer, supposedly awaiting royal commands to intervene on Audley's side.

With both sides in strong defensive formations, Salisbury took the initiative with a feint: around midday his men began to recouple the horses to their wagons, as if they were preparing to fall back from the heath. Audley took the bait and sent his cavalry out to give chase. Unfortunately, in order to do so they had to cross the brook in front of them. Wading through the water slowed their progress and made them vulnerable to attack by Salisbury's archers. A storm of arrows fell from the sky, raining death upon the advancing horses and their riders. Men were catapulted from their dying mounts, only to be chopped down by the infantry. Those who survived were forced to flee back out of the archers' range, to the lines on the other side of the brook. Audley sent a second mounted charge across the water; but they too were driven back in a vicious hail of wood and steel sent from Salisbury's bowmen.

At this point, the Stanleys' army, waiting close at hand, might have been expected to join the fray. But the Stanleys, as arch pragmatists, were always wary of committing their men to a battle whose outcome seemed anything less than completely certain. Thomas, Lord Stanley simply kept his troops back, while Sir William Stanley actually sent reinforcements to Salisbury's side. In the end, Audley had no choice but to change tactics. He abandoned the cavalry charge and led about four thousand of his men, including large numbers of dismounted knights, in an advance on foot. A furious hand-to-hand battle began, steel ripping into flesh and men hurling themselves at one another in close quarter. Although Audley was an ageing commander and his tactics had been seriously naïve, he did not lack personal valour. He fought in the thick of the battle. But in the mêlée he was sought out by one Sir Roger Kynaston of Hordley, a retainer of the duke of York, who was among Salisbury's knights. In the open field, where the ground sloped gently downwards, Audley eventually lost his valiant stand. He was hacked down and killed, and his assistant commander, John Sutton, Lord Dudley, was taken prisoner. The loyalists had lost their leader, and soon gave up the fight. The battle lasted in total around four hours and by the end of it perhaps two thousand men lay dead in the field, their blood seeping into the warm autumn soil. Audley was buried at Darley Abbey in Derbyshire and a stone cross (which still stands) was erected at

Blore Heath, where he fell. In later years local people would refer to the battlefield as 'Deadman's Den'.[12]

*

After Blore Heath, Salisbury took the majority of his men onwards to the south, to meet with his son Warwick and York. Victory had cost him considerable casualties, and he weakened his forces further by allowing his two youngest sons, Sir Thomas and Sir John Neville, to take a significant number of soldiers back north: on their way the Neville boys were both captured and imprisoned in Chester Castle. Meanwhile Salisbury's remaining forces were pursued into the marches by the main royal army, which now included around twenty of the peers of the realm. They met up with York and Warwick, but by now their ranks were disappointingly thin and they were outnumbered by around three to one. In desperation, the three Yorkist lords came together at Worcester Cathedral, and in great solemnity swore oaths to protect one another. Then they retreated to York's nearby castle of Ludlow, where on 10 October they wrote jointly to Henry VI, protesting their 'humble obeisance and reverence' before condemning the realm's misgovernment, the failure of the law and the violence rampant throughout the kingdom. They also complained of the 'impatience and violence of such persones as intend of extreme malice to proceed under the shadow of your high might and presence to our destruction'.[13]

The letters may have reached the king and his councillors, but after Blore Heath they were hardly in the mood to listen sympathetically. Just as at St Albans, a Yorkist army had been raised against the peace of the realm, and blood – some of it noble blood – had been spilled. Messages returned across the midlands from the court: the rebellious lords were to lay down their arms and beg for the royal pardon within six days. They refused, and another armed confrontation became inevitable. Audley and his men may have been dead and defeated, but another large royal army was closing in.

By the second week of October the Yorkists were camped in fields south of Ludlow. Above them, on high ground, brooded Ludlow Castle, with huge turrets and towers, vast arched doorways and narrow windows, and sheets of stoutly defended walls over which fluttered the duke of York's arms. In front of Ludlow the river Teme swirled cold and fast, the only route across it into the town passing over the thick, recently built stone thoroughfare known as Ludford Bridge. On the south bank of the Teme, below the bridge, the rebel lords' army was drawn up.

Yorkist morale was already evaporating when, on 12 October, the royal army finally appeared before them. It included an impressive group of English lords: commanded by Henry duke of Somerset, Humphrey duke of Buckingham and Henry earl of Northumberland, and including the duke of Exeter and earls of Arundel, Devon, Shrewsbury and Wiltshire. The royal standard flew above them, and although in a rather desperate propaganda move the Yorkists had spread rumours that Henry VI was dead, it was obvious he was not: in fact he and Queen Margaret were with the army, probably in the rear. It seemed clearer than ever that for all their justified grievances and maltreatment at the queen's hands, the Yorkists represented partisanship and faction, while the assembled lords in front of them stood for the closest thing that existed to the united political opinion of the realm. It may also have become commonly known that summons had been sent out for a parliament in November, at which it was certain that York and his allies would be destroyed by acts of attainder.

Evening was drawing in when the Yorkists began to fire their cannon towards the royal lines. These were the preliminary exchanges of a battle that was intended to be fought the following day: 13 October, St Edward's Day, the prince of Wales's birthday and the most auspicious day of the whole year for English kingship. To York and the Nevilles it seemed that there was only one way that the day would be marked: with their armies scattered, their lives imperilled and their families put on the road to utter ruin. York's own family was in close quarter at Ludlow: his seventeen-year-old son Edward earl of March was at his side, so too his second son, the sixteen-year-old Edmund earl of Rutland. Behind them in the castle were Duchess Cecily and her two younger boys, George, aged nine, and Richard, who had just celebrated his seventh birthday. Would the king, spurred by his vengeful wife, spare them, if it came to that?

Defeatism was seeping into the Yorkist ranks. At some point during the evening, while the irregular boom of cannon echoed over the black water of the river Teme, one of Warwick's captains, a Calais soldier called Andrew Trollope, led his hardened troops out of the Yorkist camp and over to the royal side to submit to the king, taking with him both valuable fighting men and invaluable military intelligence. Now faced with what amounted to certain obliteration, in the dead of night York and his leading allies sneaked out of camp, back to Ludlow Castle, leaving their army standing oblivious in their wake as they rode hard away from the battlefield. It was a highly dishonourable thing to do, but the only means by which they could save themselves. From Shropshire they scattered 'in to diverse parties . . . beyond the sea, for the more surety of their personnes'.[14] York and his son Rutland made for the Welsh coast, breaking bridges as they went, before taking boats across the sea to Ireland. The Nevilles, meanwhile, fled in great peril to the west country, taking with them the young Edward earl of March. From Devon they took ship to Guernsey, from where they returned to Warwick's haven in Calais.

They had saved their skins but at great cost to their reputations and honour. Their men, who rose for the anticipated battle, instead found themselves surrendering and petitioning for royal forgiveness. Queen Margaret, standing behind the royal lines, no doubt took great satisfaction in this moment. Four years on from the debacle of St Albans, her enemies had finally scurried from the royal standard like frightened mice. 'Every lord in England at the time durst not disobey the Queen,' wrote one chronicler.[15] All that remained was to return to Coventry and prepare for the November parliament, where their legal destruction, and the desolation of their families, could be completed.

Up in Ludlow Castle, another great lady of the realm viewed events unfolding with growing alarm. Cecily Neville, duchess of York, had seen her husband and second son run in one direction while her brother, nephew and eldest son (Salisbury, Warwick and March) hastened in another. On 13 October she watched from the castle as royal troops broke into the town and began its sack. It was a scene that would be repeated all across the kingdom in the coming months, as Yorkist properties were despoiled and their tenants harassed. Cecily had seen enough of the violent politics of Normandy, Ireland and England during her marriage to know that she was in terrible danger. And most immediately she had to consider the safety of the two males of her kin who had not run from her: her young boys, George and Richard. As the sack of Ludlow concluded she walked out of the castle gates, taking the children with her. A day of terror and confusion had seen some men staggering drunkenly about the streets, having robbed the taverns of their 'pipes and hogs-heads of wine', while others stole 'bedding, clothes, and other stuff, and defiled many women'.[16] The grand wife of the vanquished duke walked through the streets of the ransacked town, her sons by her side. They walked as far as the overturned marketplace, in the shadow of the castle walls, and then came to a halt: the remnants of a great family, throwing themselves on the mercy of the crown. While Ludlow 'was robbed to the bare walles', Cecily, George and Richard simply stood and waited for whatever fate was to meet them.[17]

11 : Suddenly Fell Down the Crown

Nearly two thousand men poured onto the ships that set sail from Calais on a summer's day in late June 1460. They were headed for the coast of Kent, to Sandwich, the sheltered port a few miles north of Dover, whose long, sandy stretch of coastline made landing a large force of men and munitions a straightforward task. The journey across the Channel was rapid, and the soldiers who piled aboard the invading vessels were something of a crack force: 'a strong and a mighty navy', as one chronicler put it.[1] Their leader and commander was the earl of Warwick.

For nearly eleven months, since the flight from Ludford Bridge, Warwick had turned Calais into a bristling citadel for English dissidents and opponents of Queen Margaret. There were plenty to be found. As had been expected, in the dying months of 1459 the queen had moved against her enemies with indignation and spite. An act of attainder had been passed at a parliament held in St Mary's Priory in Coventry before Christmas – a gathering that would later be nicknamed the 'Parliament of Devils' – which attempted the utter legal and financial ruin of York and his sons, and a whole raft of their friends, servants, associates and allies. The attainder had been introduced with an absurdly propagandising preamble, in which the duke of York was painted as a scheming, ungrateful monster, 'whose false and traitorous imaginations, conspiracies, feats and diligent labours born up with colourable lies' amounted to the worst deeds that 'ever did any subject to his sovereign lord', while Henry VI was cast not only as a generous sovereign whose trust had been betrayed and life endangered (at St Albans), but as a vigorous soldier who valiantly faced down his enemies on the battlefield, and whose addresses to his subjects could be described as 'so witty, so knightly, so manly'.[2]

The penalty of attainder amounted to legal death. It stripped its victims of 'all their estates, honoures and dignities, which they or any of them hath within this your realm of England, and within Wales and Ireland', including 'all honours, castles, lord-ships, manors, landes, tenements, rents, reversions, annuities, offices, fees, advowsons, fee-farms, inheritances and other pos-sessions'. It was aimed not only at York and his sons Edward earl of March and Edmund earl of Rutland, but also at Salisbury and Warwick and their noble supporter John, Lord Clinton. A whole raft of other Yorkist servants, retainers and associates were also swept up, including Sir Walter Devereux, Sir William Oldhall and Salisbury's wife, Countess Alice. John de la Pole, who had inherited the title of duke of Suffolk from his father, was said to have been demoted to the rank of earl for the 'crime' of being married to York's daughter Elizabeth.[3]

Although a few culpable figures escaped ruin – Thomas, Lord Stanley was forgiven his refusal to engage at Blore Heath – by and large the queen embarked on a severe and vengeful cam-paign against all York's affiliates. Their lands and titles were swept into royal possession, their officials dismissed and replaced, and the administration of the confiscated estates given over to men of longstanding obedience to the crown and court. High among the beneficiaries were men of the king's immediate family. Owen Tudor was given a pension of £100 a year, to be paid for the rest of his life out of manors seized from Lord Clinton. Jasper Tudor, who had spent the last four years representing the king's authority in south Wales, was given the rights of constable, steward and chief forester to York's rich and strategically crucial lordship of Denbigh, along with rights of military recruitment over virtually the whole of Wales to help him seize Denbigh Castle from its disgruntled Yorkist keepers.

Yet for all their determination to destroy the Yorkists by law, the queen and her government found themselves unable to reach their enemies in person. York and his second son Edmund were safe in Ireland, and although James earl of Wiltshire – a spineless creature of the queen who ranked among the men most hated by the Yorkists – was appointed lieutenant of Ireland, he could not physically take up his role thanks to the support that York enjoyed across the sea. The situation was more or less mirrored in Calais, where Warwick now enjoyed pre-eminence and protection from all the harm that so many in England would have dearly loved to do to him.

Now thirty-one, Warwick had not come to Calais to live in fearful exile. He was a veteran soldier, a highly regarded and popular leader and a shrewd politician who used his aristocratic pedigree on the continent to recruit allies ranging from the duke of Burgundy to envoys of the papal court. With his father Salisbury and his nephew, York's son Edward earl of March, Warwick had spent the year regrouping and rearming.

Henry Beaufort, duke of Somerset had been sent by Queen Margaret to eject the rebels and take up the captaincy of Calais for himself, but Somerset could get no further than the neighbouring town of Guînes, from where his repeated assaults were easily repulsed. Meanwhile, piratical Yorkist raiding parties arrived like Vikings on the beaches of Kent, attacking towns and kidnapping or murdering royal captains. On two occasions Warwick's men stole and scuppered ships on the Kentish coast that the Crown was assembling there specifically to use against him. In one particularly daring raid, the loyalist lord Richard Woodville, Lord Rivers, and his son, Anthony Woodville, were sent to Sandwich with instructions to launch an attack on Calais, only to be abducted by Warwick's men and taken back to the garrison as prisoners. Alongside this daring guerrilla campaign, Warwick bravely kept up communications with York and Rutland in

Ireland: indeed, in March 1460 the earl managed to sail along the entire coast of southern England and Wales and hold a conference with York in Waterford on the south coast of Ireland, where the two rebel camps discussed their return to England.

Warwick, March and Salisbury landed at Sandwich on 26 June and found the town readied for their arrival. An advance party under Salisbury's brother Lord Fauconberg had stormed the royal defences the previous day, stealing the town's weapons cache and summarily beheading the unlucky royal captain Osbert Mundford, who happened to be in command. The Yorkists had sent ahead of them their now customary manifesto, protesting absolute loyalty to the king and rehearsing their condemnation of the Crown's poverty, the absence of justice and the failure of the king's household to 'to live upon his own livelihood' (i.e. to be funded by the king's private revenue, rather than relying on taxation). They added an accusation that ever since Humphrey duke of Gloucester had been 'murdered' at Bury in 1447 it had been 'conspired, to have destroyed and murdered the said duke of York', along with his issue 'of the royal blood'. Rather than directly attacking the king or queen, scathing criticism was reserved for Wiltshire, Shrewsbury and Beaumont, the lords who had replaced the old duke of Somerset as the object of the Yorkists' scorn.[4] The manifesto broke little new ground either in tone or substance. The Yorkists rightly recognised that the Crown's popular support was strongest in the midlands, the north-west and Wales; the rumble of disaffection that had led Kent and the south-east into open rebellion during Jack Cade's heyday had never wholly faded, and could easily be stirred up with a rabble-rousing publication espousing the cause of York.

By 2 July Warwick and his men were in London, with thousands of supporters streaming to their side from across southern England. To the relief of the mayor and aldermen of London, who had seen the city turned upside down by rampaging rebel armies enough times over the preceding decade, the Yorkists stayed in the capital for only around forty-eight hours before drawing up into two large divisions: the first led by Fauconberg and the second headed by Edward and Warwick. They tramped north at pace to confront the king.

Fauconberg took with him a distinguished, if extremely pompous and slightly absurd ecclesiastic: Francesco Coppini, the bishop of Terni. Coppini had been appointed as papal legate to Henry VI, with a mandate to recruit England to a crusade against the Turks, but after meeting Warwick in Calais, he had become a very enthusiastic Yorkist partisan and propagandist. Shortly before leaving London for the march north, Coppini published at St Paul's a colourful open letter to Henry VI, emphasising the supposed 'obedience and loyalty' of the Yorkists and damning their enemies as 'clerks and ministers of the devil'. He issued the starkest warnings to the king and government, forecasting 'the danger and ruin of your state' if they failed to come to terms with Warwick and his allies. Those that 'close their ears like deaf vipers, woe to them and also to your Majesty,' wrote Coppini. 'The danger is imminent and does not brook delay.' He was absolutely right.

By 7 July the Yorkists' two columns were approaching the midlands. The speed at which they had moved took the court at Coventry entirely by surprise. Henry and Queen Margaret had no choice but to go out and meet the rebels. They rode south rattled and under-strength. There was no time for Henry earl of Northumberland or John, Lord Clifford to reach the royal army with their men, and while the king and queen were attended by great lords like Humphrey duke of Buckingham, the earl of Shrewsbury, Viscount Beaumont and a healthy smattering of Percys, the Yorkists had attracted far more noble support than at any previous foray into the field. Their supporters included John Mowbray, duke of Norfolk, who had for many years been inclined to York's cause without ever before fully committing himself to military action; Warwick could count among his men John, Lord Audley, the son and heir of the leader who was slain at Blore Heath by Salisbury. The Yorkists were also accompanied by a large group of the most important churchmen in the realm: Thomas Bourchier, archbishop of Canterbury, the legate Coppini and the bishops of London, Exeter, Lincoln, Salisbury, Ely and Rochester.

The two sides met on 10 July in the meadows outside Northampton, on the south bank of the river Nene. It was a miserably wet day, with rain pounding from the sky and churning up the turf as it was trampled over by thousands of boots and hoofs: horrible weather for fighting, not least since the water ruined the royal guns. Nevertheless, the duke of Buckingham, who was given command of the royal forces as the king and queen hung back, refused to negotiate. He lined his men up between a slight bend in the river and the nearby Delapré Abbey and prepared to give battle. The bishops retreated to a safe distance to watch.

What they witnessed was not, in overall numbers, an especially bloody battle. But within half an hour of the first exchanges, the royal forces were dealt a massive and devastating blow. Their men were divided into three groupings: Buckingham leading the left flank, Shrewsbury and Beaumont in the centre, and Lord Grey of Ruthin on the right. Early in the battle Grey decided to defect, bringing his men over to the Yorkist side, where Fauconberg, Warwick and March held command. The result was total confusion among the king's army. Battered by the rain, they abandoned their discipline, and soldiers began to desert, running for Northampton, with several drowning in the Nene under the weight of their provisions and armour. As panic and chaos descended, Warwick's men followed the ruthless tactics that had served them well six years before at St Albans. Warwick himself had called across the field that 'no man shuld lay hand upon the king nor on the common people, but only on the lords, knights and squires'.[5] Thus the rank and file were spared and hit squads moved around the battlefield, cutting down the captains. By the end, only around three hundred men lay slain on the field, out of more than ten thousand who had been arrayed for the fight. But among the dead were Buckingham, Beaumont, Shrewsbury and Thomas Percy, Lord Egremont, all hunted out and killed where they stood. The whole operation took less than half an hour. While the butchering of the lords was taking place, the king was captured, as helpless in the field as he had been in 1455. He was taken first to Delapré Abbey, then on to London, no longer a puppet of his wife, but a prisoner of the earl of Warwick and his allies.

*

Cecily Neville, duchess of York had been scooped up at Ludlow following the battle of Ludford Bridge and taken with her sons George and Richard to a place of relatively genteel confinement: they were sent to stay with Cecily's sister Anne, the wife of Humphrey duke of Buckingham. It was a favour granted when, strictly, one was not due. Cecily had been awarded one thousand marks a year to compensate for the loss of her husband's income and to offer relief to 'her and her infants who had not offended against the king'.[6] The confinement was perhaps not entirely warm – one writer heard that Anne kept her younger sister 'full straight [with] many a great rebuke' – but under the circumstances she was treated well. Cecily was still with Anne in the summer of 1460, when the awful news arrived of Buckingham's death by the hand of Warwick – who was, of course, both women's nephew. In some senses this sort of thing was inevitable, for the Nevilles were a huge and broadly married dynasty, their bloodline woven across the divide in English politics. But it still must have felt to the two sisters, who were only divided by a year in age, that their family was tearing both itself and England apart.

After the battle of Northampton Cecily and her sons were released from their house arrest. With the king now in Warwick's keep, it had become safe for Richard duke of York to return once again from Ireland, a journey that had been too perilous earlier in the summer, due to royal control of Wales, the marches and the north-west. York landed at Redbank, near Chester, on or around 8 September. But as he came, it was clear that something was different about him. In his absence his allies had fought successfully for their party to regain control of the king. They could have expected the duke, their talisman and figurehead, to try his hand once more at governing England as chief councillor or protector. Instead they found him angling for another position entirely.

Cecily was reunited with her husband at Abingdon in early October. It was a grand reunion. York had instructed his wife to meet him enthroned upon a 'chair covered with blue velvet', drawn by four pairs of coursers. He himself arrived dressed in a livery of white and blue, neatly embroidered with fetterlocks – the D-shaped iron manacles used to tether horses by the leg. The symbol had first been associated with John of Gaunt, the direct ancestor of Henry VI, but had also been used by Edward of Norwich, Richard's uncle and predecessor as duke of York, who had died at Agincourt alongside Henry V. There was no mistaking the Plantagenet pedigree that the livery implied.[7] Together the duke and duchess went on to London, with trumpets and clarions blown before them all the way. Banners displaying the arms of England caught the wind high above the procession, and to complete his majestic appearance, York 'commanded his sword to be borne upright before him'.[8] York had not returned from Ireland for a second time to serve as a councillor. He had come back to England as a king.

His peers were shocked. The central tenet of Yorkist opposition – indeed of all opposition to Henry VI's rule – had always been the assertion that those who surrounded the king were enemies and traitors. Indeed, everything that had been done in England since the death of Henry V had been to preserve the power and authority of the king and crown – whether the king was a baby, an easily swayed adolescent, a naïve young man, a dribbling lunatic or a defeated, world-weary shell of a thing, prematurely ready for the grave. This was the realm's first political principle. To depose or attempt to replace a king who was not actively tyrannical (as Edward II and Richard II had been) was not just wrong, it was nearly unthinkable. And for all his failings, Henry VI was the opposite of a tyrant.

After more than fifteen years of opposition, York had crossed the line. It was an action not openly approved by his allies (although it is possible that Warwick suspected York's intentions) and regarded with amazement by his enemies.

The most likely explanation for it lay in the person of his one remaining enemy: the queen. Edmund duke of Somerset, Humphrey duke of Buckingham, the old earl of Northumberland, the young earl of Shrewsbury and Lord Beaumont were all dead. James earl of Wiltshire, Jasper Tudor, earl of Pembroke and others survived, but they were not the principal threat. This lay, manifestly, with Queen Margaret – and with her conduit to practical power in the seven-year-old Edward, prince of Wales. A queen and a little boy could not very well be killed, yet every day that she lived increased Margaret's hatred for York. So long as her son was heir to the crown she, and subsequently he, would stand opposed to York's survival and ambition. The only solution was for York to position himself either as king or – as his cousin Henry V had done in France under the terms of the treaty of Troyes in 1420 – as the king's heir. Both options would disinherit Prince Edward and thereby neuter the queen. In terms of raw power politics, the decision made sense. Practically, though, it was a catastrophic misjudgement.

York had renounced his duty of obedience to Henry VI some

time before he met Cecily in Abingdon. The sword carried before him was the most obvious sign of this, but he had also stopped using Henry's regnal year to date his documents.[9] He seems to have been confident that, having been lauded for years by the commons of England (albeit not all of the lords) as a man with the credentials to occupy the throne, he would sweep into his new position to the sound of cheers and celebration.

In this he was sorely disappointed. At ten o'clock in the morning on Friday 10 October York arrived at the palace of Westminster, where parliament was sitting, with several hundred men on horseback. He entered the palace with his sword still borne before him and stormed through the Great Hall. High in the wooden arches of the hammer-beam ceiling, Henry Yevele's famous fifteen statues of historical English kings stared impassively down upon the latest man to lay violent claim to the crown they had all worn. York marched on, bursting into the Painted Chamber to find the parliamentary lords assembled before an empty throne. Standing before his peers as his servants held the cloth of state over his head, York 'gave them knowledge that he purposed not to lay down his sword but to challenge his right'.[10] He was staking his claim to the crown on the basis that his right in blood, descending twice from Edward III, via the Mortimer and York lines, was superior to that of the king or prince of Wales, and 'that no man shuld have denied the crown from his head'.[11] There was a stunned silence. He then retired to take up lodgings in the queen's chambers. The queen, mercifully, had fled to Wales, and was not present to protest.

If there had been any great gusto for York's plan before he announced it in parliament, then enthusiasm was extremely muted thereafter. Nobles and commons alike were immediately struck by the sheer, awful reality of deposing a king. York was asked to submit his claim to the crown, which he did on 16 October via the chancellor, his nephew George Neville, bishop

of Exeter. Neville presented to the parliament a large genealogical roll, detailing York's descent from Henry III via Edward
III, and describing how the Mortimer and York lines had inter-
twined to produce him, 'Richard Plantaginet, commonly called
duc of York'.[12] This, went York's argument, gave him dynastic
precedence over Henry VI, who was descended from his great-
grandfather Edward III's third son, John of Gaunt. Gaunt's son
Henry IV had therefore acted 'unrightwisely' (i.e. unlawfully) in
seizing the crown in 1399, and 'the right, title, dignity royal and
estate of the crowns of the realms of England and of France,
and of the lordship and land of Ireland, of right, law and custom
appertaineth and belongeth' to Richard duke of York.

It fell to parliament to debate the matter. But what was it
that they were really debating? The dynastic case was there to
be made, for if one accepted that the right to the crown could
run through the female line (as York did when he trumpeted his
Mortimer ancestry) then the duke had the better claim in blood.
And yet it was clear that the claim in blood was only a mode
of addressing a deeper argument. Had York really acted out of
the conviction that his cause was purely one of dynastic right
and wrong, he should surely have staked his claim at some previous point in the two decades. He had not. The English dynastic
argument in 1460 was as much a veil for a practical argument
about effective kingship as English claims to the crown of France
had been during the 1420s. It was not the real reason that York
claimed the throne: his real purpose encompassed a broad sense
that Henry VI's incompetence, allied with Queen Margaret's
tyrannical instincts, could be tolerated no longer, bound up with
a heavy-handed sense of self-importance. All the duke's previous efforts to amend and correct royal government had failed.
Dynasty was the last resort. Now it was up to parliament to say
whether they would accept this.

Following two weeks of debate a compromise was decided.

Given the hideous breach that was suggested by the prospect of a full deposition, a Troyes-like settlement was thrashed out.[13] First, the acts of the 1459 'Parliament of Devils' were rescinded. Then, on the matter of the succession, it was agreed that the king would enjoy the crown for the rest of his natural life, but the duke would be 'entitled, called and reputed from henceforth, very and rightful heir to the crowns, royal estate, dignity and lordship'. Young Prince Edward was thus abruptly replaced in the royal line first by York and then by his sons, March and Rutland. The agreement was publicised on 31 October 1460 and bolstered by the astonishingly efficient Yorkist propaganda machine, which had in the summer been energetically spreading rumours – quite false – that Prince Edward was illegitimate and thus in every way 'not the king's son'.[14]

The cosmos, it seemed, now pointed towards York. Indeed, while the commons were debating in the refectory of Westminster Abbey, 'treating upon the title of the said Duke of York, suddenly fell down the crown which hung in [the] midst of the said house . . . which was taken for a profige or token that the reign of King Henry was ended'.[15] But it would not be that simple. For even if the supine king was prepared to yield his title to a belligerent cousin, there remained one person who would never accept the derogation of their family's royal status. Queen Margaret was still at large.

*

As Christmas approached in 1460, the queen and her supporters found themselves scattered to the corners of the realm. At the end of November, while York sought to destroy her family's future at Westminster, Margaret was encamped at Harlech Castle with her brother-in-law Jasper earl of Pembroke. The countryside was fraught with danger, and counterfeit letters reached her regularly, 'forged things' in King Henry's hand, begging her to bring Prince

Edward south. They were delivered without any sign of the secret code Margaret had arranged for Henry to add to his letters if he were captured, so the queen gave them 'no credence'. All the same, the Yorkists would soon be coming for her and her son, realising that she would remain the focus of opposition. To use the pithy phrase of one chronicler, it was clear to the whole kingdom that 'she was more wittier than the king'.[16] Employing that wit to good effect, Margaret decided to risk the freezing western seas in order to escape from Wales. On a cold day in late November she took Prince Edward by ship to Scotland. They arrived in the northern kingdom around 3 December, and went to stay at the haunting, gothic collegiate church of Lincluden, which stood on a bend in the river Nith, just outside Dumfries. They stayed under the protection of Mary of Guelders, widow of the recently deceased King James II of Scotland and regent to the nine-year-old King James III. The two women found that they had much in common.

Soon after Margaret reached Lincluden, she learned that her ally Henry earl of Northumberland was raising an army in the north of England, riding through their enemies' estates with sword and fire, raising what hell they could, while spreading rumours about the duke of York and attempting to stir the common people to rebellion. This, Margaret realised, could be the basis of a force to strike back against the usurpers. From Scotland she managed to contact Henry duke of Somerset, Thomas earl of Devon and their capable military supporter Alexander Hody, a veteran soldier of the west country. All were based hundreds of miles south, but she instructed them to find their way by whatever means they could to Hull to muster for the counter-attack. Their party included Andrew Trollope, the treacherous Calais captain whose defection from the Yorkist side had resulted in the rout of Ludford Bridge. The queen wrote in Prince Edward's name to the city of London, denouncing York as a 'horrible and falsely forsworn traitor . . . mortal enemy to my lord, to my lady and to us' with an 'untrue pretensed claim' to the crown, and asking for the citizens' aid to free King Henry from the duke's malicious grasp.[17]

To put together any sort of army in the grip of winter, much less move it across a dozen counties along wet and freezing mud tracks, was ambitious to the point of desperation. So when news of Northumberland's mobilisation reached York's circle in London, they were taken quite by surprise. The prospect of losing control of government for a third time was enough to spur York urgently to arms. As soon as details of Margaret's movements were known, York and Salisbury set out from the south-east to put down the insurgency and 'bring in the Queen'.[18] Edward earl of March went to Wales to face down an army rampaging there under Jasper Tudor.

By 21 December York had reached Sandal Castle, near Wakefield in west Yorkshire: a large stone fortress with turreted curtain walls encircling a fearsome keep on top of a motte overlooking the Calder valley. As a result of the weather and the speed at which they had set off to defend the north, York and Salisbury were sorely outmanned by the rapidly assembled partisans of the queen. York and his supporters spent a meagre Christmas inside Sandal Castle, with supplies thin and their enemies overrunning the adjoining lands, some camped outside the walls, and others raiding from their base in the nearby castle of Pontefract.

On 30 December a foraging party was attacked by Somerset and Devon's men, and York decided to strike back. Why he did so is unclear. Possibly he was drawn out by a ruse concocted by his erstwhile captain Andrew Trollope, or else he believed a Christmas truce to be in place. He may have been given to believe that he had eight thousand men arriving, mustered by John, Lord Neville, an elder step-brother of Salisbury – although this Lord Neville had hitherto been a staunch supporter of the queen's party, and was an unlikely turncoat. Whatever his reasons, York rode out of Sandal seemingly believing that he would be able to push back the substantial forces of his enemies. He was not. He was barely out of the castle when soldiers bore down on him from four sides: Somerset, Northumberland and Neville attacked him head on, Exeter and Lord Roos closed in from either flank, and Lord Clifford closed the trap, preventing a retreat back into the castle. York was outnumbered perhaps five to one by men who not only opposed his political ambition but for the most part genuinely loathed him. As a much later writer would describe it, he was 'environed on every side like a fish in a net or a deer in a buckstall'.[19]

After an hour of heavy fighting the duke was overcome. Seeing the situation becoming impossible, he sent his son Rutland to flee. Rutland ran for Wakefield Bridge, the proud, nine-arched stone crossing of the river Calder. On the far side stood the chantry chapel of St Mary the Virgin: the seventeen-year-old earl may have hoped to throw himself inside and seek sanctuary. But he fell agonisingly short. Lord Clifford had chased him from the battlefield, and caught up with him on or near the bridge. He was surrounded. Clifford stepped forward, cursed the young man and told him to prepare for his death, 'as your father slew mine'. Then, as pleas for Rutland's life rang out from all around – including, it was later claimed, from the boy's tutor and chaplain Robert Aspall, who stood by his side – Clifford drew his dagger and thrust it through his heart.[20] The blood debt of St Albans had been paid: truly, the son had suffered for the sins of the father.

The father, however, was faring little better. Hemmed in on all sides, York was trying to fight his way back to the castle. But it was too late. He was seized in the scramble of battle – Sir James Luttrell of Devonshire was later named as his captor – and dragged away. His helmet was removed, and a rough paper crown placed on his head. Then Richard duke of York, the man who would have been many things, including a king, was paraded in front of the contemptuous soldiers of his foes and beheaded.

Many more Yorkists died on the battlefield that day. Besides York and Rutland, Salisbury's son Sir Thomas Neville was also taken and killed. Salisbury himself had escaped from Sandal Castle and was attempting to flee northwards. But he made it little further than Rutland. During the night, the sixty-year-old earl was captured and brought back to enemy headquarters at Pontefract Castle. The next day he was taken out and executed in public. Soon after the heads of the four dead Yorkists were sent to the city of York to be displayed upon the Micklegate. There the duke of York's dead eyes stared down at the passing citizens, his paper crown still jammed down on his bloodied forehead.

Years of fractious politics and growing personal enmity had come to this. 'Acts of vengeance have been perpetrated on both sides,' wrote the papal legate and Yorkist supporter Bishop Coppini to one of his associates who was camped with the queen.[21] Margaret, Prince Edward and their allies had finally vanquished their greatest opponent. But the king remained in the hands of Warwick and Edward earl of March.

The realm was now truly split: the queen's party now as much of a faction as the Yorkists. (From this point we can properly refer to the former as 'Lancastrians' after the duchy of Lancaster – King Henry's private duchy, which had belonged to kings of England since the reign of his grandfather Henry IV. The duchy of Lancaster was the source of Henry's private power, rather than his public authority, which had finally evaporated.) Neither side seemed strong enough to defeat the other. And while Rutland's death at the battle of Wakefield had settled the score with Clifford, the rest of the slaughter only served to intensify the blood feud that now dragged England's magnates towards each other, armed, dangerous and desperate: whirling in a vicious dance of death.

12 : Havoc

Clement Paston, a student in London of around nineteen years old, wrote to his brother John in a state of some anxiety. Clement was a bright and level-headed young man, who had studied at Cambridge before going down to the city in the late 1450s for a professional education. He had grown up in turbulent times, and his East Anglian family's fortunes had risen and fallen according to the ebb and flow of national politics and the success or failure of their patrons near the royal court. Even at a relatively young age he was used to seeing Fortune's wheel turn, but on 23 January 1461, when Clement sat down to dash off a communiqué to his relatives in the countryside, he admitted to his brother that he was writing 'in haste' and 'not well at ease'.[1]

Even by the standards of tumult that had become customary on the streets of London over the previous decade, the winter of 1460–1 was a disturbed and dangerous time. York's defeat at Wakefield was now well known around England. But the fact of his demise had done nothing to calm the realm. In the west, his wrathful son Edward – eighteen years old but by now a strapping man of six foot four with a warrior's temperament – was leading an army against Henry VI's half-brother Jasper Tudor. The earl of Warwick, meanwhile, still held Henry prisoner, preventing any theoretical return to 'ordinary' royal government. And most troublingly of all, Queen Margaret was loose in the north, buoyed by her allies' victory in the field and said to be travelling south to take both vengeance and the capital. Rumours were flying around on the 'common voice' and Clement Paston reported a few that had reached his ears: he told of knights of the family's acquaintance who were 'taken or else dead', he described London's apparent preference for the Yorkists over the queen, and he relayed the fear that French and Scottish mercenaries and the northern lords' English retainers who made up a large part of the queen's army were being permitted to 'rob and steal' in the towns through which they passed – a fate no Londoner wished to share. Clement advised his elder brother to muster forces – 'footmen and horsemen' – in East Anglia and be ready to join battle at any moment, making sure that the men raised were presented in clean and orderly fashion, for the sake of the family honour. 'God have [you] in His keeping', the young man signed off, and this was more than the conventional pleasantry of correspondence.

England was in a state of civil war. The battles that had been fought since 1455 were sporadic, occasional outbursts of violence. But now armies were in the field throughout England and Wales, employing foreign mercenaries, trained noble retainers and haphazardly conscripted lords' tenants alike. On 2 February 1461 Edward's army clashed with that of Jasper Tudor, Owen Tudor and James Butler, earl of Wiltshire at Mortimer's Cross, near Wigmore Castle in the Welsh marches, where the road passed between London and Aberystwyth. It was a day that would burnish the eighteen-year-old Edward's reputation and his legend like no other. The 'Rose of Rouen' – as he was nicknamed by Yorkist partisans – was joined in command by several stalwarts of his late father's Welsh lands, including Sir Walter Devereux and the Herbert brothers, Sir William and Richard Herbert of Raglan. Their enemies were formidably reinforced, for Wiltshire had brought over large contingents of Breton and French mercenaries, as well as his own retainers from his Irish estates. But they had marched at pace across Wales from Pembroke and arrived at the battlefield weary. And in Edward they came up against a commander who was learning how to inspire men with an almost devout fervour.

On the morning of the battle, the winter sky was filled with a blinding and baffling sight: three suns rising together over the horizon, which then combined to form a single blazing beacon in the sky.[2] Edward read this as a divine portent predicting his victory, and his forces tore into the Wiltshire–Tudor army, routing them in relatively short order. Jasper Tudor and the earl of Wiltshire escaped the battlefield, but Owen Tudor, now about sixty years old, was captured, along with Sir John Throckmorton and seven other Lancastrian commanders. They were taken to the nearby town of Hereford, where a chopping block had been erected in the marketplace. According to one contemporary account, Owen Tudor expected his enemies to show him some leniency, although this would have been extraordinarily naïve less than six weeks after the horrible butchery that had followed the battle of Wakefield. Any remaining confidence drained from him when 'he saw the axe and the block'. Stripped to his red velvet doublet, the old man stood before the assembled townsmen of Hereford and begged 'pardon and grace'. Then the collar of his doublet was rudely torn away and he was led towards the headsman.

One chronicler wrote that Owen Tudor's last words recalled his wife, the princess of France and queen of England who had seen fit to marry this humble Welshman and bear his children. 'That head shall lie on the stock that was wont to lie on Queen Catherine's lap,' he said. Then he put 'his heart and mind wholly unto God, and full meekly took his death'.[3]

Owen Tudor's bloodied head was set upon the highest point of the market cross. Some time later a woman, possibly Owen's mistress and the mother of his infant bastard David Owen, was seen washing the blood from the mangled head, combing its hair and setting more than one hundred candles around it. The crowd, if they took any notice, assumed she was insane.[4]

The Yorkist triumph at Mortimer's Cross barely lasted as long as the glow of the three suns that had preceded it. Jasper Tudor and Wiltshire fled, eventually to take refuge in Scotland. But theirs had not been the only Lancastrian army on the march. As Edward regrouped at Hereford, Queen Margaret was mustering her other allies, including the dukes of Somerset and Exeter, the earls of Northumberland and Shrewsbury, a large host of northern lords and the ubiquitous Calais turncoat Andrew Trollope. By 10 February this violent army of hardened northerners and foreign sell-swords had burned and looted its way as far as Cambridgeshire. By 16 February they had broken the defences of Dunstable, in Bedfordshire. London was close at hand and Warwick, in charge both of King Henry VI and the government of England, was forced to act. Earlier in the year the earl had written to Pope Pius II, telling him, 'Your Holiness must not be troubled if you have heard of the events in England and of the destruction of some of my kinsmen in the battle against our enemies. With the help of God and the king, who is excellently disposed, all will end well.'[5] Now his faith and confidence were to be tested.

Warwick took a large army out of London, aided by John Mowbray, duke of Norfolk, John de la Pole, duke of Suffolk, William FitzAlan, earl of Arundel and a clutch of his own peers, including his brother John Neville, his uncle Lord Fauconberg and the treasurer, Lord Bonville. They left Londoners in a state of deep trepidation. Another battle was fully expected, in which, as one correspondent put it, 'great shedding of blood cannot be avoided, and whoever conquers, the Crown of England loses, which is a very great pity'.[6]

For the second time in less than six years, the two forces met at the city of St Albans. But whereas in 1455 skirmishing and street fighting had taken place, on Shrove Tuesday, 17 February 1461 it was all-out war. Thousands of men descended on either side: the Milanese ambassador in France would hear stories of the queen and Somerset commanding thirty thousand men each.[7] This was a wild exaggeration, but what is not in doubt is the fear that these huge forces struck into the hearts of the ordinary people of St Albans. The abbot, John Whethamstede, wrote in his official register of the savagery, profanity and appetite for destruction among the northerners, who in his view seemed to consider any incursion south of the Trent as a divinely sanctioned opportunity to plunder and steal.[8]

In truth, the northern army was much more than a rabble with pillage on their minds. As they had shown at Wakefield, they were commanded with discipline and cunning; they also marched under one identity, with every man wearing the badge of Edward, prince of Wales, a red-and-black band with ostrich feathers. Warwick's men were blindsided by enemy troops pouring into St Albans at around 1 p.m. from the north-west, rather than the north-east, and after heavy fighting the Yorkist vanguard was scattered, fleeing in every direction as the hoofs of the Lancastrian cavalry thundered after them. Abbot Whethamstede wrote of men being rounded up and run through with lances by their vengeful enemies, until finally, around 6 p.m., the darkness of the winter evening had fully fallen, and pursuit was no longer possible.[9] As their men scampered for safety, Warwick and most of his fellow commanders and captains also melted away, until only one man of any noble dignity was left on the field.

King Henry VI sat under a tree, laughing and singing as the battle raged about him. The king's guards, Lord Bonville and Sir Thomas Kyriell, were taken prisoner and summarily executed on the orders of the queen, who allowed the eight-year-old prince to pronounce the sentences upon them. Henry, meanwhile, was reunited with his family, once more changing hands like a rag doll. Abbot Whethamstede met the king in the abbey and begged him to issue a proclamation against plundering. As ever, Henry VI did what he was told. His own army ignored him and Whethamstede's beloved city of St Albans fell to rape and robbery, as though, said the abbot, it had been invaded by rabid animals.[10]

*

As fortune swung violently back and forth between the two parties, England was plunged into a desperate mood of self-preservation. After St Albans, the queen decided to push on to London. The city, however, decided to make a stand against her. Ahead of her arrival Margaret sent requests for food and refreshment to London, which were answered nervously but favourably by the mayor. But as carts laden with supplies were being dragged through the city, towards the Cripplegate and the road leading north, a group of citizens came into the streets to block their path. 'The commones of the Cite took the vitailles from the Carters and would not suffer it to pass,' wrote a chronicler. They insisted that the city's governers send a delegation to tell the queen that she could not enter London while the feared 'Northern men' remained in her party. The rumour which Clement Paston had reported to his brother had clearly taken hold: everyone now believed that if the Lancastrian army were allowed within the city walls, then London, like St Albans, would be 'robbed and despoiled'.[11] Margaret had little choice but to take her husband and son once more back north. The move – and London's communal decision that it was safer to hold with the defeated Yorkists than the victorious queen – would prove fatal.

Warwick's escape from St Albans allowed him to reunite with Edward earl of March. At the end of the month they gathered their forces together in the Cotswolds. There they took a bold decision. Warwick had lost command of Henry's person, and without him they lacked a totem for their legitimacy. But under the act of accord that had been passed between Henry and the late Richard duke of York, March was now heir to the crown.

And since forces loyal to Henry VI had killed York at the battle of Wakefield, March could argue that he was justified in regarding the act of accord to have been broken. He no longer had to wait for Henry's death to claim the crown that the Yorkists argued was theirs by blood. He was completely justified in seizing it.

This, at any rate, was the theory. On Thursday 26 February the earl of March rode into London, accompanied by Warwick and their noble allies.[12] The city was in the early days of Lent, but if the (somewhat biased) chroniclers are to be believed, there was great cheer at his coming. Rhymes and ditties celebrated his arrival, one of which hailed him with the image of the white rose of York – one of several badges and symbols that belonged to the family: 'Let us walk in a new wineyard, and let us make us a gay garden in the month of March with this fair white rose and herb, the Earl of March.'[13]

On Sunday 1 March Warwick's brother George Neville, bishop of Exeter and chancellor of England, gave a speech in St John's Fields, just outside the city walls, which was heard by thousands of soldiers and citizens. Neville detailed the case against Henry VI and asked whether the crowd wished him to remain as king. According to one chronicler, 'The people cried, "Nay! Nay!" And then they asked, if they would have the earl of March to be their king; and they seid, "Ye! Ye!"'[14] On Monday morning London was plastered with bills detailing Edward's claim, and the next day, Tuesday 3 March, Edward held a council meeting at his family's London residence, Baynard's Castle, where a handful of bishops and lords gave their assent to his claim. On 4 March, the Te Deum was sung at St Paul's, Bishop Neville preached a political sermon at the cross outside and Edward rode out of the city in procession down to the palace of Westminster. There, in the court of chancery, which was the place traditionally associated with a king's exercise of legal equity, and therefore the ultimate manifestation of the royal will in action, 'he was Sworn afore the bishop of Canterbury and the Chancellor of England and the lords that he should truly and justly keep the realm and the laws thereof maintain as a true and a just king'.[15] He put on the robes and cap of state – although not the crown, for a coronation was not to be held for some time. Then Edward sat ceremonially on the King's Bench – the marble chair in one of the two highest common law courts in the land, which symbolised the personal authority of the king as judge. Finally, he went to Westminster Abbey church to make an offering at the shrine of his namesake St Edward the Confessor. He was yet to be anointed and crowned. But in the eyes of his supporters he was now King Edward IV, 'the true inheritor of the crowns of England and France and the lordship of Ireland'.[16]

*

While Edward was sitting on the marble throne in London, the Lancastrians were falling back to the north. As they went, the royal party sent out desperate instructions to the great families to give them military aid. One such letter reached Sir William Plumpton, a fifty-five-year-old follower of the Percy family of Northumberland and a wealthy, influential gentleman in his own right, with land and manors in Yorkshire, Derbyshire and Nottinghamshire. His letter was sent from York on 13 March 1461, and marked with the small waxen seal of Henry VI's signet. It advised him that 'our great traitor' the earl of March 'hath made great assemblies of riotous and mischievously disposed people [and] . . . hath cried in his proclamations havoc upon all our true liege people and subjects, their wives, children and goods'. Sir William was charged to raise 'all such people as ye may make defensibly arrayed' and 'come to us in all haste possible . . . for to resist the malicious intent and purpose of our said traitor, and fail not hereof'.[17] A loyal subject and an old soldier, Sir William did not delay.

As Queen Margaret and her allies raised the north of England for battle, Edward's men raised the realm below the river Trent. They sent instructions to the sheriffs of more than thirty southern counties damning 'he that calls himself Henry VI' and 'charging all manner of men between sixty and sixteen arrayed in defensive wise in all haste to come and wait upon the king'.[18] Equipping for war was no small undertaking, whether for knightly men-at-arms expected to fight in the thick of battle, the thousands of archers who protected them, or lightly armoured common soldiers who were assembled to share the allegiance of whomever happened to be their local lord. Armour, weaponry and materiel ranged from the vastly expensive bespoke suits of plate armour worn by the wealthiest lords and captains to the clubs, blades and staves wielded by the rank and file. Even to dress a man of Plumpton's rank before a battle was a task that took several pairs of hands. One fifteenth-century manuscript describes the process by which a man-at-arms' squires should dress him. He was to wear no shirt, but a satin-lined twilled-cloth doublet, slashed with holes for ventilation. 'Gussets of mail [i.e. chain-mail] must be [sewn] unto the doublet . . . under the arm'. These were vital to protect the wearer from dagger thrusts at vulnerable points, where a sly blade piercing a joint in plate armour could sever a major artery or find its way into a vital organ – so the twine used to attach the mail to the doublet was as strong and durable as that used to string a crossbow. More thick undergarments, including patches of blanket to prevent chafing at the knees, were stitched all over with tough cord loops, on which plates of heat-strengthened and highly polished metal were hung: sheet metal covered the body from throat to toe and was topped by a heavy helmet with visor, an attachment for identifying personal insignia, and a tiny slit through which to view the terror of the slaughter.[19]

A knight's horse might be as heavily protected as the rider, who would use a lance to impale his enemies if he rode with the cavalry. Otherwise weapons were long, heavy or sharp – or sometimes all three at once. Wicked little rondel daggers could be driven into a man's heart, eye or brain at close range, while massive forty-inch broadswords that were swung with two hands by the richest and best-trained men on the battlefield permitted more room to attack. Perhaps the deadliest hand-held weapon of all was the pole-axe or bill: a strong wooden shaft up to six feet in length topped with a heavy and fiercely sharpened curved blade on one side, a short, clawlike point on the other, and a thin spike at the top. Swung hard, this could crush armour and break the flesh and bone beneath; it could trip an opponent – and once felled, a man-at-arms was vulnerable, since the weight of the armour could make it desperately difficult to get back up. The thick blade could hack off the limbs of less well-protected enemies, or lop chunks out of the skull of a knight who removed his helmet either to see properly, to communicate or to drink.

Through the month of March thousands upon thousands of men bearing weapons like these assembled throughout England and beyond. They came from everywhere between Wales and East Anglia, and from Scotland to Kent. Thanks to Warwick's cordial relations with lords overseas, Edward's army included a company of soldiers sent by Duke Philip of Burgundy; they carried above them the banner of Louis, the dauphin of France and eldest son of Charles VII. The Lancastrians far outnumbered them in the numbers of English nobles under their flag: besides the dukes of Somerset and Exeter, there were the earls of Northumberland, Wiltshire and Devon, Lord Rivers and his son Anthony Woodville, Sir Andrew Trollope (knighted by the queen after the second battle of St Albans) and twelve or thirteen other peers. The Yorkists marched slowly north from London towards Pontefract, men flocking to their side as they went. By the end of March, reckoned their paymasters many years later, they had 48,660 men.[20] The Lancastrians however may have had as many as sixty thousand. Even if we account for the usual exaggerations, these were two gigantic armies.

The first engagement took place on Saturday 28 March at Ferrybridge in Yorkshire, a crossing point on the Great North Road, just a few miles north-west of Pontefract. The Lancastrians had camped close to the village of Towton – or possibly in the village of Tadcaster – nine miles away across the river Aire.[21] When they received intelligence that the Yorkist lords John duke of Suffolk and Lord Fitzwalter had been charged with rebuilding the broken bridge across the Aire, they sent a detachment of light horsemen under Lord Clifford to beat them back. A bloody fight ensued in which Fitzwalter was killed. As Edward IV pressed more men from his main army to reinforce the bridge, the Lancastrians turned to retreat. They fell into a trap: Edward had also sent Lord Fauconberg and a small contingent of men to cross the river three miles upstream from Ferrybridge. Fauconberg rode with deadly mounted archers beside him, and they stalked Clifford's men, eventually ambushing them at dusk near the village of Dintingdale. When Clifford removed his metal neck-guard to drink a glass of wine an arrow hurtled through his throat, killing him instantly. The Yorkists then fell on the rest of the party, slaughtering them where they stood. The great showdown for the crown of England had begun.

The night that followed was abysmally cold and the next day, Palm Sunday, dawned bleak and frigid. The Yorkshire countryside was frozen over and snow and sleet were falling, increasingly heavy as the early morning unfolded. Nevertheless, the two massive armies rumbled into position at Towton and by nine o'clock they were ready to fight, mustered in two huge lines, facing each other across a shallow ridge. The blizzard swirled around them, snow blowing straight into the faces of the Lancastrians and making the battlefield a slippery, half-blind nightmare. Men would have stamped and trembled with the cold, awaiting a signal that

battle was ready to begin. For those who could see, banners fluttered above the troops, advertising the presence of the dozens of
lords on either side: heraldic patterns of blue, white, red and gold
marking out the location of the commanders and lordly captains
on either side. But only on the Yorkist side was there the banner
of a king of England. Edward IV was in the field, but Margaret
and Henry VI were lingering behind the lines at York, waiting
anxiously for word of the result.

Eventually, the cry went up to begin battle and the wet snow-
flakes were joined by a bloody blizzard of arrows, carried hard
on the wind from the Yorkist archers under Lord Fauconberg.
Some fire was also exchanged by gunners – men wielding primitive artillery which fired iron-and-lead shot of more than an inch
in diameter. Even in the wind, the blasts from these hand-cannon
must have been terrific, made all the more so by the occasional
screams of the gunners whose weapons backfired and exploded
in their hands.[22]

Seeing that in this exchange of fire the Yorkists had the wind at
their backs, and being unwilling to stand in the storm and watch
his men shot to death, the duke of Somerset gave the order to
advance. The Lancastrians waded downhill towards the enemy,
crashing into the vast line of the Yorkist army and beginning a
long and exceptionally fierce battle, which would turn out to be
the bloodiest ever fought on English soil. The whitened, undu-
lating landscape of Towton plain was rent with the judder of
pole-axe and sword blade into armour and flesh, the screams of
wounded horses and dying men, the press of steaming bodies into
one another, men falling and flailing and slipping as bodies piled
high on top of one another. Orders had been given by Edward
that lords should be killed and not captured, but the death toll
was equally appalling among the well-born and the lowly. As the
armies grappled and lashed out, the fronts swayed and began to
pivot through forty-five degrees, so that from a starting position

Clockwise from top left: Henry V, 'King of all the world' and scourge of the French; Catherine de Valois, whose secret marriage to Owen Tudor unwittingly founded a great royal dynasty; Margaret of Anjou, idealised as the Virgin (the real woman was less saintly); and Henry VI – simple, pious and soft – whose reign was a disaster

Clockwise from top left: Richard duke of York, a great soldier, but a poor politician, still fathered two kings; Edward IV, who was charismatic, dashing and competent, but grew fat, louche and lecherous; Edward V, whose unlucky head never wore the crown of England; and Elizabeth Woodville, an unlikely queen, she was sexy, ambitious and hard-nosed

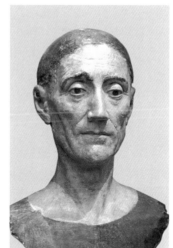

Above, a modern image of Richard III, reconstructed from his skull. Henry VII (*above right*) looks careworn and troubled in his death mask. *Below*, Perkin Warbeck, who impersonated Richard, son of Edward IV, and, *right*, the indefatigable and brilliant Margaret Beaufort: a great survivor

The battle of Barnet, 1471 (*top*), was actually fought in thick fog and Richard Neville, 'Warwick the Kingmaker', was killed in the fighting. *Bottom*, Edmund, duke of Somerset is beheaded following the battle of Tewkesbury. Edward IV watches on, impassive

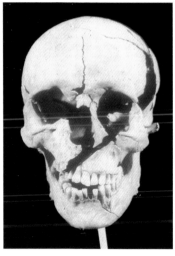

'Towton 25' – a face smashed in half. The field of Towton was known as the Bloody Meadow owing to the 28,000 men who died during the battle. *Below*, a squire dresses his knight for combat

Howe a man schall be armyd at his ese
whæn he schal fighte on foote

The Bosworth Cross (*left*) was paraded with Richard III's ill-fated army in 1485. *Below*, Edward IV in his splendour – from a genealogy celebrating his royal blood. Three royal insignia are displayed on his charger, representing the Yorkists' supposed claim to the crowns of England, France and Castile

Family history as propaganda: Bedford plastered occupied France with hand-bills illustrating Henry VI's rightful claim to the French crown. This elaborate version was presented to Margaret of Anjou before her marriage in 1445

The Tudors were masters of propaganda – roses, genealogies and new histories sold the world 'their' fifteenth century, which was immortalised by Shakespeare

in which they were arrayed on an east–west line, by the afternoon they had swung round so that the Lancastrians were fighting on a north-east–south-west axis, with their backs to the flooded meadow of a deep waterway called Cock Beck. Their right flank was menaced by Yorkist archers and their left was now fighting at the bottom of a hill, having been driven hard round when the duke of Norfolk joined the fighting on the Yorkists' right. In short, the Lancastrians were being driven into a wetland that swiftly became a deathly pool of blood: their only escape was to make their way uphill from the left flank and attempt to flee back towards Towton and Tadcaster. Doing so, however, meant scrambling up wet and churned-up turf with the blizzard on their backs. As they tried to flee they were mown down by the Yorkist cavalry, who swept over the open ground, cudgelling and lancing their enemies with abandon. Even those who made it past Towton suddenly found themselves trapped once more: before the battle the Lancastrians had broken the wooden bridge further up Cock Beck, and they were now penned in at the far end of the battle site. As the cavalry closed in on them, men threw off their armour and tried to wade or swim through the brisk water. Weary, wounded or half-frozen, they drowned by the dozen, until eventually the beck was so dammed with corpses that their colleagues could scramble to safety over what became known as the Bridge of Bodies.

With men dying in their thousands, the Lancastrian line dissolved by mid-afternoon, and the leaders took flight. The earl of Wiltshire, perhaps the greatest coward of his generation, had previously run away from the first battle of St Albans and the battle of Mortimer's Cross. He brought his tally to three desertions by abandoning Towton, but this time his luck had run out. He made it to Newcastle before being captured and beheaded. Andrew Trollope and the earl of Northumberland were both cut down on the battlefield. The dukes of Somerset and Exeter ran for their lives and escaped; the earl of Devon also ran but was too badly injured to get beyond York, where he too was caught and executed. Behind them, the leaders' abandonment of the field turned defeat into a devastating rout. On Edward's orders, no mercy was shown in victory. Skulls later found on the battlefield showed the most horrific injuries: faces split down the bone, heads cut in half, holes punched straight through foreheads. Some died with more than twenty wounds to the head: the signs of frenzied slaughter by men whipped into a state of barbaric bloodlust. Some victims were mutilated: their noses and ears ripped off, fingers snipped from hands to remove rings and jewellery in the plunder of the dying. The field of Towton was known as the Bloody Meadow, and with good reason. On 7 April 1461, Bishop Neville of Exeter wrote to the bishop of Teramo in Flanders. He reported the events of the six weeks that had just passed, including the slaughter at St Albans, Ferrybridge and Towton, and estimated that twenty-eight thousand men had been killed at the latter. (The figure was repeated by Bishop Beauchamp of Salisbury in a letter of the same day.) 'Alas!' he wrote, 'we are a race deserving of pity even from the French.'[23]

Indeed, it must have seemed to many in 1461 that all the fates that had befallen the French a generation previously, when Armagnacs fought Burgundians and the crown was tossed about and tussled over to the utter ruin of the realm, had now been visited on the islanders across the sea. England was ruled by deeds of savagery, the north country was drenched in blood, and most distressing of all, two kings were at large. Queen Margaret's decision to hold back Henry VI and Prince Edward from the battle of Towton had proven a wise one, for even though the Lancastrians were decisively defeated, they were not quite exterminated as a royal line. They retreated to Scotland with a few surviving allies: the dukes of Somerset and Exeter, Lord Roos and the judge Sir John Fortescue. Other loyal Lancastrian lords, such as Jasper Tudor, earl of Pembroke, soon joined them. They were, however, very much a rump court: militarily ruined, financially constrained and exhausted.

King Edward IV spent a month in the north mopping up resistance before returning to London in triumph in May, for the coronation that would set God's seal on his accession to the crown. He would now claim not only to be king by right *of* blood, but to have had his claim vindicated *in* blood on the battlefield. An act of his first parliament, called to Westminster in November 1461, rehearsed the legal arguments against Henry VI's kingship and put forward the righteous case for his own. By that time parliament was merely putting the legal stamp on what was already a political fact. For on Friday 26 June Edward had made a ceremonial entrance into the capital that had long supported his claim, and two days later he had been crowned as the thirteenth Plantagenet and first Yorkist king of England.

13 : The Noble and the Lowly

Edward IV was far from the youngest man to have ascended the English throne, but he was perhaps the most hastily prepared. At nineteen years old he had been raised as the eldest son of a great nobleman. He had studied hard, prayed diligently, learned to fight and dance, to speak courteously and to give his attention to the business of managing a great estate. But it was still some distance between growing up to become a duke and suddenly arriving as a crowned and anointed king of England. And yet, here he was: carried to the throne on the wave of his dead father's ambition, his hands stained with the blood of his enemies.

Fortunately, much of the outward business of kingship came naturally to Edward. As a young man he was more than six feet tall and handsome if not pretty: surviving portraits capture narrow eyes and pursed lips above a prominent chin. Edward was greatly taken with the lavish dress, manners and courtly habits that were fashionable in Burgundy and elsewhere on the continent, and to match his grand appearance the new king was possessed of courtly charm allied with a military swagger. Although he had a fierce temper when goaded, he was generally 'of a gentle nature and cheerful aspect', wrote one contemporary, also recalling that the king 'was so genial in his greeting, that if he saw a newcomer bewildered at his appearance and royal magnificence, he would give him courage to speak by laying a kindly hand upon his shoulder'.[1] He had a sharp mind and a keen memory: the author of the extended English history known as the Crowland Chronicle Continuations frequently admired Edward's 'foresight' and political acumen, and marvelled that he could recall the state and business of 'almost all men, scattered over the counties of the kingdom . . . just as if daily they were in his sight'. Edward had uncommonly clear trust in his own judgement and the ability to inspire great loyalty in the men whom he picked to counsel him. And like many of the great Plantagenet kings before him – from Richard the Lionheart to Henry V – he had proven himself on the battlefield at a young age.

Many writers contemporary, or nearly contemporary, to Edward's reign struggled to find faults with his person and his broad approach to government – with one exception. The new king was, it was frequently said, a debauched lecher. He was certainly known in his time to be fond of women, and it did not always matter whether they were attractive or not. Tongues wagged: the Italian clergyman, humanist and scholar Dominic Mancini, who visited England to write a contemporary history and saw his subjects at first hand, called Edward 'licentious in the extreme' and reported that the new king 'pursued with no discrimination the married and the unmarried, the noble and the lowly', while the Crowland continuator – although writing more than two decades after Edward's accession – scratched his pen in sadness at the fact that such a talented and confident governor could also be 'such a gross man so addicted to conviviality, vanity, drunkenness, extravagance and passion'.[2] Even if we allow for the prudishness of the writers and for the fact that some of these judgements were more appropriate to the later years of Edward IV's life than the perilous days during which he first seized his crown, the impression was consistent.

For the first three years of his reign Edward's main concern was not sensuality but survival. In March 1461 God had smiled on his claim to kingship by blessing him with victory on the battlefield. But the Lord had not given him mastery of his kingdom. Rather, at the point when Edward first wore the crown, he was still essentially the head of a faction, a private lord who needed to build his public authority in order to claim the full loyalty of his subjects. Just as Henry Bolingbroke had found when he deposed Richard II and took the crown as Henry IV in 1399, a usurper was bound to pursue two apparently opposing strategies. He was obliged to prove that he would be an impartial ruler, able to defend the realm and offer justice to all his subjects, but at the same time he was obliged to reward and favour those men who had helped him take the throne in the first place. This was no easy task at the best of times. And it was far from the only issue that faced Edward: there were also very pressing problems of violent public disorder caused by more than a decade of intermittent rebellion, plotting and civil war, and the threat of attack by foreign powers eager to seize on England's moment of desolation and distress. Charles VII of France died from longstanding infections in his leg and jaw on 22 July 1461, less than a month after Edward's coronation, but his hot-headed and belligerent son, who succeeded as Louis XI, was sure to want to discomfit the new English king as much as possible. On top of this Edward had to build from scratch a working government, staffed with men whom he could trust not only to be loyal but to be competent. Finally, he had to consider his dynastic duty: to father enough children to be sure that the future was secure and to discourage the schemes of anyone who had watched his rise and now considered the crown a bauble to be contested by anyone with old royal blood in their veins. It was a daunting task.

Edward began with the Lancastrians. A good many of the leaders had been wiped out at Towton, but a hard core of the committed still survived. Several coastal castles in Northumberland were held by Lancastrian captains, and it took a long and concerted campaign of siege warfare to winkle them out. Queen Margaret had taken Henry VI and Prince Edward back into Scotland, and for the next two years she attempted to raise support for a new invasion, allying herself first with the government of James III, and subsequently seeking finance and military aid from Louis XI. She managed to launch a land and sea invasion of northern England during the spring and summer of 1463, linking up with the defenders of the northern castles, but ultimately she was repelled and forced to flee England for good. While Henry VI remained in Scotland, Margaret and Edward were compelled to live the rest of the decade in exile on the continent. Jasper Tudor, the king's half-brother who had been stripped of his earldom of Pembroke by act of attainder, served as a go-between, travelling back and forth between France and Scotland, while also attempting to raise an invasion fleet and concentrating his efforts on harassing the Welsh coast. A small group of other diehard Lancastrians, including Henry duke of Exeter and Sir John Fortescue, remained with the queen in impoverished exile. But their efforts to return were firmly resisted, and in October 1463 Edward secured a truce with France which forbade Louis XI to engage with Lancastrian plots, effectively dashing all hopes of a swift return.

Meanwhile, sympathisers who remained actively defiant in England were rooted out. Although only a tiny number were attainted in parliament for their part in the fighting of 1455–61, there was still a move to crush the most implacable. Sweeping legal commissions visited rebellious towns and imposed exemplary justice on townsfolk about the realm. In some places, the severed heads of traitors and rebels were left to rot on poles for up to six months. Many of these heads belonged to the low-born and unfortunate, but others fell from noble shoulders. They included that of the ageing and ill John de Vere, earl of Oxford, who had been notable for his neutrality in all the armed conflicts to date. But in February 1462 Oxford was arrested with his eldest son Aubrey and tried for treason, for plotting against Edward's life. The two men were executed within a week of one another on

Tower Hill, on 'a scaffold of four foot [in] height . . . that all men might see'.[3]

Edward's early efforts in quelling Lancastrian rebellions rested heavily on Warwick and the Nevilles. Warwick was entrusted with defending the north and spent nearly three years bringing it to obedience, fighting a wearisome border war in which great castles like Alnwick, Norham and Bamburgh were reduced with 'great ordinance and guns' and the resilience of the rebels and their Scottish allies was slowly but surely ground down. In reward for these duties and his previous long and dangerous service, lands and offices taken from the defeated Lancastrians were given to Warwick on a massive scale. He was appointed great chamberlain of England, admiral of England and warden of the Cinque Ports and Dover Castle for life; he also retained his invaluable post of captain of Calais. He became warden of both the east and west marches in the north, making him the sole military authority below the king. He became steward of the whole duchy of Lancaster. He inherited all his mother's lands when she died in 1462. He took command of huge swathes of territory, particularly in the north, where he was awarded former Percy estates. He was confirmed, in short, as the wealthiest and the pre-eminent nobleman in the realm.

His family shared in the spoils. Warwick's uncle William, Lord Fauconberg was raised to earl of Kent and John Neville was created Lord Montague (and subsequently earl of Northumberland, the old Percy title). George Neville, the loyal bishop of Exeter who had preached Edward IV's accession at St Paul's in 1461, was repaid by appointment as chancellor and translation to the archbishopric of York, a promotion he celebrated with a dazzling feast at which six thousand guests were treated to several days of gluttonous roistering at Cawood Castle in Yorkshire: more than one hundred oxen and twenty-five thousand gallons of wine were said to have been enjoyed, in the presence of the king's youngest brother, Richard duke of Gloucester. The Nevilles had backed the Yorks all the way to the crown, and they received their thanks in dazzling abundance.

Of course, other noble families gained too as Edward IV set about expanding his political base. The Bourchier family was rewarded for loyalty as Henry, elder brother of Thomas Bourchier, archbishop of Canterbury, was created earl of Essex. In Edward's own family it was his young brother and heir, George, who profited most from the Yorkist victory. George was made duke of Clarence and given a large bloc of former Lancastrian lands, including the late Edmund Tudor's earldom of Richmond. In Wales, William, Lord Herbert was given most of Jasper Tudor's confiscated estates, custody of Edmund Tudor's son and heir, Henry Tudor, and virtually uncontested power in the principality. And in the household, the main beneficiary was William Hastings, who became Lord Hastings, chamberlain of the household, gatekeeper to the king's presence and will. Other new men were also cultivated: the west-country landowner Humphrey Stafford became an important ally, as did the Bedfordshire knight Sir John Wenlock – both Stafford and Wenlock were raised to the baronage for their friendship and service. None, however, enjoyed so much prestige and royal favour as the Nevilles.

Or so it seemed. Then in 1464, something extraordinary happened. Among all these old and new families coalescing in a pool of political support for the Yorkist king, there arrived another family – one who would rise to outstrip almost every other in their power and prestige, despite extremely humble roots. They were the Woodvilles, and their fortunes would be yoked to those of the house of York for the next two decades.

*

Autumn was drawing in and the festival of Michaelmas was approaching: a holiday that coincided with the end of the harvest, which all of England rose to celebrate with merrymaking, dining, drinking and good cheer. It was the middle of September 1464 and the lords of England gathered at Reading Abbey to hold a conference with their king. They met in the glorious abbey chapel, a setting intimately connected with the ancient history of the English crown, not least since it was the resting place of the great Norman king and lawgiver Henry I and his second wife and queen, Adeliza of Louvain.[4] There were several political issues at hand – not least among them a controversial recoinage, by which the value of England's money would be slashed by around a quarter and the Crown would make a handsome profit by reminting England's coins. The most pressing concern of all, however, was the most personal. The lords had gathered to discuss Edward's marriage.

Young, vigorous and single, Edward was a royal bachelor whose choice of wife was a keen matter of interest to a very great number of people. Marriage offered the chance to make a lasting alliance with one of the powers beyond the Channel. It was an opportunity for Edward to produce a son and heir – a need that was as pressing as any before him. And of course, it would allow the king to show the realm that he was growing up and taking his duties seriously, since, as one chronicler put it, 'men marvelled that oure sovereign lord was so long without any wife, and were ever feared that he had be not chaste of his living'.[5]

There was a clutch of possible wives, each of whom represented a different path through continental politics. In 1461 Philip the Good, duke of Burgundy, had suggested a marriage to his niece, a daughter of the duke of Bourbon – apparently rather a beautiful young lady – and it was hinted in 1464 that this proposal remained open. An alliance with Burgundy had strong trade advantages, and was bound to be well received by the merchant elites in the city of London, who had for so long been staunch supporters of the Yorkist cause. There was also a tentative offer for the hand of Isabella, the sister and heiress of Henry the Impotent of Castile – a kingdom with long ties to the English crown and the Plantagenet family, stretching back to the twelfth century. Or Edward could look north: at one point during the worst troubles of his early reign there were thoughts of marrying the king to Mary of Guelders, the Scottish regent and mother of James III, albeit a woman whose reputation for chastity was worse even than Edward's. Finally, and perhaps most promisingly, negotiations were advanced with Louis XI of France to create an Anglo-French alliance through a marriage with a princess of the house of Valois.

A French match was by far the most attractive offer to those who thought they held the English king's ear. Warwick and Lord Wenlock had been leading secret negotiations with the French since at least the spring of 1464, and possibly the previous autumn. By September 1464 Warwick felt that he was close to securing the hand of the French king's sister-in-law, Bona of Savoy. The most obvious advantage to a marriage alliance with Louis was that it would finally poison the stump of Lancastrian opposition – for without the support of the French and their allies, there could be no hope of Margaret of Anjou ever leading an invasion to restore her limp husband to the English crown. There were also possible trade advantages, which could compensate for the loss of business that would accompany an abandonment of Burgundy. Warwick had a certain amount of personal prestige bound up in the negotiations: he revelled in the fact that he was spoken of in the courts and corridors of European palaces as the power behind the English throne, and the man who moved the young king he had created. The ambassadors and dignitaries joked that, as one put it in a letter to Louis XI, the English had 'but two rulers, M. de Warwick and another whose name I have forgotten'.[6] This sort of thing tickled Warwick, whose landed power was quite equalled by his love of finery, display and personal grandeur. But as he discovered abruptly at Reading in September 1464, his role as the chief mover of English policy was not quite so solid as he had reckoned it to be.

Warwick came to Reading fully expecting that he and Lord Wenlock would be asked to go to a conference with Louis XI in St Omer – a town not far from Calais – to finalise Edward's marriage to Bona of Savoy. The council at large wished to hear the broad thinking behind the French alliance that would naturally proceed from the union. Yet when Edward met them in the abbey church he relayed news that shocked the realm. He announced that he would not be marrying Bona of Savoy – or indeed any other foreign princess. For he was already married, and had been for several months. His wife, the new queen consort of England, was a widow in her mid-twenties with two children by a recently deceased member of the lower nobility. Her name was Elizabeth Woodville.

She was a fair-skinned woman with dark eyes and auburn hair above a fashionably high forehead, her slender and hard-ridged nose finishing in a little bulb that mirrored the smooth, round ball of her chin.[7] At twenty-six or twenty-seven years old she was certainly still beautiful, and although she was not a member of the highest ranks of the nobility she was somewhat famous thanks to her father, Richard Woodville, Lord Rivers. Rivers had been a minor landowner in Kent and Northamptonshire until 1437, when he married Jacquetta of Luxembourg, the widow of Henry VI's mighty uncle John duke of Bedford. The spectacular match catapulted the hitherto unimportant Woodvilles into the aristocracy, with connections both to the Lancastrian royal house and various great European families including the Luxembourg counts of St Pol and the dukes of Burgundy. Rivers had followed up his own excellent marriage by providing solid noble unions for his family. His son Anthony Woodville wedded the heiress of Lord Scales, and as a young lady Elizabeth Woodville had been married to Sir John Grey, heir to Lord Ferrers of Groby, whom she had borne two children, Thomas and Richard Grey.

Appropriately, given Lord Rivers's connection to Henry VI, the Woodvilles had been loyal Lancastrians and active participants in the wars against the Yorkists. Rivers was one of those assembling a fleet for Henry VI at Sandwich in January 1460 when he and his comrades were kidnapped in a lightning raid by the earl of Warwick and taken to Calais for interrogation. It was at Calais, indeed, that Rivers had first encountered the future Edward IV: for in a humiliating torchlit ceremony before assembled Yorkist partisans, Warwick and Edward (then earl of March) had 'reheted' – that is, berated and scolded – the captive Lord Rivers for his humble upbringing, 'calling him knave's son' and scoffing at his ignoble blood.[8] Released from their ordeal, Rivers and his son Anthony had both gone on to fight on the losing side at Towton. They had survived that bloody field and been pardoned by Edward in the aftermath, but Elizabeth Woodville's husband, Sir John Grey, had been less lucky in the business of war: he was killed fighting for the Lancastrians at the second battle of St Albans.

The circumstances of Elizabeth's marriage to the king were intriguing. It was said the couple had been wed 'privily in a secret place' on the amorous occasion of May Day 1464, most likely in a ceremony in Rivers's house at Grafton in Northamptonshire.[9] The wedding had subsequently been kept secret for nearly five months. A story went about – embellished with every retelling – that the king had promised to marry Elizabeth as the most direct means to get her into bed, and that Elizabeth had attempted to defend her honour by threatening Edward with a dagger before eventually succumbing to his youthful charm.[10] This titillating tale was included in the Italian courtly poem *De mulieribus admirandis* ('Of wonderful women'), written in *terza rima* by Antonio Cornazzano some time before October 1468, so very clearly it had romantic appeal across Europe. There was probably more poetic fancy than journalistic truth to Cornazzano's account. All we know from sources immediate to the event is that within a week of Edward's marriage to Elizabeth Woodville becoming public knowledge, diplomatic channels were buzzing with the news that the king had 'determined to take the daughter of my Lord Rivers, a widow with two children, having long loved her, it appears'.[11]

The idea that the new king had married for love, rather than for hard-headed political gain, must have made a certain amount of sense to the bewildered ambassadors who gossiped together in the courts of Europe. How else to explain the astonishing rise of Elizabeth Woodville – the unlikeliest queen consort in English history? Not least among her imperfections was the fact that she was an Englishwoman. Since the Norman Conquest, a matter of four centuries, no king of England had married one of his subjects; the last to do so had been Edward the Confessor, who married the impeccably noble and virginal Edith of Wessex in 1045.[12] As an English subject Elizabeth brought with her no obvious diplomatic gain and no useful foreign alliance. Quite the contrary: her large family were already noted for their social ambition and obvious desire to advance themselves by marrying into other families' titles and estates. With two sons, a father and more than ten siblings, Elizabeth brought with her obligations for royal favour and grants that would have to be met in part out of the Crown's precious resources. She promised even less to the Crown than the impoverished Margaret of Anjou had brought when she married Henry VI in 1445.

Indeed, Edward's sudden marriage threatened to do active damage to England, both at home and abroad. The French king was completely blindsided by the news of Elizabeth's presentation: the first he knew of it was when Warwick and Wenlock failed to appear at St Omer for the conference concerning Bona of Savoy. Isabella of Castile would much later complain that she was 'turned in her hart' from England 'for the unkindness the which she took against the king . . . for his refusing of her and taking to his wife a widow of England'.[13] It is almost certain that Warwick, like most of the rest of the English peerage, was also taken by surprise. He had fair cause to 'grumble a bit', as it was reported by one chronicler, over his young protégé's eccentric, apparently lovestruck choice of wife.[14] Puzzled observers wrote that the marriage caused 'great displeasure to many great lords' and 'greatly offended the people of England'.[15]

It would be foolish totally to disregard love – the most common contemporary explanation – as an important factor in the Woodville marriage.[16] But it is also possible, with hindsight, to detect a line of political thinking that may well have allowed Edward to convince himself that his love-match was also a useful tool of public policy. Could it be that the romantic writers and tattling envoys who gossiped about the king's incontinent libido missed the broader political dimension of the Woodville wedding?

Unquestionably, in 1464 Edward was a charismatic and extremely self-willed twenty-two-year-old who had enjoyed no apprenticeship or education to prepare him for wearing a crown and was essentially inventing the role as he went along. But he was not completely reckless or heedless of convention, and his crown had been won at a greater personal cost than that of any Plantagenet king before him. Perhaps, then, we can see his choice of Elizabeth Woodville as fitting into a pattern of bold and well-intentioned, if occasionally very naïve kingship that characterised at least the first five years of Edward's reign.

In the spring of 1464 Edward was still fighting for his throne. Part of this effort was military, and part involved a concerted campaign of persuasion: an appeal to his realm for allegiance. Specifically, he made it a plank of his reconstruction to reach out wherever he could to the exiled and defeated Lancastrians.

The most prominent Lancastrian – albeit the most ungrateful – to find Edward's conciliatory hand outstretched was Henry Beaufort, duke of Somerset, one of the chief commanders at Towton, and a man whose opposition to the Yorkists had been most motivated by hate and fear. Somerset fled the realm in 1461 and had been attainted in his absence, but after becoming embroiled in the castle wars of Northumbria in 1462, he had been captured at Bamburgh and surrendered himself to the king's custody.

Instead of executing, humiliating or otherwise punishing Somerset – as Queen Margaret surely would have done had her side been victorious at Towton and a Yorkist of Henry Beaufort's status fallen into her custody – Edward treated the twenty-eight-year-old duke with an amazing degree of affection and forgiveness. One chronicler noted with astonishment that Somerset 'lodged with the king in his own bed many nights, and sometimes rode a-hunting behind the king', with the royal bodyguard containing as many of Somerset's men as Edward's. 'The king loved him well' was the chronicler's judgement, and it was quite accurate.[17] Within six months of his capture at Bamburgh, Somerset's attainder had been reversed and his estates restored; he was allowed to serve in arms alongside Warwick and he was invited to great tournaments in the south. It was a lightning political rehabilitation. Not everyone was overjoyed, and a correspondent called John Berney wrote from Norfolk to John Paston, complaining that there was much grumbling among local Yorkists, who thought that the king's 'great enemies, and oppressors of the commons' were rewarded instead of punished, while not enough of the spoils of victory found their way to 'such as have assisted his Highness'.[18] But Edward had made up his mind: he would use Somerset as living proof that he could govern as a king, drawing the whole realm and not just his partisan allies to his side.

Unfortunately Somerset's rapid rehabilitation was followed by an equally swift fall from grace. While enjoying Edward's hospitality, 'the duke thought treason under fair cheer and words'.[19] In late November 1463 Somerset rode to Northumberland to meet with the enfeebled Henry VI and rouse insurrection anew. It took two battles in the far north, at Hedgeley Moor on 25 April 1464 and at Hexham on 15 May, to squash the rebellion and rout the final embers of Lancastrian revolt for good. Lord Montague led the royal forces at both battles; Somerset was captured at Hexham and executed the following day, along with several dozen other Lancastrian renegades.

It is in the context of all of this – and not the confections of many later chroniclers and poets, who piled romantic myth onto the fact of the king's affection for his new wife – that we must see Edward IV's marriage to Elizabeth Woodville.[20] He was trying desperately – probably too desperately – both to endow allies old and new with the landed power and royal trust that he needed to secure his kingdom, and to extend the hand of friendship to those who had found themselves on the wrong side of the civil war. He had not been wildly successful in concentrating his efforts on the more senior Lancastrian families – for as well as Somerset's treachery, Edward had also tried and failed to bring Sir Ralph Percy to reconciliation and had found his generosity abused. At precisely the time that he secretly married Elizabeth Woodville, the Nevilles were once again taking to the field to defend his crown in the north, while other allies were ducking down and covering their ears against the boom of siege guns as they tried to subdue obdurate defenders of northern castles. Edward was becoming over-reliant on his longstanding friends, and frustratingly unable to bring his longstanding enemies within his peace.

Then, between the battles of Hedgeley Moor and Hexham, Edward found himself close to Grafton, in the presence of a moderately famous if second-rate Lancastrian family, a daughter of whom happened to be extremely sexually attractive to him. Elizabeth had been dealing very closely with Edward's chamberlain and confidant Lord Hastings in making a deal to protect her share of her late husband's lands from the Bourchier family who had a claim to them: her name and her situation were therefore unquestionably familiar to the king, and with Hastings's blessing, Elizabeth had probably put her case to Edward in person. Thus he knew her by sight, and understood her background thoroughly: here was the eldest daughter of a Lancastrian family actively seeking royal favour and patronage. A covert marriage must have seemed like a policy that had very few serious risks and a number of advantages: this was a bride who would demonstrate Edward's commitment to even-handed kingship, but whose family was not so grand or proud as to feel they had anything to gain by betraying his trust. There was an important foreign dimension, too, since a domestic marriage that could be explained by the romantic impulsiveness of a young and callow king also meant that Edward could avoid marrying Bona of Savoy, avoid committing his foreign policy so early in the reign to France and avoid upsetting his Burgundian allies, whose favour – and trade – was vital for the health of London's merchants.

The marriage would prove embarrassing to the earl of Warwick, who was leading the foreign negotiations, but Warwick had benefited more than handsomely enough from the Yorkist victory. To take a bride of the Neville family's choosing would have reinforced the already unpleasantly strong perception that Edward was Warwick's puppet king. To fly in the face of his ally made the point that in marriage as in all other things it was the king's ultimate prerogative to do as he and he alone chose.[21]

Still, the wedding was made in secrecy – perhaps in the hope that it could be denied if necessary – and then kept quiet until such time as an announcement became politic or unavoidable. That time was Michaelmas 1464, when his council pushed him to commit to a foreign marriage. This was the moment at which his crown was secure enough to admit to a controversial step, but also at which he could forestall a decision on a French marriage no longer. Thus the shock and surprise on Michaelmas Day when Elizabeth Woodville was presented to the English court at Reading, processing into the public presence on the arms of the fourteen-year-old George duke of Clarence, the king's heir presumptive – and a somewhat disgruntled Richard Neville, earl of Warwick.

*

Sand crunched underfoot on London Bridge as Elizabeth Woodville crossed the river Thames and entered England's capital to be crowned a queen. During the previous winter the bridge had been cleaned and cleared of its foul vapours, and forty-five loads of sand were dumped along its length to assure the grip below the feet of the many lords, ladies and dignitaries who were to cross it in the weekend of celebrations that followed.[22] It was Friday 24 May 1465, and the kingdom was about to welcome not only a new queen but also a whole new generation of nobles, all learning their places in a world still being rebuilt.

As ever when celebrating a moment of great royal dignity, London put on a spectacular show. The centre of the bridge was awash with colour, in the form of a massive stage, draped in cloth and paper in gold and green, black and white, red and purple, which provided the setting for actors and actresses dressed as blonde-headed angels, their wings made from hundreds of dazzling peacock feathers. Another actor dressed as St Elizabeth read a greeting while the high-pitched voices of boys rang out from the windows of St Thomas's chapel, singing songs of praise to the incoming queen. The whole of London, as was customary, thronged with crowds and pageants, and Elizabeth, like so many queens before her, took her stately progress through the cramped but well-scrubbed streets, absorbing the proud scenes that unfolded before her.

Two days later, on Whit Sunday, 26 May 1465, she was crowned in Westminster Abbey, having been met in the hall of the adjacent palace by the youthful figures of Clarence and John Mowbray, fourth duke of Norfolk and marshal of England (who had inherited the duchy on the death of his father in November 1461). Clarence was fifteen and a half and Mowbray only twenty – both on the cusp of manhood but gilded with the highest rank and title. They met the new queen in the saddle: riding about the crowded Westminster Hall on great thick-backed horses draped in gold-embroidered cloth. They greeted her, and the party then processed from the palace to the abbey. Beside the new queen walked the king's sister Elizabeth, duchess of Suffolk, then twenty-one, and the queen's sister Margaret, eleven years old and betrothed to the earl of Arundel's heir. These young ladies were accompanied by forty other dignified women, ranging from duchesses to knights' wives, all of them dressed in scarlet, with miniver and ermine marking out the highest-ranking from the lowest. Bobbing above the crowd were the queen's youngest sister, Catherine, aged about seven, and her ten-year-old betrothed, Henry Stafford, duke of Buckingham, who was the grandson and heir of the old duke killed at the battle of Northampton. This tiny couple was afforded the best view in the house: carried on the shoulders of squires above the throng of glorious nobility below.

Once this glittering party was in the abbey, it witnessed a long and lavish crowning. Masses and the Te Deum were sung. Elizabeth sat, stood and sat again with sceptres in her hands and a crown on her head. Then she returned to Westminster Hall for her coronation feast, surrounded and honoured by more nobles. Some, like Henry Bourchier, earl of Essex, were senior figures of the realm, but most of the prominent men in ceremonial positions were of the queen's own generation. Twenty-four-year-old John de la Pole, duke of Suffolk stood at her right hand holding one of her sceptres, while the twenty-two-year-old John de

Vere, earl of Oxford (following his father and elder brother's executions for treason), served water from a bowl held by Clarence. The hall blazed with splendour and pomp, tables groaned with food and drink, and minstrels' music blared out from every different shape and size of instrument. Trumpets blew solemnly as every course of the feast was brought before the queen's table.[23] It was a deliberately youthful pageant, wholly appropriate to a fresh and unconventional monarchy. And at the heart of it all was a group of young men and women who had been flung to the front of the English political world within the space of a few months. If the battles of the 1450s and early 1460s had been fought between ageing men quarrelling about feuds that reached back for decades, Elizabeth's coronation raised up a generation that might be freed from the bloody binds of the past.

*

The queen's coronation was followed by a great coup for Edward's rule. During the unrest that had led to the battles of Hedgeley Moor and Hexham in 1464 the exiled Henry VI had been smuggled from Scotland into England. For the year that followed he was on the run in the far north, cooped up in the few remaining Lancastrian strongholds and hiding from his enemies. At first he took cover in the massive coastal fortress at Bamburgh, but when that was shot to pieces by Warwick's cannon Henry moved on, first to Bywell Castle in Northumberland before retreating into more remote hiding places tucked away across the rugged and chilly Pennines. At some times he stayed with one John Maychell in the Cumbrian manor of Crackenthorpe; at others he hid among sympathetic communities of monks. He was more fugitive than returning king. And eventually he was neither: one day in mid-July 1465 Henry was eating dinner with another of his shelterers, Sir Richard Tempest of Waddington Hall, near Clitheroe in Lancashire, when a large party of men, including Sir

Richard's brother John Tempest, burst into the dining room and tried to arrest him. In the scramble Henry was able to flee from the house into the nearby woods, taking with him a handful of loyal servants. But his days of roaming had come to an end. On 13 July the deposed king and his attendants were tracked down and taken prisoner at Bungerly Hippingstones, a crossing point of the river Ribble.[24] Henry was lifted onto a horse, 'his legs bound to the stirrup', and marched triumphantly from Lancashire to London, where he was placed in the Tower of London, there to remain indefinitely.[25] He was fed reasonably well, given wine from the new king's cellars, occasionally allowed a new velvet gown and permitted visitors, if they were carefully vetted by his jailers. Perhaps most surprisingly of all, the deposed and imprisoned King Henry was not murdered. This had been the fate of the two Plantagenet kings who had lost their crowns before him: Edward II died while in custody at Berkeley Castle in 1327, while Richard II was killed at Pontefract in 1400, the year following his deposition. Ironically, Henry's survival was perhaps a mark of his uniquely pitiful and ineffectual approach to kingship – for it was much harder to justify killing a man who had done nothing evil or tyrannical, but had earned his fate thanks to his dewy-eyed simplicity. Permitting Henry to remain alive was a bold decision that Edward IV would come to regret. But in 1465 it must have struck the king as a brave and magnanimous act.

With Henry in gentle confinement and his enemies in the north contained, Edward's reign began to develop a sense of normality. His marriage to Elizabeth, surprising as it may have been both at home and abroad, allowed him to start growing his base of royal support. The queen's large family made it possible to start knitting many of the other great families of England within the new royal house. Two years after the royal marriage, five of the queen's sisters were married. Young Catherine was already wedded to the underage duke of Buckingham. A welter of other matches followed. Anne and Joan Woodville were married to the heirs to the earls of Essex and Kent respectively. Two more sisters, Jacquetta and Mary, were matched with Lord Strange and the heir to Lord Herbert (who would later become earl of Pembroke). Anthony Woodville – the eldest of the brothers – was married to the heiress of Lord Scales, and used the title himself from 1462. Thomas Grey – Elizabeth's eldest son – married Anne Holland, daughter of the duke of Exeter. This spider's web of matches between the queen's relations and the young men and women of the English aristocracy formed links between the new royal family and the future generations of noble dynasties with estates, interests and followers all across the realm, planting new threads of royal connection from East Anglia and the midlands to Wales and the west country. But before long, the creation of this sprawling new royal affinity became a matter of contention between Edward and the man who felt he was owed most of all by the new regime. As the Woodvilles increased their power and Edward grew in confidence, so the earl of Warwick began to feel more and more uneasy. A succession of clashes over policy and personalities was coming to a head between the king and his greatest subject. The two men whose family alliance had secured the Yorkist crown were about to blow the entire project apart.

14 : Diverse Times

From the very beginning of his reign, Edward was determined to present himself as a king not merely by right of conquest, but by right of blood and birth, even destiny. Following his coronation in 1461 he commissioned for public display a vast, twenty-foot illuminated manuscript roll illustrating his ancient claim to be a king – not only king of England and France, but also of Castile, to which the house of York occasionally trumpeted its right. The 'coronation roll' that was produced after months of painstaking work some time before the king's marriage to Elizabeth Woodville in 1464 was a mass of colours, names, heraldic devices and dynastic tables. At the top towered Edward, resplendent in plate armour aboard a bright-liveried warhorse, a huge sword in his right hand, a gold crown on his head and a smile of regal triumph on his red lips. Below this magnificent figure stretched a genealogical chart packed with detail, explaining the king's descent from Adam and Eve, down through Noah and out into all the known ages of human history, until they coalesced in the three main royal lines of England, France and Castile, all flowing through Richard duke of York and down into an eight-pointed star representing Edward once again. All over this extraordinary public demonstration of the king's blood-borne, heaven-ordained royalty were Edward's favourite personal symbols: the fetterlock that his father had worn on his robes when he first claimed the crown in 1460, the black bull representing the Mortimer family's true claim to the English crown, the arms of Cadwalladr, ancient king of the Britons, the golden sun, recalling both the true Plantagenet line descending to Richard II and, more recently, Edward's victory at Mortimer's Cross – and most frequent of all, the five-pointed white rose, the blazing symbol of the house of York.[1]

For all this magnificent visual posturing, the house of York needed to produce an heir. The king had two younger brothers – George duke of Clarence and Richard duke of Gloucester – and three sisters – Anne duchess of Exeter, Elizabeth duchess of Suffolk and Margaret of York. But his reign would only really acquire security when he produced a son and heir. For this reason, much excitement greeted Queen Elizabeth's confinement in the new royal apartments at the palace of Westminster during the early days of 1466, to be delivered of her first child.

The baby was born on 11 February in a room staffed solely by women, into which not even the queen's personal physician, Dr Dominic de Sirego, was allowed. It was a healthy child, although not the boy that the king had been hoping for. The infant was called Elizabeth, a name that had some distant Plantagenet history as well as running in the Woodville family.[2] Both the baby and the mother were treated with all honour and reverence. Remarkably, Elizabeth was the first princess to have been born to a reigning queen of England for more than one hundred years and she was given an appropriately splendid christening, at which her grandmothers, Cecily duchess of York and Jacquetta duchess of Bedford, both stood as godmothers. Beside them as the tiny baby was baptised was the princess's godfather, Richard earl of Warwick.

What Warwick was thinking at the time of the christening will never be known. If he was seriously disaffected by Edward's marriage to Elizabeth Woodville then at this point he was biting his tongue. Certainly he was still gaining handsomely from his position as the greatest magnate under the king. He presided over the lavish churching ceremony, to welcome the queen back into society following the princess's birth – a public prominence that recalled his ostentatious accompaniment of the captive King Henry VI through the streets of London in July 1465. He was commissioned to seek a treaty with Burgundy in the spring of 1466, notwithstanding his clear preference for a treaty with France. The following February, he was allowed to take a massive entourage on a diplomatic embassy to Louis XI, in which he gave the French king English dogs, and was rewarded with chests full of money, textiles and gold and silver plate.[3] At home he was showered with lands and offices: the castle of Cockermouth in Cumberland, the hereditary office of sheriff in Westmorland, custody of all royal forests north of the Trent, profits of all the royal gold and silver mines in the same region, and wardship of the lands of the wealthy peer Lord Lovell when that gentleman died and left an underage heir. Warwick was rich, and getting richer.[4] All the same, against this background of royal patronage, favour and delegated power, divisions were opening along several lines between the king and his greatest nobleman. And as the first decade of Edward's reign wore on, Warwick would come to feel that all the power and riches in the world could not satisfy his desire for more.

The biggest area of disagreement was over foreign policy. Warwick's desire to come to terms with France, rather than to pursue an alliance with Burgundy – the favoured policy of the queen's father, now Earl Rivers – had not dimmed. Edward indulged him to a degree. But while Warwick was absent courting the French, the king directly undermined his mission by receiving in great splendour a rival embassy led by Anthony, the *grand bâtard* of Burgundy – Duke Philip the Good's second son, born to one of his many mistresses. Like Edward IV, the Bastard was renowned for his taste for fine living, dazzlingly bejewelled clothes and beautiful women. He was a boon companion and an excellent sportsman, famous as one of the most skilful archers in northern Europe. He was fond of jousting, and when he arrived in England during the spring of 1467 Edward greeted him with every honour. A tournament had been arranged between the Bastard and Anthony Woodville, Lord Scales, to be held at West Smithfield, just outside the walls of the city of London. As gravel and sand from the banks of the Thames were carted to the tournament ground and a great viewing platform was built by the king's carpenters, the Bastard was treated to rides along the river in barges hung with tapestry and gold cloth; he slept in gold-hung beds at his London lodgings and was generally borne about the town with all the reverence due to a king.

The tournament, held from 11 June to 14 June 1467, was a success, despite a disappointing first day on which Scales lanced the Bastard's horse, a dastardly move held to be quite contrary to the rules of the joust, which left the animal 'so bruised that he died . . . a while after'.[5] On the second day the two men fought on foot with battle-axes, going at one another so fiercely that eventually the king had to intervene, commanding them to stop and refusing their request to finish the fight with daggers. The event ended happily, with the two lords embracing and everyone celebrating the end of the tournament with a huge feast attended by scores of stunningly dressed young English ladies.[6] There could have been no greater show of comradeship and courtly affection between the ruling families of England and Burgundy. The Bastard's visit was cut short by news of the death of his father, Philip the Good, on 15 June. Nevertheless, his departure from the realm concluded a visit that had illustrated the king's clear desire for friendship.

Duke Philip's death broke off Warwick's embassy to France. He returned laden with silver and gold, but aware that in his absence his standing in foreign affairs had been badly damaged. And things were no better at home, where the ejection of his brother George, the archbishop of York, from the office of chancellor – an event buried beneath the blaze of the Bastard of Burgundy's visit – meant that the family had been removed from their central position in the administration of domestic government, too. As the archbishop fell from grace, the king's father-in-law Earl Rivers was rewarded with promotion to treasurer and constable – a pair of offices that gave him sweeping powers over royal finance and military might. It looked like a coup designed to put the Nevilles in their place. Warwick had done too much to put Edward on the throne to bear this double slight with equanimity.

Following the death of Philip the Good, Edward's alliance with Burgundy grew steadily closer. He conceived it as part of a broad anti-French strategy in which alliances could be constructed with a ring of France's mutual enemies: treaties of friendship were also signed with Brittany, Denmark and Castile, and were pursued with Aragon and Armagnac.[7] In October 1467 the king's clever, courtly and well-educated sister Margaret agreed to marry Charles, the new duke of Burgundy (later nicknamed 'the Bold'), turning down no fewer than four matches proposed by Louis XI. Just as at Princess Elizabeth's christening, Warwick played a central ceremonial role in the king's sister's marriage. In May 1468 he accompanied Margaret as she left London by the pilgrim road to Canterbury, headed for the busy port of Margate on the isle of Thanet, whence she would set sail aboard a ship called the *New Ellen* for the Netherlands and her new life as duchess at the dazzling court of Burgundy. Warwick and Margaret rode in splendour on the back of the same horse: he in front and she right behind him.[8]

Despite his role in Margaret's departure and the continued flow of royal gifts, Warwick's discomfiture was becoming obvious. The chronicler Warkworth believed that Margaret's marriage made decisive his breach with the king: 'And yet they were accorded diverse times: but they never loved together after.'[9] Warwick had been forced to accept two other obnoxious matches. The queen's son Thomas Grey had married the king's niece Anne Holland, the only daughter and heiress of Henry Holland, duke of Exeter – despite the fact that Warwick's nephew had been promised Anne's hand. Then a far more grotesque and insulting marriage was arranged between the twenty-year-old John Woodville and Katherine Neville, Warwick's aunt and the dowager duchess of Norfolk. Katherine was not only a four-time widow but also about sixty-five years old. The medieval marriage market was more usually organised according to the principles of political advancement than romance, but there were certain limits of good taste. If anything could be said to symbolise the impertinence of the Woodvilles it was this nakedly grasping match between a vigorous upstart barely out of his teens and a blue-blooded crone. One chronicler, cattily estimating that the duchess was a bride again at 'the young age of eighty', called it a 'diabolical marriage'.[10]

Warwick had two daughters, Isabel, born in 1451, and Anne, five years younger, who were at or approaching marriageable age. He had no sons, and thus his family's future depended on their making good matches. Warwick's great desire was for Isabel to marry George duke of Clarence, but in early 1467, amid a seemingly incessant parade of matches between the king's and queen's families and the rest of the English nobility, Edward IV declined to allow it. This along with the steady drip of other insults was enough to drive Warwick into a deep sulk. By January 1468 he had retreated to his northern estates and repeatedly refused to attend the king's council at Coventry if Lord Herbert, Earl Rivers or Lord Scales was present. His appearance at Margaret of York's departure for Burgundy was one of the last times that he engaged in any meaningful public way on the side of a king whom he had made, but could no longer control. He was, as one chronicler put it, 'deeply offended'.

*

By 1468 Edward's kingly experience was growing and his family was expanding. A second daughter, named Mary, was born in August 1467 and a third, Cecily, would follow in March 1469. But the problems of a usurper king had not entirely left him. The threat to his crown was much reduced – not least because Henry VI continued to languish at the Tower of London – but it had not entirely vanished. Having offended Louis XI by allying with Burgundy, Edward had exposed himself to renewed French backing of plots against his throne. In June 1468 Jasper Tudor was funded to launch a small invasion of Wales. He landed at Harlech Castle, raided his way across north Wales, captured Denbigh Castle and proclaimed Henry VI to be the true king at 'many sessions and assizes' held in the old king's name.[11] Tudor was beaten back to the sea within weeks by an army under Lord Herbert, who captured the supposedly impregnable Harlech Castle, a bastion of defiant Welsh Lancastrianism ever since Edward's accession. (Herbert was rewarded for his efforts with his foe's old title of earl of Pembroke.) The less fortunate captains of Harlech, including one John Trueblood, were taken to London and beheaded in the Tower. But this was not the end of Edward IV's troubles.

Jasper Tudor's invasion was followed by rumours of other plots. 'That year were many men impeached of treason,' wrote one chronicler.[12] The London aldermen Sir Thomas Cook and Sir John Plummer and the sheriff Humphrey Hayford were accused of plotting and deprived of their offices, while a noble conspiracy was detected involving John de Vere, heir to the earl of Oxford who had been beheaded in February 1462, and the heirs of the Courtenay and Hungerford families. De Vere was imprisoned and eventually pardoned, but the other two were condemned and killed in early 1469. And so it was across the realm: 'Diverse times in diverse places of England, men were arrested for treason, and some were put to death, and some escaped,' recalled one writer.[13] As the plots seemed to spiral, England was becoming generally more violent: a spate of aristocratic warmongering was the subject of complaint during the summer parliament of 1467, which implored the king to deal with the 'homicides, murders, riots, extortions, rapes of women, robberies and other crimes which had been habitually and lamentably committed and perpetrated throughout the realm'.[14]

It is hard to know now whether the increased sensitivity to conspiracy was genuinely the sign of more dangerous times, or of paranoia in the king's council. From late 1467 there had been rumours that Warwick was in touch with Margaret of Anjou, who was living in uncomfortably impoverished exile with a small court of dissidents at her father's castle of Kœur, 150 miles east of Paris. Even if these rumours were nothing more than baseless gossip, the earl's cold and obstructive behaviour in early 1468 did nothing to suggest his total loyalty to the regime. And indeed, when another front of disorder and opposition to Edward's rule opened in 1469, Warwick finally decided to abandon the king and throw in his lot with a man who might prove to be more pliable. But it was not a Lancastrian: rather, Warwick decided to make use of the man who would be his son-in-law, Edward's own brother and still his male heir, George duke of Clarence.

At the beginning of 1468 Clarence was eighteen years old. Like Edward he was capable of charm and wit and he shared with the king what one writer called 'outstanding talent'.[15] He was smooth, elegantly attractive and sharp-tongued – 'possessed of such mastery of popular eloquence that nothing upon which he set his heart seemed difficult for him to achieve'.[16] His childhood under his brother's rule had been spent in large part at Greenwich Palace, where he lived with his sister, the now departed Margaret, and his younger brother Richard duke of Gloucester. He had been recognised as an adult on 10 July 1466 – still only sixteen years old – when he paid formal homage to the king and was rewarded with possession of massive estates centred on Tutbury

Castle in Staffordshire: a large and modern fortress protected with thick curtain walls and several towers with luxurious residential apartments inside, warmed by giant fireplaces hewn from huge blocks of locally quarried stone. As an important property of the duchy of Lancaster, Tutbury had once belonged to Queen Margaret, who spent a great deal on its improvements. It was a commanding position from which he could survey the sprawling patchwork of lands that he now controlled. Amid this luxury, Clarence enjoyed mastery of the biggest and most lavish household staff of any nobleman in England, consisting of nearly four hundred people at an annual cost of £4,500.[17]

But if Clarence was superficially attractive, handsomely gifted and indulged by his elder brother, he was also glib, shallow and spoiled.[18] Like Warwick, extravagant royal favour only served to increase his ambition. He was bewitched by his own magnificence, and like Humphrey duke of Gloucester (and perhaps like his own father) he saw his position as the king's male heir as licence to create an ostentatious alternative court. This instinct would lead him into trouble: for while he could at times perform as a competent magnate, settling the debates of his tenants and subordinates, he was a wilful, self-centred and infuriating man with a penchant for skulduggery and schemes.

One such scheme was to pursue marriage to Warwick's eldest daughter, Isabel. From a royal point of view it would have been considerably more useful for Clarence to have entered into a union with a foreign princess than a Neville (Charles the Bold's daughter Mary was briefly considered). This may well have been what Edward was thinking when he flatly refused to endorse the marriage in early 1467, though it is more likely that he simply wished to avoid connecting his two greatest nobles by allowing a marriage alliance between them. Warwick's power needed no bolstering via a direct link to the adult royal heir – traditionally a hub around which opposition to the Crown would gather. The politics of the midlands, meanwhile, would be thrown horribly out of balance by joining together the two most powerful lords in the region. Warwick began plainly to chafe against the restriction. To the king's clear concern, his brother George – young, impressionable and used to getting his own way – fell under Warwick's spell.

The consequences of a Warwick–Clarence alliance against the king whom each had every duty to serve and obey became clear from the spring of 1469. It began in April with a series of popular riots in Yorkshire, as large numbers of local men convened under the leadership of a figure calling himself 'Robin of Redesdale' or 'Robin Mend-all' – a sort of Jack Cade of the north, whose name was clearly a nod to the outlaw ballads that had by this time been in circulation for more than a century, and whose heroes – Robin Hood, Adam Bell and Gamelyn – embodied the ideal of the wronged man who imposes rough justice on corrupt officials. There were a number of likely causes for this disorder, high among them longstanding local disgruntlement at the demands of St Leonard's Hospital in York, which had long levied the 'petercorn' – a tax on arable farmers – in Yorkshire, Lancashire, Westmorland and Cumberland. The master of the hospital had the previous year secured his right to the tax in Edward's court of chancery.[19] Under 'Robin of Redesdale' a spate of rioting whipped across the county. It was put down by Warwick's younger brother, John Neville, earl of Northumberland, the hero of Hedgeley Moor and Hexham and one of the crown's most reliable men of the north. But within two months 'Redesdale' had sprung up again, and this time the Neville family were not the scourges of the rebels, but their covert sponsors.

The second wave of rebellion, which took place in June and July of 1469, was significantly different from the first. The leader still went under the name 'Robin of Redesdale', but was in this case either Sir John Conyers of Hornby, Warwick's steward at

Middleham Castle and an experienced soldier, or else a puppet
of the same. Whereas the disorder earlier in the year had focused
on local disaffection, now, said one writer, the people 'complained
that they were grievously oppressed with taxes and annual trib-
utes by the said favourites of the king and queen'. A regional
uprising had been stirred up into a protest against national government. The second Redesdale rising was secretly supported by
Warwick with the aim of causing the king maximum discomfort.
And it was done with great effect. There was talk of a popular
army of sixty thousand men being mustered in Yorkshire. The
disturbances were beginning to resemble what the chroniclers
called a 'great insurrection' and a 'whirlwind from the north'.[20]

Edward set off to deal with the rising in mid-June, accompanied by his youngest brother, Richard duke of Gloucester, along
with Earl Rivers, Lord Scales and a number of his other Woodville relatives. At first Edward failed to calculate how dangerous
the situation had become, but as he rode north it began to dawn
on the king that this was more than a local rising and he sent out
urgent demands to the towns and cities of the midlands to supply
him with archers and men. He also wrote to Clarence, Warwick
and George Neville, archbishop of Canterbury, sending each a
terse note on 9 July demanding that they 'come unto his Highness' with all urgency. 'And we ne trust that ye should be of any
such disposition towards us, as the rumour here runneth, considering the trust and affection we bear in you,' he added in his
letter to Warwick.[21] But as the wax was hardening on the king's
letters, Warwick, the archbishop and Clarence were on their way
to the military stronghold of Calais, taking with them the earl's
daughter Isabel.

On 11 July Clarence and Isabel were married in Calais, in
direct defiance of the king. The following day, Warwick and his
allies wrote an open letter to the king in support of the Robin of
Redesdale rising. The letter called for reform, accusing Rivers,

Scales, Sir John Woodville, the earl of Pembroke, his brother Sir William Herbert and Humphrey Stafford, earl of Devon, as well as others around the king, of allowing the realm to 'fall in great poverty of misery . . . only intending to their own promotion and enriching', and warning darkly that the fate that had befallen Edward II, Richard II and Henry VI might just as easily be visited upon Edward IV. They also named Earl Rivers's wife, Jacquetta duchess of Bedford, as a malign influence on the king. (Jacquetta would later be accused of having used witchcraft to engineer the king's marriage to her daughter Elizabeth Woodville, and of creating lead models of Warwick, Edward and the queen for the purposes of sorcery.) A manifesto for reform was attached to the letter – supposedly belonging to the rebels, although as it took an almost exclusively national outlook and was riddled from beginning to end with the sort of political jargon in whose uses the earl of Warwick was the most practised man alive, it was likely to have been either strongly influenced from or wholly manufactured in Calais.[22]

The northern rising, swelling by the day, was led by Warwick's relatives and friends. As Sir John Conyers and his son of the same name, Sir Henry Neville and Henry Fitzhugh marched their northerners towards the midlands, Warwick and Clarence returned to England from Calais, landing in Kent on 16 July. Two days later they began a push up the country to join forces with 'Robin of Redesdale'. They stopped briefly in London before sweeping up the road towards Coventry, gathering men as they rode. Edward, camped with his army at Nottingham, now found a pincer closing rapidly around him. His best hope for repelling the rebels was to receive reinforcements from Wales under the earl of Pembroke, and from the west country under the earl of Devon.

On Wednesday 26 July Pembroke and Devon's men had reached Banbury in northern Oxfordshire and were camped in the broad fields surrounding the town when they were attacked without warning by the northern forces. The main body of the royal army was separated from the archers, and they thus went into battle severely hampered. 'A great battle was fought, and a most dreadful slaughter, especially of the Welsh, ensued,' wrote one chronicler, who reckoned that four thousand men were killed on the battlefield known as Hegge-cote or Edgecote.[23] The considerable disarray among Pembroke's men was worsened when a small band of warriors bearing the earl of Warwick's arms arrived in the field, causing panic in the lines and leading many to take flight. The end result was terrible casualties on both sides. The rebel leaders Sir Henry Neville and John Conyers the younger were killed, but the battle was remembered in Wales, as the bloody fate of the Welsh infantry was shared by their commanders. The poet Lewys Glyn Cothi called it 'the mightiest [battle] of Christendom'. During the fighting Pembroke and his brother Sir Richard Herbert were captured and taken as prisoners to Northampton, where they were met by the earl of Warwick. On Thursday 27 July Warwick held a summary and utterly illegal trial, pronounced a death sentence and had both beheaded.

Panic spread. News of the disaster at Edgecote took several days to reach Edward IV, but when it did, his men scattered from his side. Alone and totally exposed, the king was taken prisoner at Olney in Buckinghamshire by a party led by Archbishop George Neville. His horse was harnessed to his captors' and he was escorted to Warwick Castle, the vast and unbreachable midland seat of the Nevilles, to be held captive while his associates were hunted down.[24] Throughout August, Warwick's men stalked England, capturing those men who had served the king and murdering them. Earl Rivers and Sir John Woodville were run to ground in Chepstow and taken to Kenilworth, where both were beheaded. The earl of Devon was taken 'by the commons' in Bridgwater, Somerset, 'and there right beheaded'.[25]

Despite the fact that Warwick and Clarence were acting effectively alone – mustering their own vast resources rather than mani-
festing the will of any wider portion of the nobility or the realm
– it had taken them less than three months to gain command of
the king, butcher his allies and assume control of the government. Edward had spent the best part of a decade establishing his
birthright, starting a new royal family, rebuilding a secure crown
and a stable government and reasserting the majesty of English
kingship. And yet in the late summer of 1469 he found himself
in the same predicament as his predecessor: two kings were now
prisoners of their own subjects. Seizing the crown had become
all too easy.

15 : Final Destruction

Like Richard duke of York before him, Richard earl of Warwick found it a great deal simpler to capture a king than to govern in his name. From Warwick Castle in the heart of the midlands, the earl moved Edward to Middleham Castle, the magnificent stone-walled stronghold that loomed over the Yorkshire Dales. But as news filtered across England and Wales of the king's captivity, the realm erupted into violence and disorder, which proved quite beyond Warwick's capacity to control: for while he had the royal person, this was by no means the same as having royal authority.

In London there was a burst of robbery, rioting and open violence, barely kept in check by the efforts of Burgundian ambassadors who happened to be in the city. Elsewhere, noble quarrels spilled over into private wars, waged from Cheshire and Lancashire to Gloucestershire and Norfolk, where the Paston family were forced to defend their castle at Caister from a siege laid to it by the duke of Norfolk, who had 'the place sore broken with guns'.[1] Warwick's realm was alive with the boom of cannon, the hum of arrows and the crackle of flames licking ruined buildings. Even in Yorkshire Warwick could not keep order as the king's teenage brother Richard duke of Gloucester took up arms in a dispute against Lord Stanley. Worst of all, rumours circulated in Wales suggesting that a Lancastrian revival would shortly be underway somewhere in the realm. And so it proved: in August two members of a renegade branch of the house of Neville raised Henry VI's banner in northern England. 'The earl of Warwick found himself unable to offer an effectual resistance,' wrote one chronicler. 'For the people, seeing their king detained as a prisoner, refused to take notice of proclamations' until Edward was set at his liberty.[2]

Warwick had no choice. Edward was free by the middle of October. Sir John Paston watched the king ride into the city of London in splendour, surrounded by a large posse of loyal lords including Gloucester, Suffolk and Lord Hastings, the mayor and all the city aldermen, two hundred guild members and what Paston described in a letter as a thousand horses, 'some harnessed and some not'. The king had crushed the northern rebellion with ease, issued a general pardon to the rank and file and was set on reasserting himself in the realm at large, an end he pursued with almost ominous good cheer. Paston noted with some trepidation that while 'the King hymself hath good language of' Warwick, Clarence and their small group of allies, including the earl of Oxford, 'saying they be his best friends', quite another message was being broadcast by the men of the royal household. Edward was almost always magnanimous after victory – but it seemed clear, to Sir John Paston at least, that a great reckoning could not be far away.

Only two serious reorganisations took place in the aftermath of Warwick and Clarence's revolt. The first was enforced: Wales had been deprived of its leading nobleman when William Herbert, earl of Pembroke was beheaded after the battle of Edgecote. In Herbert's place, Edward promoted his own brother, Richard duke of Gloucester. Aged seventeen, Gloucester was growing into an able soldier and a trustworthy lieutenant. Tall but slender and not as physically striking as either Edward or Clarence, Gloucester was a tenacious and loyal young man in whom Edward saw a great future. He made him constable of England in place of the executed Earl Rivers, justiciar of north and south Wales and steward of the whole principality. In effect Richard became the king's hand beyond the western marches. He took to his role with some enthusiasm and purpose.

Edward also moved to weaken some of the Nevilles' power in

the north. John Neville, earl of Northumberland, had remained loyal during his brother's rebellions; all the same, Edward decided that there were advantages in moving his territorial base away from northern England. The king released Henry Percy from long-term imprisonment in the Tower of London, restored him to his father's lands in the north and gave him Neville's title of earl of Northumberland. Historically the Percys had been the dominant family in the north – a fact only changed by the ascendancy of the Nevilles in the 1450s. Now Edward was moving to restore the balance of power. To compensate John Neville for his losses, he was created Marquess Montague and awarded a huge tract of lands in south-west England, another area of perpetual bloodletting and chaos, which had fallen vacant on the death of the earl of Devon. Neville's young son George was created duke of Bedford and betrothed to the king's daughter, Elizabeth of York, who turned four years old in the spring of 1470. It looked like a handsome settlement for a loyal man, which served to restore some balance to the power politics of northern England while injecting a degree of much-needed experience into the south-west. Unfortunately, it would prove to have serious consequences for Edward's rule.

In March 1470 another rebellion broke out. This time it was Lincolnshire that rose up, initially due to a bitter private feud between the local peer Lord Welles and Willoughby and Sir Thomas Burgh, a bodyguard and close servant of the king. In response, Edward raised an army and marched north to put an end to the violence. The sight of the king marching at the head of an army sent rumours whirling around the north, as speculation mounted that bloody revenge was on its way for the events of 1469. As Lord Welles and his son Sir Robert parlayed these fears into all-out insurrection, a desperate Warwick decided to raise an army of his own and throw in with the rebels once more. Once again, the unscrupulous Clarence decided to join him – despite having assured the king of his allegiance – and the pair aimed at what a government-sponsored account of the rising later described as 'the likely utter and final destruction of [the king's] royal person, and the subversion of all the land'.[3]

After most crises Edward's instinct was usually towards calmness and reconciliation rather than murderous revenge. But this time he had been provoked too much. He responded with furious aggression. He captured Lord Welles and sent a message to his son that the old man would be killed unless he submitted. This drew Sir Robert out to fight before he had a chance to combine armies with Warwick. At Stamford on 12 March 1470, a royal army routed the Lincolnshire rebels in such humiliating fashion that the insurgents ran from the battlefield, throwing their clothes away as they hastened to escape. The field was thereafter known as Losecote Field.

According to the partisan account later published of the battle, the rebels at Losecote Field ran at the king's men shouting, 'A Clarence! A Warwick!' Some of them were said to be wearing Clarence's livery, and when Sir Robert Welles was cut down in the chase, his helmet was found to contain 'many marvellous bills, containing matters of the great sedition' – in other words, implicating Warwick and Clarence in yet another round of skulduggery.[4] This time, the king's miserable relatives could expect no leniency. They refused summons to the royal presence, fled south from Lancashire to Devon, took ship at Dartmouth and escaped across the Channel, heading once more for Calais. But even here they were denied entry when Warwick's deputy captain Lord Wenlock declined to open the gates. The two men eventually landed in Normandy, in the territory of the French king. Their isolation appeared to be complete. And indeed it might have been, but for one of the most audacious and unscrupulous alliances in all of English history.

*

Margaret of Anjou and her son Prince Edward had been living in French exile for nearly ten years. The prince had been
raised in his grandfather René of Anjou's castle of Kœur, in
Lorraine, near the banks of the river Meuse. In the spring of
1470 the boy was sixteen years old and quite as unlike his father
as it was possible to be. Indeed, those who saw him suggested
that he was made in the same mould as his other grandfather,
Henry V. In February 1467 the Milanese ambassador Giovanni
Pietro Panicharolla commented in a letter to the duchess and
duke of Milan that the prince, then only thirteen, 'already talks
of nothing but of cutting off heads or making war, as if he had
everything in his hands or was the god of battle or the peaceful
occupant of that throne'.[5] He loved to ride, fight and joust with
his friends and companions. His mother had never given up the
idea that this splendid young tyro could some day return to claim
his father's crown.

Margaret's determination to overthrow the Yorkists knew almost
no limit. Since being ejected from England she had appealed for
assistance to countless allies in France, as well as to the rulers
of Scotland and Portugal. Now, in 1470, she prepared herself
to make common ground with the unlikeliest partner of all, the
man who had done more than anyone else alive to damage her:
Richard earl of Warwick. The old enemies met in Angers on 22
June, in a meeting brokered by Louis XI, and thrashed out a deal.
Prince Edward would marry Anne Neville, Warwick's youngest
daughter, and Warwick would then return to England in opposition to Edward IV, doing everything in his power to overthrow
the Yorkists and return Henry VI to the throne.

Warwick, Clarence, Jasper Tudor and the earl of Oxford set
sail from La Hougue in Normandy on 9 September. The young
Prince Edward was left behind with his mother, presumably to his
indignant frustration. After four days at sea they landed on the
Devonshire coast, announced their allegiance to King Henry VI,

called on all men to join them in their mission of restoration and set out on a march to Coventry to confront Edward IV.

Edward was at this time in the north. He had been kept well abreast of developments over the sea, writing to his subjects in the south-east to tell them that 'we be credibly ascertained that our ancient enemies of France and our outward rebels and traitors be drawn together in accord, and intend . . . utterly to destroy us and our true subjects'. He instructed them to be ready for invasion at any moment. 'As soon as ye may understand that thay land,' he wrote, 'put you in uttermost devoir [i.e. your highest duty] . . . to resist the malice of our said enemies and traitors.'[6] Violent uprisings had racked the north throughout the summer, and Edward had been torn between the need to defend a vast coastline and the pressing demand to restore order in the north country only recently restored to the management of the Percy family. When news of Warwick's landing reached him he set out for London, to defend his crown and capital.

As the rebels marched they gathered numerous powerful defectors, all with reasons to bear a grudge against the king. The earl of Shrewsbury and Lord Stanley brought substantial numbers of armed retainers, and they were followed, most damagingly of all, by Warwick's brother Marquess Montague. This was far from a critical mass of the English nobility, but the uncertainty of military campaigning seems to have convinced Edward that 'he was not strong enough to give battle', particularly if his opponents were to include the formidable Montague.[7] Rather than stand and fight for his crown with an inadequate army, Edward 'withdrew from a contest so doubtful in its results'.[8] To give battle immediately for his kingdom might have seemed like a natural course of action. But to do so also risked capture or death.

Edward boarded a ship at King's Lynn and set sail for Flanders, leaving his kingdom in the hands of his enemies. He left in such haste that he did not even stop to collect his pregnant wife:

Queen Elizabeth was forced to take sanctuary with her three daughters behind the walls of Westminster Abbey. Lodged in the abbot's apartments, she would give birth there to her first son, yet another Prince Edward, on 2 November 1470. 'From this circumstance was derived some hope and consolation for such persons as remained faithful in their allegiance to Edward,' wrote one chronicler. But to the ascendant Nevilles and Lancastrians, 'the birth of this infant [was] a thing of very little consequence'.

As Elizabeth Woodville laboured in the sanctuary apartments at Westminster, the so-called 'readeption' of Henry VI was well underway. The old king was brought out of the Tower of London on Saturday 6 October 1470. His supporters made no delay in formally returning him to his throne, for the most auspicious day in the English royal calendar was fast approaching: the feast day of the Translation of St Edward the Confessor, whose stunning shrine was the centrepiece of all the tombs of the Plantagenet kings inside Westminster Abbey. A week after Henry's release, 'after walking in solemn procession, [he] had the crown publicly placed on his head'.[9]

Henry was now forty-eight years old and jail had not been kind to him. He had, wrote his confessor John Blacman, 'patiently endured hunger, thirst, mockings, derisions, abuse and many other hardships'.[10] The chronicler Warkworth sniffed that he seemed 'not worshipfully arrayed as a prince and not so cleanly kept'. Nevertheless, many in England seemed able temporarily to convince themselves that since Henry VI had not been the author of the ills done during his reign, he was fit to be restored to the throne. The chronicler Warkworth put this down to Edward's failure to restore England to 'prosperities and peace'. So much hope had been invested in him at the beginning of his reign, wrote the chronicler, 'but it came not; but one battle after another, and much trouble and great loss of goods among the common people'.

Yet if there was any genuine hope placed in Henry's return to the throne then this, too, would be sorely disappointed. The restoration of Queen Margaret was hardly an event likely to bring reconciliation and understanding to the realm, all the less so if her son had inherited his mother's implacable temperament. It was virtually impossible to see how Lancastrian loyalists like the Cliffords, Courtenays, Somersets and Tudors might be rewarded, or even restored to their former estates and dignities, when the chief beneficiaries of the Yorkist victory had been Warwick and Clarence, the same men who had helped bring Henry VI out blinking from the Tower and placed the crown back on his head. And then there was the problem of Clarence himself: the faithless rebel had caused so much of the trouble that had descended on England through his selfish desire to inch closer to his brother's throne. With two rival Prince Edwards now alive – the one a bellicose young Lancastrian, the other Edward IV's tiny son and heir – Clarence was now further from the crown than ever. How, then, could his lasting support be bought? And how would Warwick enjoy a political role that would surely never reach the near-mastery that he had achieved in the 1460s?

In the end, these were not questions that the court of Henry VI had very long to ponder. New Year passed with Edward IV still in exile in Bruges: but he had been busy. He was discreetly supplied with ships and money by Charles the Bold and the merchants of the Low Countries, and with his brother-in-law Anthony Woodville (now the second Earl Rivers) Edward began fitting out an invasion fleet to reclaim his kingdom. Edward, Rivers, Lord Hastings, Richard duke of Gloucester and their company set sail from Vlissingen on the island of Walcheren on Monday 11 March 1471, armed with thirty-six ships and twelve hundred men. (Edward sailed aboard a Burgundian warship called the *Antony*.) This small flotilla picked its way across a sea bristling with enemy craft, heading for a landing in East Anglia. Storms, however, blew the fleet north, and they eventually landed near the mouth of the river Humber at Ravenspur. This was enemy territory in every sense, for Warwick's men patrolled the countryside, watching jealously for any sign of an invasion. By coincidence, it was the very same point at which Henry Bolingbroke had arrived in 1399, when he had come to claim his lands, and subsequently the crown, from Richard II. It was an auspicious scene for the return of a king.

*

'It is a difficult matter to go out by the door and then want to enter by the windows,' Sforza de Bettini of Florence, the Milanese ambassador to Louis XI, wrote from the French court to his master Duke Galeazzo Maria Sforza on 9 April, the Tuesday before Easter 1471. Having monitored reports from across the Channel, he held out very little hope for Edward's mission to rescue his kingdom. Wild rumours spinning out of England suggested that the earl of Warwick had the upper hand: Bettini had heard that 'the greater part of those who were with [Edward were] slain and the rest put to flight'. Queen Margaret and Prince Edward were waiting impatiently in port at Normandy for a wind to carry them across the sea and reclaim their kingdom in triumph.[11] It appeared that Edward IV's mission to rescue his realm had been strangled before it had even begun.

But Bettini was misinformed. Edward was far from routed. In fact, on the very day that the Milanese ambassador wrote his letter, he was marching south on London, with men rallying to his side.

Edward's arrival in Ravenspur had not quite thrown England into great bouts of celebration, but neither had he been immediately chased away, in part because he rode through the countryside claiming (much as Bolingbroke had before him) that he came not to take back the crown, but 'only to claim to be Duke of

York'.[12] He wore the ostrich feather badge of the prince of Wales rather than the crown, and professed to all who would listen that he was returning as a loyal subject. This was enough to gain him entry successively to the northern towns of York, Tadcaster, Wakefield and Doncaster, before he moved down into the midlands and entered Nottingham and then Leicester. At every stop he was joined by supporters; a few at first but gradually more, until 'his number was increased' with 'bands of men, well arrayed and habled [i.e. armoured] for war'.[13] On 29 March he advanced on Coventry, where the earl of Warwick was holed up with his allies John de Vere, earl of Oxford, Henry Holland, duke of Exeter and Lord Beaumont. Warwick, preferring to avoid a fight until reinforced by Montague and Clarence, retreated inside the walls of the city, barred the gates and refused to come out. Momentum now lay with Edward, and it was at this point that he dropped the obvious pretence of claiming his duchy, and announced his determination to defeat the adherents of 'Henry the Usurper'.[14]

From Coventry Edward struck out west, before turning in the direction of Oxford and London. As he went, news of his return fanned out around him. It did not take long to reach the realm's other great rebel, George duke of Clarence, who was in the west country when Edward landed. Clarence now frantically tried to raise troops, in order to rally to the earl of Warwick. But a coward and a turncoat such as he did not have the moral steadfastness to attack his brother ascendant. (Clarence had also been lobbied by two of his sisters, Margaret duchess of Burgundy and Anne duchess of Exeter, who had counselled him to make peace.) He met Edward near Banbury on Wednesday 3 April. In the company of Rivers, Hastings and Gloucester, he threw himself at Edward's feet. Edward 'lifted him up and kissed him many times', assured him that they were at peace and took him back to Coventry, in a second attempt to coax Warwick out of his bolthole. Again Warwick would not emerge, even though he was by now accompanied by his brother John Neville, Marquess Montague. Edward decided not to waste any more time seeking battle. On Friday 5 April he set out for London.

So on Tuesday 9 April London's common council, who had much better information than distant diplomats, were aware that, far from having been crushed, 'Edward late king of England was hastening towards the city with a powerful army'.[15] Warwick was also writing to the city, demanding that the council keep it for King Henry. The stress was such that the mayor, John Stockton, had taken to his bed and would not be dragged out of it. But in the mayor's absence, the rest of the city council resolved not to resist Edward. They had plenty of good reasons. Not only were Queen Elizabeth, her daughters and her newborn son as well as scores of other Yorkists still holed up in sanctuary at Westminster, close to the city walls, but the merchants of London had also loaned Edward a great deal of money, which, according to the Burgundian chronicler Philippe de Commines, 'obliged all the tradesmen who were his creditors to appear for him'. Commines, who was like all good chroniclers an insatiable gossip, added that 'the ladies of quality and rich citizens' wives, with whom [Edward] had formerly intrigued, forced their husbands and relations to declare themselves on his side'.[16]

Edward entered London on Maundy Thursday. He found that the Tower had already been secured by his friends. Supporters of the earl of Warwick, identifiable by badges of the bear and ragged staff worn on their coats, were making themselves scarce. Edmund Beaufort, duke of Somerset had left London for the coast, to await Queen Margaret's arrival. Warwick's brother, the treacherous George Neville, archbishop of York, had been left in possession of the 'other' king, but his attempt to rally the populace by parading Henry VI through the streets during Edward's approach was met with ridicule. Henry appeared as the pathetic, downtrodden old man he was: his shoulders draped not in the latest Burgundian finery but in a dreary old blue gown. In fact, the pious Henry was dressing according to the solemnity of the religious calendar – for Maundy Thursday, the day before Good Friday, was a day of mourning. Yet it looked to one London chronicler as if 'he had no more to change with'.[17] Nor was the rest of the parade impressive. Lord Zouch, commissioned to carry the sword of state, appeared old and impotent. The crowd accompanying the king was small. And their symbol of defiance – a pole borne above the parade with two foxes' tails tied to it – appeared lame and unkingly. It was 'more like a play than the showing of a prince', recorded the chronicler. It was in this context that the strapping, energetic Edward entered the city to 'the universal acclamation of the citizens', who now awaited his command.[18]

Edward went first to St Paul's, to give thanks, before riding directly for the bishop of London's palace in Lambeth, to take possession of Henry VI. Dim and vacant, the shabby figure greeted Edward with an embrace and the words, 'My cousin of York, you are very welcome. I know in your hands my life will not be in danger.'[19] Edward assured him that all would be well and sent him back to the Tower of London, with the archbishop of York for company. Then he set out for Westminster Abbey, where he gave thanks once again, this time before the shrine of St Edward: the source of all that was mysterious and holy about English kingship. Finally he made the short trip from the abbey church to the abbot's apartments, where Queen Elizabeth was waiting for him. She had received personal letters announcing her husband's return, but nothing would be a substitute for the man in person. Since the beginning of Warwick's rebellion Elizabeth had lost her father and her brother. She had been in hiding at the abbey for six months, during which time the official record would state that she had endured 'right great trouble, sorrow and heaviness, which she sustained with all manner of patience that belonged to any creature'. The queen presented Edward with his tiny namesake, 'to the Kings greatest joy, a fair son, a prince'.[20] Joyfully reunited, they spent the night back in the city, at Edward's mother's lodgings in Baynard's Castle. The following day was Good Friday, and Edward spent the morning with his brothers and allies, plotting 'for the adventures that were likely for to come'.[21]

*

'On Holy Saturday in Easter week,' wrote a chronicler of the time, Edward 'quitted the city with his army, and, passing slowly on, reached the town of Barnet, a place ten miles distant from the city; and there pitched his camp, on the eve of the day of our Lord's resurrection.'[22] There were two kings in the army, for Edward had brought Henry VI with him. It was hardly likely that Henry would have escaped, or even conceived of escaping from the Tower of London. But his presence in Edward's lines was vital, for marching in the other direction, directly towards them on the road from St Albans, came the earl of Warwick. He had finally left Coventry, 'calling himself lieutenant of England and so constituted by the pretensed authority of King Henry'.[23] Henry's physical presence on the other side rendered this claim manifestly false.

The two armies made first contact as the light was fading on Saturday afternoon, when Warwick's scouts were intercepted and chased by Edward's men. With the sun setting, there was no hope of a fight that day, but the two sides were virtually within sight of one another. Both camped on the open ground north of Barnet. The damp, cold night air flashed and boomed with fire sprayed from the muzzles of Warwick's cannon, aimed badly in the darkness and flinging shot safely over the heads of the kings' men.

Dawn broke around four o'clock on Easter Sunday. A great mist hung over the ground, clouding the short distance between the two armies and obscuring 'the sight of either other'. But almost all present – not least the veterans of the battle of Towton – had fought in worse. No sooner had the sun's thin light come up than Edward 'committed his cause and quarrel to Almighty God', raised his banners, ordered his trumpeters to blow and charged his men forward against the blaze of the enemy artillery.[24] The reckoning had begun.

The royal army was commanded by Edward, with Lord Hastings on the left flank and Richard duke of Gloucester leading the right. Opposite them were Oxford, Montague and Exeter, with the earl of Warwick commanding from the rear. The two armies were misaligned, so that Gloucester's men heavily outnumbered Exeter's at the eastern end of the battlefield, while Hastings was hobbled in his fight against Oxford on the west. Hastings in particular took terrible losses, his division routed and chased back in the direction of London, carrying the false but terrifying news that Warwick had triumphed, capturing Edward and killing Clarence and Gloucester.

It was not so. Both sides' guns were nullified by the thick fog, and the battle raged hand to hand, 'cruel and mortal'. Edward fought in the centre of it all, his vision obscured so badly that he, like the rest of his men, could 'see but a little from him'. Nevertheless, he 'manly, vigorously and valiantly assailed' his enemies and 'with great violence, beat and bore down afore him all that stood in his way . . . first on that one hand, and then on that other hand . . . so that nothing might stand in the sight of him'.[25]

While Edward was accustomed to fighting on foot, Warwick was said by one chronicler to prefer to run with his men into battle before mounting on horseback, 'and if he found victory inclined to his side, he charged boldly among them; if otherwise he took care of himself in time and provided for his escape'.[26] At Barnet, however, he was harangued by his brother Montague, who insisted that he should demonstrate the Neville family's courage by fighting on foot and sending his horses away. It was to be his undoing. After several hours of fighting the battle lines had wheeled ninety degrees, and the positions of the two armies grew very confused. The earl of Oxford, returning from his pursuit of Hastings's men, arrived back on the misty battlefield and attacked what he thought were Edward's rear lines. In fact he was encountering Montague's men. In the mist and the press of battle, the Neville retinue apparently mistook the Oxford badge – a star – for Edward's sun, and immediately turned their guns on their own allies.[27] The cry of 'Treason' went up around the Lancastrian–Neville army and its order collapsed. In the confusion Warwick turned to scramble from the field and save himself. But on foot he was fatally hampered. By the time he had found a horse and set off in the direction of St Albans, there were Yorkist men in pursuit. Warwick was driven into a little wood at a fork in the road, where he was taken prisoner and killed before he could be brought up to Edward IV. Behind him on the battlefield Warwick left his brother John, Marquess Montague to be 'slain . . . in plain battle, and many other knights, squires, noblemen, and other'.[28]

It was all over by eight o'clock on Easter morning. The battlefield was strewn with ten thousand spent arrows.[29] The earl of Oxford fled the field and escaped to Scotland. Exeter was left for dead on the battlefield, but was eventually discovered by a servant, dragged from the field towards London and spirited into the sanctuary at Westminster. Later he was taken out of sanctuary and imprisoned in the Tower, where he remained for four years.

Edward lost his allies Lord Cromwell, Lord Saye and Sir William Blount in the fighting; his brother Gloucester and brother-in-law Lord Scales were both seriously injured and thousands more lay dead on the field on both sides. Those who staggered the ten miles back to London were seen arriving with their horses lame and faces bandaged, some having had their noses cut off in the fighting. 'All men say that there was never in a hundred years a fiercer battle in England than this,' wrote one well-connected foreign correspondent.[30] There was no doubt that Edward had won an astonishing victory. St George, the Virgin and all the saints in heaven, wrote the official chronicler of the battle, had adjudged Edward's 'quarrel to be true and rightwise'. To advertise this fact, by the king's order Warwick and Montague's bodies were brought to London 'in two chests, and were set upon the stones in the body of the church of St Paul's, lying therein naked, except for a cloth tied around the private parts of either, so that everyone in London and others might see them, which many thousands did'.[31]

Just one enemy remained. On 16 April word reached the king that Queen Margaret, her son Prince Edward, his wife Anne Neville and many others, including Lord Wenlock, had finally found a favourable wind from Normandy and had landed on the south coast at Weymouth with seventeen ships, and had been greeted by their allies Edmund Beaufort, duke of Somerset and John Courtenay, earl of Devon. For all the death and destruction that had been caused, it seemed as though there might be yet more to come. Foreign diplomats, receiving their news piecemeal across the Channel, shook their heads and marvelled at England's topsy-turvy politics. 'I wish the country and the people were plunged deep in the sea, because of their lack of stability, for I feel like one going to the torture when I write about them, and no one ever hears twice alike about English affairs,' wrote Ambassador Bettini in a letter home to Milan. One thing was certain: the kingdom was not safe yet.

*

The Lancastrian army struggled through the inhospitable land north of Gloucester on the eastern bank of the river Severn: 'a foul country, all in lanes and stony ways, betwixt woods and without any good refreshing'. It was Friday 3 May, and some of them

– including their leaders Queen Margaret and Prince Edward – had been travelling for more than three weeks. Their enemy, a rival royal army under the leadership of King Edward IV, had been in pursuit for several days. Both armies were now heading for the town of Tewkesbury, where there was a crossing in the river that would allow the chase to continue on the other side, with all of Wales opening up beyond. The troops on both sides were weary. Their leaders pushed them urgently onwards. The fight, when it came, was likely to be final.

Margaret and Prince Edward had landed in England on Easter Sunday, the same day that the slaughter was unfolding at the battle of Barnet. They had immediately begun raising troops, sending requests to supporters calling for 'all such fellowship as you can make in your most defensible array', against 'Edward Earl of March the King's great Rebel our Enemy'.[32] The call was answered: large numbers of men had flocked to the Lancastrian standard from Devon and Cornwall. They formed a dangerous, undisciplined army that terrorised the towns they visited as Margaret pressed them northwards, marching through Somerset towards the Cotswolds, in the hope either of meeting up in Wales with Jasper Tudor, who might provide them with loyal soldiers from the principality, or of reaching Lancashire, 'where great numbers of men skilled in archery were to be found'.[33] As they went, Queen Margaret kept up a stream of cheerfully outrageous propaganda, sending word to the king of France that 'the Earl of Warwick was not dead, as reported, but he had been wounded in the fight with King Edward and had withdrawn to a secret and solitary place to get well of his wounds and sickness', and that Prince Edward was 'in London with a very large following of men and with the favour and assistance of the greater part of the common people and citizens'.[34]

Barely having enjoyed his victory at Barnet, Edward IV had been forced to scramble for another army, which he assembled at

Windsor on 24 April, the day after St George's Day and the annual royal feast held to commemorate the foundation of the Order of the Garter. Spies had informed him of the Lancastrians' movements, so Edward had set off in pursuit of his enemies, heading north-west to try and cut them off in the Cotswolds. He had been in Cirencester on 29 April, as Margaret's army approached Bath. Thereafter the two armies had tracked each other for the best part of a week.

On 3 May, a blisteringly hot day, as the Lancastrians struggled through the foul country by the riverbank towards Tewkesbury, Edward had flogged his chasing army a full thirty-one miles in a twelve-hour hike. The paucity of supplies in the countryside made supporting one army difficult, and two armies impossible. Thus Edward's men had covered their ground without stopping once for food and water – there was 'ne so much as drink for their horses, save in one little brook', wrote one chronicler.[35] It was an astonishing piece of leadership to have moved around five thousand hungry, thirsty men so far, so fast. But Edward managed it, and with his two brothers by his side, along with Lord Hastings, John duke of Norfolk and his stepson Thomas Grey, marquess of Dorset and many other noblemen, he was able to close in on the Lancastrians with his usual certainty of purpose. Throughout the day, his scouts watched the enemy army, travelling 'evermore . . . within five or six miles'.[36] They camped near Tewkesbury in the afternoon on 3 May, 'so extremely fatigued with the labour of marching and thirst that they could proceed no further'.[37] Queen Margaret's army arrived at Tewkesbury at four o'clock on the same afternoon. They, too, were exhausted from many days and miles of punishing marching. The two sides made camp around three miles away from each other, knowing full well what the next day would bring.

Early in the morning the following day, Saturday 4 May, Edward donned his armour and divided his army into three divisions under the same leadership that had prevailed at Barnet – himself, Hastings and the brilliant young Gloucester, who was now given command of the vanguard. Then he 'displayed his banners, did blow up the trumpets; committed his cause and quarrel to Almighty God . . . the Virgin Mary, the glorious martyr Saint George, and all the saints and advanced directly upon his enemies'.[38] The Lancastrians were arrayed under Prince Edward (assisted by Lord Wenlock and Sir John Langstrother, the prior of St John), Edmund duke of Somerset and John Courtenay, earl of Devon. Queen Margaret was some distance from the battlefield, perhaps watching events from Tewkesbury Abbey, which sat beyond a meadow and a couple of fishponds north of the Lancastrian lines. The battleground was uneven and pitted with obstacles: a road separated the two armies, and the ground between them contained 'deep dykes, [and] so many hedges, trees and bushes'. It was, said one writer, 'a right evil place to approach'.

Edward began his assault with a hail of arrows and gunshot – a 'right-a-sharp shower' –which was returned in kind. Fire was concentrated on the Lancastrian vanguard under the duke of Somerset, and 'his fellowship was sore annoyed'. They refused to stand firm beneath the hail of deadly missiles until eventually the duke was forced to order a charge on the Yorkist lines. His men ran down the hill on which they had been arrayed, heading directly for the middle of Edward's army, rather than for Gloucester's vanguard, against whom they were most directly aligned. The troops crashed into each other, Somerset's men fighting 'right fiercely' before 'the King, full manly, set for the even upon them' and began to push the attack back up the hill.

Before battle started Edward had detached two hundred pikemen and sent them to a nearby wood, instructing them to scout for a Lancastrian ambush. If they found nothing, they were to return to the battlefield 'as they thought most behovefull' and 'to employ themselves in the best wise as they could'. It was a tactical masterstroke. As Somerset's men were bowled back up the hill towards their own lines 'with great violence', Edward's detachment of spearmen attacked them from the side, sending them into total disarray. Their discipline dissolved and Somerset's whole division was scattered into the meadow and fields, 'where they best hoped to escape the danger'. Just as at Towton, the meadow ran with blood as the fight became a rout: tired, panic-stricken men run down and hacked to pieces.

Somerset's failure seems to have precipitated the collapse of the whole Lancastrian army. Lord Wenlock was killed. So was the earl of Devon and Somerset's brother, John Beaufort. Most devastating of all, Prince Edward was cut down in the first battle he ever fought, 'fleeing to the town-wards and slain in the field'. The chronicler Warkworth heard that the prince had died crying for succour from his brother-in-law George duke of Clarence.[39] As their leaders were butchered, the Lancastrian captains and troops scattered from the field. Those who escaped death in the meadow fled either for the abbey or for the numerous churches of the surrounding countryside, hoping to find sanctuary. Not all of them would be so lucky.

The battle was decisive. Edward had 'at last gained a glorious victory'.[40] And just as at Towton he was determined to secure that victory with bloody swiftness. The king marched directly from the battlefield to Tewkesbury Abbey, where Somerset and others were sheltering under the protection of sanctuary. According to Warkworth, Edward walked into the abbey church 'with his sword' in his hand, only to be stopped by a priest holding the holy sacrament, who demanded that a royal pardon should be issued to the lords who were hiding there. Edward appears to have consented, and ordered the burial of those who had fallen in battle on the abbey's consecrated ground 'without any quartering or defouling [of] their bodies'. Two days later, though, Somerset, Sir John Langstrother, Sir Hugh Courtenay and others were taken out of the abbey by force, and given into the custody of Gloucester as the constable of England, and Norfolk in his capacity as marshal. Gloucester's court found them all guilty. They were beheaded in the town on the same day.

On 7 May Edward left Tewkesbury. He was barely out of the town when news came that Queen Margaret had been tracked down and taken at a nearby poor religious house, possibly Malvern Priory, in the company of her son's widow, Anne Neville, the countess of Devon and Lady Katherine Vaux. The queen was brought, broken-spirited, to London in a cart. Her life was spared, but her fight was over. She would spend the next four years in honourable confinement, the prisoner of Alice de la Pole, the aged widow of her husband's greatest minister, the duke of Suffolk, who had once been her lady-in-waiting. In 1475 Margaret would be ransomed back to Louis XI, under whose patronage she would live out the rest of her life: lonely, defeated and stripped of her power, her days of adventure over.

There was one last serious flurry of Lancastrian rebellion: as news reached London that all had been lost at Tewkesbury, Warwick's cousin Thomas Neville, known universally as 'the bastard of Fauconberg', raised a rebellion in his father's home county of Kent. He was an extremely accomplished sea captain, pirate and soldier, and between 10 May and 14 May he sailed up and down the Thames, launching attacks by land and sea on London's gates and walls, aided by several hundred crack troops from Calais: it seems likely that they hoped to remove Henry VI from the Tower. But Edward had thought to anticipate an attack on the city. Anthony, Earl Rivers had been left to lead London's defences and he did so with great distinction. Despite the fact that Fauconberg set up cannon on the south bank of the Thames to pound the city's walls, destroying part of London Bridge and capturing the Aldgate, Rivers and the earl of Essex husbanded the Londoners' defences, counter-attacked effectively from within the city and eventually hounded Fauconberg and his men away: he took ship and fled back across the Channel. (He would later be captured at Southampton, handed over to the duke of Gloucester and executed, his severed head being placed on London Bridge, facing Kent, whence he had brought his rebels.) With Fauconberg's defeat the last serious plank of Lancastrian resistance was broken. On Tuesday 21 May 1471, Edward rode once more into London in a procession led by the triumphant Gloucester, 'with a retinue far greater than any of his former armies, and with standards unfurled and borne before him and the nobles of his army'.[41] Trumpets blared as the triumphant king returned to his city 'to the great joy and consolation of his friends, allies and well-willers . . . and to the great confusion of all his enemies'.

That same night, Henry VI died. The king's confessor and biographer John Blacman said that Henry spent his last days having visions, including one in which he successfully admonished an imaginary woman whom he saw through his window attempting to drown a child.[42] A more physically harmless inhabitant of the Tower of London it was hard to imagine, but Edward was no longer prepared to be merciful beyond reason. The official chronicler of the Yorkist royal victory said that Henry reacted very badly to the certainty of his defeat and the death of his son: 'He took it to so great despite, ire and indignation, that, of pure displeasure and melancholy, he died.'[43] This would have been an unsatisfactory explanation even were it not for the fact that Richard duke of Gloucester was in the Tower on the night of Henry's death: a more believable account is given by the chronicler Warkworth, who recorded that Henry was 'put to death' between eleven o'clock and midnight.[44] His body was wrapped in linen and taken the next day by torchlight to St Paul's for display; it bled on the cathedral pavement several times. Later, Henry's corpse was transported by boat to Chertsey Abbey for burial. (It would be exhumed and moved to Windsor in 1484.) Henry may have been bludgeoned to death: his corpse was found much later to have light brown hair matted with what appeared to be blood.[45]

It did not take long for the news of Henry's 'secret assassination' to circulate: by mid-June it was common knowledge at the French court that Edward IV, in order to bring the wars finally to an end, had applied himself to the extermination of his enemies. 'He has, in short,' wrote one ambassador, 'chosen to crush the seed.'[46] Edward's decade as king had finally taught him the value of ruthlessness. Within the space of eleven weeks and against the most desperate odds he had invaded England, raised an army, rescued his son and heir from sanctuary, fought two 'right-great, cruel and mortal' battles, put down a rebellion, killed or captured virtually every one of his enemies, slain his rival king and successor and won back his crown.[47] There had not been as successful and fortunate an English general since the days of Henry V. Edward was, as one writer put it, 'a most renowned conqueror and a mighty monarch; whose praises resounded far and wide throughout the land'.[48] He had not just staked his claim in blood: he had now earned it in bloodshed. He reigned with unarguable and well-deserved majesty: a great and glorious king.

IV

The Rise of the Tudors
1471–1525

But who will insane lust for power spare . . . ?

DOMINIC MANCINI

16 : To Execute Wrath

The fourteen-year-old boy travelled through south Wales alongside his forty-year-old uncle and a band of loyal retainers, making their way towards unstable country, thick with woods and pocked with the turrets of glowering castles. They were heading for the estuary of the river Severn, hoping to make contact with Queen Margaret and Prince Edward, and to reinforce the Lancastrian army aiming to destroy the Yorkist pretender who called himself Edward IV. The boy and the man both knew that if they could join forces with the queen, then they stood an excellent chance of victory. Ten years of exile, insurgency and plot would finally be rewarded with a return to rule. Reaching the river valley was the most important mission of their lives.

Both were well acquainted with the perils that they faced. The man was a veteran of England's wars: a skilled soldier with a fondness and talent for insurgent fighting. The boy had also seen his share of violence. His father had died a prisoner before he was even born. Then he had been brought up from the age of four as a captive – albeit a generously treated and well-schooled captive – in the heavily armed Yorkist castle at Raglan. He had been under the wardship of William Herbert, earl of Pembroke, who had bought him for £1,000, provided him with brilliant tutors and groomed him for marriage into the Herbert family. When he was twelve years old Herbert had taken him to the battle of Edgecote, to see and hear for the first time the ghastliness of men being hacked down in their hundreds. Herbert had perished there, at Edgecote: beheaded after the battle was through. The boy knew, therefore, the thin line that lay between living and dying, triumph and catastrophe. 'This world', as the old poem had it, 'is variable.'[1]

And so it proved. They had just passed Chepstow when the dreadful news arrived. The slaughter at Tewkesbury had spared no one: the queen was captured, the prince was dead, and so too were many of their allies, from Somerset and Lord Wenlock to the scores of loyal retainers who had risen up to fight for the Lancastrian right to rule. Tewkesbury was a disaster that exceeded even the horror of Towton. Edward and his brothers were triumphant. The boy and the man now knew that soon they would be targets. To march further was futile. The only rational plan now was to flee, as fast as they possibly could. Henry Tudor and his uncle Jasper halted their march and bolted for safety.

Since Chepstow was the nearest town, it was there that the Tudors went first, taking with them a part of the armed force that Jasper had raised during the earlier months of 1471. Chepstow was a relatively secure fortress town, protected by city walls and the natural defences of the river Wye, and overlooked by a large turreted castle built on the densely forested hills that rose above the town. Here the Tudors paused. Jasper tried to make sense of the fact that Edward IV had 'utterly overthrown' his half-brother the king, and debated with his friends 'what course was best to take'.[2] He did not need long to deliberate. In a bid to exterminate whatever was left of the house of Lancaster, Edward IV sent out Sir Roger Vaughan – a veteran of Mortimer's Cross, where Jasper's father Owen Tudor had been captured and executed – with a licence to kill. Vaughan was described as a 'very valiant man'; fortunately for the Tudors he was not so skilled in the art of survival as Jasper. Having received advance warning that Vaughan was on his way, the elder Tudor set up an ambush in Chepstow. Vaughan was captured when he entered the town, and Jasper avenged his father's death by having the gentleman beheaded. But there was scarcely time to take satisfaction. More royal agents were closing in, and the Tudors retreated in all haste to Pembroke on the west coast of Wales, where they were 'besieged, and kept in with ditch and trench [so] that [they] might not escape'.

In happier times during the 1450s, when Jasper had himself been earl of Pembroke and the premier nobleman in south Wales, this great coastal town had been the seat of his power. It was where Henry Tudor had first seen the world, when he was born to thirteen-year-old Margaret Beaufort on 28 January 1457. It was a place that had traditionally been very close to Tudor hearts. Now, though, it was a prison. Their tormentor was the late Sir Roger Vaughan's son-in-law, Morgan Thomas. The Thomas family had a long tradition of supporting the Lancastrian cause, but Jasper's decision to kill Vaughan had pushed his son to the other side. For more than a week he kept Jasper and Henry pinned down, cut off from supplies and finding it desperately difficult to communicate with their supporters.

Fortunately, not all of the Thomas family had lost their faith. Morgan Thomas had been camped in front of Pembroke for more than a week when he was attacked by his brother David, who brought a force of two thousand men before the town walls and distracted the besiegers just long enough for Jasper and Henry to slip out of the gates and flee again, this time four miles across the south-western peninsula to 'a town by the sea side' called Tenby. This little port town was just as well protected as Pembroke – indeed, Jasper had once helped to reinforce its defences. It was strong enough, at any rate, to keep Edward IV's forces at bay for a couple of months while the Tudors hired a barque (a small sailing boat with three masts) and corresponded with the French court, asking for assistance and in return promising to 'keep up the war and disturbance' for as long as they could. But eventually their position became untenable. In mid-September 1471 the Tudors faced the inevitable and made arrangements to leave Wales for the continent. Taking with them a skeleton crew of friends and servants, they piled into Jasper's hired barque, cast out from the shore and trusted their lives to the sea. The Channel stretching out before them churned with storms.[3]

*

When the Tudors sailed for France, they left Edward IV finally and indisputably master of his kingdom. He was still a young man – the battle of Tewkesbury took place only a few days after his twenty-ninth birthday – and he set about rebuilding his realm with his usual energetic bonhomie. A growing brood of young children by his wife Elizabeth suggested a healthy future for Edward's royal line. His eldest daughter, Elizabeth, was six; her sisters Mary and Cecily were three and two. Their brother, Edward, had been born in sanctuary in November 1470 and was still a tiny baby, but he was heir to the crown all the same. On 11 June 1471 the seven-month-old was created prince of Wales and earl of Chester in a ceremony at Westminster Abbey, followed by investiture somewhat later as duke of Cornwall. Less than a month later, on 3 July, a great council met at Westminster, where forty-seven archbishops, bishops, dukes, earls, barons and knights all swore on the gospels that they would acknowledge Prince Edward as 'true and undoubted heir to our . . . sovereign lord, as to the crowns and realms of England and of France and the lordship of Ireland'.[4] Edward and Elizabeth would produce six more children during the next nine years: Margaret, born in April 1472; Richard duke of York in August 1473; Anne in November 1475; George duke of Bedford, who was born in March 1477 but died at the age of two; and finally Catherine in August 1479 and Bridget in November 1480. All but George would survive their earliest years, creating a large and youthful family around the king.

One of Edward's first actions of his second reign was to set out a long list of protocols and ordinances for his household and those of his children. His fondness for the glittering and ritual-ised court of his brother-in-law Charles duke of Burgundy had only been increased by the months he had spent exiled in the Low Countries at a court which John Paston thought was sec-ond only to King Arthur's.[5] A long instruction manual for the organisation of an English king's domestic and ceremonial life, called the Black Book, was produced by 1472.[6] In it was set out every tiny detail of propriety and protocol in the royal presence, the deference due to visitors of every rank, and the rations due to servants and officials, no matter how lowly. The Black Book contained everything from the number of loaves, ale-flagons, candles and faggots of firewood that should be given to a baron residing at the royal court, to the precise means by which the king's tablecloth should be folded and presented when he sat to dine in the company of his subjects. It described a court whose splendour would match that of any English court before it and which would impress any foreign visitor with its command of fashion and princely worship. This was more than simply a Bur-gundian copycat court: it was a royal establishment that was singularly, dazzlingly English, harking back to the glorious days of the king's mighty fourteenth-century ancestor Edward III.[7] Its style and grandiloquence was matched in the building works that began in Edward IV's second reign, not least in his recon-struction of the chapel of the college of St George at Windsor, the spiritual home of the Order of the Garter, which became a soaring masterpiece of gothic architecture, furnished with elab-orately carved choir stalls, decorated with brilliant statues and stained-glass windows and stocked with ornate vestments for the use of the clergy of the college. Edward spent £6,572 in five years on works to improve Windsor, at the same time under-taking extensive reconstruction of the fortresses and palaces at Calais, Nottingham, Westminster, Greenwich, Eltham and the York family seat in the midlands, Fotheringhay.

Besides erecting fine buildings and marshalling the royal household, there was a kingdom to run. The deaths of Warwick, Montague and several other rebels left swathes of land to be reassigned in south-west England, the west midlands and the north. Edward also voluntarily reclaimed lands and offices that had previously been alienated from the Crown by passing an act of resumption in parliament in 1473. This was a tool that he had used before in 1461, 1463 and 1467 – and one which had the double benefit of fortifying royal finances while allowing the scope for cheap patronage by granting exemptions. Edward approached the problem of redistributing land, titles, offices and authority like a political jigsaw puzzle: fitting together sensitive areas of the country under the leadership of men whom he thought he could trust, most of whom came from the family circle. Lands in Devon, Cornwall and the south-west fell to the king's stepson, Thomas Grey, who became marquess of Dorset by 1475. The late Lord Herbert's son and namesake William Herbert became earl of Pembroke and was initially trusted to oversee Wales before the role was taken over by a council under the authority of the young Edward, who had been awarded the traditional heir's titles of prince of Wales and earl of Chester.[8] The prince's council operated from the old Yorkist seat of Ludlow, on the borders, and its power in Wales was operated by the queen and her brother, Earl Rivers.

Warwick's huge estates, which, had he died naturally, would have gone to his brother Montague and his two daughters, were largely split between the king's brothers.[9] In the midlands, the unreliable Clarence was entrusted with land and a limited degree of autonomy and power, but his authority was eventually overtaken by that of Edward's great friend, servant, military captain and companion, William, Lord Hastings. Edward kept a measure of direct control on the midlands, later marrying his second son, Richard duke of York, to the daughter of the duke of

Norfolk, who had interests in the region. A patchwork quilt of delegated royal authority was being stitched together, connecting the king's children, brothers and extended family in a way that had not been attempted since the heyday of Edward III.[10] At the centre of it all the king remained sharp, interested and focused on the business of government. He was capable in an argument of demonstrating intimate knowledge of politics to a remarkably local level. He appointed men connected to his household to serve as local justices of the peace and sheriffs, to sit on the itinerant judicial commissions known as 'oyer and terminer' ('to hear and to judge') and to do the work of the royal council in the regions.[11] The fingers of direct royal power spread deeper than at any time in living memory into the shires of England. One chronicler observed that the dominance of royal officials controlling the governance of 'castles, forests, manors and parks' was such that 'no person, however shrewd he might be' could commit any offence without being 'immediately charged with the same to his face'. Gradually, the machinery necessary for keeping law and order in the realm was being rebuilt.

Edward's reconstruction of England and of English royal power relied heavily on the use of tough and trusted lieutenants, and few were more trusted after 1471 than his youngest brother, Richard duke of Gloucester. He was awarded the Neville estates in northern England, a perpetually troubled and dangerous area of the country, bordering the unpredictable enemy kingdom of Scotland. It required a leader of unimpeachable loyalty, military skill, courage and cunning, characteristics he had displayed over the course of the recent crises. To bolster his position, in 1472 Gloucester was married to Warwick's younger daughter, Anne Neville. (His brother Clarence had, of course, married Anne's elder sister, Isabel, during his rebellion in 1469.) Gloucester was also awarded huge tracts of land from the duchy of Lancaster, the honour of Richmond (which had once belonged to Henry Tudor's father Edmund) and effective seniority over Henry Percy, the earl of Northumberland. He held land in Wales and East Anglia, as well as serving as constable and admiral of England.

Still only twenty-two years old in 1472, Richard of Gloucester was beginning to suffer noticeably from scoliosis, a curvature of the spine which caused him to walk with his right shoulder raised and his back hunched, and may have given him pain and shortness of breath.[12] In later years a German visitor to England, Nicolas von Poppelau, would remark that although Richard was tall (he stood five foot eight inches, not as tall as his brother Edward, but large by the standard of the day), he was lean, with delicate arms and legs. Whatever Richard's physical shortcomings, they did not diminish his standing either in his brother's eyes or anyone else's: during the 1470s he was roundly acclaimed as the most senior military man in England under the king, an effective prince in the north and Edward IV's foremost and most trusted lieutenant. He had, said von Poppelau, 'a great heart'.[13]

The same could not be said of George duke of Clarence. He was chief among those who benefited from Edward IV's preference for conciliation and mercy, and had been treated with extraordinary generosity, considering his pivotal role in the crisis that had forced his brother from the throne in the first place. Clarence had extensive territories in the midlands and was, with Gloucester, among the first to profit from the death of the earl of Warwick. But the partition of the Warwick estates caused a good amount of friction between Clarence and Gloucester from 1472 until 1474 – friction that translated on the ground into disorder throughout the midlands and a growing headache for the king. Edward had indulged his feckless younger brother for many years, tolerating the most appalling and disloyal behaviour, but eventually he came to realise that Clarence was never likely to redeem himself and become the dependable and astute kinsman on whom so much of his royal policy was founded. The duke's final fall from grace would be spectacular, even by the standards of this ruthless, pitiless age.

*

On Friday 16 January 1478 the great men of England assembled in the Painted Chamber at the palace of Westminster for the opening of parliament. The large room was decorated in every available space with faded murals of biblical and historical scenes arranged in six large horizontal strips, rising to the very top of the thirty-foot walls: the stories depicted included those of King David, the Maccabees and the destruction of the Temple. Elsewhere were huge seven-foot figures representing the Virtues standing victorious over Sins, angels bearing crowns swooping above the windows and a sublime rendering of St Edward the Confessor on his coronation day.[14] Amid all this splendour, sitting on his royal throne was King Edward IV. Before him were the representatives of his subjects and ready to address them was the chancellor of England, Thomas Rotherham, bishop of Lincoln.

The bishop took as his theme two texts: the first from the Old Testament and the second from the New. The first was the famous Psalm 23: *Dominus regit me et nihil mihi deerit* – 'The Lord rules me, I shall want for nothing.'[15] The Lord, explained Rotherham, was the protector of his people. He was the essence of their salvation and it was, in turn, their absolute duty to obey their master. This brought the bishop on to his second text, the letter of St Paul to the Romans, in which he warned his correspondents that 'the king does not carry the sword without cause'.[16] This ominous passage explains that those who resist righteous power will be damned, and that in bearing the sword, a godly king is appointed as 'an avenger to execute wrath on evildoers'. The bishop concluded his remarks by returning, pointedly, to the psalm, and reminding his audience that 'if the Lord will rule them they will lack nothing

but he will put them to graze in pasture'. It was obvious to everyone assembled in the Painted Chamber on that winter morning
precisely what Thomas Rotherham had in mind.

The duke of Clarence was in the Tower of London and had
been there for more than six months. Around 10 June, he had
been summoned to an audience with the king, the mayor and
the aldermen of London. Edward had upbraided him in person
before commanding that he be thrown in jail. It was no secret that
the king and his wayward middle brother looked on one another
'with no very fraternal eyes'. Nevertheless, there was something
sensational about a king summarily imprisoning his closest adult
relative and preparing to put him on trial before the lords in parliament.

Clarence's behaviour had been problematic for some time.
His feud with Gloucester over the division of the Warwick and
Neville estates between 1472 and 1474 had almost resulted in
armed confrontation and had certainly not helped Edward to
stabilise the realm following his return to the throne. The deal
that Edward imposed in 1474 to bring this quarrel to an end
had settled on both men handsome portions of the lands they
craved, but it had left Clarence highly dissatisfied.[17] He did 'more
and more to estrange himself from the king's presence', sulking
in silence through council meetings and refusing to eat or drink
in the king's company. His rage was that of a middle child overtaken by a prodigious younger brother. Gloucester was emerging
as the king's hand in the north and his most trusted magnate,
whereas Clarence was humiliated: Edward had taken away his
favourite manor and ducal seat at Tutbury in Staffordshire, and
also refused to allow him to exercise his military duties as lieutenant of Ireland.

Personal matters had also served to inflame the brotherly
resentment. When Gloucester married Anne Neville in 1472,
she immediately conceived and in the course of time bore him a

son, Edward of Middleham. Clarence's marital experience was markedly less happy. In December 1476, his wife Isabel died at the age of twenty-five. She left two children, Margaret and Edward, who would survive to adulthood, but her death made a terrible mark on her husband. It is probable that Isabel died from the after-effects of childbirth, but this was not the way it seemed to Clarence. Perhaps because he was driven mad by grief, perhaps simply because he was constitutionally vindictive, short-sighted and unwise, he determined to take revenge for his wife's death. At two o'clock in the afternoon on Saturday 12 April 1477 a mob of eighty 'riotous and misgoverned persons' loyal to the duke descended on the manor of Cayford in Somerset and seized a woman by the name of Ankarette Twynho, who had once been a personal servant of Duchess Isabel. Effectively abducted, Twynho was whisked across the country at great speed, from Cayford to Bath, from Bath to Cirencester and from Cirencester to Warwick, where she arrived as dark was falling on Monday 14 April and was locked in a cell. At six o'clock the following morning the wretched woman was dragged to the Guildhall in Warwick, where Clarence sat in personal judgement as she was accused of having killed Isabel by giving her 'a venomous drink of ale mixed with poison'. It was plainly a ludicrous charge (not least because the crime had supposedly taken place on 10 October 1477, more than two months before the duchess had actually died) but Clarence ensured that within three hours of reaching the Guildhall, Ankarette Twynho had been presented to the court, indicted for murder, tried, found guilty, dragged through the streets of Warwick and hanged. There was no semblance of justice: indeed, several of the jurors who were browbeaten into delivering a guilty verdict apparently approached Twynho with 'great remorse in their conscience, knowing they had given an untrue verdict' and 'piteously asked forgiveness' before the unlucky lady was put to death.[18]

This would have been a serious indiscretion in its own right – to subvert the judicial process and kill innocent people was no way for a duke of the royal blood to behave. But it would most likely have been forgiven, were it not for Clarence's subsequent intervention in another, far more serious criminal case.

This second case involved three men – a fellow and a chaplain of Merton College, Oxford by the names of Master John Stacey and Thomas Blake and a brutish, violent midlands landowner called Thomas Burdet, who were arrested and charged with predicting the king's death by sorcery. During the mid-fifteenth century the phenomena of witchcraft, alchemy, astrology and sorcery were taken very seriously – they had after all been instrumental thirty years previously in bringing down Humphrey duke of Gloucester through his wife Eleanor Cobham. The men were charged before a court composed of some of England's most senior noblemen with having attempted to predict the death dates of Edward IV and his eldest son, so that 'the King, by knowledge of the same, would be saddened . . . so that his life would be thereby shortened'. All three were found guilty. On 19 May 1477 Burdet and Stacey were drawn on a hurdle to Tyburn and hanged, pleading their innocence as they stood on the scaffold. Blake was pardoned, and that would have been the end of it – if Clarence had not decided to intervene, for, intriguingly, Burdet had been one of his servants. Two days after the hangings, Clarence marched into a council meeting, read out declarations of innocence on behalf of the dead men and promptly marched out again. Even if Burdet's association with Clarence had not cast suspicion on the duke, his headstrong defence of a convicted traitor most certainly did.

These, then, were the events that had convinced Edward IV in the summer of 1477 that Clarence was too dangerous to be left alone. The first sign of royal displeasure came in the king's explicit refusal to allow Clarence to marry again. Edward IV 'threw all possible impediments in the way' of potential matches with either Mary of Burgundy (the only heir of Charles the Bold following the Burgundian duke's death in 1477) or Margaret Stewart, sister of James III of Scotland.[19] Ill-feeling between Edward and Clarence began to burn from this point: stoked, according to one chronicler, by 'flatterers running to and fro, from the one side to the other, and carrying backwards and forwards the words which had fallen from the two brothers, even if they had happened to be spoken in the most secret closet'.[20]

When the January 1478 parliament assembled before the king in the Painted Chamber, it was clear to everyone in it that the duke's time was up. The autumn preceding parliament's meeting had been passed by those around the king – principally his Woodville relatives – in building a case against Clarence which extended far beyond the affronts to justice, judicial process and political common sense committed in the aftermath of his wife's death. All of the duke's past misdemeanours had been bundled together in a package of damnable crimes that could be deployed to destroy him. Parliament, when it was called, was packed with retainers, servants and associates of the king and queen. Over the next months, as proceedings took place in Westminster Abbey, it witnessed an extraordinary, ruthless piece of political drama in which Edward IV, unsupported by any other legal counsel, delivered a personal case against his brother. 'Not a single person uttered a word against the duke, except the king,' wrote one chronicler, who also noted that Clarence was refused the right of attorney in his defence: 'Not one individual made answer to the king except the duke.' Witnesses were called, but they struck observers as royal stooges. It was plain from the beginning that Clarence was doomed. Outside Westminster, the king had scheduled a series of lavish parties and pageants to celebrate the marriage of his four-year-old second son Richard duke of York to the six-year-old Anne Mowbray, sole heiress to the duke of Norfolk.

The large royal family, dominated by Woodvilles and their noble spouses, feasted and made merry, while inside a tense parliament chamber, Clarence was systematically destroyed by his own brother.

Eventually and inevitably, early in February 1478 proceedings were wound up and Henry Stafford, duke of Buckingham – the king's brother-in-law through his marriage to Catherine Woodville – stood in parliament and delivered a verdict. Clarence was convicted of treason, having been adjudged guilty on a bewildering array of charges, which were enumerated in a bill of attainder later passed against him. He was held to have engaged in a 'conspiracy against [the king], the queen, their son and heir and a great part of the nobility of the land'. Ignoring the fact that Edward had 'always loved and generously rewarded' him, he had 'grievously offended the king in the past, procuring his exile from the realm and labouring parliament to exclude him and his heirs from the crown. All of which the king forgave, but the duke continued to conspire against him, intending his destruction by both internal and external forces.' Then came the list of specific crimes.

> [The duke] sought to turn [Edward's] subjects against him by saying that Thomas Burdet was falsely put to death and that the king resorted to necromancy. He also said that the king was a bastard, not fit to reign, and made men take oaths of allegiance to him without excepting their loyalty to the king. He accused the king of taking his livelihood from him, and intending his destruction. He secured an exemplification under the great seal of an agreement made between him and Queen Margaret promising him the crown if Henry VI's line failed. He planned to send his son and heir abroad to win support, bringing a false child to Warwick castle in his place. He planned to raise war

against the king within England and made men promise to be ready at an hour's notice. The duke has thus shown himself incorrigible and to pardon him would threaten the common weal, which the king is bound to maintain.[21]

The bill of attainder noted that the duke was convicted of high treason. It was signed by Edward's own hand.

The king dithered for a few days about whether to carry out the sentence that his brother's supposed crimes demanded. But eventually the parliamentary commons complained about the delay, and on 18 February George duke of Clarence was put to death in the Tower of London. The exact method of death has never been established, but a long tradition holds that he was plunged head first into a barrel of malmsey wine and drowned.[22] His bones were later buried at Tewkesbury Abbey. It was an unfortunate end for a man who in life had been a feckless nuisance and an ingrate. He died the victim of his own rashness. Edward rued his brother's death and made many expensive provisions to tie up his finances and estate, but his reign was the more secure for Clarence's removal. By 1479 almost every threat to the rule of the house of York – both external and internal – had been erased. There was only one man left who posed even the vaguest challenge to the dynastic security of the English crown. Far away across the sea, Henry Tudor still survived, a dim beacon for the Lancastrian cause. But in 1478 he could hardly have seemed less dangerous to Edward IV, the king who had amply demonstrated what St Paul had once told the Romans: 'They that resist shall receive to themselves damnation.'[23]

17 : The Only Imp Now Left

Jasper and Henry Tudor had washed up on the shores of western Brittany, in the little fishing port of Le Conquet, in the middle of September 1471. Their crossing was rough and troubled by storms, but the wind was kind in blowing their barque ashore in the territory of Duke Francis II of Brittany. Francis was a clever politician and a courteous host. When Jasper and Henry found their way to his court he treated them 'very handsomely for prisoners', which was what they now were.[1] The Tudors would remain at the duke's mercy for more than a decade.

As Edward rebuilt England, across the sea Jasper and Henry lived the lives of honourable fugitives. Francis's ducal seat was the Château de l'Hermine at Vannes: a grand, well-fortified palace equipped with fine stables, tennis courts and its own mint. Having submitted to Francis's authority, the Tudors were treated with 'honour, courtesy, and favour' and entertained as though 'they had been [the duke's] brothers'. The duke promised that they should be free to 'pass as their pleasure to and fro without danger'. But manifestly that was not the case. In October 1472 the Tudors were moved from Vannes into the possession of Jean du Quelennec, the admiral of Brittany, who kept them at his château of Suscinio, a small but stunning moated hideaway on a peninsula between the ocean and the bay of Morbihan. Later, when it was feared that Suscinio was too vulnerable to a kidnapping raid from the sea, they were moved to Nantes. Here the men would become political pawns in the diplomatic intrigues that took place between Duke Francis, Louis XI of France and Edward IV.

Although Edward was busy in the 1470s with the pacification both of his kingdom and his brother, he never wholly forgot that the only remaining Lancastrian of any note was tantalisingly beyond his reach. Henry was, in the words of the Italian historian Polydore Vergil, 'the only imp now left of Henry VI's blood', and the English king determined on numerous occasions to solicit his return from Brittany with 'gift, promise and prayer'.[2]

He had a rival for Henry's custody in Louis of France. The French king suspected, quite rightly, that possession of the Tudors would be a very useful stick with which to prod his English rival. Louis attempted to extract Jasper and Henry from Brittany in 1474, sending an ambassador, Guillaume Compaing, to argue that since Jasper was a pensioner of France (and cousin of Louis himself) he and his nephew ought to be released into French custody. Francis refused, seeing in turn that possession of the Tudors was a stick with which *he* could prod France, but he agreed to move Jasper and Henry from Nantes. Early in 1474 Jasper was taken to the Château Josselin, twenty-five miles from Vannes, while Henry was placed in the newly constructed, maximum-security Château Largöet, under the watch of the marshal of Brittany, Jean de Rieux. He was imprisoned once again in luxury on the sixth floor of seven within the massive octagonal Tour d'Elven.[3] Not for the first time in his life, the seventeen-year-old Henry Tudor was comfortable, but he was not going anywhere.

In June 1475 Edward IV invaded France with a large army, funded by English taxation on a scale that had not been seen since the time of Henry V. He declared himself, in time-honoured fashion, to be the king of France and duke of Normandy and Gascony, evoking the claims of all his Plantagenet predecessors since Henry II and Richard the Lionheart. Using a fleet of five hundred borrowed Dutch boats, he landed in Calais with as many as fifteen hundred men-at-arms, fifteen thousand archers and 'besides a great number of foot-soldiers'. Even if we allow for exaggerations in the estimates, the English army was still thought by a close associate of the French king to be 'the most numerous, the best disciplined, the best mounted and the best armed that any king of that nation invaded France withal'.[4] Nevertheless, Edward found little support from either Burgundy or Brittany for his endeavour. After some minor and fruitless skirmishing the expedition was over by 29 August, when Louis XI and Edward met on the bridge over the river Somme in the town of Picquiny to thrash out the terms of a deal. Edward wrung from Louis a seven-year truce and a lavish pension. In comparison to the great campaigns of the Hundred Years War, which Edward was hoping to emulate, the 1475 invasion was a largely insignificant jaunt about the countryside, notable for little more than the fact that the king had managed, as he was wont, to collect a huge amount of tax without fighting the campaigns it was intended to fund. But the treaty of Picquiny also made the Tudors' position a great deal more precarious, for under its terms Louis promised not to attack Brittany. Expecting that Duke Francis might be rather grateful, Edward renewed his attempts to wheedle Henry Tudor away from Brittany and bring him to justice in England, on the understanding that he would not be ill-treated. This time, he was very nearly successful. After a year, weary of being nagged, Francis agreed to repatriate his charge.

In November 1476 English ships bobbed in the waters off the Breton coast, ready to receive the prodigal Tudor. But when he was brought to the port of St Malo, Henry, 'knowing that he was carried to his death, through agony of mind fell by the way into a fever'.[5] Whether feigned, real or psychosomatic, this illness was enough to save him. He took sanctuary in one of St Malo's churches in order to recover his health, and during the delay Duke Francis had a change of heart. He sent messengers summoning Henry back to the Château d'Hermine. Jasper joined him there from Josselin. The Tudors had narrowly escaped Edward's attempts to recapture them. The king realised he would have to choose a different tactic if he wished to wipe out for good the last remaining threat to his throne.

*

Back in England, Henry Tudor's mother, Margaret Beaufort, had trodden a more conciliatory course through the politics of the Yorkist restoration. Small of stature, shrewd and tough, Margaret was a very impressive woman. She was highly literate, a canny businesswoman and, above all, always mindful of her duty to protect what she could of her son's inheritance and future. Despite the trauma she had suffered while giving birth to Henry in Pembroke Castle during the plague-swept winter of 1457 when she was only thirteen years old, she had gone on to marry twice since the death of her first husband, Edmund Tudor. In 1461 she married Henry Stafford, the second son of Humphrey Stafford, late duke of Buckingham. This had meant separation from her son when he was only four years old, although she had visited the boy at Raglan Castle during his youth. Henry VI's readeption had permitted a brief reunion, and Margaret had taken the young Henry Tudor on a barge ride up the Thames to visit the king at Westminster. (Polydore Vergil recorded that the simple-minded old monarch had looked at the child and said, 'This, truly, this is he unto whom both we and our adversaries must yield and give over the dominion,' a cryptic statement to which Margaret would later assign great meaning.[6]) When Edward IV swept back into power, circumstance once again separated mother from son. Margaret's first cousin Edmund duke of Somerset had been dragged out of sanctuary and beheaded following the battle of Tewkesbury, while her cousin John marquess of Dorset was killed during the fighting. Jasper and Henry had fled to the continent. Margaret had last seen Henry on 11 November 1470, but in all that time she had never stopped chasing means by which she could secure her own inheritance, consisting of a considerable body of land and income in the south of England and the midlands, and pass on what she could to her exiled only child.

Margaret's husband, Stafford, died on 4 October 1471, having endured for six months bouts of illness and infirmity connected to wounds he had received fighting at the battle of Barnet. It was a mark of Margaret's instinct for survival that she ignored the social protocol suggesting widows ought to observe a year's mourning before remarriage. There is every sign that she had enjoyed an affectionate partnership with Stafford, but before he was even in the ground she had begun negotiations for a union with another baron of the realm: Thomas, second Lord Stanley, a northern magnate with extensive lands and power in the north-west and, more importantly, extremely good connections to the Yorkist court. When Edward IV formalised the lavish new arrangement of the royal household, he appointed Stanley as steward – the most prestigious post available, with regular access to the king and scope for all sorts of political intrigue. Stanley's position in the household meant that he developed a close working relationship with the Woodvilles. Over the course of the 1470s, Lord Stanley and Lady Margaret were drawn close into the Yorkist family circle. At a splendid ceremony held in 1476 to rebury old Richard duke of York in the family mausoleum in Fotheringhay, Margaret attended Queen Elizabeth and her daughters. In 1480, when Bridget, the last of Edward IV and Elizabeth's children, was born at Eltham, Margaret was permitted to carry the baby to the font during the christening. She walked at the head of a procession of one hundred knights and squires, all carrying torches, accompanied by the king's eldest stepson, Thomas Grey, marquess of Dorset.[7] Little by little she was making her way into royal favour.

Margaret Beaufort's slow but steady integration into the royal circle worked precisely as intended. After 1476, when the king had failed to drag Henry Tudor out of Brittany by diplomacy, he began to consider other means of neutralising what small threat the young man could pose. He turned to Stanley and Margaret to establish the grounds on which Henry could be brought home and knitted into the acceptable ranks of English society.

The first impediment to this was removed with the death of George duke of Clarence in the Tower of London. Clarence had held the lands of the earldom of Richmond – Edmund Tudor's old title – and with this available there was an enticing bait to dangle in front of Henry, who could now be offered a return to England as a nobleman of the first rank. Prompted by the king, Margaret and Stanley began to work on the process by which that might be achieved: at some (unknown) point a royal pardon for Henry was drafted on the back of the letter that had originally created Edmund earl of Richmond in November 1452.[8] At around the same time, there were discussions between Margaret and the king about the fact that their children were related within the degrees of kinship that prohibited marriage without papal consent: these were terms of discussion that would theoretically precede a marriage between Henry Tudor and one of the royal princesses. Finally, on 3 June 1482, a document was drawn up at Westminster in which Edward IV made an agreement with Stanley and Margaret concerning the disposal of estates belonging to Margaret's mother. From these estates, Margaret was permitted to carve out a rich inheritance for Henry. The agreement granted that the young man would be allowed to inherit on condition that he returned to England 'to be in the grace and favour of the king's highness'. Edward's seal was affixed to the document. The stage was set for Henry to come home – albeit to a home that by 1482 the twenty-five-year-old renegade had only known for a few months of his life. Then disaster struck.

*

On 9 April 1483 Edward IV died in his bed at Westminster Palace. Although he was 'neither worn out with old age nor yet seized with any known kind of malady', he had become unwell following a fishing trip during the days leading up to Easter. A short and severe illness carried him from good health to death in less than a fortnight, three weeks before his forty-first birthday. In his youth a tall and a strikingly handsome man, by the time he reached early middle age he had become barrel-chested, fat and louche – facts that were noted by men inside and outside the kingdom. Years of increasingly debauched living had finally caught up with him.[9] Feasting and fornication were the prerogative of kings, but even by royal standards, Edward had thrown himself wholeheartedly into excess. He had numerous mistresses (the most famous was Elizabeth Shore, a fast-tongued mercer's daughter from London whom the king shared with Lord Hastings) and at least two illegitimate children by different mothers: there was a boy called Arthur Plantagenet, born to an obscure lady of the court around 1472 and much later created Lord Lisle, a daughter, Grace, and probably many more. Edward 'loved to indulge himself in ease and pleasures', wrote the historian and diplomat Philippe de Commines, who had seen the king in action at first hand during the peace negotiations of 1475.[10] Polydore Vergil, who knew and interviewed many of Edward's associates, observed that the king had been 'given to bodily lust, whereunto he was of his own disposition inclined'.[11] An even more vivid description was penned by the visiting Italian historian Dominic Mancini, who wrote of Edward that 'in food and drink he was immoderate: it was his habit . . . to take an emetic for the delight of gorging his stomach once more . . . after his recovery of the crown, he had grown fat in the loins, whereas previously he had been not only tall but rather lean and very active.'[12] Commines thought that the king had died of an apoplexy – which could mean anything from a stroke to a heart attack. It was said elsewhere in Europe that the cause of death had been eating too many fruits and vegetables on Good Friday, although this was probably more a reflection of Edward's famous girth than of medical science.[13] We can speculate today that in view of his life-style, Edward may have been suffering chronic kidney disease, a fatal condition that only manifests itself in the acute final stages. Or perhaps he succumbed to a virus like influenza, which made its first significant appearances in England from the 1480s.[14] We will never know.

All his fatness and loose living notwithstanding, Edward IV had been the most capable politician and most talented soldier to wear the English crown since Henry V. He had stamped out the vicious civil wars caused by the prolonged ineptitude of Henry VI, the bullheaded politicking of Edward's own father, Richard duke of York, and the faithless scheming of Richard earl of Warwick and George duke of Clarence. He did so not merely by winning great victories on the battlefield but thanks to an acute understanding of what lay at the root of good kingship. This was an even more remarkable achievement considering that never in his life did he see another man govern England competently. His instinctive bonhomie had put him at ease in the company of everyone from the lowliest servants to the magnates who made up his natural circle of friends, advisers and counsellors. Although both halves of his reign had experienced turmoil, his second reign had been a marked improvement on the first. Dissenters had either been co-opted or ruthlessly wiped out. A great, if underemployed, army had been mustered for service in France, reminiscent of the hordes raised by his ancestor Edward III in the 1340s and 1350s, and the magnificence of the English court had been raised to a similarly exalted level. 'After all intestine division appeased, he left a most wealthy realm abounding in all things, which by reason of civil wars he had received almost utterly void as well of able men as money,' wrote Vergil. And although the coffers were not quite brimming over, on his death he left England a great deal more stable than he had found her.

If England was restored by Edward IV, it was also dealt a massive wrench by his death. For if the travails of the last six decades had taught Englishmen anything, it was that the prosperity of the kingdom was heavily dependent on the good sense of the man who wore the crown. In 1483, however, there was no man waiting, and there were several difficult problems looming. A war had been started with Scotland in 1482, which required careful royal attention and considerable military expenditure, while in the same year relations across the sea had become much more delicate: the treaty of Arras had been signed between Louis XI of France and a new ruler of Burgundy, Archduke Maximilian I of Habsburg – hobbling the traditional English strategy of playing these two great powers off against one another. These were potentially perilous times, yet Edward's son and heir was twelve and a half years old, and his brother and heir apparent Richard duke of York not quite ten. Once again, agonisingly, England's fate depended on a child: or more accurately, on the good service and goodwill of the adults who surrounded him.

*

When Edward IV died, his eldest son was at Ludlow, the sumptuous castle in Shropshire which served as the seat of the council over which he presided as prince of Wales. The prince's council was convened under his authority, but in practice all its business was transacted by the young man's governor, tutor and uncle, Anthony Woodville, Earl Rivers. For more than ten years Rivers had served as guide and mentor to the prince of Wales, keeping him busy in a life that his father had long ago abandoned. He spent long hours with 'horses, dogs and other youthful exercises to invigorate his body'.[15] The queen's forty-three-year-old brother was a paragon of chivalry and an enthusiastic patron and practioner of the learned piety of the Renaissance. Reputed to be the finest knight in England, it was Rivers who had been afforded the honour of jousting with the Bastard of Burgundy in the famous tournament of 1467. Since then he had spent much of his life in the role of a knight errant, riding around Europe making war on the infidel while wearing a hair shirt beneath his heavy armour. Rivers had fought the Saracens in Portugal, he had been on pilgrimages to Rome and Santiago de Compostela, he was on good terms with Pope Sixtus IV and he was an enthusiastic man of letters. He collaborated with the pioneering merchant William Caxton, who in 1475–6 had brought a printing press to England for the first time. Rivers made use of Caxton's new technology to publish English translations of the *Dictes and Sayings of the Philosophers* and the *Proverbs of Christine de Pisan* as well as many of his own works of moralising verse. Caxton wrote approvingly of Rivers that he 'conceiveth well the mutability and the unstableness of this present life, and that he desireth with a great zeal and spiritual love . . . that we shall abhor and utterly forsake the abominable and damnable sins which commonly be used nowadays; [such] as pride, perjury, terrible swearing, theft, murder and many other'.[16] He was, in short, the model tutor for a young king growing up in a time of war and burgeoning knowledge, and his presence at the boy's elbow had evidently been reassuring to the old king both in life and upon his deathbed. Indeed, Edward had given explicit instructions concerning the education of the prince, demanding that 'no man sit at his board [i.e. table] but [. . .] by the discretion of [. . .] Earl Rivers'.[17]

Edward IV's death, however, made Rivers's dominant position into a far more complicated matter. The earl's physical and emotional proximity to the young king now made him, potentially, the most powerful man in the land. For Edward V was at a very sensitive age. Twelve years old was the point at which a king might begin to show a will of his own and to give direction to the government flowing from his crown; yet it was also a child-ish age at which he remained highly susceptible to direction – or indeed misdirection – by those who were closest to him. Rivers understood this well, for besides being a great knight he was an astute politician. Just six weeks before the king's death Rivers had requested from his solicitor in London copies of the letters by which he was appointed as the head of the prince's household, letters which gave him explicit command of the royal person and discretion in moving him from place to place. It would therefore have been fresh and clear in Rivers's mind just how much polit-ical value was attached to his possession of Edward V in April 1483. It was certainly fresh and clear in the minds of those out-side the Woodville circle.

Edward IV's will is now lost, but it seems that on his deathbed he tried to establish a series of compromises by which kingship could have been operated during his son's early reign. He had made a concerted personal attempt to reconcile those around him who were engaged in longstanding quarrels, bringing Lord Hastings to his bedside and commanding him to make peace with Thomas Grey, marquess of Dorset, the queen's eldest son. Although Dorset was married to Hastings's stepdaughter, the two 'maintained a deadly feud': they were territorial rivals in the midlands and, according to the writer Mancini, rivals for the embraces of 'mistresses whom they had abducted or attempted to entice from one another'.[18] Next, to balance the fact that his son would remain comfortably in the care of Rivers and the Wood-villes, the dying king seems to have nominated his faithful brother Richard duke of Gloucester, next in line to the throne after the young duke of York and therefore naturally the greatest man in the realm, to take command of government, effectively in the position of protector. If this was so, then it was almost exactly the same arrangement that Henry V had attempted to make as he lay dying at Vincennes some sixty years previously, when he

had nominated Thomas Beaufort, duke of Exeter to take responsibility for the infant Henry VI's person, and another duke of
Gloucester – Humphrey – to have control of royal government.
Splitting command of the new king's household from command
of government was a logical means by which to divide power.
Unfortunately, it took absolutely no account of the realities of
politics.

As soon as Edward's death was known, those of his councillors
who were in London gathered to debate the best form for the new
government to take. Two solutions were suggested. The first was
the establishment of a protectorate, which according to Mancini
was what the old king had directed in his will. The only plausible
candidate for the role of protector was Richard duke of Gloucester, the most senior adult nobleman of the royal blood. Gloucester was away in the north of England, overseeing military efforts
against the Scots. As soon as he had heard of Edward's death he
had come to York for a funeral ceremony at which he wept for
the loss of his brother. But grief did not distract him from politics: Gloucester found time during his mourning to write to the
council, stating his claim to be protector, for which Lord Hastings
lobbied hard on his behalf in London. Hastings was motivated by
two very obvious factors. He was naturally wary of Thomas Grey,
marquess of Dorset and the Woodvilles, who bore him 'extreme
ill-will' and with whom he was so uneasily reconciled.[19] Hastings had lost his post as chamberlain of the royal household on
Edward's death; he may well have feared that under a Woodville-
led government he would also be deprived of his captaincy of
Calais. But more than this, Hastings was motivated by loyalty. No
man, save perhaps Gloucester, had been closer or more faithful to
Edward IV, and it was therefore a matter of honour that Hastings
should defend his late master's wishes.

Yet the will of a dead king and the protests of his friends
counted for nothing. Hastings was voted down by those

councillors 'who favoured the queen's family', and it was decided instead that there would be no protectorate: Edward V would begin his reign immediately. He would be crowned on 4 May, and would rule as an adult king, with a council convened to advise and assist him. Gloucester would have a seat on this council, but he would not have pre-eminence. It was a victory for the Woodvilles, and Mancini claims that Dorset gloated that 'we are so important, that even without the king's uncle [i.e. Gloucester] we can make and enforce these decisions'.[20] On 14 May letters were sent to Ludlow summoning Rivers and Edward V to London, to arrive on 1 May, accompanied by a modest force of no more than two thousand men. In the meantime, the old king was to be buried.

The obsequies for Edward IV were formidable. On the day of his death the king's broad, bare-chested body had been placed on display for twelve hours to be viewed by all the lords, bishops and aldermen present at Westminster.[21] Subsequently Edward lay in state for eight days before being drawn, black-clad, behind horses for burial at St George's Chapel in Windsor on 20 April. A grand and solemn service was held, and masses were sung for the dead man's soul. Finally, when the king's body was placed in the ground, his chief officers of state broke their ceremonial staffs and threw them on top of the coffin, signifying the end of the old reign. Directly they had done this, the royal heralds gave a great cry of *'Le roy est vive!'* – 'The king is alive!' And attention returned to Edward V.

Rivers and the young king set out from Ludlow for London in the last full week of April. Rather than taking the most direct route, they made a detour through the midlands. Gloucester, returning from the north for the coronation, had been in communication with Rivers and had persuaded him to join forces, the better to make a triumphant entry into London. On Tuesday 29 April the two parties neared one another in Northamptonshire.

Gloucester had been met by Henry Stafford, duke of Buckingham, and the two of them lodged that evening in the town of Northampton. Rivers, Edward V and the queen's son Sir Richard Grey were a couple of miles' ride away, their men having fanned out to spend the night at the villages and hamlets dotting the countryside – which included the old Woodville seat of Grafton Regis. It had been arranged that Gloucester and Buckingham were to present themselves to their new king on the following day, and in preparation for this important family occasion, Rivers and Richard Grey rode over to Gloucester's inn on the night of 29 April, to share what turned out to be a convivial meal. They were received with 'an especially cheerful and joyous countenance, and sitting at supper at the duke's table, passed the whole time in very pleasant conversation'. Talk may have involved the Scottish campaign, on which Rivers and his brother Sir Edward Woodville had both briefly served under Gloucester's command, and there may have been some discussion of the property deals that ceaselessly occupied the minds of English magnates: only a month previously Rivers had asked Gloucester to arbitrate a land dispute for him, an act that implied a significant degree of trust and kinship. Whether on these or other matters, the four great men talked late into the night before retiring to bed, agreeing to rise early in the morning.

They rose with the light. The presentation to the new king was to take place in Stony Stratford, eighteen miles south along Watling Street, the old Roman road that cut diagonally across the middle of England. Riding at a gentle pace, it would have taken three hours or so to cover the ground. But the journey was never completed. The magnates were riding together, accompanied by a large body of Gloucester's soldiers, when the two dukes suddenly drew up, told Rivers and Grey that they were under arrest, 'and commanded them to be led [as] prisoners to the north of England'.[22] Then Gloucester, Buckingham and their armed men kicked their horses and set out at a gallop for the king. They commanded sentries to ride out along the road and prevent the news of their coup from spreading, and the tactic appears to have worked. They reached a startled Edward V in quick time, arrested his chamberlain, Sir Thomas Vaughan, dismissed almost all of the royal attendants with threats to kill anyone who disobeyed, then bent on their knees before their new sovereign, caps in hands, and declared that they had come to safeguard the king's rule and protect him from the scheming impudence of the Woodvilles.

Edward V was only twelve years old, but he saw quickly through his uncle Gloucester's fine words. According to Mancini, the youth replied, 'saying that he merely had those ministers whom his father had given him . . . he had seen nothing evil in them and wished to keep them unless otherwise proved . . . As for the government of the kingdom, he had complete confidence in the peers of the realm and the queen.' At the mention of Elizabeth Woodville's name, Buckingham snapped back that it was 'not the business of women but of men to govern kingdoms and so if [the king] cherished any confidence in her he had better relinquish it'. At this point, Edward realised that the dukes were 'demanding rather than supplicating'. He was as much at their mercy as the men they had arrested: the victim of an unforecast and bewilderingly swift coup. Helpless, Edward went along with them. His last day of real freedom had come abruptly to an end.

*

Richard duke of Gloucester trotted Edward V into London on Sunday 4 May, the king dressed in blue velvet and his uncle clad head to toe in black. They were met by the mayor, aldermen and a delegation of five hundred citizens wearing robes of violet. It had escaped none of these well-apparelled gentlemen that 4 May was the date that had been scheduled for the king's coronation. This, Gloucester announced, would now be postponed for seven weeks, to take place instead on Sunday 22 June, immediately followed by the opening of parliament on Tuesday 24 June. This would allow for 'the coronation and all that pertained to the solemnity [to] be more splendidly performed'.[23] In the meantime, on 8 May Gloucester secured from the council the right to act as protector of the kingdom – an office, it struck contemporaries, that echoed the office wielded by another duke of Gloucester, Henry VI's uncle Humphrey. But whereas old Humphrey had been frustrated throughout his career by the careful impositions laid upon him by his peers, Richard duke of Gloucester now appeared to have the 'power to order and forbid in every matter, just like another king'.[24]

The Woodvilles had been cut out with extraordinary rapidity. Rivers and Sir Richard Grey were locked up in the earl of Warwick's former castle at Sheriff Hutton in Yorkshire, a huge, square fortress that had been one of Gloucester's chief residences when he had been sent to keep order in the north during his brother's reign. The horrified queen, meanwhile, had fled on 1 May for sanctuary to Westminster, 'in like condition', noted one chronicler, 'as she had done before the field of Barnet'.[25] She took with her her daughters, her nine-year-old son Prince Richard, duke of York and her eldest son, Thomas Grey, marquess of Dorset; they would soon be joined there by Lionel Woodville, another of the queen's brothers. Sir John Woodville, who was the queen's youngest brother, was at sea with a fleet detailed to defend the English coasts against French piracy. When he heard about the moves against his family he fled English waters and landed in Brittany. On 9 May, the day after Richard's appointment as protector, the young king was sent to the Tower of London, supposedly for his own security – although security was scarcely what previous royal inhabitants had found there.

Richard, meanwhile, moved into Crosby Place on Bishopsgate,

one of the most stunning and modern mansions in the whole of the city, a luxurious stone-and-timber home that towered above every other residential property in London. From here he ordered a steady anti-Woodville propaganda drive: producing wagons piled high with weapons which he claimed the queen's family had intended to use against him, and accusing them of having pilfered from the royal treasure. He was ably assisted by Hastings, confirmed in his position as chamberlain of the new king's household. According to one well-informed writer, Hastings was 'elated . . . and was in the habit of saying that nothing whatever had been done except the transferring of the government of the kingdom from two of the queen's blood to two more powerful persons of the king's . . . causing as much blood to be shed as would be produced by a cut finger'.[26] But it was not quite as simple as all that.

In acting ruthlessly to overthrow the Woodvilles, Richard had on one level demonstrated much the same instinct for swift, bold leadership that had marked his late brother Edward's finest hours. His motivation for staging a coup against the family is not hard to deduce. Prestige alone demanded that he should have full control of government during his nephew's minority, and his whole life's experience suggested that direct and decisive action against potential rivals was essential in a time of political uncertainty. The house of York was acutely aware of its own tribulations; it would have been a profound betrayal of the family's own history to have allowed parvenus like Rivers and Dorset to step in and control the kingdom while the only duke of the blood royal stood by and did nothing.

Yet having imprisoned the king and partially scattered his enemies, Richard found himself in a somewhat awkward position. His bullish actions echoed those of his father during Henry VI's reign rather too closely: seizing control of England by means of a coup was in a sense the easy part; building a long and stable royal government on the back of a factional power-grab was a rather more difficult task. On 22 June the king was due to be crowned, and at that point Richard's powers as protector would evaporate. There was every chance that the boy Edward V, who had seemed so astonished and aggrieved at being forcibly removed from the family and servants he loved and trusted, would seek to be revenged upon his presumptuous thirty-year-old uncle. At the very least, Richard could expect to be forced to release Rivers and Grey, and to see the rest of the Woodvilles emerge from their various boltholes.

It was a mark of his desperation that during the brief weeks he served as protector, Richard attempted to secure a legal judgement that would allow him to have Rivers, Grey and Vaughan condemned for treason and beheaded. Worryingly for him, the council refused to countenance it, pointing out that since Rivers and the rest had not actually committed any treasonable acts, there was no legal grounds upon which their heads could justifiably be cut off. All that came of Richard's attempts to neutralise those he saw as his rivals was to increase their alienation. When a council meeting was held in early June at Westminster, and the queen emerged briefly from sanctuary to attend, she sat in silence, spoken to by no one throughout the entire two-hour meeting.[27]

Late spring ticked by into early summer. Richard's concerns mounted. It was almost as though he was become his father. Loyalty had been his defining characteristic in his whole career to date. Yet actions taken in defence of what he believed was his brother's legacy – although begun in the genuine spirit of protecting the realm – were leading him into a corner. The minute he should lose his grip on the power he had taken, he would be potentially as vulnerable as those whom he had displaced. Somehow, loyalty had now to be balanced against the purest form of self-preservation.

Although the daily business of government progressed

unremarkably, with the coronation approaching Richard became increasingly paranoid. On 10 and 11 June letters were sent to loyal servants in Yorkshire, requesting urgent military support in the capital, and warning that 'the Queen, her blood, adherents and affinity . . . have intended and daily do intend to murder and utterly destroy us and our cousin the duke of Buckingham and the old royal blood of this our realm'. If such a plot existed outside Richard's mind, it went unnoticed by other writers. However, it would appear that the strategy of summoning what amounted to an army to London was too much for some of those who had hitherto been closest to the protector. If the business of the coup had been in part to protect the legacy of Edward IV, then Gloucester was now running dangerously close to shredding the very thing he claimed to stand for.

Some time around the period when Gloucester was summoning his northern faithful 'in fearful and unheard of numbers' to tramp down the ancient straight road from York to London, Lord Hastings appears to have begun losing his confidence in the regime he had done so much to enable. He shared his concerns with two other former loyalists, Thomas Rotherham, archbishop of York, and John Morton, bishop of Ely.[28] Whether or not he had fully worked out Gloucester's ultimate ambition, this is the only really plausible explanation for what occurred on Friday 13 June. Hastings, Rotherham and Morton all assembled for a routine council meeting at the Tower at ten o'clock in the morning, 'as was their custom'. According to Mancini, they had walked straight into a trap.

> When they had been admitted to the innermost quarters,
> the protector, as prearranged, cried out that an ambush
> had been prepared for him, and they had come with hid-
> den arms, that they might be the first to open the attack.
> Thereupon the soldiers, who had been stationed there by

their lord, rushed in with the duke of Buckingham, and cut down Hastings on the false pretext of treason; they arrested the others, whose life, it was presumed, was spared out of respect for religion and holy orders.

It was a summary execution of the most breathtaking ruthlessness, and the writers of the time marvelled.[29] 'Whom will insane lust for power spare, if it dares violate the ties of king and friendship?' wondered one. Cornered and desperate, it was now clear that Gloucester was prepared to countenance any move whatever that would help him cling to power. At any point of wavering he was supported by the duke of Buckingham, who was probably motivated by more obviously selfish desires to see the Woodvilles and Hastings discomfited and himself advanced to the position that he believed his Plantagenet blood merited, and which he had too long been denied.

With Hastings dead and London trembling in confusion and fear, a slide to murderous madness now began. On Monday 16 June the archbishop of Canterbury, Cardinal Bourchier, went to Westminster and cajoled the queen into releasing from her custody her second royal son, Richard duke of York, on the understanding that he was absolutely required to play a prominent role in the forthcoming coronation. He met his elder brother Edward V in the Tower; they were joined there by the late duke of Clarence's young son Edward, known as earl of Warwick, who was then only eight years old. The following day it was announced that the coronation was cancelled, likewise the parliament that was due to follow.

On Sunday 22 June the theologian Dr Ralph Shaa appeared at St Paul's Cross to preach the extraordinary – and wholly specious – message that Edward IV's marriage to Elizabeth Woodville had been undertaken while Edward was already contracted to marry someone else: Lady Eleanor Butler, the daughter of the great Lancastrian soldier John Talbot, earl of Shrewsbury. On these grounds, Shaa argued, Edward V and Richard duke of York were illegitimate and therefore the former could not be allowed to take the throne. Instead, Richard duke of Gloucester, who was said to bear an unmistakeable physical resemblance to his father, the duke of York, should take the throne in the place of his nephews.[30] Three days later, the duke of Buckingham appeared at the Guildhall, and subsequently at Baynard's Castle, to proclaim that since Edward V and Richard duke of York were tainted with bastardy, and since Clarence's son Edward earl of Warwick was ruined by his father's attainder, Richard, duke of Gloucester was 'the only survivor of royal stock . . . legally entitled to the crown and could bear its responsibilities thanks to his proficiency. His previous career and blameless morals would be a sure guarantee of his good government.'[31] As Buckingham spoke, far away in the north at Pontefract Castle Earl Rivers, Sir Richard Grey and Sir Thomas Vaughan were being subjected to a cursory trial for treason in front of the earl of Northumberland. The blood of all three was soon congealing on the ground.

The following day Richard duke of Gloucester formally took the crown as Richard III, elected by a group of hastily assembled noblemen, bishops and Londoners, led by his right-hand man, the duke of Buckingham. They meekly accepted his ridiculous claim that the young princes were bastards, and he accepted their acclamation as king of England before sitting upon the carved marble throne in Westminster Hall in a ceremony that evoked – probably intentionally – that by which his brother had taken power in 1461. 'Seditious and disgraceful', was the judgement of the Crowland continuator.[32] A sense of helplessness descended on a capital that had witnessed more upheaval, regime change and reversal of fortune in the previous thirty years than in all the three hundred that preceded them. Thousands of northern troops continued to march on London, swords, bows and polished breastplates clattering as they approached. Tongues wagged in the streets of London, and gossips noted that a popular prophecy – to the effect that three kings would hold the crown in three months – had come true.[33]

The coronation of a new king, which had proven so difficult for Gloucester to organise for his poor, imprisoned nephew, was now arranged with almost indecent haste. On Sunday 6 July 1483 Gloucester and his wife, Anne Neville, celebrated mass at Westminster and were crowned, and a feast was celebrated with 'all circumstances thereunto belonging'. The new king sat enthroned on a chair with cushions of cloth of gold. When the ritual demanded, he grovelled before the high altar in comfort, his knees protected by crimson damask and velvet and white damask embroidered with little golden flowers. His ears rang with the rich sound of trumpets and the playing of minstrels, some of them brought to England from as far away as Rome. Following the service in the abbey, the new king dined on forty-six different dishes, including beef and mutton, roast crane and peacock, oranges and quinces.[34] And when the solemnities and the feasting were finished, Richard held an audience with the nobles whom he had summoned to witness his usurpation, commanding them to go back to their shires and see that order was kept and no extortions committed against his subjects. As a public morality display, he had his brother's and Lord Hastings's former mistress Elizabeth Shore clapped in London's stocks and put to open penance as punishment for the iniquity of her life. 'And thus', wrote one chronicler tartly, 'he taught other[s] to exercise just and good which he would not do himself.'[35]

18 : Judge Me, O Lord

The last recorded sightings of the Princes in the Tower (as they are now popularly known) were in the late summer and early autumn of 1483, in the month that followed their uncle's seizure of the crown.[1] After Hastings's murder, all the regular servants who had been on hand for Edward V and his brother Richard were removed from the boys' presence; they were paid their last wage on 9 July.[2] It was reported in London's Great Chronicle that the boys were spotted 'playing and shooting in the garden of the Tower', perhaps as late as 29 September.[3] But Dominic Mancini wrote that they 'were withdrawn into the inner apartments of the Tower proper, and day by day began to be seen more rarely behind the bars and windows, till at length they ceased to appear altogether'.[4]

Edward V was twelve and he had been well educated. He presumably knew enough either of English history or of human nature – or both – to anticipate his fate. Deposed kings did not live. 'The physician Argentine, the last of his attendants whose services the king enjoyed, reported that the young king, like a victim prepared for a sacrifice, sought remission of his sins by daily confession and penance, because he believed that death was facing him.'[5] Indeed it was. By the time the summer's blaze had ceased to bake the whitewashed walls of the Tower of London, Edward, who 'had such dignity in his whole person, and in his face such charm', had vanished, along with his little brother. 'I have seen many men burst into tears and lamentations when mention was made of him after his removal from men's sight,' wrote Mancini.[6] By November 1483 the assumption driving

English politics was that the Princes in the Tower would never be seen alive again.[7]

We still do not know for certain how the boys died. In later years rumours would hold that they had been smothered with a feather-bed, or drowned in a butt of malmsey, or poisoned – but these were no more than rumours. It is possible that bones and teeth discovered roughly buried in a wooden box beneath the chapel stairs in the White Tower are those of the Princes, but these have not been tested adequately enough to say for certain.[8] All we can be sure of is that the boys were first disinherited, then deprived of their liberty and servants, and that they then disappeared, presumed dead by contemporaries across Europe. And the person who benefited most from their disappearance was Richard III.

Almost as soon as his reign began, Richard had gone on progress about his new realm, travelling up along the Thames, through Windsor and Reading to Oxford and Woodstock, swinging west to his ducal town of Gloucester and then moving back across to the midlands, York and the north. All of these were areas where his noble power had been strongest, and where he wished – or felt compelled – to demonstrate his fullest gratitude for their support. Richard pointedly avoided going into Wales, the west country or any of the other territories that had been most closely associated with the Woodvilles and the prince's council through which they had exercised their power. He showered grants and offices in these areas on his hitherto most loyal crony and supporter, Henry duke of Buckingham.[9] The south-east and East Anglia were largely entrusted to his loyal ally Lord Howard, newly promoted to the position of duke of Norfolk.

As Richard travelled he attempted to demonstrate that he was a king capable of dispensing good governance and justice, whereas his brother's reign had descended into lust and neglect. He would later argue that Edward IV's rule had been ruined because he delighted in 'adulation and flattery' and that, 'led by sensuality and concupiscence', he had 'followed the counsel of insolent, vicious people of inordinate avarice, despising the counsel of good, virtuous and prudent people'. Richard's appeal to the country was much the same as his father's had been in 1460: he claimed to stand for 'prudence, justice, princely courage and excellent virtue'.[10] Everywhere he went he was greeted with pageants and ceremony, and he responded by holding court with truly royal splendour and munificence.

Richard III was not exactly physically imposing. He had been born with his father's dark looks but without his brothers' extraordinary height, and although only thirty years old he had by this stage fully developed the crooked spine that must have caused him extreme physical discomfort and caused him to walk with one shoulder raised higher than the other. He had nervous tics: he ground his teeth, which the historian Polydore Vergil described, noting that 'while he was thinking of any matter he did continually bite his nether lip'. Vergil, writing later and with some prejudice, also wrote that the king 'was wont to be ever with his right hand pulling out of the sheath to the midst, and putting in again, the dagger which he did always wear'. Nevertheless, he said, not even Richard's detractors could deny that he had proven himself over his relatively short life to have 'a sharp wit, provident and subtle' and to possess 'courage . . . high and fierce'. Most notably of all, he was bright and decisive, 'a man much to be feared for circumspection and celerity'.[11]

Thus, despite his diminished bodily appearance, Richard could still project majesty. On his northern progress he travelled with a massive retinue, including numerous bishops, earls and barons, a Spanish diplomatic embassy, his wife, his nine-year-old son Edward of Middleham (who as heir apparent was now styled prince of Wales and earl of Chester) and his captive nephew, Clarence's son, Edward earl of Warwick. Richard granted charters of privileges to the towns that he visited, allowing some of them the new right to appoint mayors and aldermen. He generously refused to take the customary gifts of money that he was offered by each town: rather, he paid for repairs to castles and settled old debts including a large sum outstanding for Clarence's tomb at Tewkesbury Abbey. 'He gave the most gorgeous and sumptuous feasts and banquets, for the purpose of gaining the affections of the people,' wrote one chronicler.[12] At York he feasted in stately splendour, wearing his crown. During his long stay in the city he promised to bestow vast riches and liberties on the citizens, the minster and the people of the local area. Everywhere he went he gave out his personal insignia: little badges in the shape of a boar, thirteen thousand of which were distributed. The boar was a visual pun on Eboracum – the ancient Roman name for York, which was usually shortened to Ebor, and in handing it out Richard was making a very particular statement: he was a king of the north. The people of the north, in their turn, showed their admiration. The Warwick-based historian John Rous, who was at least in his sixties at the time of Richard's visit, and an expert in the long and varied past of the house of Plantagenet, described the new king as 'by true matrimony without discontinuance or any defiling of the law by heir male lineally descending from King Henry II'. Given the tumult and confusion of Rous's own lifetime, this extravagant statement smacked rather more of flattery than accuracy. But it was testament to the open-handed energy with which Richard went about selling his kingship to the realm.

In setting out his stall as a northern king, Richard dangerously underestimated the power of the south. At the end of July, disturbing news reached the travelling court: a plot had been uncovered to remove the Princes from the Tower. Buildings in the city of London were to be set alight, causing enough panic and pandemonium to distract the Tower's guards, at which point the Princes would be broken out of their jail. Richard responded by sending orders south commanding the plotters, at least one of whom was a former member of Edward IV's household and another of whom was a senior official in the Tower, to be tried and executed. He ordered soldiers to surround Westminster Abbey, to prevent the escape of the Woodville women who were sheltering in sanctuary there. It is extremely likely that at this point he also gave the instructions that led to the death of the Princes in the Tower. The actual murderer's name was never discovered (although Richard's servant Sir James Tyrell gave a dubious confession many years later). Philippe de Commines, writing from the French court, heard that the deed had been orchestrated by the duke of Buckingham, although this too is unlikely.[13] If Buckingham were responsible for carrying out Richard's orders to kill the Princes, then it would have been the last loyal act that he carried out. In October 1483 he turned against the king whom he had helped to create, joined a rebellion of former associates of the old king Edward IV, and switched his allegiance to the only candidate for kingship still alive and even vaguely plausible: Henry Tudor.

*

It was a sure sign of the woe that had befallen the English crown that anyone should ever have considered Henry Tudor as a potential king. His father Edmund had been a half-brother of Henry VI, and his mother Margaret Beaufort had a small measure of Plantagenet blood in her veins. In ordinary circumstances these facts would hardly have amounted to a strong dynastic claim to kingship. In 1483 Henry was essentially the heir to a disgraced and minor Welsh Lancastrian family, who had lived the majority of his life in the castles of south Wales and western Brittany and was unknown to most of the people of England, whether great or small. But Richard III's usurpation of the crown had broken every rule of political propriety, and with it opened up new and previously unthinkable possibilities. Whereas in the long distant past adult kings such as Edward II and Richard II had been forced from the throne as punishment for long and tyrannous misrule, and while Henry VI's inanity had eventually led the English polity into a civil war which cost him his crown, Edward V had done nothing whatever to deserve his fate. He was a blameless king whose only fault was to accede at the age of twelve. It was inevitable that many members of the Woodville family and the old king's affinity would never accept Richard III as their king, and would strive immediately for his replacement. More generally, Richard's violent and unprincipled coup, snatching office on entirely specious grounds and by murderous means, dealt a severe blow to the fragile dignity of a crown that had been fought over and grabbed back and forth for nearly thirty years. Not since the dark days of the 1140s, when King Stephen and Empress Matilda had carved up the realm in a civil war that contemporaries had called the Shipwreck, had kings of England been so vulnerable to assaults. If Richard could seize the crown, why should it not in turn be seized from him?

The rebels who plotted to burn London over the summer and turn the Princes loose from the Tower had attempted to make contact with Henry Tudor before they were discovered. Since they believed that Edward V was alive, they did not contact Henry with a view to making him king, but he was now 'at his own liberty' in Brittany and was therefore looked upon by dissidents as a possible ally in the struggle against the usurper Richard III.[14] Ferment was bubbling among Edwardian loyalists, and by early August a series of conspiracies and rebellions had begun, which drew Henry Tudor ever closer to their heart. All across the southern counties of England, men were preparing to rise up against the new regime. At the end of August Richard III was concerned enough to command the duke of Buckingham to lead treason commissions into counties across the south-east, from Kent, Sussex, Surrey and London to the Home Counties. A month or so later, on 22 September, the king sacked his master of the rolls, Robert Morton, evidently fearing that treason was spreading to the ranks of the royal administration. In fact, it had already penetrated far deeper into the royal circle. By the end of September, it was spoken of openly that the Princes were dead.

On 24 September Buckingham, Richard's most exalted and lavishly rewarded noble ally, defected. He wrote from his Welsh castle of Brecon to Henry Tudor in Brittany, asking him, according to one account, 'to assemble a great fleet and bring an army and a great number of foreigners from Brittany with them over the sea, and to land in this realm to destroy [Richard's] most royal person'.[15] Although Buckingham had been the most ardent follower and facilitator of Richard's usurpation, and the man who had profited most handsomely from the ousting of the Woodvilles, he was now persuaded that his fortunes would be increased even further by turning coat once again. In the years that followed it was suggested that he did so because Richard had been slow to grant him a portion of the earldom of Hereford, which he felt he was owed as the result of a marriage made by one of his ancestors in the fourteenth century.[16] More likely it was simply because he was a feckless character who was drawn to intrigue. Buckingham appears to have calculated in September 1483 that the rebellious spirit swelling across the south would be sufficient to push Richard off the throne, and that his own political survival and advancement therefore depended on backing the rebels. He was sorely mistaken.

It is telling that Edward IV never considered Buckingham a suitable figure either for a substantial landed endowment or for significant involvement in government. Like the duke of Clarence, Buckingham appears to have been essentially vain and short-sighted.[17] All the same, his defection was a serious problem for Richard III. There had already been covert communication between the circles of Henry Tudor's mother, Margaret Beaufort, and Edward's widow, Elizabeth Woodville, hidden away in sanctuary at Westminster Abbey: the women were determined to proceed with marrying Henry to Edward IV's eldest daughter, Elizabeth of York. This alliance would formally unite the rump of Lancastrian support in England with what remained of the Woodville faction.[18] In the autumn of 1483 their plans became entwined with both the general rebelliousness of the south and the self-serving machinations of Buckingham. Despite Richard III's attempts to earn his realm's loyalty and trust, he was now faced with the first serious challenge to his rule, less than four months after he had seized the crown.

In the three and a half weeks that followed his letter to Henry Tudor, Buckingham did his best to raise an army from his lands in south Wales, assembling men and munitions at Brecon Castle. He was hampered by abysmal weather: autumn skies lashed rain on the land and made troop movements difficult and unpleasant. Buckingham was also hamstrung by his own reputation as a 'sore and hard-dealing man' who was despised by the tenants he was attempting to stir into action. Nevertheless, in the end he managed to assemble a 'great force of Welsh soldiers', while also contacting the perpetually fractious men of Kent, who never needed much encouragement to rise up against the established order. He ignored letters of increasing belligerence sent to him by Richard, demanding that he give up his plotting immediately and come to the royal presence.[19]

Unfortunately for Buckingham, the men of Kent began their rebellion too early. They attempted to rise on Friday 10 October but very swiftly fell away again when the duke of Norfolk, Thomas Howard, led a resistance force out of London. Further unrest fanned out across the south of England, with local risings in Sussex, Essex, Oxfordshire, Berkshire, Hampshire, Wiltshire and into the south-west in Somerset, Devon and Cornwall. But these do not seem to have been especially well co-ordinated. Neither did the threat of yet another outbreak of civil war command any serious noble support. Margaret Beaufort's husband, Lord Stanley, declined to raise his men in the north-west, and most of the rest of the regional magnates also sat on their hands. Buckingham hesitated and did not begin his western campaign until Saturday 18 October, by which time it was too late. When the duke prepared to march east into England he found that ceaseless rain had caused the banks of the Severn to burst, flooding the surrounding lands and making the river quite impassable. The Welshmen in the duke's army were 'brought to the field against their wills and without any lust to fight for him'. They had been browbeaten in the early part of October and by the end of the month were inclined to go home, dry their feet and avoid any more contact with the man who commanded them.[20]

Buckingham headed north-east, into the marches, and did his best to raise the people of Herefordshire. Unfortunately, news had already reached them that Richard III was moving with an army from the north towards the rebellious duke, upon whose head there was now a £1,000 bounty for having 'traitorously turned upon us contrary to the duty of his liegance'.[21] Faced with failure, Buckingham abandoned what remained of his army and went into hiding in Shropshire, in the house of his servant Ralph Bannister, whom he had known and trusted since his childhood. But trust had its limits. On 1 November Bannister sold Buckingham out. He was captured and taken to Salisbury in Wiltshire by Sir James Tyrell, where Richard, having ridden imperiously through his realm in search of the rebels, now held court. Richard's men interrogated Buckingham, who confessed 'without torture' and asked to 'have liberty to speak with king Richard'. His request was flatly refused and on Sunday 2 November the duke was hauled into the marketplace in Salisbury and beheaded.

Many centuries later a decapitated skeleton, with its right arm also hacked off, was found beneath the kitchen of a pub called the Saracen's Head, on the spot where Buckingham was supposed to have been executed. As soon as the bones were touched they disintegrated, leaving only dust behind them.[22]

*

As Buckingham's head rolled in the dirt of Salisbury's market square, Henry Tudor was being tossed by the waves in the sea. His mother had kept him informed of events in England, and Henry had spent September and October in Brittany fitting out a fleet of fifteen ships, sufficient to carry a force of five thousand soldiers across to England for an invasion. His sponsor in this great adventure was his long-time jailer Duke Francis II, who gave the twenty-six-year-old exile ships, sailors and a considerable amount of money in loans to help them on their way. They pushed off with a good wind from Paimpol, a pleasant fishing village on the northern tip of the Breton coast, probably on the night of 1 November. But as anyone who had braved the Channel during the stormy months of darkness knew, the weather could quickly turn foul. Henry and his uncle Jasper were blown by 'a cruel gale of wind', which drove some of their ships north to Normandy, while others were sent back to Brittany. Eventually, Henry's ship limped in sight of the English coast at Poole, where it anchored alongside the one other vessel that had passed safely through the tempest. On land they spied a number of lookouts, clearly waiting for their arrival. But something in the scene struck Henry as ominous. He sent a small craft to investigate the situation on shore: when it made contact with the men on land, they all cried that they were sent from Buckingham to greet Henry and bring him to the successful rebel headquarters, 'which the duke himself had at hand with a notable excellent army'.[23] It was a trap, and Henry could smell it. The wind was still blowing in the direction of Normandy. He weighed anchor and followed it, leaving England to a triumphant Richard III and abandoning the fight for another day. It was a very wise move.

Henry had been proclaimed king in his absence at Bodmin on 3 November by a small group of English rebels, but as he returned to Brittany he found that his position was as weak as it had ever been. His actions during Buckingham's rebellion had confirmed him as an unrepentant enemy of the English crown. The possibility of rehabilitation into the English nobility – so close in 1482 – was now dead. The only option left to Henry was to claim the crown outright. In a ceremony held at Vannes Cathedral on Christmas Day 1483, at which his supporters swore homage to him as if he were an anointed ruler, he in return swore an oath to marry Elizabeth of York as soon as his claim to the crown was realised. How exactly it was to be realised was not very clear. International relations stood in a muddle, for on 30 August 1483 Louis XI of France had died, leaving a thirteen-year-old successor, Charles VIII, whose regent was his elder sister Anne. Henry's value as a pawn in relations between England, France and Brittany was now diminished, as was the likelihood that Francis II – whose health was beginning to fail – would wish to finance a second invasion of England.

Henry's main source of hope lay with the small but swelling community of exiles who fled England following the failure of Buckingham's rebellion with their lives in danger and their property at default. There was no shortage of outcasts. In January 1484 Richard III called his first parliament and used it to deliver a full-scale attack on his enemies, to defile the memory of his brother's reign and to secure the allegiance of all the lords of England to his own rule and the future rule of his heir, Edward of Middleham, prince of Wales. The act *Titulus Regius* praised Richard as the only legitimate heir to his father Richard duke of York and condemned the 'ungracious feigned marriage' between Edward IV and 'Elizabeth Grey' – as Elizabeth Woodville was now to be known – which, the act stated, 'was presumptuously made without the knowledge and assent of the lords of this land, and also by sorcery and witchcraft committed by the said Elizabeth and her mother Jacquetta, duchess of Bedford'.[24] At a specially convened meeting in a committee room in Westminster, 'nearly all the lords of the realm' swore an oath of adherence to Prince Edward 'as their supreme lord, in case anything should happen to his father'.[25] Then the parliament set about systematically destroying those whom Richard perceived to have crossed him the previous autumn.

The January parliament passed attainders against a large number of Richard's enemies, most prominently Thomas Grey, marquess of Dorset, John Morton, bishop of Ely, Lionel Woodville, bishop of Salisbury, and Peter Courtenay, bishop of Exeter, as well as Margaret Beaufort – who retained her life and liberty but had her lands transferred to her husband. Dorset and the bishops were therefore among those who took up residence in Brittany, where they found themselves in the company of Sir Edward Woodville, Richard Woodville and numerous loyal old servants of Edward IV, including Sir Giles Daubeney and John Cheyne, who had been personal attendants to the old king, John Harcourt, once a faithful follower of Lord Hastings, and Reginald Bray, who was connected to Margaret Beaufort and the Stanleys. All were wanted men and many had lost virtually everything. All now clung to the desperate notion that Henry Tudor might one day invade England again, to cast aside yet another anointed king.

*

Richard III may have been a usurper, but when he turned his attention to issues of more general government he was capable of being generous and sympathetic. Over Christmas 1483 his mind had been on the plight of England's poor, who found themselves unable to get justice due to the high costs of the legal system.

A grant dated 27 December shows him granting a yearly payment for life of £20 to his clerk John Harington, who served the court of requests. This court was designed to hear the 'bills, requests and supplications of poor persons', offering a route to legal redress that would not ruin them financially.[26] After the New Year celebrations he travelled around Kent, and just as he had done on his northern progress, he refused to accept expensive gifts from the towns through which he passed – a richly decorated purse stuffed with more than £30 of gold was graciously declined at Canterbury, with the king ordering its contents 'to be redelivered to the said persons from whom the said sum had been collected'.[27]

The parliament of January 1484, when it was not concerned with the business of legitimising Richard's claim to the crown, also suggested that his inclinations as king were towards the principles of justice and fairness. One law granted that 'every justice of the peace in every county, city or town shall have authority and power to grant bail . . . at his or their discretion' – meaning that all people convicted of felonies could in theory be freed until they faced trial, and not suffer confiscation of their goods before they had had a chance to defend themselves in court.[28] Forced loans known as benevolences, which had been used by Edward IV, were declared illegal. Where taxes were levied, they were imposed most heavily on foreign merchants, yet even here Richard showed himself to be relatively enlightened, ensuring that the flourishing new book trade was exempted from import duties, and that every writer, printer and bookbinder could do business freely, 'of whatever nation or country he may or shall be'.[29]

All the same, the extreme circumstances surrounding Richard's ascent to the throne meant that all the progressive policies in the world would not bring unity to his realm overnight. One of his most serious problems was the fact that he remained forced to rely heavily on the men who had brought him to power, rather than constructing a broad and inclusive government that represented the interests of the whole realm. His chief servants, who included William Catesby, Richard Ratcliffe, Francis, Lord Lovell, Sir James Tyrell and Robert Brackenbury, were all unconnected to Edward IV, and mostly men who had served Richard as duke.[30] His household was packed with northerners whom he could trust, a fact which worsened the sense of a north–south divide to his kingship.

Worst of all, Richard was simply unlucky. The king suffered the first personal tragedy of his reign on 9 April 1484 when his beloved little son, Prince Edward, died. He was about ten years old. The child had grown up in the castles of the north, including his birthplace of Middleham, where he enjoyed the life of learning and entertainment common to all boys of his class, with trips in a chariot about the countryside, the japery of fools in his household and the occasional involvement in ostentatious ceremonies at which his father had his status as heir to the crown publicly proclaimed.[31] But childhood was a perilous time of life, and Prince Edward's death, following a short illness, came as a crushing blow to Richard and Queen Anne. The news reached them at Nottingham and it threw the bereaved royal couple into 'a state almost bordering on madness, by reason of their sudden grief'.[32] The long-term hopes of any usurper's regime depended on the security of succession. While Richard had fathered several bastard children, including one John of Pontefract, whom he knighted at York in 1483 and acknowledged as 'our dear bastard son' when he appointed him captain of Calais in 1485, Edward of Middleham was the only child who could have been an acceptable heir to the crown. His death was therefore a catastrophe, even to a ruler as tenacious as Richard III.[33]

Prince Edward's death made it essential that Richard should step up his attempts to capture Henry Tudor. With Francis of Brittany ailing, the king of England made his move through Pierre

Landais, the Breton treasurer. By September 1484, he was close to an agreement that would exchange Henry's person for the title of the earldom of Richmond, which in ancient times had been given by English kings to dukes of Brittany. By chance, Henry was warned of these negotiations just as they neared their conclusion. The Tudors, with their court of exiles, had established themselves in Vannes – but it was clear that the duchy, for so long a haven, had now become a dangerous place. Early in September Jasper Tudor led a small advance escape party over the Breton border near the town of Rennes. Two days later Henry followed him, galloping over the frontier disguised as a groom. By the end of September, most of his adherents had joined them. It was a highly dangerous dash for freedom, since outside Breton territory the Tudors enjoyed no safe-conduct and none of the guaranteed diplomatic protection that for many years had kept them safe. But in 1484, with an heirless Richard determined to hunt and exterminate his chief remaining foe, it was a gamble worth taking.

Fortunately for Henry, it paid off. Charles VIII's government received the Tudors neither with trepidation nor hostility, but rather with delight. There was no excitement in the French court at the prospect of a renewed Anglo-Breton alliance, and the voluntary flight of the Tudors greatly reduced the prospect of this happening. So the renegade Englishmen were greeted with honour by the French king's envoys, presented with money, clothes and lodgings, and encouraged to continue their plans to invade Richard's realm. As they wintered in France they were reinforced by a steady trickle of defectors and sympathisers: John de Vere, earl of Oxford escaped from Hammes Castle in the Pale of Calais and joined the Tudors in November; the academic and rising cleric Richard Fox offered his support from his position at the university of Paris, and former members of Edward IV's household continued to smuggle supplies and messages out of England to the Tudor court in exile.

This was all extremely irksome to Richard, whose attempts to establish secure and broad-based kingship were undermined by the existence of a possible rival authority, no matter how small and far away. On 7 December 1484, from the palace of Westminster, the king issued a proclamation against the Tudors and their allies. He described them as rebels, traitors, murderers and extortioners 'contrary to truth, honour and nature'. The proclamation damned Henry's 'ambitious and insatiable covetice' which led him to 'encroach upon . . . the name and title of Royal estate of this Realm of England, whereunto he hath no manner, interest, right or colour as every man well knoweth'. If the rebels were to be successful in their plans to invade, Richard warned, they would 'do the most cruel murders, slaughters, robberies and disinheritances that were ever seen in any Christian realm'. All natural subjects were called upon 'like good and true English men to endeavour themselves at all their powers for the defense of themselves, their wives, children, goods and inheritances'. They would be in good company, for Richard, 'a well-willed, diligent and courageous prince will put his most royal person to all labour and pain necessary in this behalf for the resistance and subduing of his said enemies . . .'[34]

And indeed, Henry Tudor had begun to style himself as king of England. Around the time of his flight from Brittany to France he began to sign documents with the initial H, a considerable presumption which had not been adopted by any unanointed English king-in-waiting before him. His intention to marry Edward IV's eldest daughter, Elizabeth of York, remained undimmed, although it was an intention that Richard was determined to subvert. On 1 March 1484 Richard had reached a settlement with Elizabeth Woodville by which she and her girls could leave the sanctuary at Westminster, where they had been for the best part of a year. The king had sworn publicly to ensure that if the Woodvilles would emerge 'and be guided, ruled and demeaned after me, then I shall see that they shall be in surety of their lives . . . [and] I shall put them in honest places of good name and fame . . .'[35] Richard promised to marry the girls respectably and provide modest lands for their upkeep. Rumours began to circulate at Christmas 1484 that he intended to discard Queen Anne and marry his niece Elizabeth himself, despite a closeness in relationship that bordered on the grotesque, even by fifteenth-century aristocratic standards. The prospect was unpalatable – 'incestuous' and guaranteed to incur the 'abhorrence of the Almighty', was one verdict – but this was Richard, after all, whose attitude towards members of his family had proven to be anything but sentimental. Could he marry Elizabeth? 'It appeared that in no other way could his kingly power be established, or the hopes of his rival be put an end to,' wrote one chronicler.[36]

Queen Anne died on 16 March 1485. She was only twenty-eight and mutterings of poisoning accompanied her demise. These, combined with the lurid speculation about Richard's intentions, were enough to prompt the king to make a public statement in the presence of London's mayor and citizens shortly after Easter. He had been advised by his disgusted councillors that to press ahead with plans to marry Elizabeth would incur not 'merely the warnings of the voice; for all the people of the north, in whom he placed the greatest reliance, would rise in rebellions against him'. For this reason, Richard stood in the great hall of the Hospital of St John and made a denial 'in a loud and distinct voice', assuring his people that he did not intend to wed his brother's daughter. The limits of good taste had been reached.

On 23 June 1485 Richard issued another proclamation against the Tudor rebels in France, damning Henry's 'bastard blood both of father side and of mother side' and warning of 'the disinheriting and destruction of all the noble and worshipful blood of this Realm forever' should a Tudor invasion succeed.[37] Evidently, Richard was acutely concerned for his crown. According to Vergil, the king remained 'vexed, wrested and tormented in mind with fear almost perpetually of the earl Henry and his confederates' return; wherefore he had a miserable life.'[38]

Yet he was no more nervous than Henry Tudor, who was, Vergil continued, 'pinched by the very stomach' at the rumour concerning Richard's intentions towards Elizabeth of York, and had also to deal with the wavering of Elizabeth's half-brother the marquess of Dorset, who flirted with returning to England as a loyal subject of the king. By the height of summer it was clear that both sides needed a resolution. Henry in particular sensed that his chance to strike at Richard was both fleeting and immediate. He borrowed a modest forty thousand *livres tournois* from Charles VIII, took counsel with his uncle Jasper and the other leading exiles, fitted out a small fleet with four thousand men – some of them dredged up hurriedly from the jails of Normandy – and set sail from Honfleur at the mouth of the river Seine. They were headed for the western tip of Wales, the land from which Henry's grandfather, Owen Tudor, had first emerged, where Edmund and Jasper Tudor had held sway during Henry VI's reign, and from where the Tudors had fled when Edward IV had retaken his realm in 1471. Their journey, propelled by a helpful southerly breeze, took seven days: plenty of time for those aboard the invasion fleet to consider the enormity of what they were about to attempt.

Henry Tudor was described succinctly by Philippe de Commines as being 'without power, without money, without right to the Crown of England'.[39] Nevertheless, on Sunday 7 August 1485, this unlikely claimant to England's crown landed at Mill Bay near Milford Haven, waded through the salt water onto wet Welsh sand, knelt and kissed the ground, and uttered the words of Psalm 43: 'Judge me, O Lord, and plead my cause.'[40] His time had finally come.

19 : War or Life

They marched through the mountains beneath the sign of the dragon. Henry Tudor and his allies had been on the road for a little over a week, travelling on a cautious route and at a slow pace through the rolling and occasionally inhospitable Welsh country-side. Frenchmen, Welshmen, English exiles and a smattering of Scots made up this hotchpotch army, but above their heads the banners of the campaign included a few clear symbols of their intent. The cross of St George and the Dun Cow of the Beaufort family spoke of royal intent and Lancastrian ancestry. The red dragon against a background of green and white reminded those who passed by that as a Welshman, Henry could connect himself not only with Henry VI (who had granted Edmund and Jasper Tudor the right to use it as a heraldic symbol) but with ancient kings of the Britons such as Cadwaladr, whose exploits were cele-brated by the bards.[1]

Their route during the first week of their march had taken them north-east from Mill Bay, via Haverfordwest to Cardigan, then hugging the coastline up to Aberystwyth. This was by no means the most direct path towards Henry's sworn enemy, the man whom his letters to local Welsh gentry described as 'that odious tyrant Richard late duke of Gloucester, usurper of our said right'. But it was the safest road to take: partly because south Wales was well secured against the Tudors and partly because Henry entertained a keen hope that his stepfather Lord Stanley and his brother Sir William Stanley would be willing to add their substantial military might from their estates in north Wales and north-west England.

On Sunday 14 August the invaders were at Machynlleth, the small town in the Dyfi valley that had in Owain Glyndwr's day been the rebel capital of the whole country, and from which it was possible to turn directly east and traverse the mountains of mid-Wales, descending through the marches to reach England by the fertile plain of Shropshire. Even in the height of summer this was rugged and difficult countryside, but after three days Henry's men had dragged their feet and their guns over the high ground and were approaching Shrewsbury. The English midlands and their chance at seizing the realm opened up before them.

Of all the men and women who had fought for the English crown during the struggles of the century, perhaps none was less familiar to the majority of that crown's subjects than Henry Tudor. A thin face with high cheekbones framed a long thin nose, a feature shared by his mother, Margaret Beaufort. Round, somewhat hooded eyes formed a tight triangle with his thin, downward-sloping mouth, and dark wavy hair tumbled down almost to his shoulders. Having barely lived in England, he preferred to speak French. But he had already adopted the style and bearing of a crowned king, and his letters calling for support suggest that he was more than comfortable in the language of imperious persuasion that was expected of an English monarch. 'We will and pray you and on your allegiance straightly charge and command you that in all haste possible ye assemble [your] folks and servants . . . defensibly arrayed for war [and] come to us for our aid and assistance . . . for the recovery of the crown of our realm of England to us of right appertaining,' he wrote from Machynlleth to potential supporters among the Welsh gentry.[2] To many of these Welsh supporters he also dangled the alluring prospect of the principality's ancient liberties and legal freedoms being restored, should he be victorious. All the same, the Tudor rebellion struck most contemporaries as so unlikely that reinforcements trickled, rather than flowed, to his side.

As Henry rode through the mountains, word reached Richard III that the attack he had long anticipated had finally arrived. He was in Nottinghamshire during mid-August, and according to one well-informed chronicler he 'rejoiced' at the news, celebrating Henry's arrival as 'the long-wished-for day . . . for him to triumph with ease over so contemptible a faction'. The Stanley family was the one serious ally whom the Tudors could hope to recruit, but Richard had taken precautions to secure their loyalty: while Lord Stanley was absent from the king's side in Lancashire, he had agreed to leave his son and heir, George, Lord Strange, under royal supervision. Richard did not trust the Stanleys – indeed, as a precautionary measure he had declared Sir William and his associate Sir John Savage to be traitors simply as a warning to others who might consider joining the rebellion – but he had enough of a hold on them to feel that they would think long and hard before attacking their anointed king.

All the same, as the Tudors came down out of the mountains into England, they found that their association with the Stanleys was beginning to work in their favour. On their first arrival at Shrewsbury on Wednesday 17 August, the bailiff, Thomas Mitton, lowered the portcullis against them, swearing an oath that they would have to walk over his belly – implying his dead body – before they were allowed to pass through the streets of the town. After a short impasse, word reached Mitton from the Stanleys that Henry was to be afforded civility and assistance. The rebel army marched through, and in order to protect his oath and his honour, Mitton lay on the ground in front of Henry and allowed him to step over his – very much living – belly as he went.

Little by little, Henry was gaining momentum. Although the nobility remained thinly represented – of the highest ranks only John de Vere, earl of Oxford was with him – the rebel army slowly began to expand with gentlemen who either had connections to the Stanley family or else remained loyal to the memory of Edward IV, Buckingham and even the duke of Clarence. The Stanleys themselves had three thousand men in the field, although Lord Stanley refused to formally join his forces with the five thousand or so who were directly behind the Tudors. On Friday 19 August they were at Stafford. The following day they had reached Lichfield. The day after that Henry had his army camped around Atherstone, near the border between Warwickshire and Leicestershire.

By this stage, Richard III had travelled from Nottingham to Leicester and had somehow scrambled together an army described as 'greater than had ever been seen before in England collected together in behalf of one person'. The king rode out of Leicester at the head of his army on the morning of Sunday 21 August with the duke of Norfolk and earl of Northumberland by his side and the crown on his head. 'Amid the greatest pomp' and with 'mighty lords, knights and esquires, together with a countless multitude of the common people', Richard rode west towards the place where his scouts told him Henry Tudor was waiting.[3] By nightfall little more than a mile separated the armies of king and pretender, both of whom were now ready to meet their fate.

*

Richard III woke early on the morning of Monday 22 August, out of a fitful sleep, plagued by 'a terrible dream' in which 'he saw horrible images . . . of evil spirits haunting evidently about him . . . and they would not let him rest'.[4] It was so early that the king could not find breakfast in his camp, nor was there a chaplain yet awake who could celebrate the mass. But the discomfort of the night did not dissuade the king from battle; rather, it hardened his mood. His enemy was, to Richard's mind, the last true obstacle to the final security of his kingdom. He 'declared it was his intention, if he should prove the conqueror, to crush all the supporters of the opposite faction', not least since he believed that Henry Tudor would do exactly the same if the roles were reversed. That day, he told his companions, 'he would make end either of war or life'.[5] He decided at some point that he would ride into battle wearing his royal crown. Everything he was, everything he possessed, would be visibly at stake.

The two armies were camped on either side of a place known locally as the Redesmere – a marshy plain below the sharp slope of Ambion Hill, set in verdant countryside dotted here and there with towns and little villages, including Market Bosworth, some way off to the north. The royal camp was pitched at Sutton Cheney, near the hill: perhaps fifteen thousand men stretched out across the fields, all of them having been encouraged to feed and refresh themselves before the travails that lay ahead. Morale was reasonable, for none had been in the field for more than a couple of weeks, but spirits had all the same been dented by a pair of high-profile embarrassments. The royal captives Sir Thomas Bourchier and Walter Hungerford, both imprisoned in the Tower on suspicion of plotting in 1483, had escaped while being moved in custody, and managed to join with Henry Tudor. It was also suggested, some time after the battle, that during the night before the battle the duke of Norfolk's tent was graffitied with a defeatist slogan:

> Jack of Norfolk be not too bold
> For Dicken thy master is bought and sold.

The light had barely come up on the camp when, from the vantage point of Ambion Hill, the enemy was spotted on the move, marching north-east in battle formation across the corn fields that lay between the hill and the villages of Atterton and Fenny Drayton. Henry Tudor had beaten Richard's men to the start, and now the king's men scrabbled to be ready for the oncoming assault.

Richard's army certainly appeared as ferocious as the sleepless king who commanded it. Arranged in a single line, they stretched out for miles, horse and foot alongside one another: swords, armour and sharp arrowheads gleaming, and dozens of lean-barrelled serpentine guns chained together alongside their fatter cousins, the bombards. Some of the infantry carried handguns and when all the royal gunners began to fire, the early morning air would have been filled with caustic smoke, and the field rung with deafening booms. As the arrows were unleashed, the thunder would have been joined by the snap of bowstrings and the deadly fizz of wood and fletchings arcing towards vulnerable flesh.

The rebels' vanguard was led by the wily and experienced John de Vere, earl of Oxford; the left and right were led by Henry's allies John Savage and Gilbert Talbot respectively. Henry himself was behind the lines, surrounded by a very few men grouped around the Tudor standard bearer, Sir William Brandon. Mercifully for Richard III there were no Stanleys among the rebel ranks. Although Lord Stanley and Sir William were present near the battlefield they kept their forces mustered separately, arrayed about a mile away, from where they could watch the battle unfold before committing themselves. This was not entirely useful to anyone but the Stanleys themselves. In a fit of pique, Richard sent a message that Lord Stanley's son, Lord Strange, whom he had brought as his hostage to the field, should be summarily beheaded to punish the Stanleys for their lack of commitment. But as the chaos, thunder and panic of battle unfolded, the orders were never carried out.

What occurred subsequently is hard to piece together. Henry's vanguard, under Oxford, used the marshiest part of the field as a natural defence on their right flank and came upon the royal vanguard as they ran down Ambion Hill. The two vans crunched into one another, their helmets pulled down over their faces, fighting fiercely hand to hand. Oxford ordered the rebel troops to fight in tight clusters, no more than 'ten foot from the standards', according to Vergil.[6] This caused some confusion to their enemies, watched by Henry Tudor from behind his lines, and King Richard observing from higher ground on the hill.

Henry Tudor and his personal guard were still bunched in a small group below his rival royal standard. To Richard, never short of personal bravery, this seemed to offer an opportunity to end the battle in short order. His enemy was a man who had lived twenty-eight years without ever commanding troops; he, Richard, was a toughened veteran of numerous difficult battles. 'Inflamed with ire, he struck his horse with the spurs' and charged around the side of the vanguard towards where his enemy was positioned. His crown was still on top of his helmet.[7]

Richard slammed into Henry's men with lethal speed. His assault caused such terror and damage to the rebel leader that his standard bearer was killed and the standard that marked out the commander's position was hurled to the ground. This was a very perilous situation for any army to endure, since the fall of the standard was generally associated with the defeat and probable death of the man below it. But Henry clung on, although 'his own soldiers . . . were now almost out of hope of victory'.[8] And his tenacity was rewarded. Seeing Henry in trouble – perhaps also having heard that Lord Strange's sentence of death had been executed – Sir William Stanley charged his reserve army into the mêlée, casting in his lot with the Tudors at the last possible moment. Three thousand fresh men poured onto the field, scattering the royal army in despair and overwhelming Richard as he fought in plain sight of his rival.

At some point, it seems that Richard must have either lost or removed his battle helmet. It cost him his life. He was struck by several glancing blows, which cut his scalp and took small chunks of skull away. Then he was dealt a heavy blow directly to the top of the head by a small, pointed blade which pierced his skull right through. Finally, a heavy, bladed weapon – it may well have been the wickedly curved large blade of a halberd – cleaved through the air and removed a large chunk at the base of his skull, opening a huge wound, perhaps severe enough to kill him instantly.[9] 'King Richard alone was killed fighting manfully in the thickest press of his enemies,' wrote Vergil.[10] He died, if not a hero, then certainly a staunch and courageous soldier. 'An end to war or life,' the king had cried on the eve of the battle. Fate had chosen for him: as one writer at the time marvelled, 'A king of England slain in a pitched battle in his own kingdom, has never been heard of since the time of King Harold.'[11] His death brought the battle – which came to be known as the battle of Bosworth – to an end. Once the fighting had ceased King Richard was stripped of his armour, slung over a horse and taken to Leicester to be buried in the nave of the church of the Greyfriars. Somewhere on his final journey his body was abused and humiliated: a knife or dagger was stabbed so hard through the naked buttocks that it damaged the bone of his pelvis. Then his slashed and bloodied body was slung into a hastily dug shallow grave. 'God that is all merciful,' wrote one chronicler, 'forgive him his misdeeds.'[12]

*

Once the battle of Bosworth was won, Henry Tudor thanked God, clambered up the nearest hillside and addressed the men who stood exhausted before him on the battlefield. He thanked the nobles and gentlemen who had fought beside him, commanded the wounded to be cared for and the dead to be buried, and then received the acclaim of his soldiers, who bellowed 'God save King Henry!' at the tops of their voices. Lord Stanley, standing close by, saw his moment. Richard III's battered crown, dislodged along with his helmet in the mêlée, had been found 'among the spoil in the field'. As kingmaker, Stanley exercised his right to place the hollow crown on Henry Tudor's head, 'as though he had been already by commandment of the people proclaimed king'. Then the victorious party left the field, making their slow and regal way towards London.

Henry VII officially dated his reign from Sunday 21 August, the day before the battle of Bosworth – a novelty that allowed him to present victory as divine sanction for his kingship. Accordingly, since Henry's reign had been approved by God, he had been 'crowned' (in the most informal manner) by Stanley and his rival Richard III was dead (quite a luxury for a usurper) he was prepared to delay his official coronation by more than two months. Partly this was for safety, since London in the late summer of 1485 was plagued with a 'sweating sickness, whereof died much people suddenly'.[13] The date for Henry's crowning was therefore set for Sunday 30 October 1485, which allowed enough time for the epidemic to depart and a splendid ceremony to be prepared. Henry realised that he was a political unknown, whose reign demanded brilliant public spectacle in order to demonstrate that he was no interloper, but rather a worthy successor to both Henry VI and Edward IV. In that sense, extravagance was a political necessity.

Accounts of the coronation were drawn up by Sir Robert Willoughby, and they spoke of a flurry of activity among the goldsmiths, cloth merchants, embroiderers, silkwomen, tailors, labourers, boatmen and saddlers of London. Instructions went out for yards of velvet, satin and silk in royal purple, crimson and black, which were then run up into beautiful jackets, hose, hats, robes, wall hangings, cushions and curtains. Henry's henchmen were ordered hats plumed with ostrich feathers, boots made from fine Spanish leather and striking costumes of black and crimson.[14] Even the horses were smartly dressed: their stirrups were covered in red velvet, while tassels and silk buttons adorned their halters. More than £50 was spent commissioning 105 silver and gilt portcullises – the family symbol of Margaret Beaufort – for distribution to favoured guests. This was far more than was spent

even on the four ceremonial swords carried in Henry's procession: two with sharpened points and two blunt. In total, more
than £1,500 was spent on the solemnities and celebrations.[15]

From the embroiderers of London the new king purchased
great decorative trappings and hangings – presenting most clearly
the symbols of the new reign. One item in the royal accounts
for the coronation stands out: £4 13s 4d paid 'to John Smith,
broderer for embroidering of a trappour of blue velvet with red
roses with gold of Venice and dragons feet'. Many emblems were
displayed at the coronation. Some were traditionally English, like
the arms of St Edmund and St Edward the Confessor; others were
generically chivalric, such as the 'trappour with falcons' which
was embroidered by one Hugh Wright. But several were particular to the new Tudor king and his family. The arms of Cadwaladr advertised Henry's connection with the ancient British-Welsh
kings of Arthurian lore. (That claim had also been made by the
Yorkists, who proudly traced their ancient roots through the Mortimer line.) A similar lineage was suggested by the many images
of red, fiery dragons and their feet. But the greatest sums were
spent commissioning red roses detailed with gold. The image
of the rose was far from new: the white rose had been one of
the chief badges favoured by the house of York, along with the
golden sun, with which it was often combined. It was true that
red roses had occasionally been associated with Lancastrian kings
since Henry IV's lifetime, while the Welsh poet Robin Ddu had
associated the Tudors with the symbol, hankering for the time
when 'red roses will rule in splendour'.[16] But never had a king of
England so consciously or prominently adopted the red rose as
his most visible emblem.

The coronation went off with appropriate pomp, with the
most prominent roles taken by the small group of English nobles
whom Henry could count as his intimates. These included his
uncle Jasper Tudor, now duke of Bedford, his stepfather Thomas,

Lord Stanley, who became earl of Derby, and Sir Edward Courtenay, another of the Breton exiles, who was awarded his ancestors' old title of earl of Devon. All three played important parts in the pageantry, as did John de Vere, earl of Oxford, whose loyalty was rewarded at the coronation feast, where he placed the crown on the king's head. All had been well rewarded for their long suffering and faith in the Tudor cause. But none was so well rewarded as Margaret Beaufort, the king's mother: according to her late-life confessor John Fisher, she 'wept marvellously' at the moment the crown was placed on her son's head.

Margaret held the title of countess of Richmond, and was given back the lands that had been placed in her husband's name by Richard III. She was declared *femme sole*, a special legal status that gave her total independence, and given a beautiful Thames-side mansion at Coldharbour, which served as her main London residence. But the sight of her son, the boy who had been torn devastatingly from her womb in a cold, plague-ridden Welsh castle when she was just thirteen years old, being crowned king was surely the greatest reward that a mother could desire. Throughout Henry's reign Margaret was treated as a sort of demi-queen – allowed to dress in the manner of a consort and (in her later years) to sign herself 'Margaret R', an explicitly royal style. Her son consulted her in virtually all matters, from foreign policy to legal affairs and internal security. Her manor of Collyweston in Northamptonshire would be palatially refurbished and would serve as a base for the crown in the east midlands. She was entrusted with queenly status and authority, and she exercised it with relish.

She was not, of course, the queen. Henry VII had sworn a solemn oath in 1483 that he would marry Elizabeth of York. Now he was king, he was bound to make good on his word. On 10 December, at Henry's first parliament, the Speaker, Thomas Lovell, requested that the king's 'royal highness should take to himself that illustrious lady Elizabeth, daughter of King Edward IV, as his wife and consort; whereby, by God's grace, many hope to see the propagation of offspring from the stock of kings, to comfort the whole realm'.[17] The king, sitting enthroned before the whole gathering, told parliament that he was 'content to proceed according to their desire and request'. The wedding was to be held on 18 January 1486.

Henry's marriage to Elizabeth was not simply a matter of his word or of popular opinion. It was vital to his whole royal manifesto. It was no secret that his claim in blood as a Lancastrian king was weak; he was not a sufficiently obvious heir to Henry VI to be accepted wholeheartedly for who he was. In large part Henry had been made king because he was a candidate for those seeking a replacement for Edward IV: marrying Edward's eldest daughter was essential to holding that support and trying to restore some stability to the English royal line. It should be noted that Henry ensured he had been crowned and acclaimed as king in his own right, by the judgement of God, before he went about marrying Elizabeth – he could not afford to be seen as purely the puppet of the Yorkists, still less of ruling by right of his wife. (As a group of English ambassadors were instructed to tell the pope in 1486, Henry had won 'the throne of his ancestors' by 'divine aid'. He was marrying Elizabeth to 'put an end to civil war'.[18]) Nevertheless, he used the marriage to project a subtle and effective political message, summed up in a striking visual motif. His marriage was represented by another rose. This time it was not the famous old white rose of York or the rather hastily adopted red rose of Lancaster, but a perfect blend of the two: the Tudor rose, white superimposed upon red to form a visual emblem of union, instantly comprehensible to even the dullest mind. The Tudor double rose expressed an instant analysis both of the cause of the wars that had torn England to pieces during the troubled fifteenth century, and of their solution. Everything, the rose said, was down to the split between the houses of Lancaster and York. Everything, the rose also said, was now solved by the two houses' binding union. Or, as the contemporary writer and court poet Bernard André wrote, 'It was decreed by harmonious consent that one house would be made from two families that had once striven in mortal hatred.'[19] This was a simplistic reading of history, to say the least. But it was one that would endure for centuries.

The wedding was celebrated in the customary fashion, with 'wedding torches, marriage bed and other suitable decorations', followed by 'great magnificence . . . at the royal nuptials and the queen's coronation. Gifts flowed freely on all sides and were showered on everyone, while feasts, dances and tournaments were celebrated with liberal generosity to . . . magnify the joyful occasion . . .'[20] The new queen fell pregnant on or soon after her wedding night and the royal couple departed on progress to the north in March 1486, to demonstrate to the kingdom at large the power and good fortune of the new king. They encountered a few minor disturbances as they went, but largely the countryside was peaceful. And at York, heartland of the former regime, the first city pageant that greeted the new king was a mechanical device displaying a gigantic red rose, which merged with a white rose before other bountiful flowers emerged ('showing the rose to be the principal of all flowers'). Finally a crown descended from a cloud to cover the whole scene.[21] The message was clear.

*

Queen Elizabeth went into labour in September 1486, in St Swithun's Priory, Winchester. It was no random setting. The former capital of England had close connections to King Arthur and his knights of the Round Table, and the queen's lying-in was deliberately located there, in the hope that she would bear a son and heir whose life and reign would rekindle the glorious past.[22] Ever since the earliest days of the Plantagenets there had been a taste among the rich and educated English elite for national histories that began with the deeds of Brutus, Cadwaladr and Arthur. The fashion was as strong as ever. In 1485 Thomas Malory's *Morte D'Arthur* had been printed by Caxton, providing a new compendium of tales from the days of Camelot. The origins and ideals of English kingship lay in these long-distant histories of the island, and Henry VII had made it his business to be closely associated with them.[23] That extended explicitly to attempting to produce his own heir to the crown in a place with as much historical significance as possible.

In this pageant of dynastic creation Elizabeth played her part perfectly. On 20 September she gave birth to a healthy son who was christened, inevitably, Arthur. 'Let the priests chant fitting hymns with great praise and entreat blessed spirits to favour the boy, that he may magnify the splendid deeds of his parent and exceed his ancestors in piety and arms,' fawned Bernard André.[24]

Arthur was very quickly invested with all the trappings of princely status: at his birth he became duke of Cornwall; when he was three years old he was created prince of Wales and earl of Chester and made a knight of the Bath. When he was still not quite five, he became a knight of the Garter, taking the Garter stall at Windsor that had lain vacant since the disappearance of Edward V. He was appointed as warden of the north, with his practical duties carried out by Thomas Howard, earl of Surrey. He was named as the king's lieutenant when Henry VII travelled out of England. After infancy the boy was tutored by the same Bernard André who had written such exaltations on the occasion of his birth; André reported that his student was vigorous, quick to learn and well versed in the classics. Henry wished to establish his son in exactly the same role as the young Edward V: setting up a prince's council at Ludlow to deploy royal rule over Wales and the marches. Just as Edward V's council had been run by a trusted uncle, Earl Rivers, so Prince Arthur's authority was wielded by his great-uncle, Jasper Tudor, duke of Bedford, a man who was in many ways the most loyal of them all.

Prince Arthur was soon joined by a sister, Margaret, born at Westminster on 28 November 1489. A brother, Prince Henry, was born on 28 June 1491 and a second sister, Mary, on 18 March 1496. In the case of the second prince, Henry VII once again followed the protocol of Edward IV's time: little Henry was made warden of the Cinque Ports and marshal of England at around the time of his first birthday, and the boy was given the important and evocative title of duke of York. Wild celebrations attended his official investiture on All Hallows' Day, 1 November 1494. The king laid on a grand three-day tournament with glittering prizes including heavy gold rings set with rubies, emeralds and diamonds, great feasts and dances were held, twenty noble sons were knighted and virtually the entire political community of the realm attended a solemn service in the parliament chamber at Westminster, where the little boy was paraded in his finery alongside his parents, both of them wearing their crowns. The story of Henry VII's reign, played out in a series of pageants and state occasions, was a simple one: through his family he was healing the kingdom.

Yet for all King Henry and Queen Elizabeth's success in producing heirs, publicising their union and plastering the country with joined roses, there remained – inevitably – those who wished that the turmoil and violence that had tormented England for so long could somehow be rekindled: that another usurper family could be overthrown and yet another king placed beneath the crown. And indeed, Prince Henry's creation as duke of York when he was aged just three was a direct response to a very specific plot against his father. Three generations of English history had made it inevitable that anyone with even the slightest trace of old royal blood in their veins could be a plausible candidate for kingship: a fact that seemed to be true whether that person was alive – or dead.

20 : Envy Never Dies

On Ascension Day in 1487, in Christchurch Cathedral in Dublin, a young man enjoyed a rather unexpected coronation. Besides Dublin Castle and the town's other cathedral, dedicated to St Patrick, Christchurch was the greatest building in the city, and by extension, one of the most magnificent in all of Ireland. And on Sunday 24 May it was enjoying one of its most extraordinary moments, as a ten-year-old child, dazzlingly dressed and supported by Gerald Fitzgerald, earl of Kildare and John de la Pole, earl of Lincoln, was crowned Edward VI, king of England and France.

His name – or more likely his pseudonym – was Lambert Simnel. He could have been an orphan from Flanders or a boy called John from Oxfordshire. His father may have been a carpenter called Thomas Simnel, who specialised in fitting out the wooden components of musical organs for the colleges and churches of Oxford and its flourishing university. He may alternatively have been a baker or a cobbler. Of his mother very little is known.[1] What is known is that he had turned up in Dublin the previous autumn, and since that moment had been exciting the local population with his claims about his background and personal history. He was a comely youth, with 'courtly manners' according to one writer, and no doubt he looked radiant in the spring light of the cathedral, when he was crowned with a small circle of gold taken from the head of a statue of the Virgin Mary, and subsequently when he was carried through the city streets on the shoulders of a local lord, to be toasted and feasted in the castle.[2] The coins that were minted bearing his likeness were handsome, as was the great seal struck for him, showing the boy enthroned, holding orb and sceptre. But this was most certainly not a king of England.

Lambert Simnel was an imposter. He claimed to be Edward earl of Warwick, the young son of George duke of Clarence, who had lived for most of his life in confinement, variously at Sheriff Hutton, Margaret Beaufort's London palace at Coldharbour and the Tower of London – which was precisely where he was on Ascension Day 1487. Warwick had been damned by his father's rebellion against Edward IV: he had become a political and legal nonentity at the time of his father's execution and attainder, and was more or less ignored as first Richard duke of Gloucester and then Henry Tudor staked their claims to the crown. Were it not for Clarence's attainder he would have been the last direct male member of the royal house of York. Instead, he had gone from being a prisoner of Richard III to a prisoner of Henry VII. Nevertheless, his impersonator had managed, in less than a year, to rally behind him a worrying degree of opposition to Henry VII's young reign. Ominously for the real king, that support was on the verge of bringing about a full-scale invasion of England.

The earliest origins of the plot to present Simnel as 'Edward VI' are obscure, but he seems to have emerged in Oxfordshire under the tutelage of a priest called William Simonds and the political sponsorship of three renegades from Richard III's reign: Francis, Viscount Lovell, Robert Stillington, bishop of Bath, and John de la Pole, earl of Lincoln, who as Richard III's nephew had been heir presumptive at the time of the battle of Bosworth. Most importantly of all, the plot was supported by Margaret, dowager duchess of Burgundy: Richard III's older sister, who ruled the Netherlands from the palace of Mechelen, near Antwerp, on behalf of her son Philip the Fair. Margaret was a superlative politician and a strong, hard-nosed protector of what she believed to be her family's interests. She refused to accept Henry VII's accession as king, and she extended the protection of her court to exiles who shared her aim of undermining the callow Tudor monarchy from afar.

Henry VII had been aware for some time that there was a pretender at large in Ireland. His own experience must have prepared him for the fact that, having taken the crown by force, he would be tested by others seeking to do the same, and he reacted decisively. On 2 February 1487 he had tried to snuff out the plotting by parading the real Edward from the Tower through the streets of London. Subsequently he had commanded that Elizabeth Woodville should be stripped of her estates and sent summarily to begin a luxurious retirement at Bermondsey Abbey, while her eldest son, the marquess of Dorset, should be imprisoned in the Tower. There is nothing really to suggest that either was involved: Elizabeth, as the mother of the queen, had very little motivation for plotting to overthrow the crown, still less in the name of Clarence's son. Dorset was temperamentally unreliable and had not been trusted to join the Bosworth campaign, but there is nothing really to suggest that he was scheming against the king. Nevertheless, Henry VII was not willing to take risks. And his caution was to prove absolutely correct. For on 4 June 1487 an army of fifteen hundred German mercenaries and four thousand Irish peasants landed at Furness on the Cumbrian coast in the far north-west of England. They were led by Simnel and his puppet master John earl of Lincoln and marshalled by the fearsome Swiss captain Martin Schwartz, a man 'admirably skilled in the art of war'.[3]

They marched rapidly across the lower Cumbrian mountains and the Pennines to Wensleydale, then skirted past York to Doncaster, and on down in the direction of Newark. They kept up a terrific pace, and by 15 June they were approaching the river Trent, the traditional dividing line between the north and south of England. There could be no hesitation on the king's part. This was a full-scale invasion, at least as severe as that which Henry himself had mounted two summers previously. The flames of beacons would have licked the air to publicise the presence of the hordes marching down the spine of England. The crown would once again be placed in jeopardy on the battlefield.

Henry was at Kenilworth, in the east midlands, when Simnel and Lincoln landed. He threw his realm immediately into a state of martial readiness. As a royal army was assembled, Jasper duke of Bedford and John earl of Oxford were detailed to high command. The Stanleys were given an independent commission to defend their area of authority. Other loyal nobles, including Lord Lisle, Lord Scales, Sir Rhys ap Thomas and the earls of Shrewsbury and Devon, were also summoned to serve at the fore. Proclamations demanding that public order be kept were sent around the country. The king himself rode to Coventry and on to Leicester, mustering his troops and readying himself for the assault. In Leicester, Richard III's corpse, not long in its rough grave at the church of the Greyfriars, must have reminded the king of fortune's fickleness. Henry did not stay long in the city. By the time Simnel and Lincoln's army had reached the Trent, he had amassed a large force of his own – perhaps twice the size of the invaders' – which camped in the shadow of Nottingham Castle. It was the festival weekend of Corpus Christi – normally a time for processions, pageants and mystery plays. But with foreign mercenaries on the rampage in the English midlands, there was no thought for anything but beating back the enemy. 'Like doves before a black storm,' wrote Bernard André, quoting Virgil's *Aeneid*, 'the men at once seized their weapons. Now the royal army advanced to meet the throngs of barbarians.'[4]

The armies collided slightly south-east of Newark, near the lower bank of the meandering Trent, where the old Roman road cut a path directly from Leicester towards its end-point at Lincoln. On Friday 15 June the rebel army had camped overnight near the village of East Stoke – around eight thousand in total, made up of a band of highly trained foreign sell-swords carrying halberds, crossbows and long, primitive rifles known as arque-buses (or hackbuts), along with half-naked Irish backwoodsmen with spears in their hands and the various bands of northern English archers, horsemen and gunners whom the rebel leaders had managed to rally to their cause on their long march south. The royal army, packed with veterans of Bosworth and large noble retinues, overnighted around Radcliffe, several miles away in the direction of Nottingham. Henry's scouts, sent out at first light, hastened back to the camp to inform the king that they had seen rebel troops lined up in readiness to fight on the brow of a hill near East Stoke (a place that locals simply called Stoke).

The long mornings of early June meant that even with a short march, Henry's men reached the field by around 9 a.m. As they arrayed in battle formation facing Simnel's far smaller force, Henry gave a speech. André later put a fancifully poetic version into the king's mouth, but the sentiment – that Lincoln had 'bra-zenly' taken up his cause in alliance with 'a trifling and shameless woman', Margaret of Burgundy, and that the king now trusted 'the same God who made us victors' at Bosworth to 'give us tri-umph' – may well have been correct.[5]

The fight was begun by the rebels, with a swarm of crossbow bolts buzzing towards the royal lines. Fire was returned with interest by Henry VII's archers. Since many of the rank and file in Simnel and Lincoln's army were unarmoured and vulnerable Irish fighters, better used to fighting hand to hand than with-standing volleys of arrows, the result was something close to a massacre.

Rather than stand and suffer annihilation from long range, the rebels charged, and a violent mêlée at close quarters began. This suited both the sophisticated continental mercenaries and the fierce men from rural Ireland. The close fighting lasted for around an hour, but eventually Henry's superior numbers prevailed and the enemy began to disintegrate. Both armies suffered severe losses, but it was on the rebel side that the most hideous carnage was wreaked. Perhaps four thousand of Simnel and Lincoln's fighters were killed, many from arrow wounds, their blood pooling in great puddles about the field and running deep into a wooded hollow afterwards known as the Red Gutter. By the end, almost all of the rebel commanders and captains, including Lincoln, Martin Schwartz and Lord Lovell, lay dead. Lambert Simnel was captured and taken to the Tower, where he was treated chivalrously and eventually put to work in the king's service. (Over the years he would work his way up from the kitchen staff to a post in falconry.) Meanwhile, Henry VII paraded from the battlefield for the second time in as many years, and took his army to the city of Lincoln to celebrate by gorging on pike, capons, sheep and ox-flesh and hanging a few of the Irish and English rank and file who had dared to rebel. News of the victory was sent across the country, being particularly well received by Henry's supporters in London, where rumours circulated that the king had been defeated and killed. Far from it. Henry had trusted his reign to Providence, and Providence had once again appeared to vindicate his kingship. In retrospect, the battle of Stoke would take on great significance. For it was the last battle that Henry, or any other king of his dynasty, would ever have to fight to save the crown.

Yet if the last clash of armies had taken place, the danger was not quite over. For almost as soon as Simnel had been captured, another pretender was produced, who would trouble the Tudor king for many years to come.

*

Late in 1491 a Breton merchant by the name of Pregent Meno set sail from Lisbon to Ireland to sell silks. He washed up in Cork, on the rugged south-eastern tail of the country: a marshy town that spread out across several islands, in which shops and houses stood higgledy-piggledy beside one another in a grid of warren-like streets. Here walked exiles and plotters: dissidents who had reason to hate the regime of the English king across the sea, and who were constantly on the watch for ways in which they could harm him.

Accompanying Meno on his silk-selling mission was a young man from northern France by the name of Pierrechon de Werbecque. Around seventeen years old, Pierrechon (his full name was mockingly part-anglicised by his enemies to 'Perkin Warbeck') had been born in Tournai, in the borderlands between France and the Netherlands, in about 1474. He had, said Vergil, a 'sharp and artful mind' and spoke English as well as several other languages.[6] He had been apprenticed by his parents to other merchants and from the age of about ten had lived an itinerant life in the trading towns of western Europe, from Antwerp to Lisbon, where he met Meno. Finally he arrived in Ireland and came to the attention of the former mayor of Cork, John Atwater, a central figure in the network of Yorkist sympathisers in the town. Whether they saw in Warbeck a likeness to another famous young man, or whether they simply found him an enterprising lad who could be bent to their purposes – or both – they took him into their confidence and convinced him to join them in a plot. Just as Lambert Simnel had been set up as an imposter, so too would Warbeck be. Only this time, rather than impersonating Edward earl of Warwick, the subject of the pretence would be the younger of the Princes in the Tower, Richard duke of York.

Richard, had he been alive in late 1491, would have been seventeen, like Warbeck, and of the perfect age to assume the crown. It was a matter of general agreement that he was dead – Henry VII's first parliament had condemned Richard III for 'shedding infants' blood, with many other wrongs, odious offences and abominations against God and man'.[7] But since a body had never been found nor a murderer brought to justice, it was still possible for those who wished to convince themselves that Richard had escaped the Tower to do so.[8] This was precisely the wilful gullibility on which the rebels of Cork depended when they set up Warbeck to impersonate the lost prince.

Once he was established as 'Richard', Warbeck was shown to the earl of Desmond, who responded with enthusiastic support. Then he was effectively hawked around western Europe to anyone who wished to annoy and harass the Tudor king.

The first to make use of him was the twenty-one-year-old Charles VIII of France, whose initial great project as king was to marry – more or less illegally – Anne of Brittany, four years old and the heir to her ailing father Francis II's duchy. By marrying Anne, Charles intended to annex Brittany to France and strike down forever its independence from the French crown. Henry VII was long acquainted with Duke Francis from his years in exile and was understandably inclined to offer his support to the Bretons. Charles thus followed a well-trodden path in international diplomacy. Since the outbreak of the English civil wars in the 1450s, foreign rulers had understood the value of holding or sheltering alternative claimants to the English crown. (Most recently, Francis II had harboured Henry Tudor, while the dukes of Burgundy had supported Edward IV, and Margaret of Anjou had set up her renegade Lancastrian court during the 1460s under the protection of Louis XI of France.) Most credible claimants to the crown had been killed, but that inconvenient fact aside, the policy was still a sensible one. Thus from March 1492 Perkin Warbeck was put up by the French court.

Henry treated Warbeck's accommodation in France as though it were an outright declaration of war. The previous year parliament had voted him a substantial grant of taxation to send troops to assist with the defence of Brittany. Now the money was turned to a more aggressive purpose. During the summer English ships were sent to harass the Normandy coast. In September, although it was late in the year and a dangerous time for campaigning, Henry himself took ship on the south coast, heading to Calais with a very large army of perhaps fifteen thousand men at his back. They spent a few days in camp before marching twenty miles down the coast to the nearest French city of significance, which happened to be the port town of Boulogne. Four columns of English troops descended on the town and laid siege to it. According to Vergil, 'There was a resolute garrison in the town, which energetically defended it. But before there was a recourse to hard fighting, behold suddenly a rumour spread through the camp that peace had been arranged.'⁹ So it had. Charles's aim was to annex Brittany, not to involve himself in a resuscitated version of the Hundred Years War, and he was quite happy to pay Henry to accept his wishes. The result was the treaty of Étaples, sealed on November 1492, by which Henry stood down his invasion and withdrew from Breton matters, and Charles agreed to pay the English a vast indemnity for their war expenses, along with the promise of a very generous pension of fifty thousand gold crowns a year for the following fifteen years. Crucially, he also agreed to stop assisting pretenders to Henry's throne. After three months of campaigning and virtually no bloodshed (save for the death of a rather overzealous knight by the name of John Savage, who was ambushed by French soldiers in front of Boulogne, fought back rather too lustily rather than submitting and was killed), Henry took his army back across the Channel in a sort of triumph.

Henry's uncompromising actions ensured that the court of Charles VIII was only a temporary stop for Warbeck. He would not, however, be thwarted, and as the treaty of Étaples closed doors in France, the pretender moved on: this time making his way to the court that had become the main European focus of anti-Tudor sentiment: the circle of the arch-schemer of the Netherlands, Margaret of York, dowager duchess of Burgundy.

For Margaret to embrace Perkin Warbeck as her own nephew – surely knowing full well that he was a fraud – was a mark of her political ruthlessness and devotion to the memory of her brothers. Despite Henry VII's marriage to her niece, Margaret would never accept that he had the right to rule, and was happy to pursue any means of discomfiting him. 'What people commonly say is true,' wrote Bernard André. 'Envy never dies.'[10] Certainly it never died at Mechelen, and Margaret welcomed Warbeck to her dazzling court, schooling him on his backstory from her own memories of life as a member of the house of York and introducing him to the great men in her continental circle. Chief among these was Maximilian, king of Germany, who was crowned Holy Roman Emperor in 1493 at a ceremony to which Warbeck was invited. Here was another player to whom he appeared to be a well-placed pawn. The man styling himself as Richard IV was treated with the reverence due to a real king, travelling a while with Maximilian, while Margaret made contact with dissidents in England, attempting to stir them to rebellion in the name of the pretender. Slowly but surely, the plot to promote this young man, and place him on the English throne, was gathering momentum.

None of this was in the slightest bit amusing to Henry VII. According to Vergil, 'Henry feared that unless the deception was quickly recognised as such by all, some great upheaval would occur.'[11] Most disturbingly, the king began to receive reports that the rebel circle in the Netherlands had connections in England, some perilously close to the royal household. Those rumoured to be in treasonable contact with Warbeck included the ambitious and shifty John Ratcliffe, Lord Fitzwalter, Sir Robert Clifford and William Worsley, the dean of St Paul's. In the spring of 1493, the king learned that this lordly cabal had sent Clifford to the Low Countries to meet Warbeck, assess whether he was really Richard duke of York, and (if satisfied with what he saw) inform him to expect a warm welcome if he should decide to cross the Channel and claim his throne.

In response Henry flew into a state of high defence, lasting for nearly eighteen months, during which he sent spies to the continent to feed back information about Warbeck and the rebels, and attempted to plant undercover agents in his circle. He also placed the English ports under tight surveillance, circulated propaganda both at home and abroad to rubbish the pretender's claims to royal stock, and imposed trade embargoes against the merchant towns of the Netherlands. Young Prince Henry's elevation to duke of York in November 1494 was part of this strategy of undermining Warbeck: creating a legitimate princely duke of York meant there was less room for a false one.

Yet Prince Henry's investiture as duke of York did not end Warbeck's conspiracy. Rather, the danger seemed to creep ever closer to the crown. Late in 1494 Henry's agents managed to 'turn' Sir Robert Clifford from the pretender's cause, milking from him a huge amount of intelligence in the process. The most shocking revelation was that a supposed Yorkist sympathiser was to be found at the heart of the royal household and family: Sir William Stanley, the king's chamberlain and step-uncle, the hero of Bosworth and brother to the kingmaker Thomas earl of Derby, had supposedly been heard to say of Warbeck that 'he would never take up arms against the young man, if he knew for certain that he was indeed the son of Edward'.[12] If Englishmen of the highest rank were prepared to believe that Richard was alive, and might return to reclaim his crown, then Henry could not afford to treat Warbeck with anything other than deadly seriousness.

Stanley's reported wavering was a hard blow to Henry VII, but he dealt with it swiftly. Despite the risk of antagonising Derby, the king put Sir William on trial at Westminster Hall on 30 and 31 January 1495. Stanley was 'condemned of a capital crime and put to death' by beheading on 16 February. Meanwhile, security measures were stepped up even further, both at home – where coastal defences were sufficient to repel an attempted landing at Deal, in Kent, on 3 July – and in Ireland, where Sir Edward Poynings was sent with a mandate to impose royal discipline by severe and authoritarian means.

Still Warbeck remained at large. Following his aborted invasion of Kent, he sailed via a now hostile Ireland to the kingdom of the Scots, and sought the protection of King James IV. 'The inhabitants there, deceived by his hints and inventions, believed him to be [Richard IV] and tenaciously adhered to him,' wrote André.[13] The truth was that once again he served as a tool for a greater lord's anti-English ambition. And once again he was a failure. James IV recognised him as 'Prince Richard of England' and gave him shelter, men, a handsome expense account for clothes, servants and horses, and an aristocratic wife – in the form of Lady Katherine Gordon, daughter of an earl and the king's distant cousin.[14] In September 1496 the Scots invaded the north of England on Warbeck's behalf, burning and pillaging the unfortunate villages of the border country. But the sight of the pretender's flag provoked only apathy in the hearts of the Englishmen who saw it, and almost as soon as they had come, James and his would-be prince were scuttling back over the border, having achieved precisely nothing.

Henry's response to Scottish backing for the irritant Warbeck was uncompromising. The parliament of January 1497 granted heavy taxation for the purpose of sending a massive military force north 'for the proper correction of [James IV's] cruel and wicked deeds'. The invasion, intended for summer, never materialised, because the weight of the taxation on Henry's English subjects provoked a tax rebellion in June of the same year, in which thousands of Cornishmen marched all the way to Blackheath and had to be routed by a military force under Giles, Lord Daubeney, Sir William Stanley's successor as lord chamberlain. However, the seriousness of Henry's intentions convinced James IV that Warbeck was probably more trouble than he was worth, and the young masquerader was packed off to continue his adventures elsewhere. Warbeck sailed for Cork in July 1497, and two months later he made what would be his final play for recognition, invading Cornwall at Land's End in the rather forlorn hope of rekindling the rebellious spirit of the early summer. A few thousand restless yokels gathered beneath his banner and laid siege to Exeter, but they were easily scattered by Edward Courtenay, earl of Devon, and by the end of the month Warbeck was captured. At Taunton on 5 October he was brought before the king. At last he admitted that he was not Richard IV, and offered up a full confession of his origins, bringing a formal end to his pretensions.

Like Simnel, Warbeck was kept honourably at the royal court once he had been exposed as a fraud. His wife, Lady Katherine, joined the queen's service and was treated extremely well 'on account of her nobility'.[15] Warbeck, however, lacked the good sense that had led Simnel to behave himself in royal service. In June 1498, while he was travelling with the royal court, he attempted to escape. He was recaptured at Sheen and – after twice being humiliatingly displayed in the stocks and made to confess his imposture again in public – he was thrown into the Tower of London for the rest of his life. As it transpired, that would not be a very long time. One of his fellow captives was Edward earl of Warwick – the man whom Simnel had impersonated. Warwick was now twenty-four and it would seem that his long imprisonment had addled his brain: Polydore Vergil wrote that he had been 'so far removed from the sight of man and beast that he could not easily tell a chicken from a goose'.[16] In the autumn of 1499 a plot was concocted between the two prisoners and a few citizens of London (possibly agents provocateurs) who planned to break them out of the Tower and put Edward on the throne in Henry's place. Escaping – or even plotting escape

– was a serious crime and the punishment could be harsh. Both men were tried in Westminster Hall before John de Vere, earl of Oxford, holding court in his capacity as lord high steward. Warwick was beheaded on Tower Hill on 28 November 1499, and Warbeck was hanged at Tyburn, having been forced to confess for the final time that he was no Plantagenet, but an adventurer, an imposter and a fraud. As the century drew to a close, noble heads still rolled and traitors' legs still kicked pathetically in the breeze beneath the hangman's noose. If the cycle of violence that had engulfed the English crown for nearly five decades seemed finally to be coming to an end, it was only because there were so few candidates left to kill.

21 : Blanche Rose

The ships came into Plymouth harbour at three o'clock on 2 October 1501, having sailed through strong winds, huge rolling waves and the terrifying flash of lightning over a boiling sea. The fleet had taken five days to make its way from the Cantabrian port of Laredo, moving to the northern tip of Brittany before heading due north to the south coast of England. Despite the wretched weather, the valuable cargo had arrived safely: a fifteen-year-old Spanish princess, Katherine of Aragon, stepped off to receive the choreographed acclaim of the assembled crowd, who hailed her, according to one of her companions, as if 'she had been the Saviour of the whole world'.[1]

She was certainly, in a way, the saviour of England. A marriage alliance with Ferdinand and Isabella, the joint rulers of Spain, had been more than twelve years in the making: as agreed in principle under the treaty of Medina del Campo of 1489, Katherine had already been married twice by proxy to Prince Arthur, but now she was here in person, to play her part in the creation of England's new royal dynasty.

This was, in a sense, the high point of Henry VII's kingship. For sixteen years he had fought a gruelling battle to maintain his grip on the crown that he had taken at Bosworth – seeing off pretenders and plots, decorating his realm with infinite symbols and reminders of Tudor triumph and, with his wife Elizabeth, diligently creating a new royal family. He had seen off dynastic conspiracies and a major tax rebellion. He had defended his crown on the battlefield and subsequently through the diplomatic networks of Europe. He had kept a tight hold on royal finance, directing much of the business of England's revenue collection through his chamber, rather than through the exchequer – a strategy that demanded much of his time, but allowed him to ensure that he was in command of the detail of policy, and to avoid the criticisms that so many of his predecessors had faced concerning the financial feebleness of the English crown. He had sailed a large army to France and used it to extract a handsome pension. And now, to cap it all, he was about to celebrate both an alliance with a major continental power and a marriage that would be fruitful enough to secure Tudor rule for a second generation.

Arthur and Katherine were married at St Paul's Cathedral on Sunday 14 November, amid high ceremony, and with the arms of the three kingdoms traditionally claimed by the house of York – England, France and Spain – prominently displayed, alongside all the other heraldic symbols of Henry's monarchy: the Welsh dragons, the greyhounds of Richmond and the ubiquitous rose. The whole cathedral was hung with expensive arras tapestries showing 'noble and valiant acts' and 'the besieging of noble cities'. Henry and Elizabeth watched from a discreet viewing gallery – 'a closet made properly with lattice windows', wrote one eyewitness – hidden from the sight of the congregation, so as not to distract from the splendid young couple, who were both dressed head to toe in white satin.[2] Despite their restricted view of proceedings, the king and queen would have been satisfied to hear the crowds both inside and outside St Paul's cheering 'King Henry!' and 'Prince Arthur!' A greater victory would have been harder to imagine, and the royal family celebrated appropriately. Then, following a fortnight of masques, balls, jousts and celebration, the newlyweds were packed off to the seat of Arthur's authority: Ludlow and the marches in his principality of Wales.

Prince Arthur's marriage was not the only step that Henry VII had taken to extend the connections of his family. Long negotiations were also underway to marry twelve-year-old Margaret to James IV of Scotland, whose appetite for raiding and burning northern England would presumably diminish if he could be drawn into a dynastic union. The treaty was concluded two months after Arthur's wedding celebrations, and Margaret would eventually marry the Scottish king at a magnificent service of her own, held at Holyrood Palace in Edinburgh on 8 August 1503. But by that time disaster had engulfed the house of Tudor.

On 2 April 1502 Prince Arthur died at Ludlow, following a wasting disease that may have been tuberculosis, but could have been a form of cancer.[3] He was only fifteen, and his wife became a widow at sixteen. Henry VII and Queen Elizabeth were devastated, and although the queen attempted to comfort her husband with words of cheer, suggesting that they were both young enough to have more children, Arthur's death was a blow from which the king would never recover. It left all his hopes of a clean succession on the shoulders of Prince Henry, who was approaching his tenth birthday.[4] Immediately, negotiations were opened by which Henry could be married to Katherine, who remained in English eyes as promising a future queen as ever. But Henry VII's life's experience counselled against relying on such thin hopes for the future.

Another Tudor death occurred within months of Arthur's. The king's quiet and reclusive uncle Owen Tudor, the monk of Westminster, died close to the age of seventy, and was buried some time before June 1502.[5] But this was nothing to the misery that followed on 11 February 1503, when Queen Elizabeth also died, following the premature birth of her last child, a girl named Katherine. The king had been told by his personal astrologer that his wife would live until the grand age of eighty. In fact, she died on her thirty-seventh birthday. Her daughter Katherine survived her only by a week. The king paid around £2,800 for a vast and solemn funeral for his wife, for which every church in London was draped in black. His sorrow was deep, almost tangible. In less than eighteen months, all his plans for the future of his dynasty had collapsed.

The shadow cast by Arthur's death was long and dark, and it changed the whole character of Henry VII's reign. The king's general mood shifted from celebratory to suspicious as his fears of losing everything for which he had fought suddenly seemed closer than ever to being realised. Consequently, he began to cast a paranoid eye upon many of his subjects, regarding with naked hostility all those whom he thought might have a motive for challenging his rule.

Chief among the victims of the king's forebodings were the de la Pole family – a large brood born to John de la Pole, duke of Suffolk and his wife, Elizabeth Plantagenet, Edward IV's sister. The eldest of these children was the earl of Lincoln who had died in rebellion at the battle of Stoke with Lambert Simnel by his side. In the years that followed Stoke, Henry had not seen fit to damn Lincoln's siblings on account of their brother's violent treachery. After Arthur's death, however, young men with Yorkist connections did not need to do much to draw upon themselves the suspicions of the king. Four de la Pole men were alive at the turn of the century: Edmund, Humphrey, William and Richard. Humphrey was a monk, and thus politically neutral. The others, however, could be considered as potentially dangerous.

First among these was Edmund de la Pole, earl of Suffolk. Although loyal during the 1490s (he helped to put down the Cornish rebels at Blackheath in 1497), close to his cousin the queen and a regular attender at court parties and great state occasions, Edmund had some cause for disgruntlement, mainly stemming from his financial troubles. Too poor to maintain himself as a duke, he had been downgraded to the rank of earl when he inherited his title in 1493, yet even in this reduced state he held his noble title on such onerous conditions that most of his yearly income was diverted to the Crown, meaning that he was

'embarrassed by very heavy debts'.[6] He had been further humiliated by involvement in a legal case brought in 1498, in which
he was accused of murdering a man named Thomas Crue and
told to make a grovelling apology in order to receive the royal
pardon. And on top of all this he was recognised by all those who
remained inclined to the house of York as a senior claimant on
Edward IV's side. In debt, in political trouble, in demand by the
king's enemies and, if we believe the account of Vergil, 'bold,
impetuous and readily roused to anger', Suffolk began to agitate
against the king.

He committed his first act of defiance on 1 July 1499 when he
left England without royal permission and travelled to Picardy,
trying to make contact with the Yorkist doyenne Margaret of
Burgundy. This caused a serious diplomatic incident. Suffolk was
eventually brought home in October, made to apologise to the
king and fined £1,000 – more than a year's income, which further crippled his finances. His friends and associates were interrogated and his wife, Margaret Scrope, was placed under royal
surveillance. Then, as if any further warning to would-be plotters
were required, in November 1499 Edward earl of Warwick was
beheaded. King Henry was making his point.

If all this was intended to force Suffolk into obedience, however, it had precisely the opposite effect. In November 1501, as
Arthur and Katherine of Aragon's wedding was being celebrated,
he once again slipped out of England, taking with him his youngest brother, Richard de la Pole, and made his way across Europe
to the court of the Holy Roman Emperor Maximilian at Imst.
He had been assured that he would find support there for the
cause that he would now openly trumpet for the next five years:
his claim that he, and not a member of the Tudor family, was the
rightful king of England.

When he heard of Edmund's defection Henry's first step was
to round up and punish all those whom he could connect with

the White Rose, as Suffolk's supporters had begun to call him. Richard de la Pole had fled to the continent with Edmund. But their brother Sir William de la Pole had not. Therefore he was arrested and thrown into the Tower indefinitely. (He would eventually die there in the 1530s.) Then William, Lord Courtenay, the heir to the earldom of Devon who had married the queen's younger sister Catherine, was also imprisoned and remained locked up for nearly a decade. Previously loyal knights including Sir James Tyrell, Sir John Wyndham and several others connected – however weakly – to the White Rose were executed. Tyrell was conveniently induced to confess to having murdered the Princes in the Tower before he died, which was one effective means of Henry reminding his subjects that Edward IV's boys really were dead, and their cause no longer worth heralding. Beyond these grand men, dozens of other yeomen, royal servants and ordinary tradesmen were rounded up, interrogated and in many cases put miserably to death. Henry once more set to work planting spies and informants in a network fanning out across Europe. There was some good news in 1503, when the king's most vehement foreign opponent, Margaret of Burgundy, died at Mechelen on 23 November. The same year Maximilian yielded to sustained diplomatic pressure and agreed to end his financial support for the de la Poles. Still, though, Henry could not secure Suffolk's person. He attempted to arrange his assassination via royal agents in Calais – again to no avail.[7] The English parliament of January 1504 convicted the de la Poles of 'falsely and traitorously plotting and conspiring the death and destruction of the king our sovereign lord, and the overthrow of this his realm', and attainted them in absentia.[8] Still none of it resulted in de la Pole's death or return, but by 1505 Henry had succeeded in squeezing the White Rose cause so hard that virtually no court or officer in Europe would proffer any financial aid. From March 1504 Richard de la Pole was locked up in Aachen as a hostage to secure debts that the family had incurred there, and only escaped in 1506. Suffolk, meanwhile, was reduced to wandering the Low Countries with an increasingly tiny group of aides and supporters, living on debt, dressed in rags and pawning his possessions for food. At home, the violent persecution of suspected White Rose sympathisers continued. By October 1505 the pathetic Suffolk was in Namur, in the custody of Maximilian's eldest son, Philip the Fair, duke of Burgundy, and was readying himself to try and make peace with Henry VII, end his dismal penury and return home in whatever grace he could, praying that his life, at least, would be spared. But events would overtake him.

In the middle of January 1506 Philip archduke of Burgundy and his wife Joanna set sail from Flanders for Spain, where Philip was to seize possession of the crown of Castile.[9] But midwinter was a bad time to be braving the northern seas. As the couple sailed, 'an evil storm suddenly arose'. It was one of the fiercest ever known, which one London chronicler remembered as having blown 'with such sternness that it turned over weak houses and trees', taking the thatch and tiles from rooftops, flooding the countryside and blowing the weathercock from the top of St Paul's Cathedral.[10] (It crashed into a tavern called the Black Eagle and caused considerable damage.)

Out at sea Philip and Joanna were lucky not to be drowned. Their ships were blown into port at Weymouth, where Philip, 'little accustomed to the ocean waves' and 'exhausted in both body and mind', was delighted to disembark his battered craft.[11] But delight did not last long. The couple were given a splendid welcome as guests of the English king, but beneath the finery and the hospitality lay a stark political reality. Philip and Joanna were now effectively Henry's prisoners. The terms of their release were twofold: a trade deal loaded heavily in favour of English merchants and an agreement to return Edmund de la Pole.[12] By the end of March, Suffolk had been collected by English officers at Calais and transferred across the now calm Channel. On his return, Philip and Joanna were allowed to go on their way. Despite Henry's promises that he would pardon the fugitive and return him to his former estate, Suffolk was thrown into the Tower of London. The White Rose would never see the outside world again.

*

The burdens and disappointments of middle age brought about a sorry decline in Henry VII. He was forty-nine when Edmund de la Pole was finally returned to his grasp, and as his sight failed and his health began to stutter, he became increasingly withdrawn, suspicious and tyrannical. His most trusted servants and counsellors began to die. His uncle Jasper Tudor, duke of Bedford, had died in 1495, having retreated from public life since his sixtieth birthday, around four years previously. Cardinal John Morton, who had served as a faithful and diligent archbishop of Canterbury from the beginning of the reign, died in 1500. Sir Reginald Bray, chancellor of the duchy of Lancaster, who had been a loyal servant since long before Bosworth, expired in 1503. The king's stepfather Thomas Stanley, earl of Derby, died in 1504. The circle of trust around the king tightened yearly. In response, Henry's approach to government, which had always relied on heavy personal oversight, particularly with regard to financial matters, now degenerated into more or less rule by extortion. Henry came to see all external power as threatening to his own. He began to employ an extensive system of bonds and recognisances, by which wealthy and influential individuals were forced to agree to pay the king exorbitant sums in the event of his displeasure, as a means of guaranteeing their good behaviour. The system, used on a grand and virtually unprecedented scale, was associated most closely with two determined and ruthless young officers of the crown: Sir Richard Empson and Edmund Dudley, whose rule over the realm was generally loathed, and whose names were synonymous with the perversions to normal governance that afflicted the king's final years. Henry was growing sicker, his kingdom was becoming ever more badly ruled. And by the end, he was clinging on, employing methods that had not been seen in England since the darkest days before the deposition of Richard II in 1399. During the early years of his reign Henry had proven himself an extremely successful and self-consciously majestic king, even if he had never possessed the easy bonhomie that had characterised the rule of the man he claimed to succeed, Edward IV. But by the end, he governed by fear, fortunate that the best alternative candidates for kingship were either dead, exiled or locked away in his prisons.

He died, following a lingering illness, on 21 April 1509, and was succeeded by his seventeen-year-old son, Henry VIII. The succession was a nervous, secretive affair, stage-managed by the wizened and arthritis-crippled Margaret Beaufort, by now approaching her sixty-sixth birthday but still as acute a political operative as she had ever been. The effort took its toll. She died on 29 June the same year and was buried in an astonishingly beautiful tomb in the new Lady Chapel at Westminster Abbey, made by the Italian sculptor Pietro Torrigiano, who also made Henry VII's tomb. She had lived long enough to witness the coronation of her grandson: the crowning triumph of an eventful life. Not since the accession of Henry V in 1413 had an adult (or nearly adult) king inherited the throne from his father. Margaret Beaufort, an astonishing woman in any age, had been a key player in the long struggles that were waged over the English crown. Victory and vindication were hers.

Young Henry came to the throne confident and ready to rule. He was well educated, charming and charismatic: truly a prince fit for the renaissance in courtly style, tastes and patronage that was dawning in northern Europe. He had been blessed with the fair colouring and radiant good looks of his grandfather Edward IV: tall, handsome, well built and dashing, here was a king who saw his subjects as peers and allies around whom he had grown up, rather than semi-alien enemies to be suspected and persecuted. One of the new king's first acts was to issue a general pardon, although pointedly excluding the de la Poles, the detested Empson and Dudley, and around eighty named others. Shortly afterwards he married his brother's twenty-three-year-old widow, Katherine of Aragon. And then, as soon as possible following the deaths of his father and grandmother, the new king – modelling himself on his legendary ancestor Henry V – began planning for a war in France. Over the course of a century all of the French lands traditionally claimed by English kings had been lost. Like his Plantagenet forebears, young Henry made it his ambition to win them back.

Beginning in 1512 Henry would send armies over the Channel to torment the French. If not especially successful, these campaigns were at least highly enjoyable to a military society that had had precious little opportunity to fight abroad since the 1450s. Here was a young king who seemed naturally to understand the style and much of the art of kingship from the very beginning. For emulating Henry V was not a challenge limited solely to the mind of Henry VIII. In 1513–14, a book entitled *The First English Life of Henry V* had been published, lauding the memory of the hero of Agincourt for the explicit purpose of guiding the new king towards 'the example of [Henry V's] great wisdom and discretion', and praying that he might be 'provoked in his said war' against the French.[13] (In this, the author found a much more willing audience than the Italian humanist Tito Livio Frulovisi, whose *Vita Henrici Quinti* had been ignored by Henry VI in the 1430s.)

Henry VIII's purpose as king, however, was to be more than simply Henry V reborn. The new king was also, as the poets and propagandists of the new reign pointed out gleefully, the living manifestation of the Tudors' self-made myth: Henry was, to quote his tutor John Skelton, 'the rose both red and white'. He was neither Lancaster nor York, but both: the heir of both Henry VI and Richard duke of York; unity personified. The Tudor rose continued to abound as a motif of his reign: it adorned buildings and decorated royal palaces; it was painted in choirbooks and illustrated manuscripts prepared for the king's library; it was even doodled on the king's private prayer roll.[14] Hope, which had been long frozen under the later rule of Henry VII, was reawakened by the accession of his son.

Yet under his bluff and bold exterior, Henry VIII could be as ruthless as his father had been. Although his position was much improved as a king who had legitimately inherited his crown, rather than having wrenched it from a dying rival on a battlefield, he could not afford wholly to ignore the dynastic vulnerabilities that had occupied his father's mind so feverishly. In the Tower, Edmund de la Pole was a potentially toxic prisoner, while Richard de la Pole remained at large, somewhere across the sea. Ageing Yorkist diehards might still harbour a grudge, and while Henry VIII could afford to be magnanimous in his newly acquired kingship – he restored George duke of Clarence's daughter Margaret Pole to her estates and promoted her to a position of dignity and independence, giving her the old family title of countess of Salisbury – he knew he was not wholly free of the enemies whom his father had made. And he was prepared to act swiftly and savagely if necessary to contain them.

The catalyst was Henry's war in France. As a young, thrusting king with an urge to prove himself and a talented and rising new first minister by the name of Thomas Wolsey, Henry launched a second invasion of France in 1513, which he led himself, while Queen Katherine stayed at home as regent to oversee renewed hostilities with the Scottish king James IV.[15] But Henry could not in good conscience go over to France and risk his life in battle in the knowledge that he held in captivity a man who had very recently claimed the crown of England for himself. 'It was feared that when the king was out of the country, the people might perhaps be eager for a revolution; they might snatch Edmund forcibly from the Tower [and] give him his liberty,' wrote Vergil.[16]

Shortly before the king embarked for France, he gave the order that Edmund de la Pole, erstwhile earl of Suffolk, should have his stay in the prison abruptly terminated. On 4 May 1513 the White Rose was taken out of prison, hauled up to Tower Hill and summarily beheaded.

*

There was, however, one more left. One White Rose had been lopped off, but another grew from the same stem. Richard de la Pole had been loose ever since absconding from England with his brother in 1501. After his brother's capture and repatriation he had wound up in Buda, in the kingdom of Hungary, where he made an unlikely success of his career in exile, under the protection of King Ladislaus II, who paid him a pension until 1516 and made sure that he stayed far beyond the reach of the frustrated English kings. Financially secure and warlike by nature, Richard distinguished himself on the battlefield, fighting in the wars that raged in the unstable kingdoms and fiefdoms of northern Italy, southern France and the Spanish peninsula. He was a talented and brave captain, well respected by those who saw him fight, and he quickly made powerful friends, including the French dauphin, Francis. From 1513, when his brother was killed, he claimed the title of duke of Suffolk and adopted the nickname White Rose – or variations thereof, including Blanche Rose and La Rosa Blancha.[17]

As ever, in continental politics and war, the possession of a

rival claimant to the English throne was a great boon for anyone who wished to vex the king of England. Thus, when Henry
VIII invaded France in 1513, Louis XII recognised Richard de
la Pole as the rightful king of England. The transaction was clear:
if Henry wished to reopen the foreign wars of his Plantagenet
ancestors, then in return Louis was more than happy to reopen
the question of the English succession. In 1514 he equipped
de la Pole with an army of twelve thousand men, much larger
than the force that had accompanied Henry VII when he crossed
the sea and successfully deposed Richard III in 1485. They
were rumoured to be ready to depart from Normandy in June
1514, and it is very possible that they would have done so had
not Henry VIII decided against sending another expensive army
to France that summer, choosing instead to make a peace with
the ageing French king, by which Henry's eighteen-year-old sister
Mary married Louis and became queen of France. (She would
hold the position for only three months, since Louis died on New
Year's Day 1515, to be succeeded by his cousin Francis I.)

The peace was well timed, and averted the threat of a Yorkist invasion, but it was still clear that under Richard de la Pole's
tenacious challenge Henry VIII was no more able to ignore the
threat of the White Rose than his father had been. Before long
he had resorted to much the same tactics as the old king: hiring
assassins, commissioning spies to work the European channels,
and applying diplomatic pressure to try and keep the White Rose
at bay. But none of it worked. Like Henry VIII, Francis I was a
young, thrusting and lively king determined to make an impression. More importantly, he was friendly with Richard de la Pole,
so support for the White Rose continued. There were rumours of
an invasion under or a rising in the name of the would-be Richard IV in 1516, 1521, 1522, 1523 and 1524. None ever came
to fruition, but Henry and his ministers were seldom allowed
to forget that every move abroad came at a potential price in

domestic harmony. And in the end, only the unexpected outcome of a battle fought halfway across Europe would bring Henry VIII the dynastic security he so badly craved.

*

Before the sun had risen on 24 February 1525, a French army led in person by Francis I was moving around the walls of Pavia, a heavily fortified military town in the heart of Lombardy, some twenty miles south of Milan. More than twenty thousand men had been camped out in siege formation around Pavia for nearly four months, attempting to starve out the nine thousand men, mainly mercenaries, who were inside the city walls. They were about to be confronted by an equally mighty relieving force of fighters loyal to the Spanish emperor Charles V, with whom Francis was pursuing what would be a long, complex and bloody war for domination of the Italian peninsula. From first light the assault began: the crash of cannon and arquebus mingling with the rumble of cavalry hoofs as two gigantic armies flew into one another with utter ferocity.

Richard de la Pole was in command of the French infantry, fighting alongside another experienced and capable captain, François de Lorraine, who commanded a crack unit of mercenary *landsknechts* known as the Black Band. But 24 February was not to prove a blessed day for either man. During a battle that raged for nearly four hours the French army was split and finally routed by a fierce and brilliantly organised Spanish imperial effort. Francis I was knocked from his horse and pinned to the ground before being chivalrously picked up and taken as a prisoner for Charles V. The casualties on the French side were appalling, and included many commanders and captains. The French lost a miserable field, and with it their position in Lombardy, from which they would retreat at great speed almost as soon as the battle was over. And by the end of the battle, Richard de la Pole – the

White Rose, last remaining grandson of Richard duke of York and rival king of England – lay dead.

The shock and scale of the French defeat stunned many in Europe. But it absolutely delighted Henry VIII and Cardinal Wolsey. French fortunes in war, which had ridden so high for so long, now stood in tatters: their king a humiliated captive, their armies destroyed. Henry could now seriously begin to plot a repeat of the feats of his ancestor Henry V: to storm France, recover the ancient Plantagenet patrimony and restore English rule from Normandy to Gascony. He could even fantasise, if his allies should prove themselves agreeable, about taking back the crown of France which Henry VI had last worn in Paris in 1431. And all of this could be conceived without the tiresome prospect of a French king conjuring up another puppet claimant to the English throne. De la Pole was dead! The price of war abroad need no longer be plotting and intrigue at home. Now conquest would not have to be weighed against dynastic security. The ghosts of the previous century could finally be forgotten.

A French historian writing in the eighteenth century described – or perhaps imagined – the conversation between Henry VIII and the messenger who found the king in bed during the early days of March 1525 and told him the outcome of the battle of Pavia. Having discoursed at length about the capture of Francis I and the destruction of the French army, the messenger went on to report the wonderful news about the last White Rose. 'God have mercy on his soul!' Henry is said to have exclaimed. 'All the enemies of England are gone.' And then, pointing to the messenger, he cried, 'Give him more wine!'[18]

Epilogue: How Many Men, in the Name of God Immortal, Have You Killed?

The death of the last White Rose in 1525 was really the final rattle of opposition to the Crown to have its origins in the wars that had shaken the realm since the first outbreak of violence during Henry VI's reign in the 1450s. By the 1520s the generation that ruled and moved England were, by and large, not veterans of Bosworth or Stoke. Anyone who had participated in either of those battles would be in his fifties – approaching old age, by the standards of the time. Few could now remember the horrors of Towton. Henry VIII's generation were children of (relative) peace, and though the elderly would have spoken of the violence of civil war, and shared their memories of the ferocious battles that had taken place in the midlands, the marches of Wales, the outskirts of London and the far north, the truth was that most of the protagonists and the participants of the wars were long dead. The wounds were passing into the realm of history and folklore.

One very important reason for this was that the central issue that had lain at the root of the wars appeared to have been resolved. This was not a case of an overmighty nobility having been blunted, of a system we now call 'bastard feudalism' having been destroyed, or of a radical shift having occurred in the power structures of England, as has sometimes been argued. Rather, it was the result of a final restoration of determined and legitimate kingship that would have been recognisable to men who had lived a century earlier, during the heyday of the Plantagenets. Henry VIII was not merely a king who had inherited his crown by right of birth rather than conquest: he was a majestic, assertive, warlike prince who combined the swagger and grit of Edward IV with the appetite for all the trappings of Renaissance princeliness that was common to the other great monarchs of his generation: most especially Francis I of France and Charles V, king of Spain and Holy Roman Emperor. Although 'the wars of the roses' had in the 1480s become wars of dynastic legitimacy, their origins were not in a squabble about blood. Rather they had lain squarely in the English polity's inability to cope with the inane, destructively pliant kingship of Henry VI. This vacillating king, peaceful and pious, had unleased a half-century of political trauma.

Henry VIII could hardly have presented a more different character. 'Our king is not after gold, or gems or precious metals, but virtue, glory and immortality,' the English scholar-courtier Lord Mountjoy had written to the great Dutch humanist Erasmus on Henry VIII's accession in 1509. Henry had many faults, as the second half of his reign would amply demonstrate, but during his early years it was clear that personal authority had finally been restored to the crown by a king whose right to rule was stronger than that of any of his predecessors since 1422. Henry's accession thus solved two problems at once: it addressed the vague and random problem of personal authority on the part of the man who happened to become king, and the question of legitimacy as a matter of blood-right, which had been disastrously thrown open in 1460 when Richard duke of York had decided to abandon his quest for political leadership and claim the crown. The basic symbols and images of Tudor kingship presented Henry VIII as the embodiment of red rose and white rose reunited. He understood the role, and played it perfectly.

This is not to say, of course, that Henry could afford to ignore dynastic threats completely, as the Richard de la Pole saga had demonstrated. Alternative Plantagenet and 'Yorkist' lines of royal descent were thin, but they still existed. In the spring of 1521 Henry had acted ruthlessly to press charges of treason – conspiring or imagining the king's death – against Edward Stafford, duke of Buckingham, whose long line of descent from Thomas of Woodstock connected him to Edward III, and whose loud mouth, insufferable pride and arrogant bearing had been inherited all too obviously from his father, the foolish kingmaker duke who had rebelled against Richard III. Edward's crime was largely a case of grumbling about royal policy, listening to prophecies concerning the king's life and muttering that he himself might one day make a better monarch. But this was enough to bring down the greatest nobleman in England. Buckingham was subjected to a show trial at Westminster Hall, had a guilty verdict delivered to him by a tearful duke of Norfolk and was beheaded at the Tower of London on 17 May 1521. The charges against him were largely trumped up, and his trial stage-managed to produce the inevitable judgement. It is hard to imagine that Buckingham would have been so sorely treated by the king were it not for the Plantagenet blood of which he was so proud.

Other noble families might have presented Henry with concerns if he had put his mind firmly to it, but by the end of the 1520s the king's mind was occupied with dynastic matters of a different sort. His marriage to his brother's widow Katherine of Aragon had produced only one surviving child, Princess Mary, and his head had been turned by the woman who would become his second wife, Anne Boleyn. The issues of religious reform that exploded out of his search for a divorce during the early 1530s provided new political dividing lines just as deadly as those that had existed between the various factions of Lancaster, York, Neville, Tudor and the rest during the fifteenth century. To be sure, dynastic issues were still alive, but they were now fused with the politics of religion, shaped by domestic concerns and Henry's increasingly monstrous sexual psychology and hunger for power and grandeur.

It was in this context that he persecuted the Pole family, condemning the aged Margaret Pole to her hideous butchery at the block in the Tower in 1541, cursing Cardinal Reginald Pole's name all around Europe and having another of Margaret's sons, Henry Pole, Lord Montague, likewise executed for high treason on 9 January 1539 alongside Henry Courtenay, marquess of Exeter. Montague and Exeter's principal crime was to oppose the king on matters of religion, and to rebel (or be suspected of rebelling) against the royal supremacy. The fact that Margaret Pole was the daughter of George duke of Clarence, and one of the only remaining links to the wars of the fifteenth century, was not on its own enough to justify her losing her head in 1541. But it was almost certainly an aggravating factor in her execution.

All the same, the death of Margaret Pole still represents a watershed: she was the last aristocrat who could claim with much seriousness to carry Plantagenet blood in her veins. The pseudo-royal families of York, Beaufort, Holland, de la Pole and Pole were effectively all gone. The Nevilles and Staffords had been bludgeoned into submission. The old nobility had by no means been destroyed as a unit of society, but many great and ancient families had been wiped out. 'How many men, in the name of God immortal, have you killed?' wrote Reginald Pole, raging at Henry for the judicial murder of his mother. The answer was simple: enough. The politics that stirred men's hearts and moved their hands to their swords in anger had shifted decisively from dynasty to faith. After the king died in 1547 the great arguments of his children's reigns were not Lancaster versus York but evangelism versus papism, reform versus the old ways and, ultimately, Protestant versus Catholic. The wars of the roses were well and truly over.

*

And yet. On Saturday 14 January 1559, at about two o'clock, Henry VIII's younger daughter, Elizabeth, rode through London, from the Tower down to Westminster, on the eve of her coronation. As usual, a great series of pageants had been organised to illustrate the many ways in which the new queen's majesty was righteous and worthy.

At the corner of Fenchurch Street and Gracechurch Street a large stage was erected across the street, 'vaulted with battlements' and built on three separate levels. According to the official record of the procession:

> on the lowest stage was made one seat royal, wherein were placed two personages representing king Henry the Seventh and Elizabeth his wife, daughter of king Edward the Fourth . . . [not] divided but that the one of them which was king Henry processing out of the house of Lancaster was enclosed in a red rose, and the other which was Queen Elizabeth being heir to the house of York enclosed with a white rose . . . Out of the which two roses sprang two branches gathered into one, which were directed upward to the second stage . . . wherein was placed one, representing the valiant and noble prince king Henry [VIII].

Beside this Henry sat his second wife, Anne Boleyn, and on the stage above them sat a final figure, representing Elizabeth I herself, 'crowned and apparelled as the other princes were'. The whole pageant was 'garnished with red roses and white and in the forefront of the same pageant in a fair wreath was written . . . "The Uniting of the two houses of Lancaster and York."' A great play was made on Elizabeth's name: like Elizabeth of York, who brought unity to the realm through her marriage, it was explained, the new Elizabeth would 'maintain the same among her subjects'. Unity, said the official account, 'was the end whereat the whole device shot'.[1]

Those men and women of London who stood and gawped as the queen's procession passed by would have understood instantly the version of history that was being suggested by the rose pageant. It had, after all, been repeated at length for more than seventy years. Buildings were decorated with the Tudor roses and other associated emblems of the dynasty. Great stained-glass windows installed in churches during the sixteenth century blazed with red and white petals.[2] Anyone who had been lucky enough to browse the books of the royal library would have found the exquisite illustrations on the pages decorated with roses red, white and Tudor – in many cases these were added to books that had been inherited from earlier kings, particularly Edward IV. Other books, too, were emblazoned with the simplified dynastic story of the wars of the roses. Nowhere can Tudor teleology be seen more clearly expressed than in the full title of Edward Hall's chronicle, 'The Union of the Two Noble and Illustre Famelies of Lancastre & Yorke, Beeyng Long in Continual Discension for the Croune of this Noble Realme, with all the Actes Done in Bothe the Tymes of the Princes, Bothe of the One Linage and of the Other, Beginnyng at the Tyme of King Henry the Fowerth, the First Aucthor of this Deuision, and so Successively Proceadyng to the Reigne of the High and Prudent Prince, King Henry the Eight, the Vndubitate Flower and the Very Heire of Both the Sayd Linages'.[3] As if this were not clear enough, the frontispiece to the publisher Richard Grafton's 1550 edition of Hall's chronicle made things visually unmistakeable. The writhing branches of a rosebush prickled their way around the title, growing from the bottom of the page: on either side they were occupied by rival members of the broken Plantagenet dynasty. At the very top of the page, inevitably, sat the magnificently porcine figure of Henry VIII, the messiah, the end of history.

The frontispiece was such a popular motif that it was repeated and reused on other, unconnected works: the same family tree appeared unmodified in John Stow's 1550 and 1561 editions of Chaucer's works, introducing the section on the *Canterbury Tales*.[4]

Just as John duke of Bedford had plastered occupied France with genealogies advertising the legitimacy of the joint monarchy during the 1520s, and just as Edward IV had obsessively compiled genealogies tracing his rightful royal descent from centuries long gone, so too did the Tudors drive home the simple, visual message both of their right to rule and their version of history. By Elizabeth's reign, the mere sight of red and white roses entwined was enough to evoke instantly the whole story of the fifteenth century: the crown had been thrown into dispute and disarray by the Lancastrian deposition of Richard II in 1399; this had prompted nearly a century of warfare between two rival clans, which was a form of divine punishment for the overthrow of a rightful king; finally in 1485 the Tudors had reunited the families and saved the realm. It was that simple.

By the 1590s, when Elizabeth I was old, her own reign decaying and a new crisis of rule beginning to loom, the Tudor story of the fifteenth century was a matter not only of historical fact, but of public entertainment. A generation of playwrights mined the monumental histories of Hall and his successor Raphael Holinshed to unearth material for a new and extremely well-received form of spectacle: the English history play. One of the most popular eras for depiction on the stage was the fifteenth century. And the greatest of all the dramatists was William Shakespeare.

In or around 1591 – the dating is a matter of dispute – Shakespeare wrote, or more likely contributed to, the play that is now called *Henry VI Part I*. The play's events concern the early stages of the wars of the roses, charting the loss of England's lands in France and the political upheaval that resulted. In the famous 'rose garden' scene, Richard duke of York (called here Richard Plantagenet) and various other noblemen squabble and align into two factions, selecting red or white roses to represent themselves:

RICHARD PLANTAGENET

[. . .]

Let him that is a true-born gentleman

And stands upon the honour of his birth,

If he suppose that I have pleaded truth,

From off this briar pluck a white rose with me.

He plucks a white rose

SOMERSET

Let him that is no coward nor no flatterer,

But dare maintain the party of the truth,

Pluck a red rose from off this thorn with me.

He plucks a red rose

WARWICK

I love no colours, and without all colour

Of base insinuating flattery,

I pluck this white rose with Plantagenet.

SUFFOLK

I pluck this red rose with young Somerset,

And say withal I think he held the right.

[. . .]

SOMERSET

Well, I'll find friends to wear my bleeding roses . . .[5]

Above the hubbub of a late Elizabethan theatre, the nuances of political history could be lost. But the mere sight of actors dressed as aristocrats teaming off according to their choice of rose was designed to be instantly understood. *Henry VI Part I* eventually became part of the cycle of Shakespeare's two historical tetralogies: eight plays that run, if arranged by their historical chronology, from *Richard II* to *Richard III*, and which portray the whole course of pre-Tudor fifteenth-century history.[6] The message that had been concocted by Henry VII nearly one hundred years previously had become entrenched in public consciousness. And there it has remained, more or less, ever since.

*

As we have seen, the wars of the roses and the destruction of the house of Plantagenet did not really come about because two factions divided by blood were destined to atone through war for the sin of deposing Richard II. All the evil of the fifteenth century was not embodied in a villainous Richard III, any more than the marriage of Henry VII and Elizabeth of York provided instant salvation. Rather, this was a vicious and at times barely comprehensible period of deep political instability, which stemmed ultimately from a collapse in royal authority and English rule in France under Henry VI. In a system in which law, order, justice and peace flowed so heavily from the person of the king and the office of the crown, Henry VI's reign (and his afterlife between deposition in 1461 and his death ten years later) was a disaster. The English system of government was robust in the 1420s and 1430s – robust enough to deal with a minority of nearly two decades. But it was not robust enough to deal with an adult king who simply would not perform his role. For a time under Henry VII there was an attempt to rehabilitate his memory, with the old king proposed as a candidate for sainthood who had performed wonderful miracles, including healing a man who had been run over by a wagon, or a young boy who had been injured during a football game.[7] Under Henry VIII, however, this was quietly dropped in favour of reverence for the more obviously inspiring example of Henry V. It was difficult to sustain much interest in a man whose doleful and agonisingly protracted rule wreaked long-term damage on the English crown that took decades to repair.

Edward IV undid a great deal of the appalling harm that had been caused by Henry VI, repairing much of the fabric of royal government and taking to kingship with extraordinary brio and competence; but he made two bad mistakes. The first was to marry Elizabeth Woodville, whose large family could not be easily assimilated into a political system that had just endured such a rough shaking. The second was to die in April 1483 – not a matter about which he had much choice in the short term, although it is possible to argue that his physical decline in his later years was self-inflicted by his fondness for gorging and idleness. All the same, the combination of a child heir and a Woodville faction that could not or would not be accommodated was too much for a fragile and weatherbeaten political system to bear. That said, Richard III's ruthless usurpation of the crown was not and could not have been foreseen by anyone, and it unleashed a period of bloody desperation in which the crown was all but up for grabs to anyone who could show a strain of royal blood and raise a foreign army. It was this battle, fought 'hot' between 1483 and 1487 and 'cold' between 1487 and 1525, that was won by the Tudors, not the 'wars of the roses' as a whole. Nevertheless, the fact is that the Tudors did win. And like all historical winners, they reserved the right to tell their story: a story that has endured to this day.

Notes

INTRODUCTION

1 The French ambassador to England, Charles de Marillac, thought Margaret 'above eighty years old'; Eustace Chapuys, the Imperial ambassador, reckoned her 'nearly ninety'. L&P XVI 868; CSP Spain, 1538–42, 166

2 For this and below see H. Pierce, *The Life, Career and Political Significance of Margaret Pole, Countess of Salisbury 1473–1541* (University of Wales, Bangor, 1996), chapter 8 passim

3 CSP Spain, 1538–42, 166

4 D. Seward, *The Last White Rose: Dynasty, Rebellion and Treason – The Secret Wars against the Tudors* (London, 2010), 291

5 CSP Venice, V (1534–54) 104–6

6 Ibid., 108

7 M. Callcott, *Little Arthur's History of England* (London, 1835), 112. For further historical uses and development of the phrase, see OED 'Rose', 6a. Eng. Hist.

8 W. A. Rebhorn (ed. and trans.), *The Decameron, Giovanni Boccaccio* (London/New York, 2013), 351 n. 3

9 See for example BL Arundel 66 f. 1v; BL Egerton 1147 f. 71; BL Royal 16 f. 173v

10 Notably the D'Arcy family. See H. Gough and J. Parker, *A Glossary of Terms Used in Heraldry* (London, 1894), 500–1

11 Robbins, R. H. (ed.), *Historical Poems of the Fourteenth and Fifteenth Centuries* (New York, 1959), 215–18

12 B. Williams, *Chronique de la traison et mort de Richart Deux roy Dengleterre* (London, 1846), 151; see below, n. 24 to chapter 18

13 H. Riley (ed.), *Ingulph's Chronicle of the Abbey of Croyland with the Continuations of Peter of Blois and Anonymous Writers* (London, 1908) (hereafter *Croyland Continuations*), 506

14 A good example is BL 16 F II, especially f. 137: this book, commissioned under Edward IV, was unfinished on the king's death and completed under Henry VII, whose artists liberally plastered it with red roses and other Lancastrian-Tudor insignia.

I Beginnings

1 : KING OF ALL THE WORLD

1 T. Johnes (ed.), *The Chronicles of Enguerrand de Monstrelet*, I 439

2 T. Rymer, *Foedera, conventiones, literae, et cujuscunque generis acta publica, inter reges Angliae, et alios quosuis imperatores, reges, . . . ab anno 1101, ad nostra usque tempora, habita aut tractata; . . . In lucem missa de mandato Reginae* (London, 1735), IX 907

3 Charles's murdered friend was the constable of France, Olivier de Clisson.

4 For a comprehensive discussion of Charles's illness, see R. C. Gibbons, *The Active Queenship of Isabeau of Bavaria, 1392–1417: Voluptuary, Virago or Villainess* (University of Reading, 1997), 27–40

5 *Henrici Quinti Angliae Regis Gratia*, quoted in *EHD* IV 211–18

6 Ibid.

7 For a succinct account of Henry's conquests following Agincourt, see J. Barker, *Conquest: The English Kingdom of France 1417–1450* (London, 2009), 1–45

8 In return for this Queen Isabeau in particular has never been popularly rehabilitated in French history. She is regularly slandered as the greatest whore and traitor of her age, whose numerous sexual misdeeds included an affair with Duke Philip and the bastard birth of the dauphin. For a sensitive rehabilitation see T. Adams, *The Life and Afterlife of Isabeau of Bavaria* (Baltimore, 2010) and Gibbons, *Active Queenship* and 'Isabeau of Bavaria' in *Transactions of the Royal Historical Society* 6 (1996)

9 Speed quoted in A. Strickland, *Lives of the Queens of England, from the Norman Conquest: With Anecdotes of their Courts* (12 vols, London, 1840–8), III 97

10 Ibid., III 98

11 J. Shirley (trans. and ed.), *A Parisian Journal 1405–1449* (Oxford, 1968), 151

12 Rymer, *Foedera*, IX 920

13 J. Watts, *Henry VI and the Politics of Kingship* (Cambridge, 1996), 113

14 Ibid., 439

15 Gower, quoted in G. L. Harriss, *Shaping the Nation: England 1360–1461* (Oxford, 2005), 588

16 Ibid., 588–94

17 The 'Agincourt Carol' is printed in *EHD* IV 214–15

18 Quoted in Strickland, *Queens of England*, III 101

19 D. Preest (trans.), and J. G. Clark (intro.), *The Chronica Majora of Thomas Walsingham (1376–1422)* (Woodbridge, 2005), 438

20 C. L. Kingsford, *Chronicles of London* (Oxford, 1905), 162–5

21 Strecche in *EHD* IV 229

22 Shirley (ed.), *Parisian Journal*, 356 n. 1

23 B. Wolffe, *Henry VI* (2nd edn, London, 2001), 28

24 For a discussion of all the royal minorities of medieval England, see C. Beem (ed.), *The Royal Minorities of Medieval and Early Modern England* (New York, 2008), passim

25 Ecclesiastes 10:16

2 : WE WERE IN PERFECT HEALTH

1　R. A. Griffiths, *The Reign of King Henry VI* (Stroud, 1981), 51–7;
　　Wolffe, *Henry VI*, 29–38

2　For more on the history of the residence, see R. Brook, *The Story of
　　Eltham Palace* (London, 1960), passim

3　H. M. Colvin, *History of the King's Works* (London, 1963), II 934–5

4　For the best explanation of the conceptual framework and reality
　　of government in the early fifteenth century, see Watts, *Henry VI*,
　　13–101

5　The regency of France was in fact first bequeathed by Henry's
　　will to Philip the Good of Burgundy, with a stipulation that if he
　　declined the task then rule should fall to Bedford; on Charles VI's
　　death this is precisely what happened.

6　Kingsford, *Chronicles of London*, 279–80

7　Ibid., 281

8　CCR Henry VI 1422–9, 46

9　CCR Henry VI 1422–9, 54

10　POPC III 233

11　POPC III 86–7

12　PROME 1428

13　J. Gairdner (ed.), *The Historical Collections of a Citizen of London in
　　the Fifteenth Century ('Gregory's Chronicle')* (1876), 159. For a detailed
　　summary of the Gloucester–Beaufort dispute, see Griffiths, *Henry
　　VI*, 73–81; G. L. Harriss, *Cardinal Beaufort: A Study of Lancastrian
　　Ascendancy and Decline* (Oxford, 1988), 134–49; and L. Rhymer,
　　'Humphrey Duke of Gloucester, and the City of London' in
　　L. Clark (ed.), *The Fifteenth Century* 8, 47–58

14　Ibid.

15　Pedro, duke of Coimbra was the second son of Philippa of Lan-
　　caster and her husband John I. His maternal grandfather was John
　　of Gaunt and he was, therefore, a first cousin, once removed, of
　　Henry VI. He was famous for his extensive travels about Europe,
　　and would return to England later in the 1420s for Henry VI's
　　coronation.

16　Kingsford, *Chronicles of London*, 84

3 : BORN TO BE KING

1 The best analysis of the battle of Verneuil is M. K. Jones, 'The Battle of Verneuil (17 August 1424): Towards a History of Courage' in *War in History* 9 (2002), which this account follows.

2 Shirley (ed.), *Parisian Journal*, 198; Jones, 'Battle of Verneuil', 398

3 'Book of Noblesse', quoted in ibid., 407. 'Worship' was a medieval concept perhaps best translated as 'honourable respect and gentility'.

4 Shirley (ed.), *Parisian Journal*, 200

5 BL Add. MS 18850 f. 256v

6 Jean de Wavrin, quoted in J. Stratford, *The Bedford Inventories: The Worldly Goods of John, Duke of Bedford, Regent of France (1389–1435)* (London, 1993), 108 n. 15

7 Barker, *Conquest*, 74. The French text of Bedford's 1423 ordinances may be found transcribed as an appendix to B. J. H. Rowe, 'Discipline in the Norman Garrisons under Bedford, 1422–35' in *EHR* 46 (1931) 200–6

8 Barker, *Conquest*, 67–9

9 B. J. H. Rowe, 'King Henry VI's Claim to France in Picture and Poem' in *The Library* s4, 13 (1932), 82

10 BL MS Royal 15 E VI, reprinted in part in S. McKendrick, J. Lowden and K. Doyle, *Royal Manuscripts: The Genius of Illumination* (London, 2011), 379 and available in full online at bl.uk/catalogues/illuminatedmanuscripts

11 Although Bedford did not realise it, this propaganda strategy would be the model – or at least the archetype – for rival kings on both sides of the Channel for the century that followed. See pp. 224–5.

12 Rowe, 'King Henry VI's Claim', 78

13 F. W. D. Brie, *The Brut: or, The Chronicles of England* (London, 1908), II 454. For the siege of Orléans and the role of Joan of Arc in its relief, see Barker, *Conquest*, 95–124.

14 For the latest biography of Joan, see Helen Castor's forthcoming *Joan of Arc* (London, 2014), which the account here follows in several places.

15 POPC III 340

16 See n. 15 to chapter 2. For details here included of the ceremony see *Brut*, II 454; *Gregory's Chronicle*, 161–77; the traditional order of

service for English coronations in the fifteenth century, known as the *Forma et Modus*, is printed and translated in L. G. Wickham Legg (ed.), *English Coronation Records* (London, 1901), 172–90

17 *Gregory's Chronicle*

18 *Brut*, II 460

19 Shirley (ed.), *Parisian Journal*, 271

20 Ibid., 272. Parisian snobbery about the culinary efforts of other races seems to be a timeless trait.

21 H. N. MacCracken, *Minor Poems of John Lydgate* (Oxford, 1961–2), II 630–1; J. G. Nichols, *Chronicle of the Grey Friars of London* (Camden Society, v53, 1852), 16

4 : OWEYN TIDR

1 F. Palgrave, *Antient Kalendars and Inventories of the Treasury of His Majesty's Exchequer* (London, 1836), II 172–5

2 POPC V 46–7

3 For the lives of Owen Tudor's ancestors, see R. A. Griffiths and R. S. Thomas, *The Making of the Tudor Dynasty* (Gloucester, 1985), 5–24, and R. L. Thomas, *The Political Career, Estates and 'Connection' of Jasper Tudor, Earl of Pembroke and Duke of Bedford (d. 1495)* (PhD thesis, University of Wales, Swansea, 1971), chapter 1, 1–29

4 Letter of Catherine de Valois quoted in *DNB*, 'Catherine de Valois'

5 J. A. Giles (ed.), *Incerti scriptoris chronicon Angliae de regnis trium regum Lancastriensium Henrici IV, Henrici V et Henrici VI* (London 1848), 17

6 Catherine's own family history told her this: her eldest sister Isabella had been the child bride of another king of England, Richard II, and following Richard's deposition and death she had returned to France to marry Charles duke of Orléans.

7 PROME February 1426, item 34

8 Sir John Wynn of Gwydir, quoted in Thomas, *Jasper Tudor*, 13

9 PROME September 1402, items 88–102

10 Harriss, *Cardinal Beaufort*, 178–9 n. 34, has speculated that Edmund Tudor may indeed have been the son of Catherine and Edmund Beaufort, in which case the later house of Tudor would have had Beaufort roots on both sides. It seems more probable to me that if

Edmund Beaufort had any relationship to Edmund Tudor then it was that of godfather, rather than biological father.

11 See Thomas, *Jasper Tudor*, 19–20

12 National Archives SC 8/124/6186

13 Excavations in the cemetery on the site at Bermondsey Abbey found a high incidence of bodily trauma, particularly of healed fractures among those buried there. Report by the Centre for Bioarchaeology, museumoflondon.org.

14 *Brut*, II 470–1

15 The account of Owen Tudor's arrest as given to the privy council, quoted here, is in POPC V 46–50

16 Ibid., 49–50. The article accompanying the council minute detailing Owen's arrest appears to be preparatory notes for a speech to the king himself, explaining what Owen had done, and rehearsing all the reasons why Henry ought to be outraged by his stepfather's 'malicious purpos and ymaginacion'.

17 See M. Bassett, 'Newgate Prison in the Middle Ages' in *Speculum* 18 (1943), passim

18 Robin Ddu quoted and translated in H. Evans, *Wales and the Wars of the Roses* (Cambridge, 1915), 70 n. 3

19 Priests were necessary to celebrate mass – then as now a rite which women were forbidden to perform. The most complete guide to medieval life at Barking Abbey can be found in T. Barnes, *A Nun's Life: Barking Abbey in the Late Medieval and Early Modern Periods* (MA thesis, Portland State University, 2004).

20 Rymer, *Foedera*, X 828

21 Thomas, *Jasper Tudor*, 26; Rymer, *Foedera*, X 828

II What is a King?

1 *Brut*, II 516

5 : MY LORD OF SUFFOLK'S GOOD LORDSHIP

1 For the idea that England's medieval population had begun to conceive of the historical coherence of the 'Hundred Years War' by the early fifteenth century, see W. M. Ormrod, 'The Domestic Response

to the Hundred Years War' in A. Curry and M. Hughes (eds), *Arms, Armies and Fortifications in the Hundred Years War* (Woodbridge, 1994), 83–5

2 C. D. Taylor, 'Henry V, Flower of Chivalry' in G. Dodd (ed.), *Henry V: New Interpretations* (York, 2013), 218. The Nine Worthies were Hector, Alexander the Great, Julius Caesar, Joshua, David, Judas Maccabeus, King Arthur, Charlemagne and Godfrey of Bouillon, hero of the First Crusade.

3 *Vita Henrici Quinti*, translated in J. Matusiak, *Henry V* (London, 2013), 3–4

4 For dating and provenance of the famous 'Windsor' portrait of Henry VI, see notes at http://www.npg.org.uk/collections/search/portraitConservation/mw03075/King-Henry-VI

5 See Griffiths, *Henry VI*, 241

6 POPC IV 134

7 M. James (ed.), *Henry VI: A Reprint of John Blacman's Memoir, with Translation and Notes* (Cambridge, 1919) (hereafter 'Blacman')

8 Ibid., 36–8

9 Harriss, *Cardinal Beaufort*, 251

10 Now catalogued in Stratford, *The Bedford Inventories*

11 *Brut*, II 573

12 Wolffe, *Henry VI*, 87–92; Watts, *Henry VI*, 128–34

13 POPC V 88–9

14 John de Wavrin (ed.), and W. Hardy (trans.), *A Collection of the Chronicles and Ancient Histories of Great Britain, Now Called England* (London, 1864–87), III 178

15 Ibid.; Barker, *Conquest*, 121–2

16 H. Castor, *The King, the Crown and the Duchy of Lancaster: Public Authority and Private Power 1399–1461* (Oxford, 2000), 82–93

17 J. Gairdner (ed.), *The Paston Letters* (new edn, 6 vols, London, 1904), IV 75

6 : A DEAR MARRIAGE

1 The fullest modern account of Margaret's coronation procession is in G. Kipling, 'The London Pageants for Margaret of Anjou' in *Medieval English Theatre* 4 (1982); a more widely available summary

is in H. Maurer, *Margaret of Anjou: Queenship and Power in Late Medieval England* (Woodbridge, 2003), 17–22

2 *Gregory's Chronicle*, 154

3 *Brut*, II 486

4 See above, p. 39

5 Maurer, *Margaret of Anjou*, 41

6 Ibid., 21

7 MacCracken, *Minor Poems of John Lydgate*, II 844–7

8 J. Rosenthal, 'The Estates and Finances of Richard Duke of York (1411–1460)' in *Studies in Medieval and Renaissance History* 2 (1965), 118

9 For a full list of York's manors, see ibid., appendix I 194–6

10 Commission transcribed from the original document in Bibliothèque nationale, Paris, in P. Johnson, *Duke Richard of York 1411–1460* (Oxford, 1988), 226

11 T. Pugh, 'Richard Plantagenet (1411–60), Duke of York, as the King's Lieutenant in France and Ireland' in J. G. Rowe (ed.), *Aspects of Late Medieval Government and Society: Essays Presented to J. R. Lander* (Toronto, 1986), 122

12 C. Carpenter, *The Wars of the Roses: Politics and the Constitution in England* c. *1437–1509* (Cambridge, 1997), 98–103, offers a succinct articulation of arguments against York as an isolated and ambitious rival for the crown during the 1440s. See also Watts, *Henry VI*, 237–8, especially nn. 137–40. A more 'dynastic' reading of the decade can be found in R. A. Griffiths, 'The Sense of Dynasty in the Reign of Henry VI' in C. Ross (ed.), *Patronage, Pedigree and Power in Later Medieval England* (Gloucester, 1979), passim but especially 23–5.

13 All this closely follows Griffiths, ibid., 20–1

14 Blacman, 29–30. Obviously, Blacman had an interest in talking up the king's piety and chastity; nevertheless, his portrayal of a squeamish king who would swoon at the sight of naked flesh is both internally consistent and at one with our broader understanding of Henry VI's character.

15 Maurer, *Margaret of Anjou*, 41

16 The jewel was a gift when Margaret was finally pregnant in 1453. J. Stevenson (ed.), *Letters and Papers Illustrative of the Wars of the English in France during the Reign of Henry the Sixth* (1861–4), II ii 208

17 Margaret's role in the cession of Maine is discussed in Maurer,

Margaret of Anjou, 25–38; also see B. M. Cron, 'The Duke of Suffolk, the Angevin Marriage, and the Ceding of Maine, 1445' in *Journal of Medieval History* 20 (1994), 77–99

18 *Brut*, II 511

19 J. David (ed.), *An English Chronicle of the Reigns of Richard II, Henry IV, Henry V and Henry VI* (Camden Society v44, 1838), 116

20 Ibid., 62

21 Ibid.

22 Kingsford, *Chronicles of London*, 157

7 : AWAY, TRAITORS, AWAY!

1 C. A. F. Meekings, 'Thomas Kerver's Case, 1444', in *EHR* 90 (1975), 330–46, from which the following narrative is taken.

2 *Brut*, II 485

3 Quoted in Griffiths, *Henry VI*, 256

4 Indictment from King's Bench, reprinted in *EHD* IV 264

5 PROME February 1449, item 22

6 'Between 1437 and 1450 throughout the shires of England the personal influence of the king in the field of justice, law and order was at best a negative one.' Wolffe, *Henry VI*, 116–17

7 See M. H. Keen and M. J. Daniel, 'English Diplomacy and the Sack of Fougères in 1449' in *History* 59, 375–91

8 Griffiths, *Henry VI*, 521; Harriss, *Shaping the Nation*, 584; Barker, *Conquest*, 404

9 A simple cash conversion of £372,000 at 1450 prices would give us a rough figure of £202,000,000 in 2005 prices. But this does not quite do justice to the monstrous scale of Henry VI's indebtedness, which according to the parliamentary figures was nearly 3,400% of his annual income and spiralling every year, regardless of the costs of war with France.

10 We would now call this the 'structural deficit'. PROME November 1449, item 53

11 A crude modern conversion of Richard's debts owed by the Crown would be £10 million. Again, this does no justice to the scale of the financial obligation.

12 In 1345 Edward III owed Italian merchants and bankers alone the

equivalent of £400,000 – perhaps £262,000,000 in 2005 prices. Cf. E. Russell, 'The Societies of the Bardi and the Peruzzi and Their Dealings with Edward III' in G. Unwin (ed.), *Finance and Trade under Edward III* (Manchester, 1918), 93–135

13 'A Warning to King Henry' in T. Wright, *Political Poems and Songs Relating to English History* (1859–61), II 229–31

14 PROME November 1449, item 15

15 Watts, *Henry VI*, 244–5

16 PROME November 1449, appendix 1

17 Ibid., item 49

18 Ibid., items 50–2

19 Frammesley was executed after a trial before the court of King's Bench. R. Virgoe, 'The Death of William de la Pole, Duke of Suffolk' in *Bulletin of the John Rylands Library* 47 (1965), 491 n. 3

20 *Paston Letters*, II 146–7; *Brut*, II 516; Virgoe, 'Death of William de la Pole', 494, 501

21 M. Bohna, 'Armed Force and Civic Legitimacy in Jack Cade's Revolt, 1450' in *EHR* 118 (2003), 573–4. For the course of Cade's rebellion and discussions of its causes, see also Griffiths, *Henry VI*, 610–65, and I. Harvey, *Jack Cade's Rebellion of 1450* (Oxford, 1991).

22 Magdalen College, Oxford, Charter Misc. 306, reprinted in Robbins (ed.), *Historical Poems*, 63, and with slight variation in C. L. Kingsford, *Historical Literature in the Fifteenth Century* (Oxford, 1913), 359

23 Stow published this in his *Annals*: it is partly reproduced and summarised in S. B. Chrimes and A. L. Brown, *Select Documents of English Constitutional History 1307–1485* (London, 1961), 290–1

24 Kingsford, *Chronicles of London*, 162

8 : THEN BRING IN THE DUKE OF YORK

1 Bill of the duke of York, reprinted in R. A. Griffiths, 'Duke Richard of York's Intentions in 1450 and the Origins of the Wars of the Roses' in *Journal of Medieval History* 1 (1975). 'Worship', i.e. worship, may be loosely likened to the modern concept of 'respect' – which was due to a man of great birth and status.

2 Griffiths believes, in ibid. and 'Richard Duke of York and the

Royal Household in Wales in 1449–50' in *Welsh History Review* 8 (1976–7), that York did in fact disembark at Beaumaris. Cf. Johnson, *Duke Richard of York*, 78: 'It is doubtful whether York managed a landing.' York's own bill to Henry VI states that his 'proposid' arrival was 'stoppid and forebarred'. This – and the fact that York included this complaint in his bill at all – implies strongly that the attempt to prevent his initial landing at Beaumaris was successful.

3 'John Piggot's Memoranda' in Kingsford, *English Historical Literature*, 372

4 HMC Eighth Report, 266–7, reprinted in modern English in *EHD* 4, 265–7

5 Ibid.

6 Ibid., 371

7 Carpenter, *Wars of the Roses*, 102

8 For an argument in favour of York's dynastic motivation see Griffiths, 'The Sense of Dynasty in the Reign of Henry VI'. But York's dynastic arguments in the context of the 1460s were made out of desperation (see pp. 182–3), in circumstances far removed from those of September 1450.

9 York's first petition to Henry VI, printed in Griffiths, 'Duke Richard of York's Intentions', 300

10 See Johnson, *Duke Richard of York*, 84–5

11 Ibid., 301–4

12 For a sympathetic view of Somerset's conduct in France, see M. K. Jones, 'York, Somerset and the Wars of the Roses' in *EHR* 104 (1989)

13 PROME November 1450, item 1

14 'Bale's Chronicle' in R. Flenley (ed.), *Six Town Chronicles of England* (Oxford, 1911), 137

15 Kingsford, *Chronicles of London*, 162

16 York had attempted, without royal licence, to settle the Courtenay–Bonville dispute himself earlier in September 1451. For a full account of the dispute, see M. Cherry, 'The Struggle for Power in Mid-Fifteenth-Century Devonshire' in R. A. Griffiths (ed.), *Patronage, the Crown and the Provinces in Later Medieval England* (New Jersey, 1981).

17 'Colleges: St Martin le Grand' in W. Page (ed.), *A History of the County of London* (London, 1909), I 555–66

18 A. Kempe, *Historical Notices of St Martin-le-Grand* (London, 1825), 141

19 *Paston Letters*, I 97–8

20 Ibid., 103–8

21 Kingsford, *Chronicles of London*, 163. Several more chronicles carry similar versions of this story. For a persuasive argument against believing this popular vignette, see Johnson, *Duke Richard of York*, 112.

22 Ibid., 101

9 : SMITTEN WITH A FRENZY

1 'Bale's Chronicle' in Flenley (ed.), *Six Town Chronicles*, 140; Kingsford, *Chronicles of London*, 163. In modern terms Henry's illness might be characterised as a severe, catatonic episode of either depression or schizophrenia, but medical diagnosis is impossible and essentially futile at such a distance. For a recent discussion of Henry's illness with reference to modern diagnostics, see N. Bark, 'Did Schizophrenia Change the Course of English History?' in *Medical Hypotheses* 59 (2002), 416–21, although note that the author's interpretation of the historical course of Henry's reign prior to 1453 differs sharply from that presented here. For Henry's illness in context of his times and his family history, see B. Clarke, *Mental Disorder in Earlier Britain* (Cardiff, 1975), passim but especially 176–206.

2 'Bale's Chronicle', 140

3 The other godparents were Cardinal Archbishop Kemp of Canterbury and Anne duchess of Buckingham.

4 POPC VI 163–4

5 Council minutes transcribed in R. A. Griffiths, 'The King's Council and York's First Protectorate', *EHR* 94 (1984)

6 Newsletter of John Stodeley in *Paston Letters*, I 295

7 For a full discussion see H. Castor, *She-Wolves: The Women Who Ruled England before Elizabeth* (London, 2010), 339–43

8 PROME March 1453, item 32

9 Watts, *Henry VI*, 310 n. 220

10 Stodeley in *Paston Letters*, I 299

11 *Paston Letters*, III 13

12 PROME July 1455, item 18

13 Watts gives the Leicester meeting the pleasing title of a 'pseudo-parliament': Watts, *Henry VI*, 314

14 C. J. Armstrong, 'Politics and the Battle of St Albans 1455' in *Bulletin of the Institute of Historical Research* 33 (1960), 13–14. This remains the authoritative account of the first battle of St Albans, and much of the account here follows its arguments.

15 Letter to the townsmen of Coventry, quoted in ibid., 12

16 *Paston Letters*, III 25

17 For Clifford's conduct, ibid. and M. Kekewich et al. (eds), *The Politics of Fifteenth-Century England – John Vale's Book* (Stroud, 1996), 192

18 *Paston Letters*, III 27

19 Blacman, 40

20 MS Gough London in Flenley (ed.), *Six Town Chronicles*, 158

21 'Bale's Chronicle' in ibid., 142

22 *Gregory's Chronicle*, 198

23 CSP Milan, I 16–17

III The Hollow Crown

1 CSP Milan I, 1471 item 227

10 : PRINCESS MOST EXCELLENT

1 *Victoria County History*, 'Warwickshire', VIII 418–27

2 Pius II, quoted in P. Lee, 'Reflections of Power: Margaret of Anjou and the Dark Side of Queenship' in *Renaissance Quarterly* 39 (1986), 197

3 M. Harris (ed. and trans.), *The Coventry Leet Book, or Mayor's Register* (New York, 1971), I–II 287–92

4 Robbins (ed.), *Historical Poems*, 190

5 The correspondent was John Bocking; *Paston Letters*, III 75

6 *Brut*, II 526; Davies, *English Chronicle*, 79

7 *Brut*, II 525

8 Ibid.

9 MS Gough London in Flenley (ed.), *Six Town Chronicles*, 160; *Paston Letters*, III 130

10 Davies, *English Chronicle*, 80

11 *English Heritage Battlefield Report: Blore Heath* (English Heritage, 1995), 8–9
12 Griffiths, *Henry VI*, 821
13 The letter is preserved in Davies, *English Chronicle*, 81–3
14 Ibid., 83
15 *Brut*, II 527
16 *Gregory's Chronicle*, 206
17 Davies, *English Chronicle*, 83, also records that the duchess of Yorke 'unmanly and cruelly was entreted and spoyled'. It has been suggested – most recently in P. Langley and M. Jones, *The King's Grave: The Search for Richard III* (London, 2013), 73, 235 – that this reference indicates Duchess Cecily was raped at Ludlow in full sight of her children: this is a rather sensational interpretation of the evidence.

11 : SUDDENLY FELL DOWN THE CROWN

1 Davies, *English Chronicle*, 83. On Warwick and Calais see S. Rose, *Calais: An English Town in France 1347–1558* (Woodbridge, 2008), 81–3, also Richmond, 'The Earl of Warwick's Domination of the Channel', passim
2 PROME November 1459, items 7–25
3 G. Harriss and M. Harriss (eds), *John Benet's Chronicle for the Years 1400 to 1462* (Camden Miscellany 44, 1972), 224
4 Davies, *English Chronicle*, 86–90
5 Ibid., 97
6 CPR Henry VI 1452–61, 542
7 H. Stanford London, *Royal Beasts* (East Knoyle, 1956), 22–3. It is also important to note that the falcon and fetterlock had explicitly 'Lancastrian' connections. The diametric, 'Tudor' view of the whole fifteenth century as a feud between rival houses is not sufficient to explain Richard duke of York's motives at this stage.
8 *Gregory's Chronicle*, 208
9 Official papers and letters were usually dated from the accession of whichever king was reigning. To renounce this practice implicitly rejected the authority of the sovereign.
10 Letter to John Tiptoft, earl of Worcester, transcribed in Johnson, *Duke Richard of York*, 213–14

11 Ibid.

12 PROME October 1460, item 11. This is the first recorded use in the fifteenth century of the dynastic sobriquet 'Plantagenet', used thereafter and now to describe all the royal descendants of Geoffrey 'Plantagenet', count of Anjou, duke of Normandy and father of Henry II of England.

13 A successful precedent from the earliest Plantagenet history was the treaty of Wallingford of 1153, sealed between King Stephen and the future Henry II, by which Stephen's son Eustace was disinherited in Henry's favour: this ended the civil war known as the Anarchy.

14 CSP Milan I, item 27

15 *Brut*, II 530

16 *Gregory's Chronicle*, 209

17 Letter reprinted in Kekewich et al., *John Vale's Book*, 142–3

18 *Brut*, II 530

19 E. Hall, *Hall's Chronicle containing the History of England during the Reign of Henry the Fourth and the Succeeding Monarchs to the End of the Reign of Henry the Eighth* (London, 1809), 250

20 This, at any rate, is the story that Edward Hall would record many years later – his version of events is typically colourful, but the source was Aspall himself. Hall, *Chronicle*, 250–1

21 CSP Venice I, item 92

12 : HAVOC

1 *Paston Letters*, III 250

2 This is now called a parhelion or 'sun dog', and is caused by the reflection of sunlight through ice crystals in the atmosphere. Hall, *Chronicle*, 251, gives the earliest link between this and Edward's badge of the golden sun. But this may be a mistake: Stanford London, *Royal Beasts*, 30–1, argues that the 'sun shining' had been a royal symbol since at least the days of Richard II.

3 *Gregory's Chronicle*, 211

4 Ibid. The possible and quite plausible identification of the woman as Owen Tudor's mistress and David Tudor's mother is made in L. De Lisle, *Tudor: The Family Story* (London, 2013), 25

5 The letter was sent on 11 January, on which day Warwick also dictated a letter to the warlike Francesco Sforza, duke of Milan. CSP Milan I, item 55

6 Ibid. item 63

7 Ibid., item 54

8 H. Riley (ed.), *Registrum Abbatiae Johannis Whethamstede* (London, 1872), 390–5

9 Ibid.

10 Ibid.

11 *Brut*, II 531

12 The dating of March's entry into London to 26 February 1461 and a discussion of the symbolism of his inauguration and coronation can be found in C. Armstrong, 'The Inauguration Ceremonies of the Yorkist Kings and Their Title to the Throne' in *Transactions of the Royal Historical Society* 30 (1948), 55 n. 2 and passim

13 *Gregory's Chronicle*, 213

14 Kingsford, *Chronicles of London*, 173

15 MS Gough London in Flenley (ed.), *Six Town Chronicles*, 162

16 CCR 1461–8, 54–5

17 T. Stapleton (ed.), *Plumpton Correspondence* (London, 1834), 1

18 CCR 1461–8, 54–5

19 Pierpoint Morgan Library, New York, M 775 f. 122v, quoted at length in A. Boardman, *The Medieval Soldier in the Wars of the Roses* (Stroud, 1998), 126–7

20 Hall, *Chronicle*, 255. For once the notoriously inflated assessments of army sizes have the semblance of authenticity.

21 For this suggestion, G. Goodwin, *Fatal Colours: Towton 1461 – England's Most Brutal Battle* (London, 2011), 157

22 Ibid., 165–6

23 CSP Milan I, item 78; CSP Venice I, item 371

13 : THE NOBLE AND THE LOWLY

1 C. Armstrong (ed. and trans.), *The Usurpation of Richard III: Dominicus Mancinus ad Angelum de occupatione regni Anglie per Ricardum tercium libellus* (2nd edn, 1969) (hereafter 'Mancini'), 65

2 Mancini, 67; *Croyland Continuations*, 150–1

3 J. Halliwell (ed.), *A Chronicle of the First Thirteen Years of the Reign of King Edward the Fourth: by John Warkworth* (London, 1889) (hereafter 'Warkworth'), 5

4 Reading Abbey had other royal connections, too: among the hundreds of relics kept by the abbey's brothers was a portion of the arm-bone of St Edward the Martyr, the Saxon king who had been murdered at Corfe Castle in 978, while Henry II's eldest but short-lived son William lay buried within the abbey. *Victoria County History*, 'Berkshire', II 62–73

5 *Gregory's Chronicle*, p. 226

6 Wavrin, *Chronicles and Ancient Histories of Great Britain*, III 184

7 This description is based on the most contemporary of those portraits that survive, held at Queens' College, Cambridge, and Windsor. Clearly, as in all royal portraiture of the period, there is an element of idealism and fancy to these images, but perhaps less than there is in the manuscript illustrations of Elizabeth, which depict a blonde, pious generic queen in the guise of the Virgin Mary. For a guide to extant portraits, see D. MacGibbon, *Elizabeth Woodville (1437–1492): Her Life and Times* (London, 1938), appendix 1, 172–4

8 *Paston Letters*, III 204–5

9 Warkworth, 3

10 See, for example, Mancini, 63

11 CSP Milan I, item 137

12 The only vaguely contemporary royal match to resemble that of Edward IV and Elizabeth Woodville was that between Edward 'the Black Prince' and his notorious, much-wedded cousin Joan of Kent, which took place in 1361, when Edward was heir to the crown (and referred to informally as 'Edward IV'). Even in this case, however, Joan's royal stock was impeccable: her grandfathers were Edward I of England and Philip III of France.

13 J. Gairdner (ed.), *Letters and Papers Illustrative of the Reigns of Richard III and Henry VII* (London, 1861), I 32

14 *Croyland Continuations*, 115

15 Letter from Lord Wenlock dated 3 October 1464: see J. Lander, 'Marriage and Politics: The Nevilles and the Wydevilles' in *Bulletin of the Institute of Historical Research* 36 (1963) 133 n. 2(a) and C. Scofield, *The Life and Reign of Edward IV* (London, 1923), I 354 n. 3; CSP Milan I, items 137–8

16 A good historical comparison is Henry VIII's second marriage, to
    Anne Boleyn – a match of shattering political significance brought
    about principally because of Henry's romantic attachment and
    frustration. Edward IV was not, even at twenty-two, as selfish and
    self-centred an individual as Henry VIII, but he was certainly
    capable of viewing policy decisions through the lens of his own per-
    sonal desires.

17 *Gregory's Chronicle*, 219

18 *Paston Letters*, III 292

19 Ibid.

20 Amusing but fanciful sixteenth-century accounts of the royal court-
    ship in Fabyan, More, Hall and others have found their way readily
    into modern histories, particularly MacGibbon, *Elizabeth Woodville*,
    34–40, which on this matter reads more like fiction than history.

21 Carpenter, *Wars of the Roses*, 170

22 MacGibbon, *Elizabeth Woodville*, 46

23 Ibid., 48–51

24 Scofield, *Edward IV*, 380–4

25 Warkworth, 5

14 : DIVERSE TIMES

1 Philadelphia Free Library MS Lewis E 201 – this can be viewed
   in high resolution online via http://bancroft.berkeley.edu/
   digitalscriptorium/. On the golden sun and its links to Richard II,
   see above, n. 11 to chapter 10. Other similar genealogies, although
   less spectacular, include BL Harley Roll C.9 Membrane 19; BL
   Harley 7353; BL Lansdowne 456.

2 Elizabeth de Burgh's marriage to Lionel of Antwerp in 1352 had
   originally brought the honour of Ulster into the Plantagenet line.
   See A. Weir, *Elizabeth of York: The First Tudor Queen* (London, 2013),
   14

3 M. Hicks, *Warwick the Kingmaker* (Oxford, 1998), 254

4 C. Ross, *Edward IV* (new edn, London and New Haven, 1997),
   appendix III, 437–8

5 *Gregory's Chronicle*, 237

6 Scofield, *Edward IV*, 414–20

7 Hicks, *Warwick the Kingmaker*, 267
8 S. Bentley (ed.), *Excerpta Historica: or, Illustrations of English History* (1831), 227–8
9 Warkworth, 4
10 Stevenson (ed.), *Letters and Papers*, II, part 2, 783
11 *Gregory's Chronicle*, 237
12 Ibid.
13 Warkworth, 5
14 PROME June 1467, item 15
15 *Croyland Continuations*, 132–3
16 Mancini, 63
17 Roughly £2,250,000
18 'False, fleeting, perjured Clarence', as Shakespeare would later have it (*Richard III*, I iv 52)
19 For this and a general discussion of the 1469 rebellions, including problems of evidence, see K. Dockray, 'The Yorkshire Rebellions of 1469', in *The Ricardian* 82 (1983), passim
20 Warkworth, 6; *Croyland Continuations*, 445
21 *Paston Letters*, V 35
22 The letter and manifesto are printed in the notes to Warkworth, 46–9
23 *Croyland Continuations*, 446
24 Warkworth, 7
25 Ibid.

15 : FINAL DESTRUCTION

1 *Paston Letters*, V 45–6
2 *Croyland Continuations*, 438
3 'Chronicle of the Rebellion in Lincolnshire, 1470', 18, in K. Dockray (ed.), *Three Chronicles of the Reign of Edward IV* (Gloucester, 1988)
4 Ibid., 10
5 CSP Milan I, 1467, item 146
6 *Paston Letters*, V 83
7 Warkworth, 11
8 *Croyland Continuations*, 462
9 Ibid.

10 Blacman, 41

11 CSP Milan I, 1471, item 210

12 'The Arrival of King Edward IV', 4, in Dockray (ed.), *Three Chronicles of the Reign of Edward IV*. Bolingbroke, of course, claimed to be returning from exile in France in 1399 to claim his usurped right to the duchy of Lancaster.

13 Ibid., 7

14 Ibid., 10

15 Cited in Ross, *Edward IV*, 166

16 A. Scobie (ed.), *The Memoirs of Philip de Commines, Lord of Argenton* (London, 1877) (hereafter 'Commines'), 200

17 A. Thomas and I. Thornley (eds), *The Great Chronicle of London* (London, 1938), 215

18 Ibid.

19 Letter from Margaret of York, printed in Wavrin, *Chronicles and Ancient Histories of Great Britain*, III 211

20 J. Bruce (ed.), *Historie of the Arrivall of Edward IV in England and the Finall Recouerye of His Kingdomes from Henry VI* (London, 1838), 17

21 Ibid.

22 *Croyland Continuations*, 464

23 Bruce, *Arrivall of Edward IV*, 19–20

24 Ibid.

25 Ibid.

26 Commines, 201

27 Scofield, *Edward IV*, I 579–60

28 Bruce, *Arrivall of Edward IV*, 20

29 Von Wesel's letter of 17 April 1471, translated and reprinted most recently in H. Kleineke (ed. and trans.), 'Gerhard von Wesel's Newsletter from England, 17 April 1471' in *The Ricardian* 16 (2006)

30 Ibid., 10

31 Ibid. The Neville brothers were granted a decent burial by Edward: their bodies were removed to Bisham Abbey to be laid to rest near their father, the earl of Salisbury.

32 Letter to John Daunt, quoted in P. Hammond, *The Battles of Barnet and Tewkesbury* (1993), 81

33 *Croyland Continuations*, 465

34 CSP Milan I, 1471, item 216

35 Bruce, *Arrival of Edward IV*, 28

36 Ibid.
37 *Croyland Continuations*, 466
38 Bruce, *Arrivall of Edward IV*, 28–30, for all that follows, unless indicated
39 Warkworth, 18
40 *Croyland Continuations*, 466
41 Ibid., 467
42 Blacman, 44
43 Bruce, *Arrivall of Edward IV*, 38
44 Warkworth, 21
45 W. St John Hope, 'The Discovery of the Remains of King Henry VI in St George's Chapel, Windsor Castle' in *Archaeologia* (1911), 541
46 CSP Milan I, 1471, item 220
47 Ibid., 39
48 *Croyland Continuations*, 467

IV The Rise of the Tudors

16 : TO EXECUTE WRATH

1 Robbins (ed.), *Historical Poems*, 148
2 H. Ellis (ed.), *Three Books of Polydore Vergil's English History* (London, 1844), 154–5
3 Griffiths and Thomas, *Making of the Tudor Dynasty*, 86–7. Bad weather marred the Tudors' crossing of the Channel.
4 *Foedera*, XI 714, quoted in M. Hicks, *Edward V: The Prince in the Tower* (Stroud, 2003), 57–8
5 *Paston Letters*, IV 298
6 The Black Book, or *Liber Niger Domus Regis Edw. IV*, is printed in *A Collection of Ordinances and Regulations for the Government of the Household etc.* (London, 1790), 15–86
7 See D. Starkey, 'Henry VI's Old Blue Gown: The English Court under the Lancastrians and the Yorkists' in *The Court Historian*, 1999, passim but especially 20–4
8 The weak and sickly Herbert earl of Pembroke was deprived of his title in 1479, when it was given to Prince Edward, and Herbert was forced to accept a demotion to the earldom of Huntingdon.

9 Had Warwick died a natural death, his brother Montague would have inherited the Neville patrimony; the daughters would have received the rest. Since Montague also died in battle against the king, and was posthumously convicted of treason, the entire Warwick inheritance came into royal hands.

10 Carpenter, *Wars of the Roses*, 187

11 Ibid., 193–4

12 R. Buckley et al., 'The King in the Car Park: New Light on the Death and Burial of Richard III in the Grey Friars Church, Leicester in 1485' in *Antiquity* 87 (2013), 536

13 Poppelau, quoted in Mancini, 136–7

14 Colvin, *History of the King's Works*, I 499–500

15 Or, in the more famous, more modern rendering given by the King James Bible, 'The Lord is my shepherd: I shall not want.' Psalm 23:1. For a detailed excerpt of Rotherham's speech to parliament, PROME January 1478, items 1–3

16 Romans 13:4

17 In order to force Clarence to relinquish lands for redistribution to, among others, Gloucester, Edward had been forced to issue a general act of resumption in the parliament of 1473, excluding Clarence from a long list of persons exempted. For full details of the Clarence–Gloucester land feud, see Hicks, *False, Fleeting, Perjur'd Clarence: George Duke of Clarence 1449–78* (Gloucester, 1992), 111–27

18 The details of the Twynho case are contained in the petition by her 'cousin' (probably her brother-in-law) Roger Twynho, who applied for and received a royal pardon on her behalf in 1478. One John Thursby was also hanged at the same proceedings on the equally specious charge of having murdered Clarence's son Richard. PROME January 1478, item 17; Hicks, *False, Fleeting, Perjur'd Clarence*, 137–9

19 *Croyland Continuations*, 478

20 Ibid.

21 PROME January 1478, appendix 1

22 For a discussion of the malmsey wine story, see Hicks, *False, Fleeting, Perjur'd Clarence*, 200–4

23 Romans 13:2

17 : THE ONLY IMP NOW LEFT

1 Commines, I 397

2 Ellis (ed.), *Polydore Vergil*, 164

3 Griffiths and Thomas, *Making of the Tudor Dynasty*, 88–90

4 Commines, I 251

5 Ellis (ed.), *Polydore Vergil*, 164–5

6 Ibid., 135; J. Lewis (ed.), *Life of Dr John Fisher* (London, 1855), II 269

7 M. Jones and M. Underwood, *The King's Mother: Lady Margaret Beaufort, Countess of Richmond and Derby* (Cambridge, 1993), 58–9; MacGibbon, *Elizabeth Woodville*, 108

8 Jones and Underwood, *King's Mother*, 61, quoting Westminster Abbey Muniments doc. 32378

9 *Croyland Continuations*, 483

10 Commines, I 264

11 Vergil's pen-portrait was consistent with every other in also praising the king's 'wit', 'high courage' and 'retentive memory', his diligence, his tendency to be 'earnest and horrible to the enemy [but] bountiful to his friends and acquaintance' and his fortune in war. Ellis (ed.), *Polydore Vergil*, 172

12 Mancini, 66–7

13 Thomas Basin, quoted in Scofield, *Edward IV*, 365

14 R. Gottfried, 'Epidemic Disease in Fifteenth-Century England' in *Journal of Economic History* 36 (1976), 267–8, notes cases of influenza in the fifteenth century, 'although it was not particularly virulent until 1485'.

15 Mancini, 70–1

16 W. Crotch, *The Prologues and Epilogues of William Caxton* (London, 1928), 39

17 BL MS Sloane 3479, f. 53v

18 Ibid., 69

19 *Croyland Continuations*, 485

20 Mancini, 74–5

21 Gairdner (ed.), *Letters and Papers*, I 4

22 *Croyland Continuations*, 487

23 Mancini, 82–3

24 *Croyland Continuations*, 487, although the author writes with

hindsight and may well be influenced here by his knowledge of subsequent events

25 *Great Chronicle*, 230

26 *Croyland Continuations*, 488

27 C. Carpenter (ed.), *Kingsford's Stonor Letters and Papers 1290–1483* (Cambridge, 1996), 416

28 *Croyland Continuations*, 489

29 Mancini, 90–1

30 For a level-headed discussion of the arguments over Edward V's (and Edward IV's) supposed illegitimacy, see Hicks, *Edward V*, 163–6

31 Mancini, 96–7

32 *Croyland Continuations*, 489

33 Noted by Mancini 104–5: the English were well known for their fondness for cryptic prophecies of this sort.

34 A. Sutton and P. Hammond, *The Coronation of Richard III: The Extant Documents* (Gloucester, 1983), 77–9, 294–5

35 *Great Chronicle*, 233

18 : JUDGE ME, O LORD

1 The *Great Chronicle of London*, 234, reports sightings of the boys during the mayoralty of Sir Edmund Shaa, which ran from Michaelmas 1482 to Michaelmas 1483, although the chronicler misdates this by a year, and subsequently garbles the sequence of events between the disappearance of the princes, the death of Queen Anne, Buckingham's rebellion and Richard's apparent plan to marry Elizabeth of York.

2 Horrox and Hammond (eds), BL Harleian MSS 433, III 2

3 Ibid., 234

4 Mancini, 92–3

5 Ibid.

6 Ibid.

7 The *Great Chronicle* dates public rumours of their disappearance to 'after Easter', a date we can deduce to be 18 April 1484. But see n. 3 to chapter 18 for concerns over the chronicler's dating of events during this period.

8 The remains found during that excavation are now kept at Westminster Abbey. They were tested, very inadequately, in 1933 in an attempt to determine cause of death. For a discussion, see P. Hammond and W. White, 'The Sons of Edward IV: A Re-examination of the Evidence on Their Deaths and on the Bones in Westminster Abbey' in Hammond (ed.), *Richard III: Loyalty, Lordship and Law* (London, 1986), 104–47. Buckingham Palace and Westminster Abbey oppose further tests being carried out on the remains. A recent e-petition to HM Government requesting DNA analysis on the remains accrued only 408 signatures (www.thepetitionsite.org).

9 For the welter of grants to Buckingham, which effectively gave him power over the whole of Wales and the western marches, see Horrox and Hammond (eds), Harleian MS 433, II 3–4

10 As set forth in *Titulus Regius*, PROME January 1484, item 5

11 Ellis (ed.), *Polydore Vergil*, 200 ('circumspection and celerity') and 226–7. The analysis of Richard's skeleton and teeth performed in Leicester in 2012–13 confirmed his spinal deformation and worn molars.

12 *Croyland Continuations*, 490

13 Commines, II 64

14 Ellis (ed.), *Polydore Vergil*, 197

15 As described in the act of attainder passed posthumously against Buckingham, PROME January 1484, item 3

16 E.g. Ellis (ed.), *Polydore Vergil*, 192–3

17 Or to borrow the delicious phrase of Carpenter, *Wars of the Roses*, 212, 'he was a worthless man, and probably few lamented his passing'.

18 Griffiths and Thomas, *Making of the Tudor Dynasty*, 102–5; Jones and Underwood, *King's Mother*, 62–3

19 Ellis (ed.), *Polydore Vergil*, 199

20 Ibid.

21 A. Raine (ed.), *York Civic Records* (Wakefield, 1939), I 83

22 L. Gill, *Richard III and Buckingham's Rebellion* (Stroud, 1999), 68

23 Ellis (ed.), *Polydore Vergil*, 202

24 PROME January 1484, item 5

25 *Croyland Continuations*, 496

26 Text printed in P. Hammond and A. Sutton, *Richard III: The Road to Bosworth Field* (London, 1985), 151

27 See ibid., 151–2

28 PROME January 1484, item 21

29 PROME January 1484, item 27

30 R. Horrox, *Richard III: A Study of Service* (Cambridge, 1989), 325–6

31 A few entries from Prince Edward's accounts are printed in Hammond and Sutton, *Richard III*, 174–5

32 Ibid., 497. A tomb at the church of St Helen and the Holy Cross in Sheriff Hutton may be that of Edward, although another tradition holds that he was buried at his birthplace in Middleham.

33 Edward of Middleham was Richard's only legitimate son. He had two, and possibly three illegitimate children: Sir John of Pontefract, captain of Calais; Katherine Plantagenet, who married William Herbert in 1484, but died a few years later; and, possibly, a boy called Richard Plantagenet, who was born around 1469 and died in December 1550, having lived his life anonymously as a London bricklayer. The eighteenth-century antiquarian Francis Peck recorded a family legend he had heard about Richard Plantagenet: before his death he supposedly claimed to have been an observer at Bosworth and to have been presented there to his father the king on the night before the battle. The story is unproveable, but a tomb to Richard Plantagenet lies in the ruined church of St Mary's in Eastwell, Kent.

34 Horrox and Hammond (eds), Harleian MSS 433, III 124–5

35 Ibid., III 190

36 *Croyland Continuations*, 499. There is evidence, albeit difficult and inconclusive evidence, to suggest that Elizabeth was aware of Richard's intentions and may even have been considering them favourably. This has most recently been discussed by Weir, *Elizabeth of York*, 130–8, who concludes after some consideration that 'there is no evidence as to [Elizabeth's] true feelings for Richard III'.

37 *Paston Letters*, VI 81–4

38 Ellis (ed.), *Polydore Vergil*, 204

39 Commines, II 64

40 *Great Chronicle*, 237

19 : WAR OR LIFE

1 These three standards were presented later in the year at St Paul's – we assume here that they had been associated with Henry's campaign from his arrival in England.

2 Henry's letters are quoted and discussed in Griffiths and Thomas, *Making of the Tudor Dynasty*, 159–65

3 *Croyland Continuations*, 502

4 Ellis (ed.), *Polydore Vergil*, 221. Vergil uses this to suggest the king's conscience 'guilty of heinous offences'; but *Croyland Continuations*, 503, agrees, suggesting that the king woke and 'declared that during the night he had seen dreadful visions, and had imagined himself surrounded by a multitude of demons'. Neither source could be described as sympathetic to Richard – nevertheless, both were by assiduous and well-informed writers.

5 Ellis (ed.), *Polydore Vergil*, 225

6 Ibid., 223

7 Ibid., 224

8 Ibid.

9 As revealed in analysis of Richard III's skeleton carried out by the University of Leicester in 2012–13, nicely summarised by Dr Jo Appleby at http://www.le.ac.uk/richardiii/science/osteology.html

10 Ellis (ed.), *Polydore Vergil*, 224

11 *Croyland Continuations*, 505

12 *Great Chronicle*, 238

13 Ibid., 239

14 The accounts for Henry's coronation are in Wickham Legg, *English Coronation Records*, 198–218

15 Ibid. and S. Anglo, *Spectacle, Pageantry and Early Tudor Policy* (Oxford, 1969), 11

16 When the first Lancastrian king, Henry IV (then merely Henry Bolingbroke, duke of Hereford), had sallied forth for his duel with Thomas Mowbray, duke of Norfolk at Coventry in September 1398 his pavilion 'was covered with red roses': Williams, *Chronique de la traison et mort*, 153; the royal treasure subsequently taken over by Henry IV contained numerous items decorated with roses of different hues: Palgrave, *Antient Kalendars*, III 313–58. '*Rhos cochion mewn rhwysg uchel*': quoted and translated in Evans, *Wales and the Wars of the Roses*, 6

17 PROME November 1485, part I, item 9

18 Gairdner (ed.), *Letters and Papers*, 421

19 B. André, *The Life of Henry VII*, trans. D. Hobbins (New York, 2011), 34

20 Ibid., 35

21 Raine (ed.), *York Civic Records*, I 156–9

22 An interesting point of comparison is the birth of Edward II at Caernarfon Castle in 1284 – another focal point of Arthuriana.

23 The deeds of these kings were not just entertainment: often they were intended for political education, too. In 1457 the scholar James Hardyng had produced a monumental History, which expounded on the deeds of the kings, beginning in the days of Brutus. Hardyng had presented his work to Henry VI, who appeared to take no notice of the moral that was intended.

24 André, *Life of Henry VII*, 38

20 : ENVY NEVER DIES

1 Simnel's origins are discussed at length in M. Bennett, *Lambert Simnel and the Battle of Stoke* (Gloucester, 1987), 42–55

2 D. Hay (ed.), *The Anglica Historia of Polydore Vergil, AD 1485–1537* (London, 1950), 13

3 André, *Life of Henry VII*, 47 ('Admirably skilled . . .')

4 Ibid., 46

5 Ibid.

6 Hay (ed.), *The Anglica Historia of Polydore Vergil*, 63

7 PROME November 1485, part I, item 8

8 As, indeed, it still is.

9 Hay (ed.), *The Anglica Historia of Polydore Vergil*, 56–7

10 André, *Life of Henry VII*, 60

11 Hay (ed.), *The Anglica Historia of Polydore Vergil*, 67

12 Ibid., 75

13 André, *Life of Henry VII*, 66

14 Warbeck's Scottish expenses are printed in Gairdner (ed.), *Letters and Papers*, II 326–35

15 André, *Life of Henry VII*, 68

16 Hay (ed.), *The Anglica Historia of Polydore Vergil*, 67

21 : BLANCHE ROSE

1　Licentiate Alcaraz, quoted in G. Tremlett, *Catherine of Aragon: Henry's Spanish Queen* (London, 2010), 69

2　G. Kipling (ed.), *The Receyt of the Ladie Kateryne* (Oxford, 1990), 39

3　J. Guy, *The Children of Henry VIII* (Oxford, 2013), 4; D. Starkey, *Six Wives: The Queens of Henry VIII* (London, 2004), 76–7

4　A third son, Prince Edmund, had been born in 1499, but died in 1500.

5　Thomas, *Jasper Tudor*, 19–20

6　Hay (ed.), *The Anglica Historia of Polydore Vergil*, 123

7　Seward, *Last White Rose*, 138

8　PROME January 1504, item 21

9　Philip claimed the crown in right of his wife; Joanna's mother, Queen Isabella of Castile, had died in November 1504. Isabella's other daughter, of course, was Katherine of Aragon.

10　*Great Chronicle*, 330

11　Hay (ed.), *The Anglica Historia of Polydore Vergil*, 135

12　In Flanders the treaty was known as the *Malus Intercursus* – the Evil Treaty – because it was so skewed towards English interests.

13　Kingsford (ed.), *The First English Life of Henry V* (Oxford, 1911), 4

14　See for example BL Royal 8 G. vii; BL Royal 11 E. xi; BL Add MS 88929

15　The battle of Flodden was won on Catherine's watch, on 9 September 1513.

16　Hay (ed.), *The Anglica Historia of Polydore Vergil*, 203

17　L&P IV nos 1123 and 1131

18　This conversation is reported by R. Macquereau, *Histoire générale de l'Europe* (Louvain, 1765), and repeated in Scarisbrick, *Henry VIII*, 136. It is unsourced and may be apocryphal. The first mention of de la Pole's death in the official record is to be found in L&P IV no. 1131: a letter of a clerk to Wolsey dated 28 February 1525. Yet Macquereau's anecdote captures very well the relief that Henry surely felt at the termination of the de la Pole line.

EPILOGUE

1 J. Osborn (ed.), *The Quenes Maiesties Passage through the Citie of London to Westminster the Day before her Coronacion* (New Haven, 1960), 31–3

2 See, for example, the large Tudor rose in the stained-glass window at Great Malvern Priory, which sits to the left of the arms of Henry VIII and Katherine of Aragon, or Katherine of Aragon's window in the Quire at St George's Chapel, Windsor.

3 Hall, 'Union of the Two Noble and Illustre Famelies'. As if the point were not sufficiently made, in his introduction addressed to the young King Edward VI, Hall pointed out that 'I haue compiled and gathered (and not made) out of diurse writers, as well forayne as Englishe, this simple treatise whiche I haue named the vnion of the noble houses of Lancaster and Yorke, conioyned together by the godly marriage of your moste noble graundfather [i.e. Henry VII], and your verteous grandmother [i.e. Elizabeth of York]. For as king henry the fourthe was the beginning and rote of the great discord and deusion: so was the godly matrimony, the final ende of all discencions, titles and debates.' Hall, *Chronicle*, vii

4 Stow's 1550 edition of Chaucer, Trinity College, Cambridge, STC 5075, 5076

5 *1 Henry VI*, II iv 27–73

6 Arranged according to historical chronology, the full list of plays is *Richard II*, *Henry IV Part 1* and *Part 2*, and *Henry V* (known as the 'second tetralogy' with regard to the time of its composition); followed by *Henry VI Part 1*, *Part 2* and *Part 3* and *Richard III* (the 'first tetralogy').

7 BL Royal 13 C VIII f. 22v, f. 62v, f. 63

Bibliography

ONLINE SOURCES

Froissart, Jean, *The Online Froissart* (hrionline.ac.uk, V1.3/5 May 2012)
The Oxford Dictionary of National Biography (oxforddnb.com)
Letters and Papers, Foreign and Domestic, Henry VIII (via british-history.ac.uk)
Parliament Rolls of Medieval England (via british-history.ac.uk)
Victoria County History (via british-history.ac.uk)

UNPRINTED PRIMARY SOURCES

Additional MSS 18850 and 88929 (British Library)
Arundel MS (British Library)
Book of the Fraternity of the Assumption CLC/L/SE/A/004A/
    MS31692 (Guildhall Library/London Metropolitan Archives)
E101 (National Archives)
E361 (National Archives)
E404 (National Archives)
Egerton MS (British Library)
Harley MS 7353 (British Library)
Lansdowne MS (British Library)
MS Lewis E201 (Philadelphia Free Library)
Royal MS 13 C VIII (British Library)
Royal MS 15 E VI (British Library)
Royal MS 16 F II (British Library)
Sloane 3479 (British Library)

PRINTED PRIMARY SOURCES

André, B., *The Life of Henry VII*, trans. D. Hobbins (New York, 2011)

Armstrong, C. (ed. and trans.), *The Usurpation of Richard III: Dominicus Mancinus ad Angelum de occupatione regni Anglie per Ricardum tercium libellus* (2nd edn, Oxford, 1969)

Bentley, S., *Excerpta Historica: or, Illustrations of English History* (London, 1831)

Brie, F. W. D., *The Brut: or, The Chronicles of England*, vol. II (London, 1908)

Brown, R. (ed.), *Calendar of State Papers Relating to English Affairs in the Archives of Venice* (1873)

Bruce, J. (ed.), *Historie of the Arrivall of Edward IV in England and the Finall Recouerye of His Kingdomes from Henry VI* (London, 1838)

Carpenter, C. (ed.), *Kingsford's Stonor Letters and Papers 1290–1483* (Cambridge, 1996)

Chrimes, S. B., and A. L. Brown, *Select Documents of English Constitutional History 1307–1485* (London, 1961)

Collection of Ordinances and Regulations for the Government of the Household etc., A (London, 1790)

Crotch, W., *The Prologues and Epilogues of William Caxton* (London, 1928)

David, J. (ed.), *An English Chronicle of the Reigns of Richard II, Henry IV, Henry V and Henry VI* (Camden Society v44, 1838)

Devon, F. (ed.), *Issues of the Exchequer* (London, 1837)

Dockray, K. (ed.), *Three Chronicles of the Reign of Edward IV* (Gloucester, 1988)

Ellis, H. (ed.), *Three Books of Polydore Vergil's English History* (London, 1844)

Flenley, R. (ed.), *Six Town Chronicles of England* (Oxford, 1911)

Gairdner, J. (ed.), *The Historical Collections of a Citizen of London in the Fifteenth Century ('Gregory's Chronicle')* (1876)

—— (ed.), *Letters and Papers Illustrative of the Reigns of Richard III and Henry VII* (2 vols, London, 1861)

—— (ed.), *The Paston Letters* (new edn, 6 vols, London, 1904)

—— (ed.), *Three Fifteenth-Century Chronicles: With Historical Memoranda by John Stowe* (Camden Society, 1880)

Gayangos, P. de (ed.), *Calendar of State Papers, Spain* (1890)

Gibbs, V., et al. (eds), *The Complete Peerage* (2nd edn, London, etc., 1910–98)

Giles, J. A. (ed.), *Incerti scriptoris chronicon Angliae de regnis trium regum Lancas-triensium Henrici IV, Henrici V et Henrici VI* (London, 1848)

Grose, F., *The Antiquarian Repertory* (4 vols, London, 1807–9)

Hall, E., *Hall's Chronicle containing the History of England during the Reign of Henry the Fourth and the Succeeding Monarchs to the End of the Reign of Henry the Eighth* (London, 1809)

Halliwell, J. (ed.), *A Chronicle of the First Thirteen Years of the Reign of King Edward the Fourth: by John Warkworth* (London, 1889)

Harris, M. (ed. and trans.), *The Coventry Leet Book, or Mayor's Register* (New York, 1971)

Harriss, G., and M. Harriss (eds), *John Benet's Chronicle for the Years 1400 to 1462* (Camden Miscellany 44, 1972)

Hay, D. (ed.), *The Anglica Historia of Polydore Vergil, AD 1485–1537* (London, 1950)

Hinds, A. B. (ed.), *Calendar of State Papers and Manuscripts in the Archives and Collections of Milan: 1385–1618* (1912)

Hingeston, F. C. (ed.), *The Book of the Illustrious Henries* (London, 1858)

Horrox, R. and P. W. Hammond (eds), *British Library Harleian Manuscript 433* (4 vols, Gloucester, 1979–83)

James, M. (ed.), *Henry VI: A Reprint of John Blacman's Memoir, with Transla-tion and Notes* (Cambridge, 1919)

Johnes, Thomas (trans.), *The Chronicles of Enguerrand de Monstrelet* (2 vols, 1844)

Johnston, D. R. (ed.), *The Poetical Works of Lewys Glyn Cothi* (Oxford, 1837)

Kekewich, M., et al. (eds), *The Politics of Fifteenth-Century England – John Vale's Book* (Stroud, 1996)

Kingsford, C. L., *Chronicles of London* (Oxford, 1905)

——, *English Historical Literature in the Fifteenth Century* (Oxford, 1913)

—— (ed.), *The First English Life of Henry V* (Oxford, 1911)

Kipling, G., *The Receyt of the Ladie Kateryne* (Oxford, 1990)

Lewis, J. (ed.), *Life of Dr John Fisher* (2 vols, London, 1855)

Luders, A., et al., *The Statutes of the Realm* (11 vols, London, 1810–28), vol. II

MacCracken, H. N., *Minor Poems of John Lydgate* (2 vols, Oxford, 1961–2)

Macquereau, R., *Histoire générale de l'Europe* (Louvain, 1765)

Malden, H., *The Cely Papers: Selections from the Correspondence and Memoranda of the Cely Family, 1475–1488* (London, 1900)

McKendrick, S., J. Lowden and K. Doyle, *Royal Manuscripts: The Genius of Illumination* (London, 2011)

Munro, C. (ed.), *Letters of Queen Margaret of Anjou and Bishop Beckington and Others* (London, 1863)

Nicholas, N. H. (ed.), *A Chronicle of London: From 1089–1483* (London, 1827)

Nichols, J. G., *Chronicle of the Grey Friars of London* (Camden Society, v53, 1852)

Nichols, J., and R. Gough (eds), *A Collection of All the Wills Now Known to Be Extant of the Kings and Queens of England* (London, 1780)

Nicolas, N. H. (ed.), *Proceedings and Ordinances of the Privy Council* (1834–7), vols III–VI

Osborn, J. (ed.), *The Quenes Maiesties Passage through the Citie of London to Westminster the Day before her Coronacion* (facsimile edn, New Haven, 1960)

Palgrave, F., *Antient Kalendars and Inventories of the Treasury of His Majesty's Exchequer* (London, 1836)

Preest, D. (trans.), and J. G. Clark (intro.), *The Chronica Majora of Thomas Walsingham (1376–1422)* (Woodbridge, 2005)

Pronay, N. et al. (eds), *The Crowland Chronicle Continuations 1459–1486* (Sutton, 1986)

Raine, A. (ed.), *York Civic Records* (Wakefield, 1939), vols I and II

Riley, H. (ed.), *Ingulph's Chronicle of the Abbey of Croyland with the Continuations of Peter of Blois and Anonymous Writers* (London, 1908)

—— (ed.), *Registrum Abbatiae Johannis Whethamstede* (London, 1872)

Robbins, R. H. (ed.), *Historical Poems of the Fourteenth and Fifteenth Centuries* (New York, 1959)

Rymer, T., *Foedera, conventiones, literae, et cujuscunque generis acta publica, inter reges Angliae, et alios quosuis imperatores, reges, . . . ab anno 1101, ad nostra usque tempora, habita aut tractata; . . . In lucem missa de mandato Reginae* (London, 1735)

Scobie, A. (ed.), *The Memoirs of Philip de Commines, Lord of Argenton* (2 vols, London, 1877)

Shirley, J. (trans. and ed.), *A Parisian Journal 1405–1449* (Oxford, 1968)

Society of Antiquaries, *Household Ordinances and Regulations, Edward III to William and Mary* (London, 1790)

Stapleton, T. (ed.), *Plumpton Correspondence* (London, 1834)

Stevenson, J. (ed.), *Letters and Papers Illustrative of the Wars of the English in France during the Reign of Henry the Sixth* (London, 1861–4)

Stow, J., *The Annals, or a General Chronicle of England* (London, 1615)

Stratford, J., *The Bedford Inventories: The Worldly Goods of John, Duke of Bedford, Regent of France (1389–1435)* (London, 1993)

Thomas, A., and I. Thornley (eds), *The Great Chronicle of London* (London, 1938)

Ursins, Jean Juvenal des, *Histoire de Charles VI, Roy de France* (Paris, 1836)

Wavrin, John de (ed.), and W. Hardy (trans.), *A Collection of the Chronicles and Ancient Histories of Great Britain, now called England* (5 vols, London, 1864–87)

Wickham Legg, L. G. (ed.), *English Coronation Records* (London, 1901)

Williams, B., *Chronique de la traison et mort de Richart Deux roy Dengleterre* (London, 1846)

Wright, T., *Political Poems and Songs Relating to English History* (London, 1859–61), vol. II

SECONDARY SOURCES

Adams, T., *The Life and Afterlife of Isabeau of Bavaria* (Baltimore, 2010)

Allmand, C., *Henry V* (Yale, 1997)

——, *The Hundred Years War: England and France at War; c.1300–c.1450* (Cambridge, 1988)

Anglo, S., *Images of Tudor Kingship* (London, 1992)

——, *Spectacle, Pageantry and Early Tudor Policy* (Oxford, 1969)

Archer, R., *Crown, Government and People in the Fifteenth Century* (Stroud, 1995)

Armstrong, C., *England, France and Burgundy in the Fifteenth Century* (London, 1983)

Arthurson, I., *The Perkin Warbeck Conspiracy, 1491–1499* (Stroud, 1994)

Ashdown-Hill, J., *Richard III's 'Belovyd Cousin', John Howard and the House of York* (Stroud, 2009)

Baldwin, D., *Elizabeth Woodville: Mother of the Princes in the Tower* (Stroud, 2010)

——, *Stoke Field: The Last Battle of the Wars of the Roses* (Barnsley, 2006)

Baldwin, J. F., *The King's Council in England during the Middle Ages* (Oxford, 1913)

Barker, J., *Conquest: The English Kingdom of France 1417–1450* (London, 2009)

Barron, C., *London in the Later Middle Ages* (Oxford, 2004)

Beem, C. (ed.), *The Royal Minorities of Medieval and Early Modern England* (New York, 2008)

Bell, A., A. Curry, A. King and D. Simpkin, *The Soldier in Later Medieval England* (Oxford, 2013)

Bennett, M., *Lambert Simnel and the Battle of Stoke* (Gloucester, 1987)

Boardman, A., *The Medieval Soldier in the Wars of the Roses* (Stroud, 1998)

Bramley, Peter, *The Wars of the Roses: A Field Guide and Companion* (Stroud, 2007)

Brook, R., *The Story of Eltham Palace* (London, 1960)

Brooke, R., *The Battle of Stoke Field* (Liverpool, 1825)

Burley, P., et al., *The Battles of St Albans* (Barnsley, 2007)

Callcott, M., *Little Arthur's History of England*, (London, 1835)

Carleton Williams, E., *My Lord of Bedford, 1389–1435: Being a Life of John of Lancaster, First Duke of Bedford, Brother of Henry V and Regent of France* (London, 1963)

Carpenter, C., *Locality and Polity: A Study of Warwickshire Landed Society, 1401–1499* (Cambridge, 1992)

——, *The Wars of the Roses: Politics and the Constitution in England c.1437–1509* (Cambridge, 1997)

Castor, H., *The King, the Crown and the Duchy of Lancaster: Public Authority and Private Power 1399–1461* (Oxford, 2000)

——, *She-Wolves: The Women Who Ruled England before Elizabeth* (London, 2010)

Cheetham, A., *The Life and Times of Richard III* (London, 1972)

Chrimes, S. B., *Henry VII* (London, 1972)

——, *Lancastrians, Yorkists and Henry VII* (2nd edn, London, 1966)

Clarke, B., *Mental Disorder in Earlier Britain* (Cardiff, 1975)

Colvin, H. M., *History of the King's Works* (London, 1963), vols I and II

Curry, A., and M. Hughes (eds), *Arms, Armies and Fortifications in the Hundred Years War* (Woodbridge, 1994)

De Lisle, L., *Tudor: The Family Story* (London, 2013)

Dockray, K., *William Shakespeare, the Wars of the Roses and the Historians* (Stroud, 2002)

Dodd, G. (ed.), *Henry V: New Interpretations* (York, 2013)

Evans, H., *Wales and the Wars of the Roses* (Cambridge, 1915)

Famiglietti, R. C., *Royal Intrigue: Crisis at the Court of Charles VI, 1392–1420* (New York, 1986)

Fiorato, V., and C. Knussel (eds), *Blood Red Roses* (2nd edn, Oxford, 2007)

Foarde, G., and A. Curry, *Bosworth 1485: A Battlefield Rediscovered* (Oxford, 2013)

Foarde, G., and R. Morris, *The Archaeology of English Battlefields: Conflict in the Pre-Industrial Landscape* (York, 2012)

Gairdner, J., *History of the Life and Reign of Richard the Third* (Cambridge, 1898)

Gill, L., *Richard III and Buckingham's Rebellion* (Stroud, 1999)

Goodman, A., *The Wars of the Roses: The Soldiers' Experience* (Stroud, 2005)

Goodrich, N., *Charles Duke of Orleans: A Literary Biography* (New York, 1963)

Goodwin, G., *Fatal Colours: Towton 1461 – England's Most Brutal Battle* (London, 2011)

Gough, H., and J. Parker, *A Glossary of Terms Used in Heraldry* (London, 1894)

Griffiths, R. A., *The Reign of King Henry VI* (Stroud, 1981)

Griffiths, R. A. (ed.), *Patronage, the Crown and the Provinces in Later Medieval England* (New Jersey, 1981)

Griffiths, R. A., and R. S. Thomas, *The Making of the Tudor Dynasty* (Gloucester, 1985)

Gristwood, S., *Blood Sisters: The Hidden Lives of the Women behind the Wars of the Roses* (London, 2012)

Gunn, S., and L. Monckton (eds), *Arthur Tudor, Prince of Wales: Life, Death and Commemoration* (Woodbridge, 2009)

Guy, J., *The Children of Henry VIII* (Oxford, 2013)

Haigh, P., *The Military Campaigns of the Wars of the Roses* (Stroud, 1995)

Halsted, C., *Richard III* (2 vols, London, 1844)

Hammond, P., *The Battles of Barnet and Tewkesbury* (Gloucester, 1993)

Hammond, P. (ed.), *Richard III: Loyalty, Lordship and Law* (London, 1986)

Hammond, P., and A. Sutton, *Richard III: The Road to Bosworth Field* (London, 1985)

Harriss, G. L., *Cardinal Beaufort: A Study of Lancastrian Ascendancy and Decline* (Oxford, 1988)

——, *Shaping the Nation: England 1360–1461* (Oxford, 2005)

Harvey, A., and R. Mortimer, *The Funeral Effigies of Westminster Abbey* (Woodbridge, 1994)

Harvey, I., *Jack Cade's Rebellion of 1450* (Oxford, 1991)

Hicks, M., *Edward V: The Prince in the Tower* (Stroud, 2003)

——, *False, Fleeting, Perjur'd Clarence: George Duke of Clarence 1449–78* (Gloucester, 1992)

——, *Richard III* (Stroud, 2000)

——, *Warwick the Kingmaker* (Oxford, 1998)

Hookham, M., *Life and Times of Margaret of Anjou* (London, 1872)

Horrox, R., *Richard III: A Study of Service* (Cambridge, 1989)

Hughes, J., *Arthurian Myths and Alchemy: The Kingship of Edward IV* (Stroud, 2002)

Johnson, P., *Duke Richard of York 1411–1460* (Oxford, 1988)

Jones, M., and M. Underwood, *The King's Mother: Lady Margaret Beaufort, Countess of Richmond and Derby* (Cambridge, 1993)

Kempe, A., *Historical Notices of St Martin-le-Grand* (London, 1825)

Lander, J. R., *Crown and Nobility, 1450–1509* (London, 1976)

Langley, P. and Jones, M., *The King's Grave: The Search for Richard III* (London, 2013)

Laynesmith, J., *The Last Medieval Queens: English Queenship 1445–1503* (Oxford, 2004)

Lindsay, P., *On Some Bones in Westminster Abbey: A Defence of King Richard III* (Bath, 1969)

Lyle, H., *The Rebellion of Jack Cade, 1450* (London, 1950)

McFarlane, K. B., *England in the Fifteenth Century* (London, 1981)

——, *The Nobility of Later Medieval England* (Oxford, 1973)

MacGibbon, D., *Elizabeth Woodville (1437–1492): Her Life and Times* (London, 1938)

Matusiak, J., *Henry V* (London, 2013)

Maurer, H., *Margaret of Anjou: Queenship and Power in Late Medieval England* (Woodbridge, 2003)

Murray, Stephen, *Building Troyes Cathedral: The Late Gothic Campaigns* (Bloomington and Indianapolis, 1987)

Page, W. (ed.), *A History of the County of London, Volume I* (London, 1909)

Pollard, A., *The Wars of the Roses* (2nd edn, Basingstoke, 2001)

Ramsay, J., *Lancaster and York* (Oxford, 1892)

Rebhorn, W. A. (ed. and trans.), *The Decameron, Giovanni Boccaccio* (London and New York, 2013)

Richardson, G., *The Hollow Crowns: History of the Battles of the Wars of the Roses* (Shipley, 1996)

Rose, S., *Calais: An English Town in France 1347–1558* (Woodbridge, 2008)

Ross, C., *Edward IV* (new edn, London and New Haven, 1997)

Ross, C. (ed.), *Patronage, Pedigree and Power in Later Medieval England* (Gloucester, 1979)

Rowe, J. G. (ed.), *Aspects of Late Medieval Government and Society: Essays Presented to J. R. Lander* (Toronto, 1986)

Scarisbrick, J., *Henry VIII* (new edn, New Haven and London, 1997)

Scofield, C., *The Life and Reign of Edward IV* (2 vols, London, 1923)

Seward, D., *The Last White Rose: Dynasty, Rebellion and Treason – The Secret Wars against the Tudors* (London, 2010)

Smith, G., *The Coronation of Elizabeth Wydeville* (London, 1935)

Spufford, P., *Handbook of Medieval Exchange* (London, 1986)

Stanford London, H., *Royal Beasts* (East Knoyle, 1956)

Starkey, D., *Six Wives: The Queens of Henry VIII* (London, 2004)

Steel, A., *The Receipt of the Exchequer 1377–1485* (Cambridge, 1954)

Strickland, A., *Lives of the Queens of England, from the Norman Conquest: With Anecdotes of Their Courts* (12 vols, London, 1840–8)

Strong, R., *Tudor and Jacobean Portraits* (London, 1969)

Sutton, A., and P. Hammond, *The Coronation of Richard III: The Extant Documents* (Gloucester, 1983)

Tremlett, G., *Catherine of Aragon: Henry's Spanish Queen* (London, 2010)

Twemlow, F., *The Battle of Bloreheath: The First Major Conflict of the Wars of the Roses* (1912; repr. 2011)

Unwin, G. (ed.), *Finance and Trade under Edward III. By members of the History School* (Manchester, 1918)

Watts, J., *Henry VI and the Politics of Kingship* (Cambridge, 1996)

Watts, J. (ed.), *The End of The Middle Ages?* (Stroud, 1998)

Weightman, C., *Margaret of York, Duchess of Burgundy, 1446–1503* (Gloucester, 1989)

Weir, A., *Elizabeth of York: The First Tudor Queen* (London, 2013)

Wilkinson, B., *A Constitutional History of England in the Fifteenth Century* (London, 1964)

Wolffe, B., *Henry VI* (2nd edn, London, 2001)

ARTICLES

Anglo, S., 'The British History in Early Tudor Propaganda', *Bulletin of the John Rylands Library* 44 (1961)

——, 'The London Pageants for the Reception of Katherine of Aragon in 1501', *Journal of the Warburg and Courtauld Institutes* 26 (1963)

Archbold, W., 'Sir William Stanley and Perkin Warbeck', *English Historical Review* 14/55 (1899)

Armstrong, C., 'The Inauguration Ceremonies of the Yorkist Kings and Their Title to the Throne', *Transactions of the Royal Historical Society* 30 (1948)

Armstrong, C. J., 'Politics and the Battle of St Albans 1455', *Bulletin of the Institute of Historical Research* 33 (1960)

Autrand, F., 'France under Charles V and Charles VI', *The New Cambridge Medieval History c. 1300–1425* 6, ed. M. Jones (2000)

Bark, N., 'Did Schizophrenia Change the Course of English History? The Mental Illness of Henry VI', *Medical Hypotheses* 59, no. 4 (1 October 2002)

Barnes, T., 'Work as a Manifestation of Faith in the English Nunnery: Barking Abbey, Essex', *Quidditas* 32 (2011)

Bassett, M., 'Newgate Prison in the Middle Ages', *Speculum* 18 (1943)

Bennett, A., 'A Fifteenth-Century Middle English Sermon on the Decline of the World and the Age of Stone', *Medium Aevum* 80 (2011)

Blauuw, W. H., 'On the Effigy of Sir David Owen in Easebourne Church, near Midhurst', *Sussex Archaeological Collections* 7 (1854)

Bohna, M., 'Armed Force and Civic Legitimacy in Jack Cade's Revolt, 1450', *English Historical Review* 118 (2003)

Brown, A. L., 'The King's Councillors in Fifteenth-Century England', *Transactions of the Royal Historical Society* (1968)

Brown, L., 'Continuity and Change in the Parliamentary Justifications of the Fifteenth-Century Usurpations', *The Fifteenth Century* 7, ed. Linda Clark (2007)

Buckley, R., et al., 'The King in the Car Park: New Light on the Death and Burial of Richard III in the Grey Friars Church, Leicester in 1485', *Antiquity* 87 (2013)

Carpenter, M. C., 'The Duke of Clarence and the Midlands: A Study in the Interplay of Local and National Politics', *Midland History* 11 (1986)

Cron, B. M., 'The Duke of Suffolk, the Angevin Marriage, and the Ceding of Maine, 1445', *Journal of Medieval History* 20 (1994)

Cussans, J., 'Notes on the Perkin Warbeck Insurrection', *Transactions of the Royal Historical Society* (1872)

Davies, C., 'A Requiem for King Edward', *The Ricardian* 114 (1991)

Dockray, K., 'The Battle of Wakefield and the Wars of the Roses', *The Ricardian* 117 (1992)

——, 'The Yorkshire Rebellions of 1469', *The Ricardian* 82 (1983)

'English Heritage Battlefield Report: Blore Heath 1459', English Heritage (1995)

Gibbons, R. C., 'Isabeau of Bavaria, Queen of France (1385–1422): The Creation of an Historical Villainess: The Alexander Prize Essay', *Transactions of the Royal Historical Society* 6 (1996)

Gill, P., 'Politics and Propaganda in Fifteenth-Century England: The Polemical Writings of Sir John Fortescue', *Speculum* 46 (1971)

Gottfried, R., 'Epidemic Disease in Fifteenth-Century England', *Journal of Economic History* 36 (1976)

Griffiths, R. A., 'Duke Richard of York's Intentions in 1450 and the Origins of the Wars of the Roses', *Journal of Medieval History* 1 (1975)

——, 'Henry Tudor: The Training of a King', *Huntington Library Quarterly* 49 (1986)

——, 'The King's Council and York's First Protectorate', *English Historical Review* 94 (1984)

——, 'Queen Katherine de Valois and a Missing Statute of the Realm', *Law Quarterly Review* 93 (1977)

——, 'Richard Duke of York, and the Crisis of Henry VI's Household in 1450–1: Some Further Evidence', *Journal of Medieval History* 38 (2012)

——, 'Richard Duke of York and the Royal Household in Wales in 1449–50', *Welsh History Review* 8 (1976–7)

——, 'The Trial of Eleanor Cobham: An Episode in the Fall of Humphrey Duke of Gloucester', *Bulletin of the John Rylands Library* 51 (1968)

Grummitt, D., 'Deconstructing Cade's Rebellion: Discourse and Politics in the Mid-Fifteenth Century', *The Fifteenth Century* 6, ed. Linda Clark (2006)

Head, C., 'Pope Pius II and the Wars of the Roses', *Archivum Historiae Pontificiae* 8 (1970)

Hicks, M., 'Unweaving the Web: The Plot of July 1483 against Richard III and Its Wider Significance', *The Ricardian* 114 (1991)

Horrox, R., 'Financial Memoranda of the Reign of Edward V', *Camden Miscellany* 29 (1987)

Ives, E., 'Andrew Dummock and the Papers of Anthony, Earl Rivers, 1482–3', *Bulletin of the Institute of Historical Research* 41 (1968)

Jones, M., 'For My Lord of Richmond, a Pourpoint . . . and a Palfrey: Brief Remarks on the Financial Evidence for Henry Tudor's Exile in Brittany, 1471–1484', *The Ricardian* 13 (2003)

Jones, M. K., 'The Battle of Verneuil (17 August 1424): Towards a History of Courage', *War in History* 9 (2002)

——, 'York, Somerset and the Wars of the Roses', *English Historical Review* 104 (1989)

Keen, M. H and M. J. Daniel, 'English Diplomacy and the Sack of Fougères in 1449', *History* 59 (1974)

Kekewich, M., 'Edward IV, William Caxton and Literary Patronage in Yorkist England', *Modern Language Review* 3 (1971)

Khalaf, O., 'Lord Rivers and Oxford, Bodleian Library MS Bodley 264: A Speculum for the Prince of Wales?', *Journal of the Early Book Society* (2011)

Kipling, G., 'The London Pageants for Margaret of Anjou', *Medieval English Theatre* 4 (1982)

Kleineke, H. (ed. and trans.), 'Gerhard von Wesel's Newsletter from England 17 April 1471', *The Ricardian* 16 (2006)

Lander, J., 'Attainder and Forfeiture 1453–1509', *The Historical Journal* 4 (1961)

——, 'Marriage and Politics: The Nevilles and the Wydevilles', *Bulletin of the Institute of Historical Research* 36 (1963)

Lee, P., 'Reflections of Power: Margaret of Anjou and the Dark Side of Queenship', *Renaissance Quarterly* 39 (1986)

Martin, F., 'The Crowning of a King at Dublin, 24 May 1486', *Hermathena* 144 (1988)

McCulloch, D., and E. D. Jones, 'Lancastrian Politics, the French War, and the Rise of the Popular Element', *Speculum* 58 (1983)

McKenna, J. W., 'Henry VI of England and the Dual Monarchy: Aspects of Royal Propaganda 1422–1432', *Journal of the Warburg and Courtauld Institutes* (1965)

Meekings, C. A. F., 'Thomas Kerver's Case, 1444', *English Historical Review* 90 (1975)

Myers, A., 'The Household of Queen Margaret of Anjou', *Bulletin of the John Rylands Library* 40 (1957)

——, 'The Jewels of Queen Margaret of Anjou', *Bulletin of the John Rylands Library* 42 (1959)

Pollard, G., 'The Bibliographical History of Hall's Chronicle', *Historical Research* 10 (1932)

Ransom, C., 'The Battle of Towton', *English Historical Review* 4 (1889)

Rhymer, L. 'Humphrey Duke of Gloucester, and the City of London', *The Fifteenth Century* 8, ed. Linda Clark (2008)

Richmond, C., 'The Earl of Warwick's Domination of the Channel and the Naval Dimension to the Wars of the Roses, 1456–60', *Southern History* 20/21 (1998–9)

Rosenthal, J., 'The Estates and Finances of Richard Duke of York (1411–1460)', *Studies in Medieval and Renaissance History* 2 (1965)

Rowe, B. J. H., 'Discipline in the Norman Garrisons under Bedford, 1422–35', *English Historical Review* 46 (1931)

——, 'King Henry VI's Claim to France in Picture and Poem', *The Library* series 4, 13 (1932)

St John Hope, W., 'The Discovery of the Remains of Henry VI in St George's Chapel, Windsor Castle', *Archaeologia* (1911)

Sayles, G. O., 'The Royal Marriages Act of 1428', *Law Quarterly Review* 94 (1978)

Scofield, C., 'The Capture of Lord Rivers and Sir Anthony Woodville, 19 January 1460', *English Historical Review* 37 (1922)

Solon, P., 'Popular Response to Standing Military Forces in Fifteenth-Century France', *Studies in the Renaissance* 19 (1972)

Starkey, D., 'Henry VI's Old Blue Gown: The English Court under the Lancastrians and the Yorkists', *The Court Historian* (1999)

Styles, D., and C. T. Allmand, 'The Coronations of Henry VI', *History Today* 32/5 (1982)

Thomson, J. A. F., 'The Arrival of Edward IV: The Development of the Text', *Speculum* 46 (1971)

Virgoe, R., 'The Death of William de la Pole, Duke of Suffolk', *Bulletin of the John Rylands Library* 47 (1965)

——, 'The Parliamentary Subsidy of 1450', *Bulletin of the Institute of Historical Research* 55 (1982)

Winston, J., '*A Mirror for Magistrates* and Public Political Discourse in Elizabethan England', *Studies in Philology* 101, v4 (2004)

Wolffe, B., 'Acts of Resumption in the Lancastrian Parliaments, 1399–1456', *English Historical Review* 73 (1958)

——, 'When and Why Did Hastings Lose His Head?', *English Historical Review* 89 (1974)

UNPUBLISHED THESES

Barnes, T., *A Nun's Life: Barking Abbey in the Late Medieval and Early Modern Periods* (Portland State University, 2004)

Brown, A., *Recession and Recovery in the North-East c.1450–1540* (University of Durham, 2011)

Camidge, L. M., *The Celebration of Kingship in Fifteenth-Century England* (University of Exeter, 1996)

Gibbons, R. C., *The Active Queenship of Isabeau of Bavaria, 1392–1417: Voluptuary, Virago or Villainess* (University of Reading, 1997)

Millard, F., *Politics and the Creation of Memory: The Afterlife of Humphrey, Duke of Gloucester* (University College London, 2009)

Pierce, H., *The Life, Career and Political Significance of Margaret Pole, Countess of Salisbury 1473–1541* (University of Wales, Bangor, 1996)

Rhymer, L., *The Political Career of Humphrey, Duke of Gloucester c.1413–1447* (University of Cambridge, 2010)

Thomas, R. L., *The Political Career, Estates and 'Connection' of Jasper Tudor, Earl of Pembroke and Duke of Bedford (d.1495)* (University of Wales, Swansea, 1971)

Index

The index headings mirror the text as far as possible. Noblemen are indexed by title and listed in chronological order; there is a cross-reference if the text uses their family name instead. Titled females and children are indexed by their given name; if their surname or title is sometimes used, there is a second entry or a cross-reference.